GRACE OF THE GHOSTS

# Grace of the Ghosts

## A THEOLOGY OF INSTITUTIONAL REPARATION

*Jeannine Hill Fletcher*

FORDHAM UNIVERSITY PRESS    NEW YORK 2025

"Spiritual Exercises for Deep Reckoning" in Chapter 6 was first published as "The Sins of White Supremacy: Institutionalized Racism and a Composition of Place" in *Praying for Freedom: Racism and Ignatian Spirituality in America*. © 2024 by Laurie Cassidy. Published by Liturgical Press, Collegeville, Minnesota. Used with permission.



Fordham University Press also publishes its books in a variety of electronic formats. Some content that appears in print may not be available in electronic books.

Visit us online at www.fordhampress.com.

Library of Congress Cataloging-in-Publication Data available online at https://catalog.loc.gov.

Printed in the United States of America
27 26 25    5 4 3 2 1
First edition

*With a grateful heart this book is dedicated*
*to preserving the witness of*

*Susannah, Nelly, Henrietta, Dolores,*
*and all the Grandmothers*
*and to all my institutional relations*
*that we might carry on their legacies for transformation*

# Contents

Introduction 1

1 Truth Telling about Institutions 7

2 Sucky's Scream:
Hearing the Ghosts and Heeding Their Call 38

3 The Complexity of a Complicit Church:
Henrietta and Elizabeth in a Catholic Network 78

4 Institutional Networks and Nation Building:
Collaborating with the State through Systems of Education 126

5 Leveraging Capital:
Church Institutions for Change in the Twentieth Century 168

6 Confronting a Culture of White Supremacy:
Spiritual Strength for Mobilizing Capital 211

ACKNOWLEDGMENTS 255

NOTES 257

BIBLIOGRAPHY 297

INDEX 315

# GRACE OF THE GHOSTS

# Introduction

There is work to be done if we want to become a truly antiracist, multicultural church and a witness in our multireligious nation. Living in the United States of America more than fifty years after the civil rights movement, the nation still needs to be reminded that *Black Lives Matter* and called to address the persistence of #Anti-Asian Hate. We continue to struggle to live out a faith that does justice when facing dangerous White supremacies in our nation. We are living through America's ongoing intergenerational crisis, and Christian faith struggles to keep up. At times we seem baffled that a faith tradition committed to the love of God and love of neighbor could be part of a society so riddled with hate. Where does all this death-dealing division stem from, and how might Christians finally transcend it? Or, more pointedly, will we ever understand the depths of the damage that has been done, and can we ever hope toward reparation, reconciliation, and repair? As people of faith in a racialized nation, we seek answers to these questions. But we might be afraid to consider that the roots of today's challenges are embedded in the very places we are looking: in the theo-logic of an American Christianity and the cultural production of our Christian educational institutions.

The historian Craig Wilder points in this direction when he demonstrates how institutions of higher learning and the seminaries embedded within them were engines of anti-Blackness and White supremacist ideology during the nation's earliest days. Wilder's *Ebony and Ivy: Race, Slavery, and the Troubled History of America's Universities* demonstrates how colleges and universities produced so-called knowledge about peoples of African descent that fed the logic of enslaving them—and generated funds for those very institutions.[1] Wilder's work helps us understand the number of US universities and colleges that are reckoning with their particular histories embedded in the American project of chattel slavery. Wilder's realization and institutional reckoning further press the question: If colleges and universities, seminaries and congregations were engines of evil in the production of White supremacies, could they now become distinct locations to produce lasting patterns of thought and practice for change? The hope of this book is precisely this possibility: that as we step into institutional accountability for failings in the past, we break open the space to become transformative locations for the future. In the Christian perspective, such an in-breaking of hope toward healing has theological significance.

I write as a scholar who wants to be part of this transformative work. Having been trained as a Christian theologian, shaped by the Catholic tradition, embedded in my life's work within a Jesuit institution in a multireligious nation, I tap into the inheritance of many intersecting institutions. Such a nesting of identities opens for me an opportunity *both* to consider the range of institutions in our national history *and* to settle into the work to be done in some of them. Because I have benefited from being in the company of the Jesuits, I want to be part of the powerful reckoning begun at Georgetown and rippling out across the nation to all the Jesuit institutions that have a share in this history. Simultaneously, having been raised in Catholic educational and parish life, I am compelled to face the benefits that have accrued to me through those systems of thought and practice. But as Catholic and Jesuit, we share our stories with the broader collective of Christian institutions—congregations, schools, and media—through which we find ourselves connected across the nation (and, indeed, around the world). Together we can support one another in the truth telling about institutions that might set us free.

You'll see in these pages that not only am I a theologian drawn to history but that I also narrate history in a particular way: through the frame of struggle, sometimes indicated with the more technical term as "agonistic." My premise reflected in this choice of terminology is that humans have always been in the negotiation of survival-in-community and that the stories of Christian faith invite us into a particular way of doing that with love. Yet because Christians have lived out the story of the faith imperfectly (indeed as an epic failure to love throughout much of US history), the struggle that "agonistic" names is not only "out there" in the world of society but also "in here" within our Christian institutions. What this helps us imagine is that our moment in theological and institutional history is part of a much longer agonistic reality in which our American Christian ancestors have long been struggling.

In the pages to come, I invite us to situate our moment in the broader history of the struggles with White supremacy in American life.[2] As we do so, we'll have to reckon also with the history that has been passed down to us. That is, too often our Christian histories want to render Christians as the "good guys" in this struggle, and in order to make such a history plausible, injustice is erased. This erasure renders some among our ancestors merely ghostly presences, while others take center stage. When reckoning with our histories, we meet the ghosts of those ancestors whose lives were taken in the creation of our institutions yet whose names have not yet been written in their histories. Remembering the ancestors whose ghostly presence is only a trace in White histories performs two functions. On the one hand, it more faithfully tells the story of the church with a wider range of racialized actors. The church in America became what it became *because of* the land, lives, and labor of Indigenous, Black, Latinx, and Asian peoples. On the other hand, when we tell their stories as part of a single US Catholic history, it sheds light on the injustices delivered to these ancestors in the faith *by members of their own faith community.* We are wrestling with our heritage as a multiracial, multiethnic community when we wrestle with our ghosts, who are also our ancestors.

Here, the reader will recognize that our "ancestors" are not blood ancestors alone but include our institutional ancestors and our spiritual ancestors (something like a communion of saints—or a communion of saints and sinners). While perceptive readers will rightly experience my shifting use of "ancestors" as destabilizing, such disorientation toward our own histories and our place within them is purposeful. With the goal of embracing a more racially diverse history in the Catholic Church and its institutions, I would like readers to consider members of diversely racialized groups to be *their* ancestors in the faith. I would like readers to recognize that although they may want to distance themselves from the actions of some among their institutional forebears, *all* of us who reap benefits from these institutions are inheritors of past actions. The agonistic runs not only through our American history and through our American Catholic history but through our church institutions (of parish and school) even today. This is the tension of living together in diversely constituted institutions, but it can be a productive tension when we feel it, name it, and work toward a resolution together.

The premise of this volume is that *all* of our institutions need to participate in this reckoning if America as a nation will ever emerge from the cloud of despair that hovered over the summer of 2020. We read books and we marched, but the real work of transformation was forecast as yet to come. Disappointingly, in many places, 2020 has already become America's latest expression of unfulfilled promises. Simultaneously, in the years since 2020, key political actors have moved further and further toward erasing this history, rejecting Diversity, Equity, and Inclusion initiatives and the Critical Race Theory that sustains our transformation. It is within this agonistic landscape that I see Catholic institutions poised to become leaders in the educational work of racial justice. Accounting for our roles in the sins of White supremacy, with the specific textures of our institutional histories, we might each take up the mantle of an antiracist education as *part* of our Catholic faith.

In what follows, I invite the reader to consider the landscape of US history and the particularity of institutions to travel across the geography of sin and grace that our histories reveal. Before we begin that journey, let me provide something of a map for what is to come. Chapter 1 will present the foundation for conceptualizing the work of repair embedded in the institutional network of the Catholic Christian tradition in the United States. Readers will be introduced to the overarching framework provided by Maria Yellow Horse Brave Heart in response to the historical trauma of White supremacy. Here, I lay out the theoretical framing of an "institutional ontology" so we can see how institutions shape our being human in the world. This consideration of institutions introduces "ghosts" as a sociological phenomenon that alerts us to patterns of erasure and exclusion. Further, the discussion hones in on the ways in which institutions are the conduits of "capital" in its economic, social, and symbolic forms. It is from this location that we might imagine the work that *our* institution might do in the twenty-first-century world. As a Christian theology of institutional accountability, this chapter closes with a Christology that makes sense of the story of Jesus with an "institutional" lens. For those readers less theoretically or theologically inclined, you might jump right to the story of American Catholic history that begins in Chapter 2.

Chapters 2 through 5 tell a story of Catholic institutions in the United States as they are embedded in the story of the nation. Chapter 2 begins the journey with a reconstruction from the archives at Georgetown University. Mirroring the work Rachel Swarns has gifted to us in *The 272*, this chapter uses the archives not only to remember some among the ancestors enslaved by the Jesuits at Georgetown but to theologize with their witness.[3] It is in this chapter that I introduce the grace necessary to face White supremacy, and I name this as the grace of the ghosts. For the theologically attuned, here is where we will explore a pneumatology that learns from Ashon Crawley's invitation to "otherwise possibilities" in our histories.

In Chapter 3, the history of a multiracial Black Catholic Church tradition in South Carolina leads us into an ecclesiology of complexity and complicity in the sins of White supremacy. This ecclesial location of "frontier Catholicism" provides a glimpse into White Catholic theology and piety within an economy of enslavement and simultaneously envisions the spiritual capital of enslaved Black Catholics. It is a story of the Catholic Church—as Black and White—that created a network of institutions South and North. The complicity of my own institution in New York City becomes an unexpected place of reckoning drawn forward by our ghosts. The complexity of intimately intertwined histories raises the pointed question of whether repair is even possible but leaves open the conclusion as to what we might do together.

While the preceding chapters take as their focus the history of US Catholicism within an economy of enslavement, Chapter 3 reminds us that this history is simultaneous with the dispossession and erasure of Indigenous people. This chapter aims to widen the lens of our consideration and weave together the institutional Catholic configurations and their relation to Black and Indian "missions." Centering the experience of women religious, the history of the Oblate Sisters of Providence (OSPs) and the Sisters, Servants of the Immaculate Heart of Mary (IHMs) provides one lens on this era (rooted in Baltimore), while the expansion of Catholic and Jesuit missions to the Midwest and Plains in Indian Boarding Schools adds another dimension. Catholic legislators (like Roger Taney, who wrote the *Dred Scott* decision) and benefactors (like Katharine Drexel) ask us to consider multiple locations in which the church plays a part in US history. Theologically speaking, perhaps this chapter is pressing forward a "critical missiology" that opens to the intercultural and interreligious.

So much of this history is saddening, almost paralyzing, so in addition to the struggles the preceding chapters trace across the nation, we might benefit from some dwelling in the salvation that comes through the struggle. Chapter 4 allows us to witness the ways that Catholic capital—of built environments, of spirituality, liturgy, community, and witness—*has* created opportunities for transformative multiracial solidarities. To elevate this otherwise possibility, we will walk with the United Farm Workers movement in the twentieth century. It is in this chapter that we'll examine more closely the benefits of conceptualizing our lives together as "agonistic." Theologically, the chapter opens us toward a soteriology, as we think with Gustavo Gutierrez's in-breaking of salvation in history.

Chapter 6 draws from all of this truth telling of American Catholic history to envision the possibilities of repair, guided by the theoretical framework of Duke Kwon and Gregory Thompson in their 2021 *Reparations*. This chapter orients the reader forward with some among the practical steps that might be taken to be part of the ongoing reckoning with our institutional histories as agents of change for the repair of our world. Recognizing that this is long and ongoing work, the chapter closes with the spiritual capital that might sustain us to write our chapter in the nation's long struggle. An extended exploration with the *Spiritual Exercises* closes the book.

The premise of this volume is that the work of transforming our nation from out of its White supremacist patterns is *holy work*. As a theologian, I see it as the tangible opportunity to witness Christ-followers making faith real in the world. But we do not do this work alone. We join in solidarity and struggle in the coalition of activism, and we are carried forward by the call of the ancestors whose voices we have not yet heard. As we journey together, may we be surrounded and enveloped by the grace of the ghosts.

# 1
# Truth Telling about Institutions

They are written onto the walls and imperceptibly adorn the brick and mortar; their names are found in the stone along the pathways and among the leaves on the trees. As part of a capstone project, Joy Kang, an undergraduate in the Fine Arts program at Georgetown University, remembered the ancestors. Aware of the way in which our Jesuit forebears undertook a transaction of sale to transfer enslaved Catholics in order to keep the Jesuit Catholic institution of Georgetown solvent, Kang sketched in charcoal pencil the flagship building of the university's main campus. Adorning the bricks, styled into the landscape, and flying as leaves from the trees are the names of the 272 persons listed on the Jesuit registry of the sale and some among their descendants.[1] Kang's artistic representation drew out from purportedly nonliving blocks of stone the living, breathing people whose life and breath went into their making, proposing that those ready to witness might recognize our enslaved Catholic ancestors still present among us. In the pages to come, we will meet some of these people who have shaped and been shaped by Catholic educational and ecclesial institutions. The women and men, the many, the children and elders who served the institutions with their lifeblood and their creativity: Susannah, whose renowned culinary skills fed Jesuits for years; Nelly, whose sacred practices sustained them in their liturgies; Nancy, whose sacrifice had a salvific effect upon her family; Harry, whose skills saved the Jesuits from economic destruction.[2] Georgetown is a striking example of what was true in Catholic institutions across the nation: They derived benefit from and were entangled in the systems and structures of White supremacy.

For the purposes of our investigation, "White supremacy" names the ways in which the United States was formed with a legacy that sorted people into distinct race categories and directed benefits to those who were categorized as "White."[3] From an economy of enslavement and transfer of land from Indigenous nations through many and diverse forms of directing well-being to White Americans while exploiting the work of others, the history of Catholic institutions bears the imprint of prioritizing White well-being throughout the United States. So our story will not dwell only on Georgetown and our Catholic ancestors there but will move through time and across the nation to meet them in the many places that they lived and labored: New York, Charleston, Michigan, North Dakota, Spokane, and San Francisco. The ancestors will invite us into a history we may not have known, since so many of us have never met them before.

In the work of creating such a history from the archives at Georgetown, Rachel Swarns describes the challenging task of reconstructing just one Catholic family in the early American Church. Swarns writes:

> Denied literacy by priests who deemed them unworthy of an education, the Mahoney sisters, like millions of other enslaved people were effectively silenced. As a result, there are questions about their lives that I cannot answer, personal experiences that I cannot depict. Sometimes, as I studied the spidery script of the Jesuits' handwritten letters, the sisters and their ancestors seemed like ghosts passing through this world, leaving barely a trace.[4]

The proximity of ancestors to ghosts in Swarns's description asks us to consider the ways in which most of the people who went before us in the history of the Catholic Church have been lost to memory, such that our histories often rely on the most prominent figures to advance a narrative of who we are today. When some among those forebears in the faith were actively erased in the creation of ecclesial histories, they are, in effect, rendered as ghosts. The work of reconstructing a fuller picture of Catholic history in America asks us to consider some whom we may not have recognized as our ancestors being written back into our shared memory.

Kang's portrait, drawn and presented as visual memory, and Swarns's detailed accounting of one family's story might be situated as part of a long and arduous task of retelling the history of Catholic institutions in the Americas. And as we allow the story of previously ghostly shadows to come into view as our ancestors, a painful truth also enters our present. That is, while Catholic schools, churches, and universities might understand themselves to be in pursuit of manifesting signs of the grace of God among us, they are simultaneously storehouses for the illicit benefits of the sins of White supremacy. Many among those who were written out of the history of the Catholic Church in America were actively erased so that the truth of ecclesial violence against them would not be part of the story. A fuller telling of our story as an American Catholic Church is warranted, both for the sake of restoring our ancestors and for the healing that might happen today. Indeed, the widespread project of Catholic institutions in our day needing to reckon with the dual facets of our history might be illuminating for us a present reality of trauma—that is, unresolved violence, unmitigated terror, unconscionable atrocities, and "un-Christian" behaviors were the mortar that enabled the building of Catholic institutions in our history. Historical trauma and moral injury name the dressings of the houses we inhabit today. We inhabit these houses of trauma and are still seeking a way to release the pain of our presence within them.

The Indigenous scholar and social worker Maria Yellow Horse Brave Heart (Hunkpapa/Oglala Lakota) outlines a framework for healing from historical trauma. Historical trauma, she notes, "is defined as cumulative emotional and psychological wounding across generations, including the lifespan, which emanates from massive group trauma."[5] In her work, Brave Heart proposes a process for developing a response to historical trauma and empowering communities in social and mental health. The steps she develops are fourfold and include (1) confronting historical trauma and embracing our history, (2) understanding the trauma, (3) releasing our pain, and (4) transcending the trauma.[6] Brave Heart's work is intended for those harmed by historical trauma, in particular, the survivors of Euro-American assault on Indigenous people. But as a process akin to the global projects of Truth and Reconciliation, this cycle might be useful for naming and pursuing a theology of reparation also for those in the lineage of the perpetrators of past harms. What our exploration will show is the deeply interwoven histories of those who bore the burden of pain and those who produced it.

The first step in Brave Heart's recommendation, however, requires that we know or learn (or relearn) our own histories in order to name and to recognize the national trauma in systems of White supremacy entangling both White Christians and Christians of African descent, Indigenous nations, Latinx, and Asian heritage. That some within our nation in the third decade of the twenty-first century cannot bear to face this history is reflected in the resistance to Critical Race Theory—evidence also that there are currently systems in place that thwart our necessarily painful truth telling. This "truth telling" invites the retelling of stories perhaps from perspectives for the first time and complicates the historical narratives that have been received in systems of education, (civil) religion, and church. Initiatives like the 1619 Project, efforts of land acknowledgment, repudiating and dismantling the doctrine of discovery, reclaiming the cultural studies curriculum, reconsidering history from the perspectives of people of color and persons on the margins of power—all these constitute and contribute to some form of truth telling to consider and name more fully the historical trauma that *is* the history of the United States. Resisting the romanticization that erases the painful, traumatic, and inhuman aspects of this history, we are asked to face this history head-on.[7] Cultural pushback toward such programs and legislative refusal to entertain a history informed by critical approaches to race and theory reveals the power that history holds in the push and pull of human life today. Such truth telling is a necessary first step in confronting historical trauma—acknowledging the realities of White supremacies woven into US history in legislation and also in institutions. The project of this book develops as a task of "unlearning history" in its dominant and White-serving forms and "relearning history" as a necessary first step in recognizing painful realities. The histories received through systems of education in the United States, told from the perspective of those who have been racialized as White and who benefited from structures of White supremacy, were constructed to render White violence invisible, so we must relearn the same histories from the point of view of those who struggled to resist the systems and structures of White supremacy.[8] To refuse to see this history participates in the sin of White supremacy by which the histories of the struggles of people racialized as Black, Indigenous, Asian, and Latinx are erased. To refuse to hear their voices today participates in the racism that stole history from us all.

At the same time, this story of White America has been told as a religious story as well, often in the genre of hagiography, celebrating the expansion of Christendom at any cost. In this version of American history, the symbolic capital of God's blessing rested on Christians even as Christians stole Indigenous land and lives and African labor and lives and erased the diverse cultures and religions of the globe. The death and destruction wrought by White Christians throughout American history can be named in no other way in the Christian framework except as "sin": the sin of White supremacy breaking the fundamental Christian promise to love God and love neighbor. Through an alternative lens, we might see things through the critical eyes of Christian faith and like Rev. Dr. Jeremiah Wright proclaim "God Damn America" where others plead for the promise of God's blessing on the nation, even in the face of its most vicious atrocities.[9] Truth telling and confronting the history of trauma, then, is a crucial first step in the project of transformation and healing from the sins of White supremacy.

Truth telling aligns with Rev. Dr. Iva E. Carruthers's roadmap presented to the World Council of Churches in providing a "conceptual framework and spirit guide of accompaniment" in response to systems of oppression.[10]

Carruthers helpfully presses forward truth telling as "remembrance." Where structures and systems of White supremacy were projects of dismembering and deleting persons from the body politic, retelling history is designed to put bodies and a diverse body politic back together. To re-member. The process of our remembering, of putting the body of America back together, involves writing our histories with a fuller recognition of the actors who made them possible, facing squarely both how our ancestors have been erased *and* the evils our ancestors have perpetrated (these also conveniently erased). In the same way, we re-member a fuller communion of saints when we view ecclesial history through a new lens. But writing histories anew requires also that we recognize how we, in the twenty-first century, remain involved in our ancestors' drama. We must re-member the fullness of our histories in order to recognize how their drama continues today in the inheritance of institutions in which our stories continue to unfold.

Imagining the names of enslaved Catholic Christians etched into the bricks of Catholic Christian institutions, we might be anchored in an understanding that history is not just past, distant from us in time, and the remembering of repentance is not just "out there" in recalling some actors of the past proximally removed from us. Rather, truth telling touches down in the specific locations of our inheritance. The challenge is that so many White Christians distance themselves from systems of evil both temporally and spatially. Temporally, the response to history is often that it happened so long ago that no actors can be held responsible. Spatially, there are far too many opportunities to distance ourselves from actions of the past that happened "out there" or "somewhere else." Naming the harm done in the category of "history" may too quickly absolve Christians today from the evil done by the Christian communities of our forebears. Yet thinking through history as the foundation of inheritance closes the gap and bridges more directly the span of responsibility both spatially and temporally. The illicit gains acquired through systems of evil were embedded in institutions and wealth transferred from one generation to the next that remain with us today. If we can uncover the systems of evil upon which our Christian institutions were built and simultaneously recognize the benefits passed on to us through these institutions in the present, we might formulate a different set of responses to historical evil and historical trauma, ones that might call forth the Christian responsibility of repair. We seek a remembrance "to counter the dis-membering, trauma and woundedness inflicted by systems of acts of white supremacy, racism, patriarchy, and male privilege."[11] As Christian communities, this is essential before even imagining reconciliation.

But, closely related to the project of truth telling in Brave Heart's four-step approach is the necessary accompaniment of "understanding" this history. By this, I take Brave Heart to be opening the door to the rigorous analysis leading toward understanding the dynamics of these histories. If truth telling unearths the "what" that happened and the "who" that was involved, then understanding and analysis unearths the "why" and "how" of its happening. We might think of this second step in the model of a tree whose leaves can be made visible in the truth telling of our stories but whose deeper roots require digging in order to be seen.[12] Here, too, the truth telling of history that we bring forth provides the basis for addressing deeper root causes that might persist through the passage of time. *That* African peoples were enslaved by White European Christians, stealing life and labor over generations, causing social death and requiring resistance, is an essential project of articulating a shared history of the foundations of our nation; this becomes clear in our truth telling. *That* Indigenous peoples were dispossessed of their land, their language, and culture is similarly a necessary chapter in narrating US history to include historical trauma. *How* both of these projects of evil were made reasonable, normalizing inhumanity on the part of White Christians and undertaking these practices as God-ordained, requires deeper analysis of the patterns of thought and practice—educational, legal, theological—that made these projects viable. Whether these practices remain with us today in White Christian anti-Blackness and resistance to the sovereignty of Tribal Nations our analysis must consider as well. We do this because the same patterns of harm we can see in the past might still be patterns deeply embedded in institutions today.

Truth telling and analysis, as first steps on Brave Heart's path, reveal an entangled history of Christians who have been racialized as Black, White, Latino/a/x, Asian, Indigenous, and more, creating the past in the agonistic struggle for the fullness of life and well-being. Driven by ideologies of Christian supremacy, White Christians constructed systems and structures to benefit primarily themselves, betraying the fundamental command to love God and love neighbor. Revisiting these histories and understanding their contours can help us as we work together across racialized lines to dismantle White supremacy in fulfillment of the command to love God and love neighbor. Those first two steps, adopted from Maria Yellow Horse Brave Heart's roadmap, might be collaboratively engaged by all of us across the lines of racialized difference that have separated us as we seek repair and a transformed nation beyond our historical traumas.

But Brave Heart's third step cannot simply be adopted for the purposes of the work to come; it must be adapted. This is because Brave Heart's third step in working with Indigenous communities who have been harmed by the trauma of White supremacy is a process of "releasing the pain." The subject position of those of us who have been racialized as White and who have received direct benefits from the sins of White supremacy must recognize that the project is a different one. So while this history to come and our analysis of it must learn from scholars located within Indigenous, Black, Latinx, and Asian communities, as a White theologian situated in a historically and predominantly White institution, I must wrestle in a particular way in conversation with those like me who have "gained" from systems of White supremacy. The third step will be to loosen the grip on those gains and to "release the gain" so that others may be aided in their release of pain. It is the same entangled history, so a shared analysis may help us, but the path toward transformed institutions (a modification of Brave Heart's fourth step) may be different. Each reader will need to ask: Where am I situated in this history and in the project that Brave Heart sets forth?

The chapters to come follow Brave Heart's call to revisit history equipped with the lens of analysis in order to seek the possibility of transformation and healing from the trauma of White supremacy in our nation, our church, our education system, and our society. Revisiting history with the tools of analysis not only asks the *what* and the *why* but also the *who* and *where*. The structured and legislative buildup of racism did not manifest as a looming cloud that descended from the ether; it was manufactured by people who inhabited the category "White" to secure gain. This didn't happen "anywhere and therefore nowhere" but in particular places and from out of particular social and institutional settings that each of us inhabits as an "I." Once we unearth the who and where, we can ask about the "I" in this investigation. That is, the "I" of the investigation turns the scope of history from the past to the present to ask: What does this history have to do with me today? This volume invites each of us to think not just nationally but locally, to use the particularity of certain histories as a model for considering one's own history. The approach we will take in *Grace of the Ghosts* is to recognize that the national history we aim to "relearn" did not take place in the abstract but in concrete and specific locations. It is a geography of sin and grace that our history reveals, and those systems of sin and grace were transferred through institutions and form the basis of our inheritance today.

Embracing the "I" of investigation toggles between the information of a national history and the inheritance of that history as it lands on the investigator. The "I" of this investigation will be nested in a particular frame to see this "I" not as an individual alone but as fully and radically shaped by the institutions in which we are found. As we pursue this history, the reader will understand that this investigator has a particular relationship to the institutions under investigation. As institutions, they have been storehouses of capital passing down benefits to a collective beyond this investigator.

Here the nesting of Jesuit, Catholic, and Christian is worth explaining. I am situated as a theologian and educator within a particular Jesuit tradition, that is, a subset of the category "Catholic" within the broader global reality of the Christian tradition. I have earned my living and acquired capital as a member of the institution of "Fordham University." We advance our brand as "Jesuit" (*The Jesuit University of New York City*) in such a way that renders us connected symbolically, as well as practically and sometimes economically, with other "Jesuit" institutions. And simultaneously, we understand ourselves to be one among many institutions in the Catholic tradition, that particular strain of the wider Christian tradition that has hierarchically ordered itself toward the symbolic leader of the Pope. In embracing the "I" of this investigation, I simultaneously speak as a member of the Jesuit, Catholic, and Christian traditions. At times, the histories pursued in the following chapters will focus explicitly on Jesuit institutions, and at others, we will recognize the broader networking with Catholic institutions, always with the recognition that the patterns we identify among Catholics may be shared by American Christians more broadly.

For those similarly embedded in the particularity of these institutions (particularly of Jesuit and Catholic church and school) a similar "I" of investigation might unfold to ask what the reader has inherited from these institutions. For those embedded in other institutions, the frame offered in our investigation might be turned on your particularity. Each reader must ask: Where did *I* receive benefits from institutions that pass along illicit gains from the sin of White supremacy? An institutional frame for our "I"s enables us to capture a localized, shared history but to keep attentive to different experiences within these institutions, within our shared history.

## Institutional Ontology

If you peel back the layers of your institution, what injustice will you find? *The approach of this study is to consider history in order to identify the inheritance from injustice embedded in the capital of institutions.* That is the framework you will find in each chapter of this work: history retold in order to analyze the unjust inheritance that flows through our institutions. In order to orient the reader to the pages that follow, in this section we will work our way through each of the concepts embedded in the descriptive overview just stated. Working our way backward through the stated approach, this section identifies four interrelated concerns, which can be posed as questions. First is the question of what constitutes an "institution." Second, is the category of "capital"—what is capital, and how is it found within institutions? The third concern focuses on injustice as it interrelates with capital and institutions. And fourth is the recollection of history. This section takes each of these (institution, capital, injustice, history) up in turn to see the connections among these concepts as the framework to shape the investigation of this book.

The question of our study, then: How does revisiting history help identify the capital inheritance from injustice embedded in the institutions from which I draw benefits? Let's begin with "institutions" as a location that constitutes the framing of our inquiry. Modern theologians have tended throughout the centuries to consider our human existence primarily in the form of the individual, secondarily in the form of the social, and only vaguely through the lens of the institutional. An individual approach focuses on the solitary soul, the singular person tasked with crafting their life and their choices. In theological terms, the person stands as an individual before God. Such an individual approach has dominated Western Christian thought as the primary conceptualization of who we are as human beings (by comparison, many other cultures of the world prioritize the collective in which the human is embedded). This individualized approach still functions in many systems of Christian thought and practice. But, even Western Christians have, in the twentieth century, begun the work of shifting the conceptualization of what it means to be human toward recognizing the impact of the social upon the individual. Thus, late-twentieth-century theological anthropologies have moved away from the solitary soul making its way through the world in relation to God and toward the embeddedness of the human person—body and soul—always already among its "others." Movements in Christian thought that recognize the communal dimensions of our human existence and the social shaping of our lives have come to be recognizable within the theological landscape. Such a social frame for conceiving our lives as human beings has enabled us to expand the aperture for seeing the human in relation to other humans as the primary unit of theological concern, or even the human in relation to the broader world of sentient beings of the four-legged/two-legged/those who fly ecological theologies, or even in relation to the nonsentient whole of the created world in environmental concerns.

But, we have yet to fully consider the human person embedded in the quasi-sentient form of institutions—those places where persons and ideologies of the past have come to rest and take up residence in ways invisible to us. If "the social" points toward living, breathing networks of the present by which the human person is shaped in the encounter of the push and pull of relationships, then "the institutional" might point toward the nonliving locations that are nonetheless networks in which the push and pull may have ceased but the resultant forces of past agonisms remain. Here we might pause to consider the shift of our frame from the individual to the social through systems to institutions.

If the social, or "society," designates a group of people living together, then social systems are those structures put in place by the collective for people's needs to be met as they live together. In a society (or in social perspective), persons don't get food simply by individually hunting or planting or harvesting by themselves alone; rather they meet their food needs through a food system that organizes their activities alongside others' to meet this biological need. In the geographical location of what is now known as the United States, the food system may have previously consisted of nations Indigenous to the land coordinating their efforts of hunting, planting, and seasonal settlement among themselves and in negotiation with other nations. Today, the food system includes everything from restaurants, grocery stores, farmers markets, and home gardens to local ordinances, factory production, the Food and Drug Administration, multinational corporations, and more. What we need for biological sustenance is coordinated in unseen and complex configurations, which nonetheless are essential to our bodily functioning as humans. Without a food system within our society, the biological need for food to survive would not be met. Add to this image the water system, the housing system, the transportation system, and our systems of safety and security, all of which similarly meet our basic needs, and we begin to adjust our vision to the invisible structures in place that support our being human. This is the unit of "the social" read through a "structural" or "systemic" lens. Our social reality in the United States is further expanded with a recognition of the systems in place to meet a wider range of human needs—for expression, for spiritual growth, for recreation, for intellectual development. Here, we witness that some systems endure *and* produce ideological connections over time. In the words of Anthony Giddens: "Institutions by definition are the more enduring features of social life."[13] The fundamental systems that govern not only our biological needs but our developmental, psychosocial, intellectual, and spiritual needs have been identified by the theorist Pierre Bourdieu as a fourfold set of interlocking domains: the family, the religious field, educational systems, and the state.[14] Each of these has come to be a foundational structure in Western society. For our investigation, this facilitates a subtle shift into the domain of institutions insofar as these structuring systems communicate deep and lasting values.

If "the social" is the recognition of the ways in which we get what we need to live through collective distribution, and if "systems" are the containers for accessing those needs, then "institutions" might be seen as the settled repositories bearing the imprint of the past on the systems of the present. In unpacking the concept of "institution," we can consider how "contemporary sociologists use the term to refer to complex social forms that reproduce themselves such as governments, the family, human languages, universities, hospitals, business corporations and legal systems."[15] To this, of course, we must add churches.

## Institutions as Systems That Shape Us

Within a structural approach to understanding our human experience, one thing that is distinctive about institutions is their role in connecting us temporally and grounding us geographically. Insofar as they endure historically, institutions are among those structures that not only shape us in the present but connect us to the past. These two features of institutions bear unpacking: the shaping function in the present and the connecting function with the past. In the present, institutions are distinctive in the systemic landscape because they are informed by specific ideologies. Thinking systemically, something like the "water system" (the coordinated ways that members of a society access the needs of human survival) bears very little ideology except insofar as its function is to get "water" to the members of the society. Water, because of its biological necessity, is a "good," and clean water is "better" than water that has been tainted. Because of the very close proximity between the system and humans' biological needs, there is little room for divergence in relation to our assessment of water systems. Its biological functionality moves it in the direction of the ideologically neutral. The water system is simply a way to meet our biological need. Similarly, with the "transportation system," the shared value that is the foundation of the system is the human need to move from one place to another and human abilities of ambulation. Ideologically, it's not a particularly controversial idea that humans *can* move and that we might desire a system that enables us to do so. As we will see, while in principle systems may be neutral (they are functional conduits for getting members of a society what they need to live), ideologies do inform the functioning of the systems in context. Wealthy communities control access to various systems, and systems are often set up to serve some members of a society better than others (think public transportation access in rural communities or the suburbs or accessibility for persons with devices to aid their mobility, or think about access to clean water in some of America's cities). But in principle, systems themselves are *functional* and thus ideologically lean in the direction of neutrality.

Institutions, however, have been imbued with ideological commitments expressly articulated by the institutions themselves. The institution of "the state" for example, conveys visions of the human person embedded within it, as evidenced in writings like the Constitution (which puts forth the ideology of a more perfect Union, that establishes Justice and secures the Blessings of

Liberty) or the Pledge of Allegiance (that we are a nation "under God") and countless other expressions of what scholars have named our "civil religion" insofar as it elevates particular ways of being human and makes them ideal: Liberty, Justice, Union under God.[16] The truths of the state purport to be "self-evident," but when comparing them with other cultural contexts perhaps we can see that they are not so. The institution of "the church" similarly distinguishes itself by self-reflective expression of its highest values as *assertions* about the nature of the human person. For Christians, the institution of the church might be recognizable as a collective that makes claims upon us: that humans *are* made in the image of God, that Jesus Christ *does* reflect what it means to be fully human, that some actions are "righteous" and others not. As a final example, the institution of "education" similarly (although perhaps less evidently) also makes claims about what it means to be human and structures its curriculum around particular values. Each of these examples points to the conceptualization of "institutions" as normative structuring systems. As Vefa Saygin Ögütle describes: "Mainstream sociology tends to define institutions through systems of norms and/or normative social practices. The norms that regulate these practices present themselves as the rules laid down by legal systems, religious beliefs or cultures."[17] A distinctive feature of institutions is that they are structures that convey particular ideologies and foreground norms that project particular ways of being human and shape human practices. Institutions are value-laden structures that shape distinctive practices.

## Institutions as Connections in History

In addition to shaping us as humans in particular ways, institutions simultaneously connect us temporally to those who inhabited the system before us. Christians, for example, understand themselves to be continuing a tradition within the institution of "the church" in a way of being human stretching backward in time more than two thousand years. The institution of the church functions for those within it as a connection to the past: We articulate our values today with reference to those values as they were expressed by those who have gone before us within the institution. The stories written by Christians in the first century continue to inform how we understand our human condition today; the developments of patterns of thought—by medieval or modern theologians—are embraced as worthwhile ways of thinking about the human from past to present. The church may promise to deliver to us what we need for our spiritual lives, but it also does so in a way that is particular in relation to other religious institutions (diverse denominations and other religious traditions). In a parallel way, the institution of education also looks back to the past as foundational for practices in the present. The comparison of educational institutions cross-culturally may provide us with the recognition that institutions shape us distinctively and that ours is not the only way of proceeding, thus illuminating the values that were selected by our institutional predecessors. And wherever one is situated nationally, the institution of "the state" puts forward key ideologies to shape its citizens and all who reside within its territorial boundaries, drawing connections to the past and its founding values expressed in originary documents. Our human-being-in-the-world is shaped not only by the others with whom we are in relation (the lens of the social) but also by the systems that structure our interactions (the lens of the systemic) and further by the institutions that anchor collective values over time (the lens of the institutional).

## Institutions as Conduits of Capital

To the structural consideration of institutions as (a) shapers of our way of being human and (b) connections with the past, we might add an examination of the ways in which institutions are value laden as (c) conduits of capital. To pursue this point, a discussion of "capital" in its many forms will aid the investigation.

The sociologist and social theorist Pierre Bourdieu analyzed social systems and the currency that flows through them by distinguishing between various forms of capital. For the purposes of an investigation of institutions, three of these forms are critical: (1) economic, (2) social, and (3) cultural. Economic capital is the form that most readily comes to mind when many hear the term "capital." Money, currency, and material goods all fall within the category of economic capital as the means of securing needs in human lives: One can barter to get what one needs in the exchange of material goods, or one can dip into one's bank account and produce an exchangeable currency to purchase the material necessities (and luxuries) of human life. This form of capital is, of course, crucial in the modern world and our global *capitalist* social being. Participation in social systems so often depends on capital to gain a fundamental access to what we need to live. Our housing system, food system, water system, education system, and transportation system, in a capitalist society, all require economic capital.

But economic capital is not the only form of capital Bourdieu names; there is also social capital. In order to get what one needs for human life, one might also tap into the resource of "people power." If I need the resource of shelter, for bodily protection against the elements, I can put in the effort to construct a home for myself, I can dedicate some of my economic capital (money or barter) to enlist the help of another, or I can tap into the social capital of my network of family, friends, and acquaintances to help me build what I need. The importance of social capital in considering our human experience through a collective lens is central, especially as we think about how collectives enact the systems that enable members of a society to meet their needs. Institutions of the state, the church, and education all are wrapped up in these forms of capital, both economic and social, which we will unpack throughout this investigation.

But a third form of capital is uniquely associated with institutions, and bringing it into focus is crucial for our project. This third form of capital Bourdieu names as "cultural capital," or "symbolic capital," and while more ephemeral, it is nonetheless powerful as a resource for acquiring a range of human needs. Like economic capital and social capital, cultural (or symbolic) capital can be leveraged to achieve particular aims, but unlike economic capital and social capital, there is no object or person to leverage but a more intangible mode for exchange. Bourdieu would propose that our ability to access other locations of capital (economic and social) relates directly to how we are seen and what symbolic/cultural capital we hold. With the concept of cultural capital, Bourdieu asks us to see the ways in which the social collective enhances access to the systems of goods, services, and *power* by assigning a value to certain forms of being within the society.

In the United States, the systems are such that not every person moves through them with the same ease. As our bodily capacities change with age, we may not be able to navigate the systems of transportation in order to access what is available through the food system. Without the resources of social capital or economic capital, the limitations of our bodies may make our access to the systems of our society even more difficult. Although food is provided to all members of society via the same system, our location as persons within that system and our ability to navigate that system will change across our lifespan as we age. In the United States, the systems have also developed so that not every person has access to them to the same degree. Consider the housing system and the many years during which discrimination on the basis of race or sexual orientation made access to the goods of the system difficult or impossible. Or the transportation system, which even in the twenty-first century has points of access that deny participation by virtue of differently inhabited bodies (the curbs on sidewalks or stairs to the subway station precluding persons with wheeled accompaniment of stroller or chair). Or the water system, which has been demonstrated to serve wealthy communities differentially from poorer ones, a feature also of the people power of social capital and the ability to call on someone who can "get things done." The assigning of value—the recognition of being "seen" as a member of the society whose needs have a priority in being met—is the root of cultural capital.

Several features are important here to illuminate the functioning of cultural/symbolic capital and the way it adheres to institutions. First, cultural capital is *created by the power of the collective.* That is, members of society (past and present) assign value to certain persons beyond their fundamental reality as *persons* and to certain objects beyond their functionality. The example Bourdieu uses is that of the "luxury car," whose functionality may be embedded in the transportation system but whose presence on the road conveys a value beyond that of getting its occupants from point A to point B. New clothes of the latest design are functionally equivalent to hand-me-downs insofar as meeting the human need of covering, but the former leverages a symbolic capital that the latter does not. Symbolic capital inheres in material objects (crowns, gowns, and diplomas) "invested with value in the eyes of those who want to be of [a particular social world]." In Bourdieu's words:

> Every recognition is misrecognition: every type of authority, and not only that which imposes itself through commands, but that which is wielded without having to be wielded, that which is said to be natural and which is sedimented in language, a demeanor, manners, a lifestyle, or even things (scepters and crowns, ermines and gowns in another time, luxury cars and lavish offices nowadays), rests on a form of primeval belief more profound and more ineradicable than what we ordinarily convey by that word. A social world is a universe of presuppositions: the games and the stakes it proposes, the hierarchies and the preferences it imposes, in short the ensemble of tacit conditions of membership, what is taken for granted by those who belong to it and which is invested with value in the eyes of those who want to be of it, all of this rests upon . . . a perception of the social world as natural and taken for granted.[18]

In Bourdieu's exploration of "symbolic capital," some objects with an equivalent functionality are imbued with greater value than others within a given social world. It is the members of the social world, over time in history and culture, who have invested the currency in symbolic capital to make some objects more valuable than others and some persons appear more valuable than others, as well. As the values have been laid down over time, the evaluation itself is rendered "natural," accompanied by an endless field of presuppositions about what is recognizably of value and what is not.

From the institution of religion, one of the most evident examples of symbolic capital is the Bible—a book that has a power that a person can leverage, aligning their way, their truth, with the meaning that has been poured into that object. But to understand the power of that book, Bourdieu facilitates an understanding of the wider social world that has created the network of meaning empowering that book to be the repository of symbolic capital. What Bourdieu asks us to see is that the book itself may be no more than paper and ink but that the members of the social world in which it is situated have imbued it with significance.[19] The insight that Bourdieu's analysis yields is that the symbolic capital of the Christian tradition (and other religious traditions) is essentially relational: Over generations, human beings have produced this particular book as "sacred," through countless operations of "credit and discredit" of this book in relation to other books. When persons today leverage the symbolic capital that has been accounted to the Bible, they are drawing on the reserve that countless persons have deposited as "credit" into that sacred text across time and place. Indeed, countless accoutrements of religion are storehouses of symbolic capital. The collar, the sanctuary, the host, and the icon all convey symbolic capital. Symbolic capital inheres in ideas as well; think "pagan" or "heretic" or "sinner" and the power such words wield. Religious institutions are especially rich in the currency of symbolic capital—making them both highly effective and seriously dangerous. Other institutions similarly function as storehouses with symbols that can be mobilized. In educational institutions, "the degree" functions in this way, as do "grades" and "mastery"; in the institutions of the state, postures toward the flag or the national anthem indicate the power of symbolic capital. In addition to connecting past and present and shaping the social present with expressed ideologies, institutions are the bank accounts of capital: economic, social, and cultural. Access to all of these forms of capital affects the way that people move through the world and navigate the invisible realities of social systems.

## Institutions as Storehouses of Economic, Social, and Cultural Capital

The point of focusing on institutions is to ask each reader to consider two things. First, what institutions have shaped you? And second, what benefits have accrued in those institutions, and how were they passed on to you? Recall Bourdieu's identification of the four key institutions that shape Western social life: family, religion, the state, and education. Think for a moment of your family of origin. What values were conveyed within this social unit such that you look out on the world and recognize some ways of being human as having value and others not? Did your family of origin convey the importance of work and/or of taking care of one another? Were social occasions and celebrations of importance? Did the family communicate particular gendered and sexually oriented ways of being? Importantly, was your family of origin or a family you lived into afforded particular economic, social, and/or symbolic capital for you to tap into? What financial resources did the family convey? What social networks and status markers were available simply by being a member of this family, in relation to other families?

Importantly, "the family" is intimately related to the most ubiquitously structuring institution, "the state" and the symbolically rich institution of "religion."[20] For your "family" and its values (both conveyed and accrued) was not alone in its formation of what "counts." In fact, "the state" preceded the particular formation of your family and structured its values prior to its coming into being. Although we may experience the relationships of "the family" as "natural," it is through legislation and economic advantages that certain forms of "the family" were (and are) granted symbolic, social, and economic capital through the systems of "the state."[21] For the better part of American history, heterosexual partnering of persons named as "male" and "female" formed the basic unit of the family and were granted rights of ownership, decision making, and mutual care and responsibility *by the state*. Similarly, children taken care of within this heterosexual unit have been recognized in a particular way first by the state and subsequently by "society." But even this basic family unit, recognized and governed by the invisible workings of the state, was informed by an even more basic designation by the state in the value-and-rights-laden recognition of "the citizen." Enslaved people in America, for example, may have forged patterns of human partnership that were *not* recognized as rights-bearing precisely because of their prior status as enslaved rather than citizen. State designation of some family units being "unfit" similarly denies rights conferred to other family units. While we may think of "the family" as a self-determined and self-determining unit, it is deeply embedded in the systems of "the state" for its constitution. In pursuing the "I" of this investigation, each reader might ask, *Where have I been embedded in the institution of the state?* Do I continue to be located within the struggle of recognition and rights afforded to "the citizen" (a most potent conveyor or denier of symbolic/cultural capital)? Or at what point did my ancestors become "citizens"? How has the unit of my family of origin or my current family been assigned or denied recognition in the institution of the state? What financial gains or losses have I or my family experienced as a result of my location in the rhetorical and judicial fields of "the state"? Access to housing, education, and health care; the impact of incarceration; and the denial of protections—all access to the workings of the state *through* the family remind us of our embeddedness in these interlocking, foundational institutions of our society.

In addition to its embeddedness in the institution of the state, the institution of the family has for the better part of the modern period been embedded also in the institution of religion. In nearly every era of American history, in fact, the state and religion were co-constitutive, sharing the same values and functioning in a mutually reinforcing way to grant and guarantee rights. The kinds of humans who were recognized by the state as citizens, for example, had been articulated by religious institutions as worthy of recognition: adult, male, rational, in control, and partnered with adult, female companions as envisioned in a biblical narrative. The values of religion and the state formed the institution of the family, conferring rights, privileges, and recognition. Here, again, each reader can ask themselves the question of how the institution of religion shaped the generations of their forebears and continues to shape them today. How did affiliation with a religious institution in the past provide access for recognition among my forebears? How did the values of religious institutions inform the values of other institutions of society: state policy, business exchange, the media? How does affiliation with religious institutions continue to convey access to social and symbolic capital? Where do "I" fit in relation to the institutions of religion?

The institutions of religion, the family, and the state have all been wrapped up in the institution of education in the fourfold structuring of our lives embedded in institutions. While we may think of the education system as simply passing down knowledge, the analysis of capital asks us to see education as an institution that passes down capital, first and foremost "cultural capital." The education system determines what types of human living are normative and conveys values for the next generation of humans to inhabit. Think for yourself which lives mattered and were centered in the study of humanity at work within the education you received. How was "knowledge" rendered as both natural and normative in the various educational settings of your life? Which lives matter in the US system of education? And how did access to education create the cultural and economic capital of "class status" in your personal and familial history? The institution of education conveys not only cultural capital (to be recognizable as a citizen with a diploma or advanced degree) but that cultural capital opens doors of social capital and economic capital. Thus, in addition to seeing institutions conveying values to those formed within them, institutions also serve as conduits of capital from one generation to the next, capital that is social, economic, and symbolic.

## Institutions in America and the Shape of White Supremacy

At this point, an arresting statement from the Christian scholar-activist Joseph Barndt is poised to ask us to consider the systems in which we are embedded in a new way. That is, he asks us to consider that our institutions have been built upon injustice and have been conveyors of injustice. Considering the history of racism in the United States and how Christian communities might analyze it, Barndt asserts, "In the United States, every system and every institution were created originally and structured legally and intentionally to serve white people exclusively."[22] We could return to each section of the chapter thus far to trace the ways in which the systems, structures, and institutions in the United States served the needs of White Christians first and devalued Black, Indigenous, Asian, and Latinx persons at the same time. Even systems as biologically essential and seemingly value neutral as the water and food systems have been structured to provide clean water and healthy foods to some communities and not others: the Flint water crisis and the recognition of "food deserts" that affect primarily communities of color provide the evidence of this institutionalized White supremacy functioning even today. The system of education acted as a site of exclusion both from access and from the way histories are passed on; this is a location of institutionalized White supremacy that culturally specific studies and Critical Race Theory aim to address. The embeddedness of White normativity (as a form of White supremacy) within education and higher education is a reality that is not only in the past but evident in the struggles over the curriculum at today's school board meetings and departmental curricular decisions. Our systems of American religion, when designed and defended by White Christians, also are institutions that continue to be White serving at a time when Whiteness has become so embedded as to be invisible. White Christian (and White Catholic Christian) churches advance the perspectives and interests of persons who have been racialized as White, with all the past and present material advantages that racializing has entailed. Barndt explains: "Institutionalized racism takes place when an institution is shaped and structured in a way that effectively it serves and is accountable to only one racial group, while at the same time, it does not effectively serve nor is accountable to other racial groups."[23] It is the fundamental aim of this book to engage in the truth telling of White Catholic Christian institutions that will allow us to understand them as structured by institutionalized racism, that is, that will allow us to understand them as structures of institutionalized White supremacy.

Barndt also elevates in his history the reality that the Christian Church as institution has been mobilized in directions that resist institutionalized White supremacy. He names the simultaneity of the church both advancing and subverting White supremacies as a "tale of two Churches" in American history.[24] This tension of the "otherwise possibility" that the church might have developed as an antiracist institution will also be considered in our investigation. But this truth telling leads to an analysis that understands the history of American Catholicism (within Christianity more broadly) as holding agents responsible, insofar as actors make choices within institutions to pursue some values and not others. This truth telling and analysis will be for the purpose of realizing our inheritance *and* recognizing patterns in today's practices. With this more clearly in view, we might leverage our places within institutions to transform them.

The aim of approaching the sins of White supremacy through an institutional locus is that it enables us to forge an intimate link between past and present. While a "social" approach asks us to think in terms of the collective, an institutional approach allows us to think in terms of a collective *over time.* In this way, the sins of the past are recognized to have been planted as seeds that have grown into the situation of the present. Thus far, I've spoken of patterns and practices of the past that endure in the practices within institutions of the present as locations of White supremacy that need to be disrupted. A past practice of centering White actors in educational systems lingers today in decisions about the curriculum, reproducing the harmful proposal that only White actors created this history, that only White histories "count." A past practice of assigning leadership to White male elected (or appointed) officials—in church or state—shapes deep assumptions about who is prepared to step into leadership roles and whose leadership "counts." The mobilization of political and ecclesial bodies in broadening the field of representation demonstrates that this pattern of practice is still being struggled against. Institutions, as conveyors of values, forge a link of past practices with today.

But the link between past and present through institutions is even more pressing when we recognize institutions as conduits of capital in its many forms. For the purposes of our investigation, the institutions of church and school have also been *repositories* of capital—even capital illicitly gained. In the functioning of these institutions, these locations continue to be places where the recognition afforded by symbolic/cultural capital continues to be produced. *Who* is recognized as a person before God is an idea woven into institutional practices and is messaged through the institution of the church. The cultural capital of recognition accessed through the institution of the church is distributed to some and withheld from others. *Who* is a person worthy of consideration as producer or agent in our education system similarly confers cultural/symbolic capital that is accessible to some and withheld from others. These two institutions (church and school) will inform access to the symbolic/cultural capital of *who* is worthy of consideration as a person before the law. The residual decisions of recognition from the past continue to inform the recognitions afforded by the generators of cultural capital of the present. More pressingly for the purposes of this volume, however, are the forms of *economic* capital that have come to inhere in White institutions, which are the illicit gains from the sins of White supremacy. White institutions built upon land transferred/stolen from Indigenous nations have the buildup of capital illicitly gained as the very foundation of their being. White institutions that benefited (in any number of ways) from an economy of enslavement have the buildup of capital from the systems of White supremacy illicitly forging the built environments that persist as evidence of capital over time. White institutions that generated messaging that prioritized some at the expense of others had a part to play in the retention of illicitly gained wealth through the practices of institutions. Institutions, in their presence over time, are locations in which the deficits and benefits of the past reside—even those illicitly gained.

In pursuing this investigation of history to identify the inheritance from injustice embedded in the capital of institutions, *each* reader is encouraged to identify the institutions in which they are embedded. Peel back the layers of your institutions. What injustices will you find? An institutional locus for our investigation will draw each of us in and make us personally responsible for how we benefit from the sins of the past. An institutional lens, in the ways that institutions perform a connecting role over time, is useful in calling us to accountability. An institutional lens is useful also because institutions are homes to ghosts.

## A Christian Theology of Ghosts

The past is never merely past; it is woven into the structuring realities of the present, and ghosts reside in the warp and weft, the brick and mortar, the sense and sensibility of institutions. The sociologist Avery Gordon invites us to make room for ghosts. For Gordon, ghosts are presences in our social matrix of persons who have been violently written out of our sociological landscape yet whose wounds remain as a feature of our complex relationality.[25] They are absent, yet the gap that marks their absence is felt as a discomfiting reminder of those whose exclusion was part of the constitution of the event, the moment, the place, the reality. Like the "disappeared" whose absence creates the nation or the missing women in old photographs of school settings, the ghosts are people who are *not* there but whose presence is. In Gordon's rendering, ghosts are "phantoms of modernity's violence"[26] who remain as an active presence that might call us to see reality in a new way and force us to face the changes that must be enacted. In their haunting, the ghosts ask us to

> reliv[e] events in all their vividness, originality and violence so as to overcome their pulsating and lingering effects. Haunting is an encounter in which you touch the ghost or ghostly matter of things: the ambiguities, the complexities of power and personhood, the violence and the hope, the looming and receding actualities, the shadows of our selves and our society.[27]

In attuning our senses to the absent-presences of the ghosts, we meet our ancestors, whose lives were given over into the creation of our social and institutional landscape as it is today. Such attentiveness to the grace of the ghosts is not only an awareness of our past but a call to our future. The ghosts cry out to us with a "something to be done"; our reckoning with them is for the purposes of a transformed present. "Indeed, to fight for an oppressed past is to make this past come alive as the lever for the work of the present."[28] By encountering the ghosts, we are suspended between a time that has passed, a present that remains terrifying, and the possibilities of a future that might be otherwise. The ghosts in their requirement of a reckoning with the past open up for us also what Ashon Crawley names an "otherwise possibility."[29] This way that things were, this way that things are, is but one among countless ways that we might be in the world, that we might be together. These "otherwise possibilities" are "alternative modes, alternative strategies, alternative ways of life [that] *already* exist."[30]

Guided by ghosts, we enter into the complicity of institutions in the evils of the past: those whose elimination made the nation possible, those whose bodies worked to build institutions but of whom no trace remains. But attunement to ghosts should always render our discussion complex in recognizing that no single human being can take responsibility for the damage that has been done and in recognizing that no human being can be reduced to the damage they have done. Similarly, no human being can be reduced to the damage that has been done to them, and the ghosts in their present-absence press their agency and power both present and past.

In what follows, I'll admit, I've been graced by ghosts: drawn forward in the investigation by unseen forces that I "stumbled on" in the archives. It began when the historian Craig Wilder put forward in clear detail the ways in which religiously affiliated universities in this country both manufactured the cultural capital of religious "knowledge" of African peoples *and* used that knowledge to propel the trade in human beings that brought economic capital back to the very university producing the knowledge. And I started to wonder . . . where did the capital come from to found my institution? The one from which I draw my livelihood (in economic capital) and through which I experience an abundance of symbolic/cultural capital (in the doors it has opened up, in the people I have met, the experiences it has afforded me, the recognition of the ways I spend my time)? This question led me to the archives and the present-absence of Henrietta (who you'll meet in Chapter 3), whose trace remains in a letter penned to a southern slaver by a Jesuit seeking a portion of slaveholding wealth for tuition payment. From there, the question of where the wealth of institutions comes from led me to the many who had been written out of our forebears' accounts. And yet it was they who helped in the creation of the network of Catholic schools and churches. The connections the ghosts have called me to make in the stories that unfold throughout this book I can call nothing but a grace: the presence of God at work imperceptibly in the world to make things new. As a Christian, I'm guided by another ghostly presence: the absent-presence of a man who lived attentive also to the demons that reside among us.

For Christians, our primary ghost is Jesus. He is the one whose haunting presence claims our witness in the sanctuary space, the one who is present in his absence, calling us forward to the otherwise possibility of a world that might be transformed. But how we understand Jesus, whose life was erased in history but whose witness as the Christ lives on, is crucial in making the connection of seeing Jesus Christ as living witness to the ghosts of our Christian institutions. To pursue this thread—to listen for the voice of Jesus through the ghostly presence of our institutions—requires that we resituate Jesus also in a new frame. Not the frame of the individual or the frame only of the social but the frame of the institutional. For Jesus conveyed to principalities and powers a way of being that we too might follow today.

## A Christian Response to Institutionalized White Supremacy

The extinguishing of human life that renders people into ghostly presences is nothing new in Christian tradition. In fact, the central witness to the person of Jesus as the Crucified One can be rendered eerily similar to a twenty-first-century sociologist's consideration of ghosts: a presence that witnesses in its absence to the otherwise possibility of what could have been. Such a ghost, the presence of a person crushed by "powers and principalities" (Ephesians 6:12) in structures and systems that kill, who calls forth a better world seems precisely the witness of the first Christians to the alternative grace of Jesus. Fundamentally represented breathing his last breath as a torture victim on a first-century cross of state-sanctioned violence, the crucifixion runs throughout Christian history as potent symbolic capital conveying an essential meaning of the faith.

Two elements of the Christian story hook us into this particular rendering of the faith. Situated in the Creed—proclaimed by Christians from the fourth century to today—is the affirmation that the Jesus who lived in history is not dead upon death on a cross but living witness to the otherwise possibility of the renewal of life: "On the third day he rose again." This rising to new life has been the cornerstone of a Christian faith in the otherwise possibility that Jesus of Nazareth announced. And like our forebears in the faith, we might link this future possibility (that we too might rise to new life, as he was the first fruits of an abundance to come) with the present reality of our failure to heed the redeemer's call: to love God and love one another. The thirteenth-century mystic Mechtilde of Hackeborn recalls being visited by the ghost of the Jesus. Her biographer reports: "One day our Lord appeared to Mechtilde as though suspended, with hands and feet tied, and said to her: 'Every time a man sins mortally he ties Me thus, and as long as he perseveres in his sin he keeps Me in this torture.'"[31] Written forward into the twentieth century, Ignacio Ellacuria heard the ghost of the savior in the cries of the Crucified People: Every time we sin socially, politically, institutionally, we torture again the presence of the Living Christ among us. But to conceptualize more fully a savior who announced the otherwise possibility of a new life beyond the crucifying death of principalities and powers, we must revisit also our Christian history with an institutional lens.

Like the modern, Western traditions of theological anthropology, modern Western approaches to Jesus have most often thought on the level of the individual; they are only newly attentive to the social and only rarely through the lens of the institutional. But the Christian faith confession that Jesus was a revelation of God *in history* means that Jesus, like us, was an individual embedded in the social realities of his time and context *and* moving within the reality of his society through systems. As Richard Horsley describes, even scholarship surrounding the person of Jesus has been molded in a form that expects a consideration of Jesus as a "great man" standing apart from the rest of humanity and primarily concerned with the spiritual or religious dimension of human life. But, as Horsley offers instead, we might see Jesus embedded in the very movements of Jewish resistance in his day, and indebted to Horsley we might read this Jesus-in-movement forward to consider the transformative power of God precisely coursing through the structures and systems of first-century Jewish and Roman institutions. Recent work among biblical scholars might ask Christians reading the sacred text through an institutional lens and the lens of empire to see that while Jesus was a Jew situated in the wisdom traditions of his people, he was also a Jew at a particular time under the dominating systems of the Roman Empire. Two institutions—religion and an occupying state—form the nexus of reconsidering what it might have meant to be a Christ follower in the first century as well as what it means today.

Horsley paints the scene of structures and systems in Jesus's ancient Jewish world with excruciating detail. As an expanding empire, the Roman military led the charge in the system of land acquisition, brutalizing uncooperative peoples and destroying entire cities with its campaigns. Conquered peoples were terrorized by military presence as Romans underwrote their programs advancing ideologies of supremacy and putting into place the systems for a new and better "civilization" with roads, aqueducts, and buildings. As is the case with many imperial projects, land that had been used for sustenance in agriculture was taken over by "the state," and people were displaced. To finance this enterprise, a system of tribute was established by which the conquered peoples would be required to "buy in" to the imperial project, with heavy taxation. But not all Jews experienced the terror of occupation in the same way. While many Jewish movements of the first century emerge as demonstrations of resistance in response to Rome imposing its new institutions of governance, some among the Jewish elite found ways to benefit by cooperating with the occupiers. In fact, as had been done in acquiescing to earlier occupying empires, the temple that was the center of Jewish life had become an institution facilitating Jewish exploitation in cooperation with Rome. Thus, what was once an institution of religious-social-political self-governance among the Jewish people in relation to God (the Temple in Jerusalem) became a location in which the occupying power of Rome was served. The Jesus movement arose in this milieu, and it was one among many movements of resistance aiming to shake off the oppressive and dehumanizing institutions of Rome and reestablish the sacred institutions of the Kingdom of God, where love of God and neighbor were the values that animated the people. Like the prophets before him and Jewish contemporaries among whom he was found, Jesus called people back to the heart of Torah and sparked a movement that would seek this Kingdom of God as an unfolding reality in their midst.

As Horsley and others have recognized, Christians tend to read their scriptures with a spiritualizing and individualizing lens that does not sufficiently bring into focus the structures of the society in which the story of Jesus unfolds. "Empire" is a particular kind of system characterized by organized power over others and that sees the negation of "political freedom, liberation and self-determination" for those under its control.[32] Joerg Reiger characterizes this political system as "massive concentrations of power which permeate all aspects of life and which cannot be controlled by any one actor alone."[33] In the context of ancient Palestine, where the story of Jesus takes place, the controlling agents were a foreign nation (Rome) who took over the systems in place (transportation, water, taxation, built environment, housing, farming, and more) and reconstituted them to serve not the people residing in that place (the Jews who made up the land-bound agricultural peasantry) but to serve the invading and occupying political power. However it was that the people had gotten their water in the past, it now would be supplied by aqueducts. However the people had traveled from one location to the next, they now would be moving along Roman-built highways. While the land once served small units of family and village, it would now be given over to the projects of the Roman Empire. In this context, the institution most aligned with the modern category of "the state" was the occupying power of Rome. Ideologically, Rome understood itself to be the bearer of a superior culture, so that all of these improvements were a "salvation" for a backward people.

Occupying the geographical location that was the homeland for the Jewish people, Rome implemented its own institutions employing the systems already in place. Crucial here was the function of the Temple for the Jewish people, an institution that connected the people temporally to their past and geographically in both horizontal and vertical directions. A horizontal geography connected Jerusalem to all of Israel, even out into its hinterlands. To be a Jew in the ancient world was to be connected to the Temple in Jerusalem, even if one's primary place of residence was a day's journey away. A vertical geography connected the Temple to God as "a place where heaven and earth meet."[34] Serving the religious needs of the people, the Temple served also as the center of culture, politics, and other elements of life for Jews. Rome left the Temple in place to serve the Jews but commandeered it toward service also to Rome. This is why Horsley names it as the "temple-state," bringing into focus not only its social meaning but its structural and institutional ones as well. In Horsley's words:

> Herod and the Romans kept the temple-state intact as a key institution of the imperial order. The temple-state had been set up in Jerusalem in the sixth century B.C.E. by the Persian imperial regime as an instrument of imperial control. The temple provided a religious-political-economic formation in which the Judean people could serve their own "God who is in Jerusalem" (Ezra 1:3) while providing economic support for a priestly aristocracy who both controlled the area and rendered tribute to the Persian court. The Romans and their client king Herod, like the Ptolemaic and Seleucid empires before them, simply perpetuated the temple-state as an instrument of imperial rule.[35]

Not only was the temple-state an arm of imperial rule in which a small minority of the Jewish elite could play a role in keeping the Roman peace, but "they also used their positions of power to feather their own nests of privilege."[36]

So the displaced peasant in the Galilee—more than a day's journey from the Temple—felt the betrayal of the religious elite in Jerusalem acutely in their daily lives. As Horsley describes:

> The impact of Roman conquest and tribute, along with Herodian and high priestly rule, would have been severe on the peasantry, the 90-plus percent of the society that formed the economic base. . . . The brutality of Roman conquest and re-conquest left collective trauma in its wake. The demand for tribute to Rome and taxes to Herod in addition to tithes and offerings to the temple and priesthood dramatically escalated the economic pressures on the peasant producers. . . . The impoverishment of families meant [also] the disintegration of village communities, the fundamental social form of such an agrarian society. It should not be surprising that the Gospels and other sources represent Jesus and other prophets as addressing conditions of hunger and debt.[37]

It is within this social, political, and economic milieu that Christians believe a Word of God was spoken as the Jesus movement proposed that another world was possible. Grounding deeply in their Jewish faith, Jesus and those who followed him drew forth the heart of Torah to respond to the terror and trauma, the disadvantage and dispossession with an alternative vision: not the Kingdom of Rome but the Kingdom of God. We hear this as the beginning of the Christian story, expressed in the literary tradition that comes to us as the Gospel of Mark: "The time is fulfilled, and the kingdom of God has come near; repent, and believe in the good news" (Mark 1:15, NRSVUE). The reign of God now at hand, "which was opposed to and opposed by both the Jerusalem rulers and the Romans," was the Jesus movement's overarching theme for the renewal of Israel, made manifest in their very movement.[38] But as we situate that announcement in the Gospel story, we see that bringing forth a new world required submitting to a baptism of repentance for the forgiveness of sins, and John's movement paved the way for Jesus to call out again to "repent and believe in the good news." The good news at the heart of Torah was that love of God and love of neighbor remained a real possibility even in the time of trauma, even under duress. And as Horsley explains, "The renewal of mutuality, cooperation and solidarity in village communities would surely have been what enabled people in the Jesus Movements to resist the pressures of the Roman imperial rule."[39]

It is into this milieu that the Jesus movement emerged, casting a net and fishing for people who might repent and believe in the Gospel, that this renewal of the mosaic covenant of a Kingdom of God, of love and righteousness, could be a reality. The announcement of the Kingdom of God was the in-breaking of an otherwise possibility. If we can feel not only the brutality and trauma but also the temptation that bowing to or even benefiting from empire might offer, we start to get a feel for the transgressive and transformative nature of an otherwise possibility. And the earliest Christians accepted the invitation into the Jesus movement when the empire was in full strength and had an extensive regime of ideology, backed by military presence. From within the Christian framework, only Jesus can be named the "Son of God," but in the ancient world this was heard as a direct challenge to the emperor, who had already been named as such. Hearers in the ancient world would have expected any announcement of "the gospel" or "good news" to be the proclamation of Rome's latest military defeat, by which the "pax Romana" the peace of Rome would be set in place. Citizens of the Roman Empire saw the power and peace of Roman civilization as the source of "salvation." In the ancient world, Providence had ordered all things and set them in most perfect order by the virtues and beneficence of the Emperor Augustus, sending him as savior; celebrating his birthday as the beginning of the good news. So when Christians said it was *not* the Kingdom of Rome but the Kingdom of God, they were willing to forgo every benefit that empire might bring and bring upon themselves the wrath of imperial power.[40] The announcement of Jesus might be thrown forward to us as it is thrown back into the beginning of his ministry: "Repent and Believe that there *are* Otherwise Possibilities."

The condition of empire might be thought of as a sociopolitical framework through which institutions are put to use not for the good of all within society but for the good of only some. Romans used the institutions of governance and the institution of the military as a brutal force to benefit citizens of the empire, at the expense of the dominated people. Elite Jews accommodated the institutions of the Roman Empire in order to divert resources into their own hands, using the institution of religion (their own religion) to facilitate this transfer through the temple-state. The brutality and exploitation of an imperial configuration of institutions created the conditions for widespread suffering and widespread revolt among the Jews of Jesus's day. And like the many Jews put to death by the powers of Rome in its legal institutions and ruthless military institution for being insurrectionists who resisted the configuration of empire, Jesus too was put to death by a crucifixion that served as a warning to those who would seek to change the institutional course of things.

Thinking through a Christology with the frame of institutions, we might also consider a Jesus who could leverage the capital that institutions make available. As Howard Thurman describes, the Jesus of the Gospels was denied the cultural capital distributed by the Roman Empire. "Jesus was not a Roman citizen. He was not protected by the normal guarantees of citizenship—that quiet sense of security which comes from knowing that you belong and the general climate of confidence which it inspires."[41] Made vulnerable by the systems of the occupying state, we see a Jesus rooted firmly and deeply in the symbolic capital of the Jewish tradition. Throughout the text of the New Testament, Jesus expresses the ultimate longing of the people in the horizon of the Hebrew Bible—in the witness to the God of Abraham and the prophets. With a vision made possible from the generations invested in the story of Israel, the Jesus of Christian faith mobilized the people power of social capital to pursue God's justice and righteousness in the Kingdom of God. The presence he appears to have embodied was one of connecting diversely situated people, providing a healing touch and challenging powers and principalities. Using the built environment of the religious community, he challenged also the vested interests of the few over the many. And people gathered to hear him envision a way of being in the world, one both old in its ancient roots and new in the particularity of its telling.

The spiritual capital of the Jewish tradition of love of God and love of neighbor as the heart of Torah, in the expression of Jesus of Nazareth, had the power once again to rekindle resistance to structures and systems that kill. In Christian history, the raw data of a Jesus who had been crucified is made central. In reconstructing this Jesus of history, we ask not only what kind of systems employed a cross and enacted crucifixions but also what kind of life led to the cross. As Ignacio Ellacuria presents: "Jesus . . . is killed . . . because of the historical life he led, a life of deeds and words that those who represented and held the reigns of the religious, socioeconomic, and political situation could not tolerate."[42] That is, Jesus was killed by those who held the balance of power within institutions designed for their benefit.

But the writers of the Gospels, who chronicled the people's witness to Jesus after his death, also knew that the temptation toward embracing empire and drawing benefit from unjust institutions was strong, not only for the powerful few who benefited the most but also for all those who participate in structures and systems that kill. The Gospel writers thus spread more widely responsibility for Jesus's death. In the Gospel according to Luke, both Pilate and Herod (figures who held the reins of the power within the ancient institutions) exonerate Jesus and offer his release. It is the crowds of people who insist on his death. Thus, the cross of Christ indicts a much wider range of human participation when Luke's crowds shout, "Crucify, crucify him!" (23:21). This places *us* at the foot of the cross, indicted for the many ways we have been the crucifiers, aligning ourselves with structures and systems that kill. In the words of Karl Barth, Jesus Christ is "the point at which is perceived the crimson thread which runs through all history" reflecting back to us from the cross the depths of our sinful condition, which requires God's justice and enacts the mercy that might save us.[43] Although Christians have been called to be an anti-imperial people, time and again Christians across history have chosen reap the benefits of empire.

Yet, in the stories of Christian tradition Jesus Christ does not remain a passive object of contemplation resident on the instrument of torture. Christ lives! In the words of their creed, ancient Christians expressed a belief that the one who died under state-sanctioned torture was not diminished by the power of death:

> He suffered under Pontius Pilate,
> was crucified, died, and was buried.
> He descended to the dead.
> On the third day he rose again.
> He ascended into heaven,
> and is seated at the right hand of the Father.
> He will come again to judge the living and the dead.

While Christian empire has extolled the virtues of Christ-victor "seated at the right hand of the Father," another thread of the tradition might be teased out with the idea that Jesus "comes again" as judge. This thread of Christ as judge coming again (and again) to haunt the living was God's love and judgment, justice and mercy held together in the mystical visions of Mechtilde when Christ visited her with his *Ghostly Grace*.[44] Christ's justice is not reserved for those who put him to death on Calvary but visited upon all those who participate in the sinful condition of our world.

Like the visits upon the mystics, Christ's ghostly grace might haunt Christians in the altar space of liturgical practice when in the artful communication of the cross the Crucified One hovers as an embodied presence over the gathering of the community. Yet if Christ on the cross is not only Jesus of Nazareth but reflects back to us the crimson thread that runs through all history, is it not accurate to say that ghosts of the crucified people haunt as Christ's presence among us? In Ellacuria's description: "What is meant by the crucified people . . . is that collective body . . . the majority of humankind [which] owes its situation of crucifixion to the way society is organized and maintained."[45]

The haunting presence of the Crucified One points to the concentrated bodies of the Crucified People, so that the Concentrated Bodies of the

Crucified People become “a haunting presence . . . anonymous and exponential”[46] and given expression in the broken body of Jesus and his ghostly presence as judge. The expression of Concentrated Bodies also has a transformative potential that might be the presence of the Divine emanating from the judgment of the Crucified. Mark Lewis Taylor writes:

> Concentrated bodies are a perpetually [festering] wound, where bodies and beings are compressed. And yet, there is from the wound a transformative action that at least points, however desperately, to world amid “unworld.” . . . Key to any such transformative impact is a gesture’s or action’s capacity to haunt, to unsettle those concentrations of power and knowledge where weight is amassed.[47]

The Crucified One makes present in the sanctuary space the perpetual wound of the concentrated bodies of the Crucified People. The cross reflects back to those gathered the extinction of bodies that runs through history, which demands God’s justice in response.

In what follows, in the re-membering of Christian history in America, the lens of the Crucified People as Christ’s presence across time brings into focus serious and challenging questions. When White Christians in America created institutions through the death and dis-membering of Others, were they not crucifying Christ? And what if the response of God’s justice was not directed only toward individuals or even only with a social scope but also directed toward institutions? What would it look like to consider the power and possibility of God at work in the world, in “Christian” institutions built through the death-dealing projects of White supremacy? When we see the way that institutions have been conduits of the capital that directed benefits to people racialized as White and denied the fullness of life and even life itself to those racialized otherwise, will we hear the ghostly grace and the call of the Crucified in our day? In revisiting history, those of us who inhabit and benefit from the unjustly accumulated capital residing in White Catholic institutions of church and school might be visited by the ghostly grace of the Crucified One and the seething presence of the Crucified People. In the journey that follows, we will encounter in the ghostly grace of our ancestors the call of the Crucified toward the otherwise possibility of our redemption.

# 2

# Sucky's Scream

## *Hearing the Ghosts and Heeding Their Call*

The institution of the Christian Church has been the structure of meaning and coordinated action by which persons through time have witnessed to the life and ministry of Jesus. Jesus followers from the first century to today have been shaped by the same stories and seen in them a reservoir of values that might anchor the collective over time. Those of us shaped by and residing within institutions of the church—both congregation and school—allow ourselves to be shaped in the symbolic capital conveyed through the Christian Testament and Hebrew Bible. Informed by the ideology of the Crucified One, the institution of the church has passed along the values of a first-century Jew, and they remain formative values even in the twenty-first century.

But throughout the history of the church, the formative values and collected stories have served a range of purposes. "The church" is simultaneously "institution" and "institutions"—bound by common stories but enacting them in different ways. The term "church" itself forms an imagined community, while on the ground it represents diverse denominations and, indeed, diversity within denominations. As the previous chapter has advanced, the history of "the church" as imagined community began in the first century CE, with patterns of resistance to the Roman Empire. But "the church" as institution had a fateful transformation when it was elevated to state practice *through* the Roman Empire. From the ancient expressions up to today, "the church" has taken many forms; some empire resisting, others empire accommodating, and indeed still others as even empire embracing.

In exploring the history of the Catholic Church in America, this recognition of internal and external diversities in the institution of the church allows us to distinguish patterns of Christian expression we might want to carry into the twenty-first century and others we might want to overcome. In particular, as we turn to explore the stories of American Catholics for the purpose of seeking transformed institutions that might equally value *all* persons, we hear the cries of the Crucified even within the church itself. And thus hearing, we might reassess the church as conduit of capital toward greater humanity. As we do this work, we meet our ancestors and consider how their deposit into the symbolic universe of the faith might serve us in the work of seeing our history clearly, understanding its contours, releasing its pain/gain, and recreating transformed institutions of the church. Reaching back into our American Catholic Christian histories, we arrive at the origins of an American Catholic faith in which the institution of the church served both the systems of a harmful status quo and was the location for otherwise possibilities.

## An American Christian Faith in an American Christian Empire

Sometime around 1721, a young Christian girl witnessed a shocking display of harm perpetrated by a Christian man whom she took to be a leader in the faith. She tried to intervene. The setting was colonial America, and this Catholic girl had heard that a priest in her community had as part of his spiritual practice the pain of flagellation, a whipping that he inflicted upon himself that emulated the suffering of Jesus. Such a practice had been widespread in the medieval church of Europe and was adopted in the New World locations of Catholic presence like New Spain and, in this case, Maryland.[1] Presumably curious or perhaps concerned that this sort of violence ran contrary to the Jesus she knew, the young girl peeped in on the cleric's practice and let out a scream at the sight of his self-harm. Susannah, or Sucky, as she was known, worked within a Jesuit Catholic community that grew out of a Christian empire that would become an American Christian empire of its own. But despite the imperial context in which she was embedded and her lack of status in this context, nevertheless she was willing to sound an alarm on the structures and systems of harm conveyed within Christian institutionalized practices. The location of Sucky's context and those who have heard her scream will be the focal point of this chapter's investigation of the institution of the Catholic Church, built paradoxically by the hands of those enslaved by it.

Like the Romans who occupied first-century Palestine, it was Christians who put forward a claim in the fifteenth century that theirs was a superior culture and a more perfect way of being human, attempting to occupy the geography on which persons had lived for millennia, embedded in lifeways on their ancestral land. Through brutal military campaigns, Spanish Christians terrorized Indigenous peoples and taxed them with forced labor to build a Christian empire. In violent conflict with Indigenous residents, New France and New England attempted to secure new systems for their colonial governance, building Christian institutions on land forcibly taken and manipulatively purchased. Hearing Sucky's scream is part of the truth telling necessary to understand our national Catholic history as part of this Christian empire *and* release the pain of the past toward institutional transformation. Sucky's scream was let out from within the depths of the Catholic Christian institution of Georgetown, buried in the past of our collective ignoring of Catholic Christian empire building.

We hear her scream and search for her story in the archives as a way to reconstruct and retell a history with which American Catholics have not yet reckoned. Even as we are willing to turn to the archives, our difficulties in hearing her story are multiple, but the necessity of hearing her scream compels us. As Chapter 1 explored, the turn to history is for the purpose of a truth telling that might foster an analysis that could lead to releasing the pain of historical trauma and, ultimately, to transformation.[2] We are entering an economy of enslavement precisely because of the necessary repair that might emerge from that location of truth telling.

But allowing Sucky's scream to be the productive impulse of our work in truth telling about the Christian institutions of US history poses difficulties insofar as hers is among those stories, accounts, and persons whose witness has been nearly erased. Like the women of Torah and the Christian Testament erased by the scribal account and storyteller's elevation of male characters, the accounts of an America Christian past captured in text and found in the archives privilege those with the power to recount an experience through their writings. The storytellers in our American Catholic past are largely those who had been granted the time, resources, leisure, space, occupation, or vocation of writing. The speeches and sermons of Christian clerics reflect persons with the time to dedicate to such pursuits; the newspaper accounts reflect institutions with the capital to create a public sentiment. So when Catholics created the ideas that would come to us as "tradition," they were mobilizing the capital they had received (economic, temporal, material, and symbolic) and using it to create the conditions for their ideas and practices to take root. Those whose perspectives from the past we have access to are those who were already granted various forms of capital to direct their present and pass it on to us as our past. So when we turn to the archives as a resource for truth telling about the vast number of exchanges that took place in Catholic locations, we have access to partial truths and half-truths written by those with the power to write, the resources to do so, and the prominence for their perspectives to be preserved.

Because people exploited or marginalized by the church often lacked the time, prestige, and material resources to tell their stories, the sources infused by such capital have become the received version of history. New tools are currently being mobilized to tell a more complex and multisided story, for example, in reading legal briefs brought to court by enslaved persons. But, as this example demonstrates, we can envision the difficulty of the full truth emerging when the court system (for example) is controlled by White persons and White interests. Reading against the grain of capital-rich scribes who capture the counterperspective of the capital-poor may be of service in presenting a fuller account in our truth telling. New theoretical frames will also help us examine the diverse elements of the truth-telling account, to tease out its theological importance. Sucky, as one rich but modest example, helps us see the thousands upon thousands of stories that have yet to be told.[3]

This recognition also illuminates for us the capital necessary to recover our histories. First is the capital of creation, by which some writings came into being with the necessary resources just recounted: ability, time, space, leisure. Second is the capital of selection: the symbolic capital of whose writings would be kept and which writings were worth keeping. Third is the capital of preservation: Who has the capital to create and maintain an archive that protects the material evidence of past lives from the destruction of the elements? Fourth is the capital it costs today to access the archival resources: Who has the time/leisure and travel resources to access the material in the archives? Who can dedicate the work hours or pay for others to dedicate the work hours to translate and/or transcribe what capital has preserved in the archives? Who is providing the capital necessary for digital access? All of these questions of capital help us see the resources necessary for the fuller picture of truth telling of our past. The Catholic Church in America is a capital-rich institution with resources for telling a more complete history to fulfill our aim of truth telling and analysis. Could the church be a model for leveraging these illicitly acquired benefits by helping increase access to these resources, in order to help undertake the truth telling required in the process of a national healing from historical trauma? Here, we ask also the question: What capital is required to *read* and *interpret* the past? The capital of *our* time, *our* interest in writing and reading these stories indicates a willingness on our part to dedicate some of the capital *we* have available to this truth-telling project.[4] Is our investigation into this history and the truth telling it pursues a piece of the repair necessary for too many years of "willful ignorance" on the part of Catholic Christians and Christian institutions?[5] Couldn't the project of truth telling be a grace of our day in facing Catholic Christian sinfulness in the process of seeking reconciliation and repair? The sacrament of reconciliation requires first a confession and penitence before the grace of God again might flow in and among our personhood.

The resources of institutions are crucial for our truth telling because they have created the conditions for our walking through the world of the past, of our ancestors and ghosts. Institutions are storehouses of the past in their dedication to maintaining archives and in the capital they mobilize to make those archives available for research in the present. The digital archives at Georgetown University share with a reading public those necessary components for making resources available for us today to walk through the past and tease out its truth telling and its meaning for us today.[6] We turn to Georgetown *both* because it is an institution that has dedicated the resources to create, maintain, and make available the archives *and* because of the symbolic capital it holds as America's first Catholic college. The longest-standing Catholic religiously affiliated institution represents and confers symbolic capital to the various institutions in the Catholic network and the Jesuit network. To work our way through to theological truths we will encounter in the archives, we rely not only on the original actors in the drama of the past but also those who took the time to write about it, all those who were stewards of the archives over many years of its existence, all those whose hands touched the material object carefully to maintain its preservation, all those who made the resources available to digitize the material object, and all those who put in the effort of transcribing.[7] History never comes to us directly. We must move thoughtfully and critically through the "history" that the sources yield, remembering the way that power and capital flows through the construction of the past.

## Creating a Catholic Christian Empire

As the historian Shannen Dee Williams reminds us, the Catholic Church was the first and largest corporate slaveholder in the Americas, and Jesuit roots are embedded in this soil.[8] As Craig Wilder illuminates, religiously affiliated universities were among the engines that made an economy of enslavement run, through the ideologies produced as "knowledge" about African peoples.[9] The layers of cultural capital produced by deriving "sacred knowledge" of African peoples from the Bible enhanced their justifications. Reciprocally, the money generated through an economy of enslavement was an engine for creating religiously affiliated institutions, like Catholic colleges and the very buildings of Catholic churches that still stand today.

America's oldest Catholic college has its roots in colonial patterns of land acquisition. Lord Baltimore's 1636 policy was that

> two thousand acres would be given to any person responsible for bringing five men to the colony. By 1642 there were sixteen private manors established in the colony, and on average they were about two thousand acres each. . . . The early Jesuit priests used these policies to acquire land, as various priests brought with them Catholic servants to work in Maryland. . . . By this method and others, the Jesuits acquired more than 9,133 acres on their plantations by 1727.[10]

The androcentric construction of Lord Baltimore's "five men" in many cases might have distributed wealth partially in the generations to come. Imagine a wealthy entrepreneurial landowner bringing his five sons or sons-in-law, with wealth then distributed through their lineage. In contrast, the patriarchal hierarchy of the Catholic Church created the conditions for wealth to be amassed, since the Jesuits bore no responsibility for equitably compensating their five male Catholic servants (note how the symbolic capital of the historians' gaze centers the priests and places on the periphery those who served them). Surely other manors employed unpaid laborers and exploited the efforts of the servant class, but religious institutions dependent upon celibate males maintained the wealth from unpaid work in a unique way. Wealth begets wealth in a religious institution sufficiently endowed to distribute priests as landowners drawing on the work of the requisite "five men." But Jesuit landholding of such vast expanse would require additional workers to maintain and reap the benefits of such land owning. The historian James Woods reports:

> The oldest surviving record of the Jesuit plantations is dated July 13, 1765, by which time the Jesuits operated eight plantations, primarily in southern Maryland, with total acreage numbering 12,677 and a yearly income of 696 pounds sterling in 1764. This record also indicates that the Maryland Jesuits owned 192 slaves.[11]

This is fundamentally a foundation of injustice, when we pause to consider that the wealth amassed by the church was withheld from those 192 people who labored to create it.

But it is precisely because of the wealth passed along into and stored within the institution of Georgetown University that many hundreds of years later we have access to some among the stories of those whose unpaid labor supported the Jesuits in their wealth building. The capital that allowed the Jesuits leisure to write their histories captured some of the unrecountable stories of those who were enslaved. The record keeping that was the Maryland Jesuits' management of their capital provides some of the structure to reconstruct the skeleton of their stories. And the social capital that gave rise to an interest in keeping personal records, diaries, and letters preserved for us these accounts, from the time of their writing through the care of maintaining archives across the many generations. Our work in the archives is a complex and double-edged sword. The exploitative labor practices that helped build wealth through illicit gain from the life and blood of enslaved Catholics were passed on as the inheritance of an institution that therefore *had* the economic capital to preserve the resources that provide a glimpse for reconstructing some among the stories of the Catholic enslaved.

The complexity of the archives also gives insight into the dynamic reality of history and our attempt to recall it. The archives provide glimpses of enslaved Catholic lives (in letters and diaries) and structures/skeletons on which to place these glimpses (in accounting books and tax records), but they create for us the challenge of re-membering, piecing together fragments of what was and who they were.[12] Even as we attempt to re-member the ancestors, we nearly can never tell a story in its fullness. For even when multiple records provide multiple attestation with names and places, the reassembly of fragments means that sometimes we are blending stories of multiple persons. And even when we can be relatively sure the sources are pointing to the same person and their life in history, the variability of the storyteller's recollection of the contours of this enslaved Catholic's life and the unreliability of *their* memory makes *our* story one necessarily seen as through a cracked prism. But this asks us to recognize that this is true for all memory and therefore for all history. We are always working in fragments. As Christians, a story in fragments is our inheritance. Willie James Jennings describes:

> This is the first fragment. We have the words of Jesus, the words of the prophets, the stories of Israel, the lives of so many who have called themselves Christian through the centuries—their thoughts in texts, reports and secondhand reports, deliberations, confessions, decisions, meditations, interpretations—*everything is in slices and slivers, pieces and shards.* We have no whole here—no whole picture of ancient Israel, or the prophets, or their families, or Jesus, or his family, or early, middle or late Christians, or the entirety of their thinking, no full uncovering of their desires, angers, frustrations, hopes, and dreams. No complete picture of any theologian, or heretic, or faithful or unfaithful priest, monk, nun, missionary, mystic. All of it is merely fragments, large and small.[13]

And so, like the reconstruction of any period of Christian history, we reconstruct enslaved Catholic lives through the re-membering of fragments. As Christians re-membering our enslaved ancestors, we are re-membering the church as the body of Christ.

## Sucky's Scream

The oldest surviving record of the first Catholic college in the United States bears witness to the women and others who supported the Jesuits in their project of wealth building. By 1765, the Jesuits owned eight plantations, and it is almost certain that the Susannah we meet was working on one of them. At her death (sometime between 1806 and 1812), she was reported to have served the Jesuits under the leadership of more than twenty-three persons: a lifetime of service.[14] Susannah labored for the Jesuits even through the period when "the Jesuits" were not allowed to labor under that name, the order having been suppressed in 1773 and not reestablished until 1814. In this stretch of time, Susannah and the nearly two hundred other enslaved Catholics helped maintain the Jesuit institution, even while the institutional church had no interest in its survival. And while we know this to be the case from the archival record of Susannah's timeline, we do not know which Susannah we encounter when we read the records. An 1804 tax assessment identifies a Susanna, age eighty-six, with her nearest companions in age identified as Cate, sixty-two, "always sick and helpless"; Judy, fifty-five; Dorothy, forty-nine, "bedrid for life"; and Suck, aged forty-six.[15] If it is the same Susanna/h, the 1804 record might have a minor miscount, as the family record of our Susannah has her death at the age of ninety-six, but she is reported to have said that she was more than one hundred years old, which would make the date of her birth somewhere between 1705 and 1715 and her age at the 1804 tax record between eighty-nine and ninety-eight. Susannah's story places her within one generation of the very first enslaved American Catholics and among those who labored for the Jesuits' survival under suppression.

Susannah comes to us as Sucky (sometimes Old Sucky, to distinguish her from other Susannahs, like Suk, who is at least forty years her junior, and any Suckys that might be named in subsequent generations). The shortened form of her name is not only a convenient shorthand but potentially revelatory of the paternalistic and infantilizing naming by her Jesuit enslavers. At the time of her death, Sucky was among a community of roughly fifty-five enslaved Catholics who worked for the Jesuits on the plantation of St. Inigoes.[16] Over the course of her life in unpaid employment for the church, Sucky worked for between seven and twenty-three Jesuit overseers: a lifetime of work that built up White Catholic wealth. By the end of her life, Sucky was renowned for her culinary skills; she supported the work of church building from the kitchen as a cook.[17] Historical evidence points to Sucky as a flesh-and-blood human being. But she comes to us also as a legend, as breath and as scream. In these ways she is *theological*, coming to us as witness to the power of God at work in the world.

While the fullness of Sucky's story may be lost, her sound and her scream remain. She comes to us through the hand of several different Jesuits, some who encountered her (as body, blood, and breath) and through whose telling she became a legend. We first meet her as "Old Sucky" through the hand of Brother Joseph Mobberly, who managed St. Inigoes and accounted for her death sometime between 1806 and 1812.[18] Mobberly's recalling of her story, however, is found in his diary, which was written around ten years after her death (in 1820).[19] We might pause to think about what was so compelling in Sucky's story that Mobberly had occasion to write about it in his personal papers so many years later. But because her story had already become legend, it is also recounted by Fr. John Beschter in a letter written to a Fr. Leavy in 1836. More than twenty years after her death, Sucky remains in Beschter's memory as worthy of recollection. Having earned symbolic capital as worthy of recalling, Sucky's story is available to us for our re-membering. This invites us to look closely at the context in which Sucky's story is retold in order to see the purpose to which it is put. Susannah's experience with the Jesuits does not end in their nineteenth-century writings. In 2001, another Jesuit, Thomas Murphy, lifted up Sucky's story for a new purpose in his historical investigation of over one hundred years of Jesuit slaveholding. Interrogating the fragments and the purposes to which each puts Sucky's story will invite us to re-member her once again.

From the earliest record (Mobberly's 1812 accounting), we meet Susannah as "Old Sucky," but in Mobberly's diary, we meet her at a time when she is just a "girl."[20] In the two separate nineteenth-century accounts (Mobberly's and Beschter's), she seems to bear an affection for the priest under whose charge she lives. Mobberly's hand conveys that "she said that she loved her master most cordially,"[21] and Beschter describes a relationship by which young Sucky could approach her Catholic priest and "master" with authentic concerns. The concern both Mobberly and Beschter recount is an episode in which Sucky witnesses a Father Bolton undertaking a penitential practice of self-flagellation. Shocked by this self-harm, she intervenes. Sucky witnesses the priest "taking the discipline": Seeing him having "just bared his shoulder & begun his pious work,"[22] she let out a sound of shock that he was "giv[ing] himself a dreadful wipping."[23] Her involuntary sound was followed by her audible protests as she "begged him not to wip himself"[24] (as Beschter conveys), "begged her good master not to be so cruel to himself" (as Mobberly reports).[25] In Mobberly's account, Sucky is one to intervene where others in her community did not. He writes,

> One of her masters (the name I do not recollect) was accustomed to retire to an old neglected barn for the purposes of taking the discipline.

> This, it seems, after some time, was discovered and whispered among the blacks. Sucky was then a girl—She was resolved to see if this statement was true, and therefore followed her master at a distance. She arrived in good time, & peeping through a crevice, found that he had just bared his shoulders & begun his pious work. She immediately screamed aloud, & running to the barn door begged her good master not to be so cruel to himself.[26]

In the second account, Beschter adopts Sucky's speaking voice, recalling her from a time he met her when he was a Jesuit novice. In his memory, she remembers the event in this way:

> I heard some noise in his room, I went to the windows to see what was the matter there, I saw Fr. Bolton give himself a dreadful wipping, the next morning I went to him, and on my knees, I begged him not to wip himself . . . [27]

Through the Jesuits' accounts, we meet an enslaved Catholic woman in both her youth and her old age, recalling a significant event in which she clashed with the Catholic Jesuit priest on whether and how to undertake pious practices. We might begin to envision the contours of their relationship: Apparently, she cared about the well-being of his body and about the practices he undertook, and she was able to muster the courage to intervene. What does this tell us about the faith lives of enslaved Catholics and those of the Catholics who enslaved them?

As the Roman Catholic bishop Robert Barron explains of "taking the discipline," "it was a staple of the asceticism of most of the mainstream religious orders up until the time of Vatican II." Barron continues:

> It is a means of imitating Christ by participating in his suffering. The goal of the spiritual quest is to allow Jesus to live his life in us fully. . . . This means that we must strive to conform ourselves to Jesus' humility, his compassion, his joyful prayer, his identification with sinners, his teaching, his manner of thinking and feeling, and his vicarious suffering. By taking upon himself unmerited suffering, Jesus atoned for the sins of the world. We can enter, however imperfectly, into this dynamic by accepting—for our own sins or those of others—some physical or psychological discomfort.[28]

While Barron's contemporary account views flagellation as an invitation to humility by entering willingly into suffering, Sucky may have witnessed this "vicarious suffering" as a portal to the Christ *she* knew, whose sufferings accompanied her in the absurdity of enslavement. From that place, Sucky may have been reaching out in care to Fr. Bolton in the pattern of the Christ who accompanied the enslaved. Shawn Copeland envisions that

> because Jesus himself was beaten, tortured, and murdered, the enslaved people believed that he understood them and their suffering like no one else. They believed that he was one with them in their otherness and affliction, that he would help them negotiate this world with righteous anger and dignity. They were motivated not out of despair but out of love and faith when they sang, "*Nobody knows de trouble I've had / Nobody knows but Jesus.*" Caught within the labyrinth of the social oppression of slavery, black people fixed their eyes on Jesus and his cross as they grappled with the absurdity of enslavement . . . a *fellow sufferer* who knew in his body the sting of the lash, enduring with them what was their daily portion. Bloodied and nailed to rough wooden planks, he was the One who went all the way with them and for them. . . . In the paradox and promise of his life and suffering, they found their own.[29]

The multivalence of experience requires that we say and unsay the relationship of violence to Christ. But Sucky's scream announces an otherwise possibility: that violence is *not* redemptive. "I went to him on my knees and I begged him not to wip himself." [30] "She immediately screamed aloud, & running to the barn door begged her good master not to be so cruel to himself." [31]

Confronting a tradition that embraced self-flagellation as a pious practice, Sucky breathes out the power of a Spirit that says no. Sucky's scream, her gasp, the involuntary moving of air focuses in on the power of her breath, an activity which Ashon Crawley links to the power of the Holy Spirit, or "pneumatology . . . the study of *pneuma*—the Greek word for 'breath.'"[32] Expanding, Crawley explains:

> In the Septuagint (LXX), the Greek term *pneuma* is almost always equivalent of the Hebrew *ruach*. . . . The idea behind *ruach* is the extraordinary fact that air should move; the basic meaning of *ruach* is, therefore, "blowing." Both terms in the Bible, the Old Testament *ruach* and the New Testament *pneuma*, carry the same ambiguity of multiple meanings: "breath," "air," "wind," or "soul." [33]

The soul-force of the Spirit at work in Sucky's scream may be interpreted as the power of God interrupting our labors. But it also bespeaks the polysemic expression of the Spirit at work in relationship and the polyvalence of the encounter/experience. Citing David Jensen, Crawley continues:

> Theologians speak about the radical sociality—as hospitality—of Spirit: "The Spirit who gives life is evident in hospitality shown toward strangers." Such that we might say that Spirit—*pneuma* breath, that which animates the body—is grounded in the necessity for sociality. Not only does Spirit give life, but that life is evident in how one leans toward others, how one engages with others in the world. We do not merely share in sociality; we share in the materiality of that which quickens flesh; we share air, breath, breathing through the process of inhalation and exhalation.[34]

The theological frame offered by Crawley invites us to read Sucky's scream as the breath of the Holy Spirit at work in the world for the care of self and other. Sucky's scream, her gasp, her breath announces a world in which two Catholics could console each other, could wrap each other in the care of companionship and concern for the other's well-being. Shocked out of her silence she cries out, stunned at the prayer-practice that would inflict harm.

While we may read Sucky's interruptive scream as the breathing forth of the Spirit in new forms of sociality and care, the priest toward whom she extended this holy care did not hear her scream in that way. The recollection of the encounter continues in the Jesuit archives and completes the exchange that both accounts recall. When Sucky screams, the tables turn from the physical violence of the whipping of self-flagellation to the whipping of violent control of master over slave. First from Beschter (in Sucky's voice):

> I begged him not to wip himself, so what you say, said he, how you know that I wip myself? Why I saw you wip yourself last evening . . . Well, you say, you saw me . . . Yeas Fr. said I . . . Well come here to me after half an hour . . . Well I went to his room, he bid me kneel down; I did so, and then he gave me a dreadful wipping for my curiosity.[35]

And Mobberly (in the third person):

> She immediately screamed aloud, & running to the barn door begged her good master not to be so cruel to himself. She said that she loved her master most cordially, but that on this occasion, he gave her so sound a thrashing . . . [36]

While Sucky interrupts what she perceives to be a practice of self-harm with an intervention of self-care (she "begged her good master not to be so cruel to himself"),[37] the Jesuit interrupted her Spirit-breathed care of sociality by turning his violence onto her. Here, too, we might walk our way around this episode and ask what it reveals about the past and the structure of relationships in an economy of enslavement. *How likely it is that one so willing to curse one's own flesh would turn the cord on the other?* Imitatio Christi the priest's barbs inflict on his own skin; imitatio Christi the sufferer endures the scourge. Is it paradox or contradiction that the spiritual capital of the Catholic tradition could be used in such conflicting ways?

Already you'll recognize my authorial voice drawing meaning out of the episode and analyzing some features of the accounts in order to advance an examination of Catholic sensibilities within an economy of enslavement. My own re-membering of Sucky is for a particular purpose, following Maria Yellow Horse Brave Heart's fourfold path of remembering and analyzing history to release its pain for the creation of transformed institutions. The pause here asks us to consider whether practices of self-and-other harm still reside in the institutions of American Catholicism. But the purpose to which we will put Sucky's story in the twenty-first century is not the first purposeful retelling. In fact, the very sources we are employing were telling Sucky's story for particular ends.

## Three Uses of Sucky's Story: The Tangle of Our Stories in the Archives

Not only did Jesuits within the institutions of church and school use enslaved laborers to create capital; they also put the memory and stories of those enslaved laborers to use for their own purposes. Thus, archival work introduces us to enslaved Catholics through a glass darkly, the murky waters of memory and storytelling presenting to us shrouded figures for the retelling of our history. But the shrouds within which our ancestors are wrapped are also illuminating of the institutions and ancestors who ran them, as well as the persisting patterns within those institutions today. Three different uses of the story of Sucky draw out three different patterns within Jesuit institutions for our consideration today.

### Never but Once: Joseph Mobberly's Use of Sucky

To get a sense of how Joseph Mobberly uses the story of Sucky for his own ends, we might approach our analysis of this element within an artifact of history (his *Diary*) by placing it in Mobberly's wider corpus of writings. So, we come to meet Sucky within a *Diary* situated in a broader field of Mobberly's writing within the wider scene of Jesuit plantation and college and the expanded scope of nineteenth-century Catholic Christian practice in a slaveholding economy. We're not getting Sucky directly but instead wrapped up within all of the tangles of what this represents. While Sucky may have, indeed, experienced the encounter with Bolton and shared her story with Mobberly while he was at St. Inigoes, his retelling within this tangle requires that we approach his narrative with a hermeneutic of suspicion as to whether and how it captures what happened. Such a suspicion of Mobberly's motives in recounting Sucky's story rests on the knowledge that in the same year that he is remembering Sucky, he is also penning texts that illuminate his presuppositions about the enslaved of whom he is writing. In 1820, the Jesuit brother is afforded the leisure to write an extended account of the Catholic reasoning around the nature and condition of the enslaved. His *On Cham* betrays his outlook as an author who perceives enslaved Catholics (like Sucky) through a lens of his own superiority. A reading of *On Cham* demonstrates the sophisticated reasonings within Jesuit institutions as Mobberly draws on the wider scene of "knowledge" in so-called race science, explorers' writings, biblical text, and the Catholic moral theological tradition. Throughout the text, Mobberly uses the capital afforded to him within a Jesuit institution (room and board, material access to "scholarship," the leisure time to write) in order to justify inhumane practices of enslavement (with the "best" that "scholarship" has to offer), which in turn will make more capital for the Jesuits (when they use these justifications for their own unpaid labor and when ideas about the justification for withholding the wages of laborers reaches a wider Catholic slaveholding audience who might support their work). Mobberly mobilizes the range of arguments to "demonstrate" the impracticality of all people being free and equal; he concludes: "We know it is the will of Heaven that one man should be subject to another."[38] Not only does the celestial hierarchy bear itself out in a hierarchical society on earth (wife to husband, child to parent, servant to master), but the widespread reality of poverty across the globe demonstrates practically the need for some to be under the care of others. "Slavery is good—is necessary. It may be asserted with confidence that at least two fifths of the human family are deficient in point of intellect and know not how to manage for and take care of themselves."[39] Blending political writings (of Thomas Jefferson), the doctors of "race science," and biblical reasoning, Mobberly reads the hue of Black skin to "denote the enormity of Cham's [Ham's] offense."[40] The excessive construction of the natural "inferiority" of black-skinned Africans in Mobberly's musings has as its twin the supremacy of White Catholics. This supremacy was rooted, for Mobberly, in the evidence provided by "race science" and the philosophical deductions of the races, wherein, in Mobberly's words, "whiteness is the colour to which mankind naturally tends."[41]

These writings, external to the account of Granny Sucky, form an intratextual lens through which to read Mobberly's remembrance, for his purpose seems to be announced in the description of Sucky's lifetime of work with the

Jesuits. In Mobberly's account, it is important that "the cook, who was called Granny Sucky . . . told me that she had had 23 masters, and that she never had had a bad one. She observed that she had never been whipped but once."[42] Mobberly, a Jesuit who had contemplated the enslaved condition and advanced theological justifications for it, uses Sucky's story to highlight the extraordinariness of physical violence. Mobberly's elevation of the unusualness of this event—which he bolstered through Sucky's lifelong work with twenty-three masters, all of whom were good and only one of whom ever resorted to violence—allows Mobberly to advance the narrative of benevolent Catholic Christian enslavers (rhetorically placing himself among them). That the violence is a result of Sucky's interruption of the priest's pious practice intimates justification of violence as the priest puts the impious/transgressive girl-woman in her place. Gender, status, age, and more frame the analysis of this account and reveal something of its complexity. Here, Mobberly's *use* of Sucky allows us to glimpse Sucky but to also see her legend at work in advancing his own interests. This suspicion of whether the enslaver might faithfully convey the experience of the enslaved is borne by the historian's view.

But even as Mobberly's aim may have been to elevate physical punishment as an unusual event, one justified in certain circumstances, reading his account against the grain to hear Sucky's scream asks us to listen for the screams of other women like Sucky, enslaved by the Jesuits and witnesses to their cruelty.[43] If we are to begin to train our eyes to see and our ears to hear the ghosts of our institutional past, we need to look for women whose lives were erased in the building of our institutional home; these erasures, these absent-presences are the ghosts who might speak.

The dialectic of Black inferiority and White supremacy was a governing premise in the treatment of enslaved Catholics, and Mobberly reflected upon the need for great oversight on the part of the slavers when he wrote in his *Diary*, "Some years ago Blacks were more easily kept in due subordination, and were more patient under the rod of correction, than they are now, because then discipline flourished but now it is going to decay. The present white generation seems to lose sight of the old observation, 'the better a negro is treated, the worse he becomes.'"[44] As Robert Emmett Curran proposes, "Mobberly's own attempts to discipline his slaves had just the opposite effect. By the time [the Jesuit Peter] Kenney visited the plantation in 1820, the blacks compiled a litany of complaints to cite against the brother. Kenney listened (as he had elsewhere), and the corporation removed Mobberly within a month."[45] In contrast to the depravity of those Catholics who had been enslaved, Mobberly advances the supremacy and benevolence of Catholic enslavers and Catholic slave traders.

Sucky's scream interrupts Mobberly's falsification of the facts on the ground. The Spirit shouted forth in sociality opens wide our ears to hear the many women whose lives were given over to Jesuit institutions under the cloak of congeniality and the ideology of supremacy. Women whose children were sold to raise capital for the fledgling Jesuits and girl children ripped from their family network as profit for the institution,[46] women who were sold because their agency in acts of resistance to enslavement was too much for the Jesuits to bear, pregnant women bearing the brunt of Jesuit rage, women whipped in the parlor of the Jesuits who "owned" them.[47] These women whose bodies bore slavery's injustice had their lifeblood poured into the Jesuit institution that outlasted them. Their life-breath was transferred into the institutional network in which I earn my living. The institutions have outlived the women themselves, but their ghosts remain with us. Indeed, the theologian Shawn Copeland reminds us that "we Christian theologians in the United States live and work in a house haunted by the ghost of chattel slavery."[48] This is doubly true for Christian theologians who live and work in the Jesuit house haunted by the ghosts of these strong and Spirited women. Perhaps one of the reasons Sucky's scream was erased was that the repercussion that followed her scream challenged the portrait of Catholic slaveholders as "benevolent" when her so-called master, Fr. Bolton, turned from his practice of self-discipline and "bid [<u>her</u> to] kneel down"[49] gave her "so sound a thrashing,"[50] a "dreadful wipping."[51] Why have we not yet heard Sucky's scream?

## Go and Do Likewise: An Analysis of Beschter's Account

As a Jesuit in the same time period, Beschter was also active in the production of symbolic capital on the supremacy of enslaver over enslaved. He advances in his writings a notion akin to Mobberly's argument on the benevolence of Catholic Jesuits and the depravity of the Catholic enslaved. Quoting him at length may give texture to the consistency of these arguments across the Jesuit enslavers. Writing a letter to report on activities in Jesuit mission, Beschter conveys:

> There is one group entrusted to our care which, by mostly spurning teaching, continues to sink; this group is made up of our slaves, who are so depraved that there is this proverbial saying amongst the locals, who wish to point out the worst sort of person: "he is as bad as a Priest's Slave." I think this situation arises especially because of this circumstance: the slaves of others are harshly punished for their sins, negligence, and disobedience, and when they are found incorrigible, they

> are sold to outsiders; but our slaves for the most part corrupt and are corrupted without punishment. Because of this the idle, the fornicators, the adulterous, the drunks, and the thieves get away with it; they know the priests will not sell them to outsiders. From this arises our poverty and the fruitlessness of our plantations. The reason for this does not escape our neighbors, and now they would not buy our slaves at half price. *Often it occurs to me that those slaves who in our sight and under our care are damned would perhaps abandon their sins under harsh Masters and be saved.*[52]

The stories of sins and salvation are mixed together and mixed up in this account: The sins of the enslaved in their idleness, fornication, adultery, drinking, and theft leads them to their damnation because of the benevolence of the Jesuits toward them, who do not punish these "transgressions." This foregrounds a portrait of the Jesuit slavers' benevolence that brings about the ruin of the plantation and the souls of the enslaved workers who run them. Yet if the enslaved Catholics were under the mastery of harsher means, it might lead to their salvation in the correction of their "sins": violent and harsh punishments deemed the rod that corrects and saves. Further, in this reasoning it is because of Jesuit benevolence that the sins of the enslaved cause the damnation of the Jesuits, insofar as their material comforts are concerned. An analysis of this passage indicates Beschter as a Jesuit with a very high opinion of his priestly brothers, who could do no wrong: At present they are not wrong in their benevolence, but if they were to be more violently corrective toward their enslaved Catholic workers, they would not be wrong either.

With such a high view of Jesuit practice, an unlikely elevation is exhibited in Beschter's recollection of Sucky's scream and the purpose to which he puts it. In his account, Beschter introduces us by name to the Jesuit who turned violent toward one who extended her care: Fr. Bolton. In his account, however, Sucky serves as a counterwitness advocating for self-care among the Jesuits. Beschter's account turns immediately from the "dreadful wipping" Sucky received to a hortatory encouragement to follow her lead. Retelling the story in Sucky's voice, Beschter is writing to a fellow Jesuit, Fr. Leavy, and uses the story of Sucky's scream for a new purpose:

> I asked her if she had never got a wipping of them? Yeas, Father, she said; when Fr. Bolton lived he gave me a good whipping; why? Because I deserved it; I heard some noise in his room, I went to the windows to see what was the matter there, I saw Fr. Bolton give himself a dreadful wipping, the next morning I went to him, and on my knees, I begged him not to wip himself, so what you say, said he, how you know that I

> wip myself? Why I saw you wip yourself last evening . . . Well, you say, you saw me . . . Yeas Fr. said I . . . Well come here to me after half an hour . . . Well I went to his room, he bid me kneel down; I did so, and then he gave me a dreadful wipping for my curiosity . . .[53]

But immediately Beschter interrupts the recollection of the past to advocate action in the present, using Sucky as his guide. He alerts Fr. Leavy to the practices of a fellow Jesuit held in high esteem by his community.[54] Beschter closes his telling of Sucky's story with a clear purpose in mind:

> I hear, Fr Dzierozynski is getting poor and thin, I fear he does as Fr. Bolton did, should any one see him do so, I wish he should beg of him not to do so . . . and wait for the consequence.[55]

Seeing his fellow priest practice a piety similar to Bolton's self-harm and judging the practice negatively, as Sucky had, Beschter advocates intervention, using Sucky as his model. We can feel the literary layering in this purposeful retelling as Sucky "begged" Bolton (the word used in both Beschter's and Mobberly's account of the interaction). This is the precise action enjoined for Dzierozynski as well, should anyone see him doing as Fr. Bolton had done: "I wish he should beg of him not to do so." The younger Jesuit has already professed his care for "my dearly beloved Father Dzierozynski,"[56] and the recommendation of care is genuine; he can find no other way to convey his concern and recommend a course of action than to reach back into his memory, of a time "whilst I was with the Novices at S. Inigoe's" and mobilize Sucky's witness of care for the care of his beloved.[57] This care Beschter recommends whatever the consequence. Sucky becomes a model of care that disrupts practices of Jesuits in relation to their brothers and invites them to adopt a new course of action.

## She May Have Been Trying to Seduce Him: How Murphy Uses Sucky

Sucky was more than just a bondswoman whose life and labor supported the church; she is used by the Jesuits to convey other dimensions of their own story. For Mobberly, the recognition of her whipping in its unusualness allows him to maintain the Jesuit façade of benevolent slaveholding. For Beschter, the courage of her intervention is an unusual maneuver that should be emulated. But it is not just nineteenth-century Jesuits who use Sucky to tell their story. In the historical reconstruction of Thomas Murphy SJ, Sucky is used to tell another story, perhaps with a tinge of desire toward elevating Jesuit benevolence and violence as an "unusual" practice, but now also with the inclusion of another form of desire. In the mode of the modern historian, Murphy writes:

> The one specific recorded case of a Jesuit whipping a female slave would seem to have had nothing to do with sex. This incident was recorded by Brother Joseph Mobberly in 1806 [note: although Murphy cites Mobberly's diary page 21, the Georgetown archives have that written in 1820], but had taken place many decades earlier, in the youth of Granny Sucky, the old woman who recounted the incident to him. She resolved to find out whether rumors among the slaves that her Jesuit master engaged in nightly self-flagellation were true. Therefore, she hid in the barn where he was said to come after nightfall for this practice. Upon seeing that he was indeed beating himself, she screamed at him not to be so cruel to himself. The Jesuit's response was to turn his whip on her, as punishment for disturbing his prayer. *The possibility exists that the Jesuit responded as he did because he feared this young woman had come to seduce him at a time when he was particularly vulnerable.* If nothing else, this episode shows that Jesuits and slaves had little enough collaboration in prayer, let alone ministry.[58]

At this point, I would advocate for the reader to go online to the Georgetown digital archive. Read for yourself the selection from Mobberly's diary that Murphy cites. You can also read the second account from Beschter there. It is not clear where either source supports Murphy's rendering of Sucky's motivations. It is not clear whether anything in the two accounts could lead a reader to propose "the possibility" that Bolton "feared this young woman had come to seduce him" as Murphy does in his 2001 history. It is also not clear how this episode "shows that Jesuits and slaves had little enough collaboration in prayer, let alone ministry," as Murphy concludes from it (especially when other glimpses from the archives tell another story, as we shall see). Here we must interrogate not only the nineteenth-century Jesuits who use Sucky's story but analyze our twenty-first-century Jesuit practices as well.

Let us first situate Murphy in the longer institutional practice of justifying Jesuit violence toward enslaved Catholic women. Murphy reproduces for a contemporary audience the pattern of presupposing the *unusualness* of such Jesuit violence with his emphasis on "the *one specific recorded* case of a Jesuit whipping a female slave." Here, Murphy's expert reconstruction of history leans toward portraying the Jesuits as innocent unless their transgressions are directly "recorded" (presumably by the Jesuits themselves). He paints all the other Jesuits in the era of enslavement as innocent of violence, in contrast to the "one specific recorded" case, as if its being specific and recorded renders it an isolated incident and not a pattern of practice.

The reason for Fr. Bolton turning his pious practice of self-harm into a practice of harm inflicted on Sucky in her youth has been variously reported. In the 1836 letter from Fr. Beschter in the archives, it was a punishment for her "curiosity." But, curiously, Thomas Murphy, a twenty-first-century Jesuit, manufactures an alternative interpretation for this "punishment for disturbing [Bolton's] prayer." Note how the twenty-first-century historian places "the youth" hiding in the barn, waiting for the Jesuit to arrive. But you, dear reader, can read Mobberly's account for yourself, in which she "followed her master at a distance."[59] And Beschter's Sucky heard the noise and *went to* the window. Having put Sucky's pieces back together as a sexualized young woman (in contrast to Mobberly's "girl"), Murphy introduces his own sexualized supposition that "the possibility exists that the Jesuit [Fr. Bolton] responded as he did because he feared this young woman had come to seduce him at a time when he was particularly vulnerable."[60] Murphy once again renders the male Jesuit(s) *justified* in his (their) violence toward Catholic women.

While Murphy tells us that this episode shows that Jesuits and enslaved Catholics did not collaborate in prayer or ministry, Sucky's sisters will soon tell us otherwise.

## "In the future, she was determined never to much care . . .": How I Am Using Sucky

In the fragments available to us, multiple attestation to Sucky as an elder at St. Inigoes provides a starting point for our re-membering. The common identifiers—a cook, employed over many years, who died at ninety-six or one hundred years old—allow us to begin to construct a portrait of Susannah. The common contours of her story in the priest's practice and the girl's intervention—taking the discipline of self-flagellation; peeping in on him out of concern and curiosity; the desperate intervention, "begging" him not to hurt himself. While Sucky may not have been provided the capital to write her own story, her encounter had clearly become legend and her presence among the Jesuits substantive. Her presence at St. Inigoes and her unusual story make her a vessel for symbolic capital, which can be leveraged as a resource for recognition and misrecognition. What we do with our own peeping into the history of their story is up to us: We could enhance our use of this vignette for our reconstruction of history by comparing the practice of self-flagellation with other practices of piety in mid-eighteenth-century America. We could walk around the kind of relationship reflected in this account and perhaps find threads of care and concern and even intimacy in those relations. What I'd like to do is consider what Sucky screams as announcing an otherwise possibility.

While Sucky provides evidence of how the Jesuits "used" those they had enslaved in their storytelling, she also becomes a model of affective labor in different ways in the two accounts of her scream. As we have seen, in Beschter's hand, Sucky's scream becomes an extension of care as he writes to a fellow Jesuit concerned about the continued practice of self-harm among his Jesuit brothers. Just as Beschter concludes describing Sucky's encounter, he writes: "I hear, Fr Dzierozynski is getting poor and thin, I fear he does as Fr. Bolton did, should any one see him do so, I wish he should beg of him not to do so . . . and wait for the consequence."[61] Beschter lifts Sucky up as a model for his Jesuit companions to follow in their care for one another, despite the consequences that this care might bring. But Sucky as she is captured by Mobberly offers her words as witness to an alternative course of action in an institution full of harms. Mobberly's hand conveys: "She said that she loved her master most cordially, but that on this occasion, he gave her so sound a thrashing, that she was determined never to care much about his self-cruelties in future."[62] What is captured in the traces of Sucky's story might also be of interest to our particular concerns, conveyed unexpectedly in Mobberly's account, as we witness the strategy of one woman caught in the web of relationships in an economy of enslavement and nevertheless rooting herself into a form of self-determination in navigating them. Withholding her emotional labor, Sucky offers a pattern of practice and the kind of creativity under constraint we might be well served to look for as we contemplate the human condition as it is shaped by institutions that benefited from an economy of enslavement. Sucky shows us the strategy of withholding care—being part of an institution yet distancing oneself from the affective labor expected from an institution replete with violent practices.

Sucky's scream was a legend among the nineteenth-century Jesuits, and it comes down to us announcing the violence of a slaveholding institution yet witnessing also what Crawley has named an "otherwise possibility." He describes: "Otherwise [is] a word that names plurality as its core operation, otherwise bespeaks the ongoingness of possibility, of things existing other than what is given, what is known, what is grasped."[63] There is surely more to Sucky's story than what has been told so far; perhaps her scream from the archives will allow us to hear even more things in a new way.[64] Sucky screams back into the claim that Jesuits were exemplary in their care for enslaved people, a claim the Jesuits themselves perpetuated in their writings, but their self-disclosure simultaneously discloses their cruelty: "The Negroes at Saint Thomas and in our other lands love us. The greatest threat we can do to them is to tell them: I will sell you."[65] In an emotional battlefield in an economy of enslavement, Sucky determined never to care for her abuser again.

## The Interruptive and Otherwise Possibility of Sucky's Scream

Generations of Catholics in White Catholic institutions have not heard Sucky's scream. Despite the ways in which the life and labor of Black Catholics, enslaved by the institutional church, contributed their creativity to care for the Jesuits and others; despite the unjust conditions in which the fruits of their work was taken from them; despite the illicit gain transferred from the blood and backs of our siblings in the faith, White Catholic institutions are only now reckoning with the inheritance of this illicit gain. Sucky's scream—legendary in the storytelling among the Jesuits—has not been heard or has been willfully misidentified as the justifiable punishment for sexual advance, childhood curiosity, or insubordination. These alone should say something about the patterns of relationality cultivated in Jesuit institutions, but we'll leave them aside to hear *not* the screams of her pain erased by the Jesuit storytellers but her interruptive breath announcing an otherwise possibility to the self-induced harm she witnessed in her lifetime and witnesses to us in ours.

Ashon Crawley offers the sounds of the Spirit exhaled in breath, captured in his volume *Blackpentecostal Breath: The Aesthetics of Possibility.* Presuming the landscape of White supremacies scattered across US history, Crawley attends to the irrepressible life pressing forward and through that choking system. The preacher's whoop and pause, the unconstrained shouts of the congregation, the outrage of the journalist, the choreosonic "joyful noise of Blackpentecostal testimony service songs" and the dance that they evoke, the collective groan of deep sorrow, speech in tongues, the preacher's word and the congregation's response[66] give witness to an ontological presence of the more, the open-ended, the uncontainable. Each instance of life surging, expressed in breath, shout, noise, and tongues, gives voice to the is-ness of being and simultaneously witnesses the failures of White Enlightenment thought and White structures of governance advanced as if truth. This life, this surging, opens space for alternatives in time, that is, "otherwise possibilities."

Crawley offers an analysis of basic, biological human practices as they become social and, more specifically, as they become expressed in and through the racialized context of US religious institutions, writing, "I want to consider specific performances of breathing in black, breathing in Blackpentecostal performance practices, to think about more fully how breathing is not just a sign of life but is an irreducibly irruptive critique of the normative world."[67] In the normative world of White supremacies, the breath of the preacher's pause and of the whooping assent of the congregation creates new contours of space into which those who have been racialized as Black might find life.[68] But the expression of life is found also at the site of resistance to White violence, "the scream, heart-rending shriek" crying out against the exhalation/expiration of the lynched "performance of air, breath, breathing [as] the enunciation of excess . . . creative spirit was not destroyed but was continually enacted by reconfiguration of otherwise modes of sociality."[69] It is through the various forms of breath, exhalation, shouts, and other air-moving expressions that the various forms of Black life in a White supremacist society forge resistance: "If air was there at the scene of subjection, and breath was the desired object to be stolen, this slightest breath at any moment of enframing, of eclipsing, evinces the life that escaped, through screams, through moans, through pleas."[70] The shout and noise giving witness to the most fundamental presence of breath, of life, of spirit, the possibility of an "otherwise" immediately in reach, an other-than-White supremacy.

With Crawley's analysis in a theological key, Sucky might come to us as a conduit of the Spirit, a vessel for God's work of relationship and sociality in this moment as a theophany of revelatory arrest. But Bolton turns the opportunity for relationship into the reassertion of his aloneness and distance from those so close to him. He does not treat Sucky as Spirit and life, as witness and companion, but as capital.

> The foundational grounds for capital accumulation was based upon African bodies, African workers, African labor, according to Cedric Robinson. He discusses how "the significance of African labor for the development and formation of the commercial and industrial capitalist systems can only be partially measured by numbers," and that "first, African workers had been transmuted by the perverted canons of mercantile capitalism into property. Then, African labor power as slave labor was integrated into the organic composition of nineteenth-century manufacturing and industrial capitalism, thus sustaining the emergence of an extra-European world market within which the accumulation of capital was garnered for the further development of industrial production."[71]

Bolton refuses relationship in the way he has created Sucky as capital, standing his ground that violence was required to protect his property. "The black body as chattel is essentially the valued commodity of whiteness."[72] And Bolton could not allow those whom he considered his property the agency of personhood conveyed in Sucky's act of care, refusing at once the divine care that might be in his midst.

Like other witnesses captured in the archives, Bolton was incapable of enabling the personhood of persons who might disrupt his sense of selfhood in their acts of relationship. The hierarchical conception of humanity his Catholic

Christian tradition conveyed, of male over female, ordained over lay, White over Black, shaped the Jesuits to narrate and envision themselves as masters of their domain, self-sufficient and in control. But their reliance on the labor of women like Sucky betrays the neediness of men who could not succeed by themselves. Reading Bolton's refusal of care against the grain, we see the otherwise possibility in Sucky's scream as a pattern of relationality the Jesuits fostered. Not only a woman but a woman of color advanced herself as a fellow Catholic in an expression of care that Bolton, as self-controlled and controlling Jesuit Catholic male master, could not allow. His refusal was not only a refusal of care but of relationship and partnership in the mission of being Catholic Christians in colonial America and in the church. Bolton's refusal of care and cooperation is metonymically repeated in striking lines from fellow Jesuits in the archives. When Fr. Steinbacher "airs his grievances," he repeats the kind of relationality Bolton has shown. Revealing the collaborative agency Black Catholic women had in creating the conditions of the Jesuits in the nineteenth century, Steinbacher complains: "A colored woman has ruled and partly rules this house, but she will not rule me."[73] His complaint reveals *both* the reality that enslaved Catholic women were "ruling the house" in their labors *and* the refusal of the Jesuits to see their dependence upon them. When Jesuits account for their success as the result of their mastery, we need to re-member our Catholic Christian history as one that fundamentally could not have taken root without the lives and labors of Catholic women and men who were pressed into service and collaborated in the creation of Georgetown and, by extension, the wider growth of the Catholic Church in the United States.

While Jesuit practices in relation to enslaved Catholic women revealed in the archives suggests an incapacity for collaboration and the creation of collaborators as capital, in the legend that Sucky's scream becomes, Bolton is rendered impotent in his attempt to create her as capital. Divine presence cannot be contained, for she has already been created in Spirit and in flesh, and her scream sounds through the centuries as an otherwise possibility. "Otherwise is a word that names plurality as its core operation, otherwise bespeaks the ongoingness of possibility, of things existing other than what is given, what is known, what is grasped."[74] In their exchange, Sucky's scream announces that it could have been otherwise and that it *was* otherwise, as she determines from then to withhold her emotional labor from the priest. She becomes an otherwise possibility when her memory is mobilized to extend care and concern for a future generation of Jesuits. She is an otherwise possibility for us: to hold her memory as a testimony to the polyvalence of experience and complexity of encounter. The saying and unsaying of Sucky as chattel and agent, the saying and unsaying of Bolton as priest and oppressor, the saying and unsaying of mutuality and care in their relationship, the saying and unsaying of their shared Catholicism.

## An Economy of Enslavement and the Creation of Capital

In a lifetime of work, Susannah provided for the Jesuits and supported them as they amassed the capital that will come to us today and as they weathered the changes in fortune that would come from living off the resources of the Jesuit plantations. But, the Jesuits' amassing of wealth through the hands of enslaved labor was not a straightforward task. We can see the changing fortunes when Brother Mobberly in his management of St. Inigoes calculates the costs and reasons in 1815 that it would be cheaper to emancipate enslaved Catholics and to hire independent laborers who would be responsible for their own room and board.[75] This emancipation did not take place. In an 1820 register, Georgetown College collected $14,000 from students for tuition to run the school for their benefit, but at the same time approximately "45 religious" were also undertaking studies there. Their debt was not collected as tuition, but the profits at St. Inigoes ($1,233) was received to cover part of the $4,500 required for their keep.[76] This means that the life and labor of enslaved Catholics at St. Inigoes was poured into, transferred over to, and given up for the creation of the next class of male "religious" in the Catholic Church. We might pause to take in the particular kind of evil that drew the life and breath from enslaved female Catholics to sustain the spiritual progress of male seminarians. But we must also reckon with the reality that we are indebted to women like Sucky, who made the life of the next generation of the Catholic Church in America possible. Her work was even more essential given it took place during an era in which the Jesuits were denied certain protections of Rome. Together Black Catholic women like Sucky and countless others were partners in the creation and sustaining of the Jesuit tradition in America. And yet, Sucky and her companions were seen as of secondary importance to the maintenance of the institution.

Nowhere is it clearer that the Black Catholics who sustained the American Catholic Church at Georgetown were valued less than the institution itself than in the 1838 sale of 272 enslaved Catholics to save the institution. The recently published work by Rachel Swarns gives the most comprehensive account to date. Swarns chronicles the lives of enslaved members of the Mahoney family, whose skills over several generations enhanced the creation of the church at Georgetown. As their story demonstrates, the project of transferring the life-labors of enslaved Catholics and pouring them into the creation of the church was undertaken over lifetimes. And yet when the Jesuits reasoned about the value of those enslaved Catholics, a fundamental evil is clearly in view. One week before the sale of these 272 enslaved Catholics was finalized, the Jesuit Thomas Mulledy reasons out and reflects on the value of human beings (whom theologians assess as inestimable). Mulledy writes:

> I find it difficult to dispose of our servants to persons in a Catholic neighborhood. I have now a fine opportunity if we agree upon prices. Purchasers wish to price each individual servt giving high prices for the young & stout & diminishing for the elder & children. One yesterday presented his prices for men young say 20 years $800 [ditto] women $650 & so on diminishing something for everyone above 25 & under 18. I told him that I wished an average price—he made out one by adding his different prices together—which amounted to $345 per head I told him that he must make his average come to $400 at least—before I would even deign to consider his proposition. Tell me what do you think of $400 round for young & old—leaving out all of 60 & above for separate agreement—& counting all under one year with the mother as one. Fr. McSherry thinks it a fair price—let me know what you think of it. I would be willing to take $450.[77]

But even after the 1838 sale, writings in the archives convey a sadness not so much for the *fact* of the sale but with regret that it was not more profitable to help the Jesuits weather future fortunes. Five years after the sale, the treasurer in Maryland reports to the Jesuit superior in Rome on the financial disappointments of the sale:

> We draw with pain from our properties the necessities for the support of the Novitiate and the Scholastics and other incidental expenditures. The unhappy idea of Fr. Thomas F. Mulledy to sell the slaves at a 10-year term in place of on account as is the custom, exposes us to the loss of the 80,000 dollars due for them, or at least the two thirds of this sum due per year by one of the two buyers who should already [owe] two years of interest, and from whom I cannot get a cent.[78]

The "unhappy idea" of Fr. Mulledy was not that he determined "to sell the slaves" but that he had agreed "to sell the slaves at a 10-year term." The Jesuit is regretting not the sale of human beings but that it was not more profitable. However complex some relationships of Jesuit Catholic enslavers with their "Jesuit"-Catholic enslaved workers, the creation of capital and the dollar amount appears to provide a serious bottom line. The inestimably saddening reality that our Jesuit forebears dedicated their energies to putting profit over people for the continuation of the institution is something each of us in Jesuit institutions must remain vigilant to: We must ask whether this charism for calculation still lurks in the practices sustaining institutions today.

But the many stories of those enslaved by the Jesuits indicate a diversity of relations to Jesuit capital. From the archives we can also reconstruct a portrait of enslaved Catholics as collaborators in the workings of the Jesuits over hundreds of years. The Bennett family, for example, traces the efforts of an ancestor to the defense of St. Inigoes during the War of 1812: "while foreman of the Jesuit Manor at St. Indigoes, [Harry Mahoney] was single-handedly responsible for saving the treasury of the Jesuit religious order at St. Indigoes from an attack by the British and leading to safety the women and children on the St. Indigoes farms during the devastating raid on St. Indigoes by troops from the British Navy."[79] It is Harry's family story that Swarns recounts. Intersecting with our investigation, Harry would have been a companion of Sucky's if he is the Harry listed on the 1804 tax assessment at age thirty-three (there a Harry is described as "consumptive and sickly," but nearly a decade later he remained smart and skillful enough to keep the Jesuit treasury intact). Harry's ancestral line opens our Jesuit family tree to the many of us whose families have moved in Jesuit networks for many generations. As Marva Cecilia Bennett Kelly conveys, "I know that my Bennett ancestors were slaves to the Jesuits, probably as long as the Jesuits have been in America, and would you believe that for all these hundreds of years, a Bennett is still working for the Jesuits. My sister, Gladys Bennett Kemp continues to work as a cook for the St. Alphonsus Church."[80] The Bennett family reveals how many hands over how many generations of lay people and lay women have supported the work of the Jesuits.[81]

At the same time countless ancestors built the church, some among the enslaved Catholic women found ways to leverage their work in the church for their own creative and constructive ends, tapping into the resources of capital even while not fully free. The archives yield to the otherwise possibilities of enslaved women. A single line in an archival register witnesses to what has not yet been seen in White-centered histories: that Black Catholic women possessed enormous ingenuity in how they made a way out of the no-ways that were given to them. For example, a single line in an 1803 register provides a fragment for an otherwise possibility, capturing a time when the Jesuits recorded the financial transaction: "To Cash from Nancy for her Daughter Sophia sold and set free $50."[82] It appears that Nancy took advantage of the practice among the Jesuits to afford enslaved workers the opportunity to work overtime for money they might earn, and with hours of industry she was able to purchase her daughter's freedom. Who will tell Sophia's story of a life of freedom that could only come from the sacrificial actions of her mother?

Actions by which Nancy gave over her life—day by day—so that Sophia might live? What kind of a Christology is written in this line? And what of a theological anthropology? What does human relationality look like when we contemplate our indebtedness to one another? How did Nancy enact her creativity under the constraint of an exploitative relationality that slavery entailed? These female faces are theological resources for contemplating the human condition and the divine life that reveals "God as Author and Source of Freedom," as Copeland has written.[83] In her study of spirituality among the enslaved, Copeland sees that "the enslaved people faced their suffering and oppression through nourishing their interior lives in prayer."[84] Did Nancy and Sophia pray the prayers that circulate in Jesuit institutions: *Lord, teach me to be generous* . . . Did Nancy's prayers provide nourishment to face suffering and oppression—*to give and not to count the cost*—and to persevere for the sake of her daughter?[85] Did Nancy instill in Sophia the theological conviction that "the power of God in the cross was the power to live and to love—even when violence does its worst"?[86] In setting her daughter free, did Nancy witness the power of the resurrection in which God's promise of triumph over evil was made real? Was God the liberator incarnate in Nancy's action? Do we have new theologies of redemption embedded with the grace of the ghosts?

This is one among countless portraits of exploitative relationality by which our institutions have been built, where persons who will not be served by institutions give their lives to build them. But they are also portraits of potential realized and possibilities opened up. Nancy's life's work was given over to the Jesuits; that is clear. As an enslaved woman, she worked for the benefit of the Jesuits in 1803 as they built the institution that more than two hundred years later still stands. In this complex economy of exchange, Nancy's extraordinary work not only set her daughter free, but the fifty dollars that set her daughter free went back into the institution as a credit. It's not much, you might say, fifty dollars didn't keep the institution afloat, but it was one of the hundreds of thousands of imperceptible exchanges that *did*. Resources transferred from the work of women of color to enhance the work of White men. If Nancy had been paid for the work she was doing all along and had not funneled every ounce of her energies back into Jesuit institution building, there would be one less source of institution building. But Nancy represents the countless women and men whose lifeblood and life's work *were* directed to building our institution. And Nancy *didn't* funnel every ounce of her energies for her enslavers' benefit; she also reserved some for herself and her daughter. In re-membering the lives of enslaved Catholics, there will always be many ways to piece together our fragmented histories.

## Gospel Interpretation as Symbolic Capital in an Economy of Enslavement

The same is true when we consider the stories of enslaved and enslaver, Black and White Catholics together. Recall the twenty-first-century historian Thomas Murphy, who used Sucky to say that enslaved and enslaver "had little enough collaboration in prayer, let alone ministry." The response to an 1812 sermon puts the pieces together in a different way. In reporting on the preaching of a visiting priest, Fr. Francis Neale conveys that the preacher had broken open the Word in a way that spoke to enslaved workers demanding the care due to them. In Neale's complaints, we see not only that enslaved and enslavers were praying together but also that the reception of the Word by enslaved Catholics was a hermeneutic consideration. How enslaved Catholics would hear and interpret the Gospel when it was preached in mixed community was a consideration the Jesuits were forced to face. Neale writes:

> If Rev. Rantzau should return I suppose he will, he must endeavor to retrieve what he lost by the last sermon he give in our church of this place. It was on duty of masters towards their servants. I beg to be excused from nothing what is generally said on the subject, suppose it to say that it has given much alarm. His zeal was ill timed, his expressions caused several persons of other denominations to go out of the church before he concluded. These persons had admired his discourses before but at this I am tolled [*sic*], they were fitted with indignation, the Catholics, who remain, (as some do inform me) suffered the keenest sensations at his expressions & on seeing ^ at the same time, the conduct & exultation of the servants ~~during the time.~~ If the expressions, which are said that he made ^use of they may suppose they are exaggerated or not understood as delivered & be necessary. They shall be noted in a future letter. It has been observed, that if such be the doctrine of the church, the circumstances of the times, surrounded by the English & under very strict & military laws as to the slaves, ought to have caused Mr. Rantzau to have said these things either in private, or in the absence of the slaves.[87]

Key elements invite our attention in envisioning beginnings of otherwise possibilities, even in the conditions of enslavement. Rev. Rantzau appears to have been preaching on Paul's directives governing a "master"-"slave" relation, a favorite of enslavers throughout the antebellum period. Rantzau might have followed the pattern of Catholic enslavers who argued that biblical rules concerning the governance of such relations reflected the affirmation of enslavement as part of God's design. And he could very easily be one of the examples of Catholic enslaving hermeneutics where interpersonal "kindness" is advocated while leaving untouched the institutional evil of slavery, a Christian interpretive practice that through the centuries has left institutional harms undisturbed. But the *way* in which he preached it seems to have caused a stir, as it elicited a certain "conduct and exultation of the servants" ("servants" being a term used throughout the era for certain bondspeople in the condition of enslavement). Reading Neale's letter against the grain, we can envision those hearers in the condition of enslavement glimpsing an otherwise possibility in the patterns of practice in the early Christian witness. We pause to recognize that Catholic and those "of other denominations" were worshipping together as a community of enslaved persons and those who claimed mastery over them. Here, too, is a counterwitness to Murphy's authoritative pronouncement that Sucky's scream suggests otherwise. When Rev. Rantzau proclaimed a gospel of care for the enslaved (although not advocating for the abolition of their position as enslaved), he reminds us of the complexity of locations inhabited by our forebears *and* the transformative possibilities of the Gospel proclaimed with a particular hermeneutic. As it was in the first century, is now, and was as well in the nineteenth century, the position of Catholic Christians embedded in complex relationships is part of an ongoing struggle for meaning and human well-being. In this struggle in 1812, the scriptural text did not stand alone; its meaning was shaped by the "circumstances of its time," including the context of the war, the presence of the English, and the law with regard to enslaved people. In all of this, enslaved Catholics were also partners in the interpretive and life endeavors in their hearing of the Gospel; how the preaching would be heard by *their* ears informed part of the scriptural scene our Jesuit forebears considered.

White-centered histories ask us to think from the perspective of Jesuit institutions, Jesuit decision making, and Jesuits as the primary actors in the drama. But the archives allow us to read the memories they have bequeathed to us for otherwise possibilities and as gifts of the Spirit that might have allowed enslaved Catholics to survive.

## Grace in the Face of White Supremacy

In the writings of the archives, Black Catholic women, men, girls, and boys, children and elders, were agents in the creation of an American Catholicism and Jesuit institutions. What kind of grace must it have taken to weather the storm of changing fortunes for the Jesuits as they bore down on the life and relationships of our ancestors in the faith? What kind of presence of God grounded them and walked beside them in the cruelties, mundanities, and otherwise possibilities of their life among the Jesuits?

In order to pursue a reading of the Jesuit archives with this question of "grace," we might learn from the womanist theologian Katie Cannon, who sheds light on the workings of grace in the face of oppression. She writes of how "God's freely given gift of grace enables us to resist the forces of death and degradation arrayed against us and to affirm our dignity as beloved persons created in the image of God."[88] Cannon is specifically amplifying the flow of grace in the face of White supremacies as she draws out two dimensions of God's goodness: grace as spirit indwelling that confirms each person as imago Dei and grace as gift of redeeming love that transforms reality. These represent grace as both a *present*- and a *future*-oriented power of God at work in the world, one not tethered to abundance and flourishing but situated as sources of endurance and transformation.

The present power of God's grace as spirit indwelling confirming *each* person as imago Dei would have been necessary for persons who endured the two hundred years of our Christian nation's enslavement. It is not news, but it bears repeating that the Christian practice of enslavement was foundationally an affront to the Christian witness of imago Dei. As Diana Hayes paints the picture, women who survived the middle passage found

> their situations had not improved but worsened. They were separated from family and friends, from those who understood their language or shared their culture, and sold to men . . . to serve as breeders, field hands, wet nurses, and maids of all work. Cuffed and shackled, they were taken to distant farms and plantations and quickly realized that this was to be their fate in life: to work from "can't see to can't see"; to be treated as . . . beasts of labor; to be bred to strangers, to give birth only to see their offspring sold from them over and over again.[89]

But imago Dei could not be erased. It was the form of grace that grounded the freedom of the mind and freedom of the spirit that Shawn Copeland helps us see among enslaved persons despite the context of their captivity.[90] Copeland asks us to consider the depths of their faith practices of prayer and witness how "enslaved people negotiated this ontological and metaphysical assault by audaciously asserting their essential humanness in the face of dehumanizing conditions by choosing transcendence."[91] When, in the midst of her enslavement Sucky maintained the presence of personhood to reach out to Jesuits in care, was this the work of grace in the world? What was the grace necessary to wake up each morning and care for little ones if I know that once they "attained an age to be valuable in market, perhaps ten or twelve, the master sold them.

One after another was taken away and sold to the slave dealers."[92] Grace in this era might be seen as the enduring power in the present to affirm oneself as a child of God, as Howard Thurman proposes.[93] We might think of grace as God's indwelling spirit providing, in the words of Charles Long, "a new power of being . . . a power that would sustain their being because the powers-that-be would not sustain them."[94] Grace in this framing is the power to "hold together your personhood" in the face of powers bent on destroying it.[95] In Cannon's estimation, "Grace has to sustain those of us whose identities are shaped by multiple forces at odds with the dominant culture (primarily race, sex, and class)."[96]

Cannon identifies grace as the indwelling of God's spirit "that enables Christians of African descent to live conscious lives of thanksgiving . . . so that even in situations of oppression we celebrate our status as beloved creatures made in God's image."[97] In so articulating, we see Cannon present Christ's grace not only as a tool for survival but also as transformative of present circumstance when it is recognized, in Cannon's words, as "a divine gift of redeeming love that empowers African Americans to confront shocking, absurd, death-dealing disjunctions in life, so that when we look at our outer struggles and inner strength we see interpretive possibilities for creative change."[98]

To see grace at work in the lives of the ancestors at Georgetown, we might reconstruct any one of the many names Joy Kang had inscribed into the bricks and bones of the body of Georgetown's Healy Hall. To see grace at work in our ancestors, we might examine any one of the many references to persons held captive by the Jesuits responsible for sustaining them and helping our Jesuit ancestors create wealth through their life, blood, and breath. Following through on the invitation into the archives, we've met Harry, Nancy, Sophia, and Sucky, each one evidence of the grace that sustains in the face of White supremacy. But before we close, as an openness to the innumerable ancestors who tapped into such grace, we might meet Nelly.

We meet Nelly from the hand of much beloved Fr. Francis Dzierozynski, whom we met as the frail Jesuit in 1836 and as the target of care modeled on the witness of Sucky.[99] To the Jesuits, Nelly embodies all the key qualities they will need for their support: In 1843, she is described as "an excellent cook and industrious servant and house keeper and sacristan, belonging to us."[100] Nelly worked a lifetime with the Jesuits, having been "born and raised" at St. Inigoes, but we cannot be certain which of the traces in the archives belong to her.[101] Nelly not only opens the otherwise possibility of personhood withstanding the assaults of exploitative relationality, but her name opens us also to the many who shared her name, becoming a single representative of the many lives we must remember. We're simultaneously reminded of how difficult it is to re-member her. In 1839, Nelly appears to be forty-three years old and with three children.[102] The Georgetown Memory Project proposed that her surname might be Mahoney, although with uncertainty; in their 2019 document, they propose this Nelly was "age 38 in 1838." These datings would have her born sometime between 1796 and 1800, with the possibility that she was in her youth when Sucky was elderly. Since Nelly is an excellent cook, perhaps she learned her life-sustaining craft from Sucky.

What more do we have to re-member our Nelly?

Might we create a portrait of Nelly by the size of her feet in 1818, when the Jesuits kept records not of her life but of her expenses? In 1818, which of the shoes belonged to Nelly? Was she at that point: "8¾ Little Nelly—No. 8," or "9½ Nelly Aston—No. 11," or "Big Nelly 10½ No. 30"?[103]

In 1821, which Nelly was she, and how was she assessed for tax purposes among the other Nellys? Nelly age twenty-three, Nelly age forty-six, Nelly age thirty-eight.

Recognizing the instability of record keeping, we do not know which of the remaining Nellys might be her on the 1831 tax assessment:

> Nelly age 33, $60 . . . Nelly [infirm] age 53, $0 . . . Nelly age 50, $10.[104]

Or taxes owed again in 1833 on:

> Nelly $60 . . . Nelly $150 . . . Nelly $250.[105]

Our Nelly was at St. Inigoes with Fr. Carbery until about 1838.[106]

On the eve of the 1838 sale, our Nelly, the excellent cook and industrious housekeeper, would have been among those enslaved Catholics counted and accounted for as the Jesuits forecasted what profit they might have in the upcoming sale. From a document titled "List of slaves on each estate to be sold," the Nellys at St. Inigoes are listed as following:

> St. Inagoes F21 Nelly age 6
> St. Inagoes Nelly age 38
> St. Inagoes Nelly age 55 / her daughter Eliza age 22
> St. Inagoes Phil age 55 / Nelly his wife age 53[107]

All except Nelly age thirty-eight are listed with an accompanying number for the ship to which they would be assigned; three additional Nellys resided at White Marsh (aged thirty-eight, sixty, and sixteen). In the legal documents that contain the writ of sale, we know that at least three of the Nellys were transferred to Louisiana:

> Know all men by these presents, that I Thomas F. Mulledy of George Town District of Columbia, have bargained and sold, and by these

> presents do bargain, sell and deliver with Henry Johnson, of the Parish of St James, State of Louisiana . . . Nelly black cook 30, Nelly 17 . . . Nelly Harrison 50.[108]

And then again additional documentation:

> Thomas F. Mulledy sells to Jesse Beatty and Henry Johnson two hundred and seventy two negroes, to wit: Isaac, a man sixty five years of age . . . Nelly his daughter, thirty eight years of age . . . Nelly a woman thirty eight . . . Nelly a woman sixty.
>
> [and in an appended list] Nelly, age 6.[109]

The description of our Nelly's skills in her support of the Jesuits and her resourceful service to the Jesuits renders her identifiable for reconstruction in the twenty-first century. In her history of the families sold by the Jesuits in 1838, Rachel Swarns identifies *this* Nelly (our Nelly) as Nelly Mahoney, recognizable precisely by the skills she leveraged in support of the Jesuits, as the daughter of Harry, whose ingenuity had formerly saved their funds.

The occasion for Dzierozynski's recollection of Nelly's skill is to recommend her to another priest in 1843: "I think Nelly which formerly was with Fr. Carberry, and these four, five years in Alexandria with Fr. Dubisson and [Deitz?], and now by Fr. Young sent to Newtown. . . . If you choose, you may ask her from Fr. Woodley, perhaps he will consent to give her to you."[110] Like Sucky, who served somewhere between seven and twenty-three of the Jesuits, Nelly has had a long service to the church in many different capacities. We might imagine Nelly moving through the network of Jesuit placements and creating a web of relationality between the differing locations on the land that the Jesuits claimed as their property.[111]

As a foremother, Nelly was among those women whose hands helped build the church in America. She cared for the Jesuits body and soul as cook, housekeeper, *and sacristan*. We need to imagine Nelly with her breath and her body in hushed places as she tends the holy body of Christ resident in the chapel. Her acts of care for the bodies of the Jesuits, her enslaved companions, and the body of Christ in the tabernacle made these places fit for the dwelling of the divine. Theologizing from the dirt and depths of Auschwitz, the Jewish theologian Melissa Raphael envisions the possibility that our role as human beings is to make "space for the holy" even in the most desecrated places.[112] Activating creativity within the constraints of her legalized captivity, Nelly may have expanded her imaginings of the God who accompanied her. By the early nineteenth century, we have literary evidence that women's roles could be imagined in patterning and partnership with the "holy hospitality" of Jesus in his ministry of presence and the sacred acts of feeding. Although we do not have Nelly's words, we have the autobiographical account of Harriet Jacobs, who narrated her life story in enslavement, at times seeing in her own practices of hearth care a sacred connection to Jesus feeding the five thousand or dining with his companions and announcing himself as the "bread of life."[113] Just as the earliest Christians lifted up this practice of Jesus, they placed themselves in the extension of them: "New Testament writers reiterate this feeding commission by commanding Jesus's followers to feed the poor, to feed their enemies, and to feed the flock of the church (Acts 20:28, Rom. 12:20, 1 Pet. 5:2)."[114] Is there any reason why we cannot imagine Nelly also finding glimpses of grace in the agency she enacted in the creative process of cooking?

Nelly was not only a valued chef. The archives tell of her role also as preparer of the Eucharistic meal in her role as sacristan. Here, in the quiet space of the chapel at St. Inigoes Nelly enjoyed "the privilege . . . of touching the sacred vessels."[115] As described within a nineteenth-century ecclesiology, "The sacristan, who having permission to touch the sacred vessels and linens may do so also for the purpose of dressing the chalice."[116] Historical documents demonstrate that women regularly filled this role, and through the wider practices we might re-member Nelly. As a nineteenth-century account indicates, "We find in most cases that religious who realize these limitations of reverence, only handle the sacred vessel with gloves especially used for the purpose."[117] Slipping sturdy or slim or scoured hands into special gloves, we can imagine Nelly engaged in the spiritual practice of meal preparation crossing over into a mutually enriching Eucharistic meal preparation, a seamless landscape of her sacramental work. Given her dual occupations in the kitchen and in the sanctuary, was Nelly also enjoined in the task of baking Eucharistic bread? Her fingers spreading wide the dough and her arms enlisted in kneading, the full length of her frame given over into the pressing of flour and water, so that when the priest intoned over the Eucharistic celebration, "fruit of the vine and work of human hands," it was Nelly's hands that were incorporated into the sacred mystery. When the priest professed the words of Jesus, "this is my body," was it not Nelly's body and lifeblood that went into its making? In the imagined enfleshment of Nelly's sacred sanctifying she offers to us the possibility to see in the work of the church the holy work of women.

The skill with which Nelly served our Jesuit ancestors was recognized by them, and it is holy to us. And while the passing along and transferring of locations would surely have been disruptive to both Nelly's and Sucky's life, we know that both were spared the trauma of the 1838 sale, Sucky because of her death in 1812 (or 1811) and Nelly because Dzierozynski still writes of her in 1843. We might hold in our hearts the pain of loss that Nelly experienced when her skills saved her from the sale but when 272 of her companions, her friends, her intimate relations, her coworkers, and the many who filled the sanctuary that she kept were sold by the Jesuits in order to enable the institution to remain solvent. Among her companions did she hold any special place in her heart for those who shared her name, those Nellys listed on the manifest of the Katherine Jackson that stole them away to New Orleans for sale?

Nelly Merrick f 40 5–2 Black
Nelly Barns f 60 5–2 Black
Nelly Blacklock f 70 5–1 Black
Nelly Blacklock f 17 4–11 Black
Nelly Harrison f 50 6–0 Black[118]

These Nellys and the nearly three hundred friends and relations that Nelly would have counted as her Catholic, sacramental, and prayer community, gone. What kind of grace sustains us through that kind of trauma? Is it too much to imagine that the spiritual capital of her work as sacristan was a sustaining practice throughout her remaining years?

While Nelly comes to us in fragments, she witnesses the presence of faith-filled women serving spiritual roles among the Jesuits. Born and raised with the Jesuits, she escapes the sale and suffers the trauma of a life left behind. But she continues to serve. Even amid the Jesuits who cannot bear to part with her. When in 1843 Fr. Dzierozynski commends Nelly for the many laudable talents she dedicates to her care of the Jesuits and the wider community, he simultaneously reveals the limitation of Jesuit partnerships as he confesses to Fr. Lancaster at St. Joseph's that while she is "the best servant," "her only fault, is too long [a] tongue."[119] This partner among the Jesuits provides another attestation to the difficulty of our Jesuit forebears engaging in partnership with enslaved women. And the last we hear of Nelly, in 1850, suggests that she maintained her character, stood her ground, and kept her personhood even when powers were bent on destroying it. This letter also reveals the overturned estimations of a White racial frame, where enslaving White women could be "a very good Catholic" and "a first rate Lady" while an enslaved sacristan serving the Jesuits for a lifetime could be named "an embarrassment." Fr. Woodley writes,

> I have parted from Nelly to a very good Catholic, near Medley's Neck Church. He has her for an indefinite period,—<u>no sale</u> ratified, so that if the society should ever choose to be embarrassed with her again, it can take her back—not to Newtown necessarily. She went originally from St. Inigoes, where she was born and raised, to Alexandria, from Alexandria to Newtown after leaving Newtown she will be <u>common</u>

> property again, subject to the Procurator General—who may ratify a sale, or dispose of her otherwise. A first rate Lady has secured her, one with whom you are somewhat acquainted, she is the sister of Mrs. Hammet of St. Nicholas, the tall lady who wanted one in St Nicholas, Ms. Combs. All who have heard of my solution are delighted.—I know her well.[120]

In this and countless other documents of White Catholics in an economy of enslavement, the symbolic capital of "goodness" (of a "first rate lady") and "good Catholic" served to misrecognize the evils of enslavement, and we must ask: How can slavers be "good"?

We might hold Nelly in the esteem of Dzierozynski and in our hearts for the trauma she endured, and with our spirit for the ways she made the world holy. And yet both Dzierozynski and Woodley remark negatively on her character: "Her only fault too long a tongue," the men remain "embarrassed" by her. These comments we might read with a hermeneutic of suspicion, and we might wonder what provoked such commentary by the Jesuits. Were they perturbed by any woman who demonstrated initiative? Or was there something particular to Nelly's character they sought to suppress?

We know that Nelly survived the 1838 sale and continued her work among the Jesuits. The intimate reconstruction of the Mahoney family offered by Swarns gives us another possibility for reading the Jesuits' rendering of Nelly. Here archival evidence indicates that at least some among the Jesuits disapproved of the sale, including Fr. Joseph Carbery, who publicly and privately made his position known. Nelly helped convey through the network at Georgetown that not all the Jesuits approved of the sale of enslaved Catholics. Carbery's disapproval of his fellow Jesuits shows us both an internal disagreement and an otherwise possibility. It is Nelly who may have been a witness to this, and this opens space in our imagination for what might have been. In Swarns's account, "It was Nelly . . . who told Father Dubuisson about Carbery's response to the sale."[121] While Dubuisson affirms Nelly's character—"full with religion and very intelligent"—there may have been others like Woodley and Dzierozynski who supported the sale and sought to discount Nelly's truth telling. Her "too-long a tongue" was the tongue of telling the truth, and, indeed, such truth telling might have been an "embarrassment" to our Jesuit ancestors who would have preferred silence around the sale. Such truth telling had repercussions for the Jesuits who were now in the process of losing symbolic capital for what was seen as "the scandal [Mulledy] had created with the slave sale."[122]

Swarns reconstructs that the unwillingness of the Jesuits to admit their reliance on the work of Black women (*she rules the house but she will not rule me*) "seems to be a clear reference to Nelly."[123] At this point in our progress through the archives and the Catholic-Jesuit institution it reveals, are we yet willing to name the institution as a cultivator of untruthful practices as well as the refusal of collaboration? If the embarrassment of too long a tongue was because of her truth telling, how do we see patterns of an institution that maintains power with its self-serving narrative that conceals the truth? Are we capable of considering that maybe God wasn't at work in the exploitation that built the Jesuit system but rather at work among those who endured their exploitation? Are we prepared to see the institution of the Catholic Church in America rooted in the sin of White supremacy? And are we willing to recognize God at work among the enslaved insofar as the God we meet in the cross of Christianity is not the God of the oppressor but the God of the oppressed? What does this affirmation of faith say about oppression within institutions?

Nelly's care for the Jesuits as housekeeper, cook, and sacristan has both economic and theological significance. She also represents the countless women who built the Jesuit institution at Georgetown through their house labor and sewing, their field work and feeding, and clothing and cleaning for the Jesuits, even as the Jesuits were producing theological tracts that argued that their enslavement was God's design. Privately in the writings of their diaries, like the one produced by Joseph Mobberly (1823), the Jesuits contemplated the goodness of slavery with a theological anthropology that believed that *some* people would be better off in an enslaved condition.[124] Publicly, on the platforms of their public speaking, Jesuits like James Ryder (1835) presented proslavery views that the "God of order" and the "gospel of peace" required the continued practice of enslavement and that the peace of this God was reflected in the beneficent relationship between the enslaved person and the "maternal kindness of his compassionate mistress."[125] Br. Mobberly, Fr. Ryder, Fr. Mulledy, each theologically trained and each arguing theologically that enslavement was for the benefit of humanity. These men scribing in their diaries, writing in their studies for lectures and published works, practicing for their public speaking—all the while fed and cared for, clothed and living in clean rooms by the women they enslaved. An exploitative relationality fueled the Jesuit theological defense of enslavement. While we can see this exploitative relationality creating the theology of slavery from within the Jesuit system, we also imagine our Jesuit forebears writing themselves *above* the evil of the institution. Spiritualizing the condition of enslavement, Superior

General Jan Roothaan signed his letter approving the sale of 272 human beings in 1838, and with his parting words named himself "a slave in Christ."[126]

## Institutional Complicity and Re-Membering for Accountability

What do these women do for the overarching concern in this book for the transformative truth telling at Jesuit and Catholic institutions? Our forebears in the faith show us the many ways that these lay Catholic women helped build the original Catholic Church in the United States. In order to repair the breach created by the many forms of thievery practiced by the Jesuits—theft of lives and labors, theft of identity and history—we must seek their stories and remember them.[127] Moreover, Sucky and Nelly help us tease out the otherwise possibilities of their day and our own. Sucky's scream and Nelly's too long a tongue point to the possibilities of speech to create new modes of relationship, both women willing to announce otherwise possibilities despite the cost. The story of each lay Black Catholic woman offers an alternative to the story passed down about them and about the church by the White Jesuit Catholic priests in their company. Sucky and Nelly remind us of the multiplicity of ways our histories might be read and our presents might be enacted.

Duke Kwon and Gregory Thompson advocate that American Christians must face the theft of history that both erases the stories of those enslaved and elevates by "romanticization" the story of Christian enslavers.[128] Such theft is, the authors argue, its own form of racism, whereby the only actors in our histories are those White Christians who benefited from the purchase and sale, exploitation and torture, of human beings. Those of us in Jesuit institutions can no longer allow our Jesuit forebears to narrate their own story—centering as they do the claim of benevolent practices. We must return to our ancestors their own stories as we aim to repair the breach. In re-membering our ancestors, we are also guided socially, theologically, and practically by the witness of the Black Catholic women in this chapter. They are our ghosts, whose presence not only can be felt, seen, and remembered but whose insights might be leverage for changing our institutions in the present. Re-centering them, they move from ghostly presences to spiritual ancestors in the faith.

When we remember that Susannah screamed, we also might find our voice in speaking out the otherwise possibility that calls out practices of harm (to self and to others) and calls us in to care across locations of difference *and* the freedom to withhold our emotional labor. Nelly (whose only fault is too long a tongue) sounds forth the necessity of speaking this truth, even in institutions that do not value our voices both for our own sake and for the transformation of institutional practices. And Sophia, set free by the industry of Nancy, recalls for us the real opportunity for leveraging what is made available to us through the institutions as we engage this transformative work but also tap into the resources that will build fully human lives for ourselves and our children. Re-membering them and countless other enslaved Catholics provides rich resources for the hard work that lies ahead. They bring to us a grace, the grace of the ghosts.

# 3

# The Complexity of a Complicit Church

## *Henrietta and Elizabeth in a Catholic Network*

Those who call ourselves Catholic and those of us who benefit from Catholic institutions of church and school (in the social and symbolic capital they convey) might find ourselves reckoning with the history of Catholic racial injustice in the creation of our institutions. In the preceding chapters, we've entered into an examination of the Catholic tradition in the United States in order to engage in the truth telling that might lead to transformed institutions of church and school. As we've seen, an economy of enslavement fueled the establishment and foundations of the church in the Americas, and in chapter 2 the first Catholic (and Jesuit) institution of Georgetown provided an entry point into Catholic complicity in this evil. But it also provided an entry into imagining the life-worlds of some among the enslaved Catholic women whose work sustained the institution in its early years. Sucky, with her culinary skills; Nelly, who served spiritual needs as sacristan; Nancy, whose industry set her daughter Sophia free. Their stories reveal the complexity of Catholic institutions as storehouses of capital, where guardians of the church attempted to convert these women's Spirit and Breath into capital, but the women's stories reveal much more about the possibilities of a God who sustained them. Despite the many years of unpaid labor and the attempt of those in power to erase her presence, Sucky's scream echoes through the years as counterwitness to narratives of Jesuit Catholic benevolence and the otherwise possibility of living in institutions where one can navigate strategically how to withhold one's emotional labor. Nelly proved herself in a lifetime of work to be an invaluable partner to the first American Catholics as the Jesuits drew on her many skills to sustain them; the gendered assessment of willingness to speak truth and her communicative resourcefulness acted as a mirror reflecting the limits of the men in their inability to work collaboratively with women. Nancy's industry and commitment exceeded the expectations of her unpaid labor, and her economic astuteness was demonstrated in her saving sufficient funds for the release of her daughter from slavery. These are remarkable stories of Black Catholic women whose work not only sustained the church and university in their day but come to us in the cloud of witnesses for the needs of church and university today.

While historians have long known that Catholic and Jesuit institutions benefited from the evils of enslavement—Sucky, Nelly, and Nancy's stories have been available in the archives for any who might look there—the return to the truth telling with adjusted lenses allows us to draw forward new ways of understanding both the Jesuit Catholic complicity in evil *and* the complexity of lives lived under the conditions of an economy of enslavement. In the process recommended by Maria Yellow Horse Brave Heart, this truth telling is followed by our understanding history better (in the complexity brought forth by analysis) in order to seek paths to release the pain of the historical trauma of inhumanity that ran through our Jesuit Catholic Christian institutions. This unfolding and spiraling movement aims toward *transformed* institutions. The several hundred years of building Catholic institutions of school and church with unpaid and underpaid workers require that we investigate the employment practices of our institutions today. Do we pay a living wage for the work that those committed to our institutions undertake in their many and diverse forms? The structure of male leadership and hierarchical power asks us to consider what forms of shared governance structure our church and school today: Are women's lives, insights, analyses, and contributions equally valued in our communities? Are the insights from the full range of gendered and sexual expressions taken into account? Ideologies of White supremacy intersect with male dominance, raising the question today of whether White supremacies still reside in the places and practices of Catholic communities. As we work for transformed and transformative institutions, where will we apply our expansive industry, as Nancy did, and where will we withhold our emotional labor, in the footsteps of Sucky?

But the flagship Catholic institutions of church and school that come to us through the archives of Georgetown University are by far not the only opening to the many, varied, and countless Catholic locations in need of truth telling and healing. Indeed, the practices of Christian slaveholding speak across the wide range of Christian denominations in our nation's history. At the same time, scholars and historians have noted that the Catholic Church was "the first and largest corporate slaveholder in the Americas."[1] The raw fact of this data must have us looking to *all* the places where the illicit gains from an economy of enslavement have enriched our American Catholic traditions. But as we peel back the layers of our histories, we will also find some surprising complexities in the complicity of the Catholic Church in the national evils of enslavement. Like the witness of the Black Catholic women of Georgetown, more members of our ancestral community ask us to consider American Catholicism from new vantage points. In this chapter, we will follow Black and White Catholic women as they lead us into intimate relationships of congregation, home, work, and campus. These locations yield further stories to expand our imagination about the complexity and complicity of Catholic institutions in the historical trauma of White supremacy. Like our introductions with Nancy, Nelly, and Sucky, this is not a story of defeat, yet it is also not entirely a story of triumph. It is a story of creativity under the constraints of the particularity of a historical moment. In this chapter, we'll enter into American Catholicism through a clearing in the woods, at the crossroad of an economy of enslavement and a growing Catholic Church in the mid-nineteenth century, in the story of St. James the Greater, in Colleton County, South Carolina. But this story will lead us also to the network of Jesuit Catholic Christian institutions across the nation and ask us to experience the extended matrix of complicity and complexity in our shared history, as the story ends in the twenty-first century in New York City. Through the singular location of St. James the Greater, our imaginations expand to consider Catholic institutions in an extended web connected imaginatively and economically across the distances of nation and globe. In the networking of institutions and the conveyance of capital, how might we experience *today's* inheritance from the sins of the past on both expansive and intimate scales?

## St. James the Greater: Institutions of the Church at Center and Periphery

> Saint James the Greater Catholic Church is situated at the crossroads of the Charleston-Savannah highway and the old plantation road that linked Walterboro with the area where the Ashepoo and the Combahee Rivers converge and flow into the Atlantic. The parish was established by Bishop John England, first Bishop of Charleston. The church was dedicated on December 10, 1833.
>
> In 1856 the frame church burned to the ground catching fire from the burning fields nearby. No immediate effort was made to rebuild the church. In only a few years the War between the States began and the story of St. James fades for over forty years. No accounts of the area are

> available from 1856 until 1897. In that year, a priest by the name of Daniel Berberich accidentally discovered the presence of Catholic people in the vicinity of Thompson's Crossroads which was now known locally as "Crossroads" or "Catholic Crossroads." He found a group of people with a thriving Catholic Faith.[2]

The story of St. James is a curious account of the Catholic Church as an institution, from the perspective of those who kept the faith. It was at the request of lay Catholics that the Diocese of Charleston first was called into this particular locale, after many years of Catholic gatherings in private homes. At the time (1833), the Diocese of Charleston had just two parishes within the city limits (established in 1791 and 1822), so when the diocese dedicated a church building at the Crossroads of Colleton County, we can mark the formal expansion of the institution of the Catholic Church on the "frontier." The conferral of formal recognition made the community "Catholic" in a new way, with a new level of symbolic capital recognizable to others *as* Catholic and the formal endorsement of church authorities. But the distance of forty-six miles from the center of ecclesial power in Charleston, at a time governed by horse travel and footpaths, made the location of Colleton County peripheral, with traveling priests attending to the faithful only on occasion. Suzanne Krebsbach writes: "Those few Catholics in rural South Carolina were fortunate to see a priest once or twice a year."[3] The visit of such a priest was often announced in the diocesan newspaper, the *United States Catholic Miscellany*, which connected even fledgling communities like St. James with a broader network of Catholic institutions and identities across what was emerging as the United States. With articles on Catholicism locally, nationally, and globally, the print media could imaginatively embed Catholic identities in an international network while simultaneously shaping local practices and ecclesial patterns. The newspaper provides a window on the community at St. James the Greater:

> Though by reason of death and removals the number of Catholics in the vicinity of this church is diminished, yet the families and individuals for many miles round regard it as their centre. The Rev. Mr. O'Neill, celebrated Mass there for a small congregation on Sunday, the 22nd of March, and after having visited some of the stations, returned to its vicinity on Friday the 27th. The Bishop arrived on the next afternoon and celebrated Mass at an early hour on Sunday the 29th . . . a good congregation was assembled, one half of which consisted of Negroes, and amongst the whites were several other religious denominations.[4]

Describing the way ecclesial resources would be distributed on the periphery, the paper announced that Colleton and Beaufort counties "will be visited by a clergyman from this city in the next week and that ensuing. The Mass will be celebrated, God willing, at St. James's Church on Sunday the 17th [1841]."[5] The social capital of priests visiting indicates a willingness to spread economic capital from the center of the diocese, as it would take some resources to get him there. The symbolic capital of "God's will" might cover any change in diocesan plans.[6]

In the span from 1833 to 1845, St. James the Greater, at the Crossroads outside several frontier communities, was the center of Catholic life for Colleton County. But in 1845, the diocese saw fit to construct a second church in the area, announcing that "on Thursday morning at seven o'clock, the Bishop [Reynolds, accompanied by Rev. Dr. Lynch] celebrated Mass, and at 11 A. M. dedicated [a new] Church under the Patronage of St. Philip."[7] The construction of this second Catholic Church about ten miles away in the more formally settled town of Walterboro diminished the number of faithful attending St. James and stretched the visits of clergy to the community even thinner, since the Diocese of Charleston (covering all of South Carolina, North Carolina, and Georgia) was now "twenty-six churches, sixty mission stations," yet still only "twenty-two clergy."[8] When a priest would visit, he would attend to both parishes, and the prominent families in the area would be celebrated in the diocesan paper as hosts for even the bishop, the appearance of these names potentially enriching the symbolic capital of those named and serving them well within the paper's extended network of relationships. As the *U.S. Catholic Miscellany* reports on Bishop Ignatius Reynolds's visit to the area in 1848, he "arrived at St. James' Colleton District, on Saturday evening last . . . and was hospitably entertained during his brief sojourn amongst us by Mrs. Hurcell and Miss Harriet Bellinger." Reynolds gave a sermon on salvation (setting Catholic identity in competition with the surrounding majority Protestants), and "the Bishop left on the following day for Walterboro in company with our pastor where he was kindly entertained by Mr. Freysse and Mrs. Pinckney."[9] Like the wealthy women whom the Gospels describe as sponsors to Jesus and his movement, the news account points to Miss Harriet Bellinger and Mrs. Elizabeth Perry Bellinger Pinkney as pillars for the two church locations, one at the Catholic Crossroads of St. James the Greater and the other at the in-town location of St. Philip's in Walterboro. These female converts to Catholicism leveraged their economic capital to establish and support the church on the frontier (enhancing their symbolic capital in the wider Catholic network). According to the firsthand account of Fr. Jeremiah J. O'Connell (a Benedictine who served at St. James and wrote the authoritative history of the diocese), it was Elizabeth's sister, "Miss Sarah Bellinger, [who] at her own expense, erected a church at Walterboro, dedicated to St. Philip [in 1845]."[10] And, like the priests caring for multiple flocks, Elizabeth Pinckney and Harriet, Susan, and Sarah Bellinger continued also to maintain their care for the communities at both churches.

Yet when the church building of St. James at the Crossroads was destroyed by fire, the diocese chose *not* to dedicate the resources to rebuild. In his description as a historian, Fr. O'Connell offered that the reason for the refusal to rebuild was predicated on a loss of the "old Catholics" who were its prominent members. His history recounts:

> Collins Cross-Roads, or the Blue House, in Colleton district was about the first Catholic mission organized by Bishop England outside of Charleston. . . . The McGees, the Maloneys, the Purcels, the Foxes, the Bretts, the Ryans, and some others formed a respectable Catholic settlement. . . .
>
> By the year 1847 all the old Catholics had died but one. . . . I repaired the church, which had fallen into decay; and said Mass and preached there on the second Sunday of each month. It was visited at this time by Bishop Reynolds. A year or two after, it was burnt by a fire originating in the woods. I said the last Mass in that venerated shrine. Not a soul of those who flourished in its day was then living.[11]

O'Connell reminisces about the flourishing of St. James under the guidance of those named with the symbolic capital of "respectable Catholics" descended from Irish immigrants, and with regret he reports that "not a soul" was still living at the time of the fire in 1856. Recall the 1840 assessment of the parish published in the *Catholic Miscellany*, laying the foundation for what twentieth-century histories describe: "that the congregation had been greatly diminished by 'deaths and removals.'"[12] O'Connell looking out from 1878 describes: "This mission is very thin, and there are few Catholics west of Barnwell except the children of Mrs. Pinckney at Walterboro, and a few in Beaufort. It was at the beginning the most promising portion of the diocese, and like all other country missions, shrunk after the death of the first Catholics."[13] From the ecclesial center of Charleston and the ecclesial vantage point of its ordained historian, the Catholic Crossroads at St. James died a natural death after the deaths of its most prominent congregants, already in a diminished state in 1847, which was nearly ten years before the fire. The 2020 documentary *We Came a Long Way by Faith* offers interviews with twenty-first-century church representatives and scholars to create a multilayered hypothesis for why the church was not rebuilt: An expansive diocese and still thin priesthood, the interest of the bishop to build up the church in the center in Charleston, and an impending war all added to the retraction of institutional support for the Crossroads, particularly with its status as a "mission" church.[14] In the logic of the institutional church, there was little reason to rebuild a church that was already "greatly diminished" and lacking a sufficient number of "respectable Catholics." Nevertheless, church records indicate a steady flow of baptisms, including a flurry in the years between 1848 and 1856, so while O'Connell mourns the loss of "all the old Catholics" by the year 1847, a new generation of Catholics had already emerged in their place.

It may be the case that the "new Catholics" incorporated into the church were not only peripheral to the ecclesial center in Charleston and marginalized in relation to the in-town church of Walterboro, but we might also ask whether a female-led baptismal increase of the faithful wasn't a source of its marginalization as well. Reproducing the church through a spike in baptisms, Elizabeth Pinckney and her Bellinger sisters demonstrate the role lay women might play in a hierarchically ordered church in the absence of institutional oversight (while rich in economic capital, they remained poor in status afforded by symbolic capital in a patriarchal church). Nevertheless, in the period from 1848 to 1855 as lay Catholic women, Elizabeth Pinckney and Sarah and Susan Bellinger were involved in more than two-thirds of all baptisms recorded at St. James. The names of forty-nine children baptized at St. James between 1848 and 1852 might be imagined as forming the new Catholic community taking the place of the old: Jenny, Julia, Sarah, Jane Caroline, Isack John, Esther, John Edward, Elizabeth Johanna, Maria, Frederick Joseph, Charity, Benjamin, Joseph Pompey, James, Mary Augusta, Mary Priscilla, Sara, Mary, Michael, Eleanor, Mary Augusta, Joseph, Emiline, Monday, Carolina Abraham, Ben, Julia, Elizabeth, Lucian, Elizabeth, Daniel, Joseph, Hannah, Eliza, Ben, Sully Sophia Magdaline, Anne Elizabeth, Gabriel, Frank, Edward, Frank, Francis Xavier.[15] This community of young Catholics was obviously not out there on their own; their parents, too, helped birth a new Catholic community on the Carolina frontier, increasing the church list. Some among the parents were themselves receiving the sacrament of baptism at this time: Samuel and Dorcas, Francis and Lucy, Samson and Juns, Jenny and Jacob. Some stand out as leaders, taking on the role of sponsors/godparents at the baptism of the next generation: Hetty, Carolina Joanna, Vincent of Paul. The rolls of the new community that replaced the "old" Irish Catholics might have looked something like this in the years just before the fire:

| Baptized Youth | Adults in the Community | Sponsors |
|---|---|---|
| (1848) Jacob, Valentine, Peter "Cuffey," Jack, Samuel, Adam Scipio, Mary, Anna "Dinman" Ellen, Minda, John Edward, Elizabeth Joanna | (1840) Saul, John Davis and Patty, Ben Scott and Betty, Supphis Bellinger and Damian Bellinger | Susan Bellinger (1840 ff) × 10<br>Sarah Bellinger (1848 ff) × 9 |
| (1849) Maria; Frederick Joseph, Charity, Benjamin, Joseph Pompey | (1841) Robert Gaugh and Della | S. Bellinger × 6<br>Mary Augustus Pinckney (1850) |
| (1850) James, Mary Augusta, Mary Priscilla, Sarah, Mary, Michael | (1848) Benjamin Joseph, Lia and John, Samuel and Dorcas, Anna, Thomas, Sampson and Maria, Edward and Joanna | Elizabeth Pinckney (1851) × 3<br>Jenny (1841) |
| (1851) Eleanor, Mary Augusta, Joseph | (1850) Cyrus and Dyah, Sam, and Margaret, Francis and Lucy, Maria, Sarah, Shirley | Peter Garrison (1848)<br>Carolina (1848) |
| (1852) Emiline, Monday, Carolina, Abraham, Ben, Julia, Elizabeth Pinckney, Lucian, Elizabeth, Daniel, Joseph, Hannah | (1851) MaryAnn, Samson, Juns Mary, Peggy, Anna, Sibby | Vincent of Paul (1849) × 5<br>Carolina Joanna (1850) |
| (1854) Eliza, Ben, Sully, Sophia Magdaline, Anne Elizabeth, Gabriel, Frank, Edward, Frank Francis Xavier | (1852) Jacky, Leah, Mary, Sarah, Sandy, Louisa, Ben, Jane, Elizabeth, Caroline, Edward, Joseph Mal, Henrietta Rebecca Ford, Eustace & Mary Bellinger | Hetty (1850)<br>Theodore<br>Peggy (1854) |
| | (1854) Lucy, Lucy, Francis, Louisa, Martha, Mary, Dina, Joe, Maria | Thomas Pinckney (1850)<br>Rev. Dr. Lynch (1852)<br>Sally B. Pinckney (1854) × 2 |

That this Catholic community of more than one hundred strong was "forgotten" on the Carolina frontier after a fire in 1856 says something about the periphery and the peripheral locations within the church and the material consequences that come from the recognition and misrecognition attendant with symbolic capital.

Yet, in examining the dynamic of center and periphery, the logic of loss of the old guard is insufficient explanation. St. James in the clearing competed with the in-town location of St. Philip's; St. James was a young church with a predominance of children; St. James was also women led (as reflected in the sponsorship by the Bellinger-Pinckneys). Each of these is an important element at work in diminishing institutional interest in a mission church, which favored the social and economic capital that male adults could lend. But through the lens of institutional systems of White supremacy, a key feature must be pressed to the foreground: As evidence marshaled to recognize St. James on the Registry of Historic Places describes, "Originally biracial, the parish evolved into a predominantly black congregation by the middle of the nineteenth century."[16]

St. James at the Catholic Crossroads of a clearing in the woods on the frontier of the Catholic Church in a predominantly Protestant South Carolina is one of the oldest continuous Black Catholic parishes in the nation.[17] Yet it was nearly extinguished for lack of institutional attention.

The continuity of the faith makes the story of St. James the Greater even more compelling, as Shawn Copeland describes:

> When fire destroyed the church in 1856 and war grew imminent, the slaveholding families fled the area, leaving church buildings in disrepair. A small group of black Catholic slaves was left behind. Historian Cyprian Davis writes, "without a priest, church, or sacraments the Catholic faith was kept alive [among them] over a period of forty years through the efforts of Vincent de Paul Davis, a former slave and storeowner, who instructed the children."[18]

While the congregation's published history credits the rediscovery of the community to Fr. Berberich in 1897, additional evidence suggests that knowledge of this community resurfaced periodically in letters to diocesan officials. Instead of a passive "lost" and "now found," there seems to have been an active agency on the part of the diocese to ignore the call to attend to the Black Catholic community on the frontier. Not only J. J. O'Connell's history published in 1878 but several years prior a letter from a visiting Jesuit brought concern for the mission church back to the attention of the diocese. Fr. Folchi SJ offers this correspondence from his visit in 1875: "As for Walterboro and adjoining missions, I would respectfully suggest that they should be visited by missionaries for the colored people, as I found here a good many of them who still retain enough of the faith and are anxious for a priest."[19] But the Jesuit's concern did not appear to register: It was a full two decades later that the church officially "rediscovered" the Catholic Crossroads. This was an active refusal to see the thriving Black Catholic community at the Crossroads, which was reversed only toward the turn of the century with the activity of Fr. Berberich.

That members of the congregation at St. James the Greater "kept the faith" and were recognizably Catholic offers another lens through which to view the idea of "institutions." While we might say that the "institutional church" represented by the diocese of Charleston had abandoned these Catholics, the Catholics themselves, maintaining the practices of Catholicism, *were* the church. Here we might embrace a fundamental shift in the definition of "institutions" precisely as the places where people *practice*. The story of St. James returns us to a consideration of how we are shaped as human beings through the network of relationships that run through institutions. Our minds may conjure institutions as "functional organs of the body called society" necessarily anchored in the physical space of buildings.[20] But theorists also describe institutions as manifesting themselves "as a *site of action*," locations that create collectives through ideologies and practices.[21] When the community of St. James was named as part of the institution of the Catholic Church through baptism and instruction, they continued the centuries-long tradition of relating to world-and-other in distinctive ways, guided by the practices of the Catholic Church and bound to one another in their "Catholicity." In describing institutions being manifest as "places of practice," we are asked to recognize the continuation of the institution of the church among the community at St. James even without an "institutional home" in the form of a church building. In the years after the fire of 1856 and before "rediscovery" by the official arm of the institutional church (the diocese), the institution of the Catholic Church was maintained by the practices of the community members themselves. The unbroken presence of Catholics at the Catholic Crossroads gives us new dimensions of institutions for our consideration: It is not only place and physical structure but the people and practices that continue the presence of institutions.

Our examination thus far has highlighted some of the many forms of capital that run through institutions, and St. James the Greater offers here also new aspects for our consideration. The institution of the Catholic Church, as we have seen at Georgetown, was a location for the conveyance of economic capital derived from land acquisition and passed along through patriarchal networks of formation. In a very different mode, St. James the Greater, ignored by the diocese, did not enjoy the benefits of economic capital that might have infused the community in the years of the Civil War and through the tumult of Reconstruction. The institution of the Catholic Church also conveys symbolic capital, the affirmation of value within a social collective that is visible to those within and outside the network of the church. It's not clear what impact the loss of oversight by the diocese might have had on the symbolic capital of the community at St. James, but given the tumult of war and Reconstruction, it is possible that a Catholic identity may have been counted among the resources that held people together. The social capital of people power was surely a sustaining source among the Black Catholics of St. James.

The experience of the Catholic community of St. James the Greater, Colleton County, South Carolina, provides an opportunity to explore an element of capital unexamined thus far. In addition to economic capital, social capital, and symbolic capital, we might also consider the institutions of the Catholic Church offering unique forms of *spiritual* capital. In the discourse on capital complexified by contemporary sociologists, "capital" conveys the idea of resources that help human beings navigate their worlds: economic capital providing access to material needs in capitalistic societies, social capital pointing to networks of relationships that sustain our being human, and symbolic capital denoting assessments of value by which humans account for their status in a social world. *Spiritual* capital might be imagined as another form of capital, one that fosters an overarching sense of well-being with an ultimate horizon in view. That is to say, the proposal here is that religious institutions are conveyors of capital in the many forms just denoted that pertain to our everyday experience of the world but that they might also be considered as conveying a type of capital that grounds our everyday experience of the world in the broadest possible horizon. An imaginative plane of ultimacy—of God's design or the universe unfolding—is narrated through the traditions of religious institutions so as to render the everyday practices meaningful either in their alignment with this ultimate horizon or in contrast to it. If "spirituality" helps humans integrate their lives in the broadest horizon possible, religious communities might be seen as the conveyors of spiritual capital.

In Christian tradition, the term "spirituality" has its roots in early writings identified with Paul in the first century CE, who used the term to designate those activities that aligned with the work of God in the form of the Holy Spirit.[22] Yet contemporary studies also unyoke the spiritual from a distinctively Christian connotation to see spirituality as an aspect of lived human experience transcending the bounds of any singular religious tradition. As Sandra Schneiders has proposed, one definition of spirituality might be "the experience of consciously striving to integrate one's life in terms not of isolation and self-absorption but of self-transcendence toward the ultimate value one perceives."[23] In so defining, Schneiders elevates spirituality as a project by which persons seek "personal integration through self-transcendence and toward the horizon of ultimate concern."[24] The importance of loosening the grip of a singular religious institution or tradition informing spirituality is central insofar as persons might inhabit multiple traditions simultaneously and as traditions themselves are informed by distinctive historical, social, and cultural contexts. Thus, Christian spirituality may be conveyed through the institution of Christian churches and schools, while persons practicing in those locations may also be shaped by values of other institutions that inform their self-transcendence, vision of integration, and understanding of an ultimate horizon. In the case of St. James the Greater, such loosening is especially relevant for many reasons. First, the spiritual capital derived from participation in the Catholic tradition itself was unmoored from the guardians of Catholic capital in the form of the diocesan representatives; note the way that this could be a good thing, inviting the incorporation of other values, like lay leadership and shared governance. Second, the distinctive cultural and geographical context of a minority Catholic community in Protestant-dominated South Carolina could also inform the spiritual practices developed by members of the community. And third, the cultural heritage of Black Catholics, including both the experience under the conditions of White dominance *and* the longer traditions of African spiritualities, may have helped the community tap into distinctive forms of Catholic spirituality to sustain them. For the members of the St. James the Greater congregation, we might imagine that their participation in the community and their persistence in the practices of Catholicism provided some of the resources enabling them to integrate their lives—in the tumult of the Civil War and Reconstruction—in self-transcendence toward the ultimate value they perceived. Given the limits of the archives and the loss of connection with the institutional home of the diocese, it is difficult to determine precisely what that spiritual capital might have been. The social capital that sustained St. James the Greater in the years between 1856 and 1894 is a remarkable testament to the spiritual capital this group of people found in the tradition of the Catholic Church and in one another. Even an institution that held them on the geographical, social, and symbolic periphery could convey something of the life-giving values by which people orient themselves through the tradition.

An 1895 letter from the hand of Fr. D. Barberich PSM helps us piece together a picture of St. James the Greater from *both* an institutional/ecclesial perspective *and* an institutional/practice-based perspective.[25] Barberich writes:

> The Mission of the Catholic Cross Roads, with its 60 Catholics, has given me until now the greatest satisfaction. These good people were once the slaves of a respected Catholic family. Although it was unlawful to instruct slaves, this Irish family tried to their best to teach their slaves religion and other elementary subjects. The small chapel, that once stood on the plantation, was burned down during the war. The Priest who visited the plantation from time to time, became a chaplain and followed the soldiers to the battlefield.
>
> Amidst the confusion that followed the war, the white man who owned a certain number of slaves lost everything.
>
> When peace came and freedom was proclaimed, the plantation and other properties were sold at a low price. Many Negroes who had a little money bought some acres of woods and cultivated land and so they were able to reach a satisfactory financial condition. . . . And what about their spiritual condition? Of course, they possessed the great treasure of faith, without which it is impossible to please God. But to what avail is faith, unless it is increased and enriched through religious instructions and the worthy reception of the Sacraments?

> It was God's will that, after 28 years of oblivion, our Fathers, traveling by train from a distance of 50 miles, came to their village to have a picnic. Upon finding out that they were Catholics and would love to have a Priest, our Confreres informed the Bishop, who sent one of our Missionaries among those Negroes.
>
> It was only three years ago that the Lord sent His Laborers to His Vineyard, and judging from the fruits, the Mission has been blessed by the same Lord.
>
> With God's help, the building of the Chapel was started at once, and on January 21, 1894 it was dedicated, as the original chapel, to St. James.[26]

Following Barberich's intervention, the spiritual and social capital already flowing through St. James the Greater was now infused with symbolic capital of recognition, which made possible the dedication of economic capital to rebuild the church and add to it a school. In the years of Reconstruction and the hostile terrain of Jim Crow, the school was funded by Mother Katharine Drexel and was a place where Black Catholics thrived. Imagining the descendants of the very first Catholics in this area invites us to see the thread of Black Catholic thriving rooted in spiritual resources within the institution of the church even if not directly flowing from the institutional church.

It is worth returning to the origins of a renewed St. James as the home of a Black Catholicism to press further into the insights we gain from an investigation of this church in the truth telling and analysis that might release the pain of our historical trauma of White supremacy and recreate transformed institutions. In the matrix of Catholic complicity and complexity, we meet Catholic women in the archives who might expand our understanding further.

## Henrietta and Elizabeth at St. James

If we think about institutions as places where people practice, we might think of the institution of the Catholic Church in South Carolina not only at the center of power in Charleston but on the ground with the people who are practicing. Of course, as we move from the center of power, we encounter enhanced challenges of archival research insofar as the record of whose practices "count" leaves us slim resources for the reconstruction of the periphery. Yet archival reconstruction does provide some glimpses from which we can investigate and imagine the people who practiced at St. James. We know that St. James persisted as an institution among those who practiced an identifiably Catholic way of being in the world from 1856 to 1894—a community no longer supported by priests or the diocese. The era under investigation was one of great upheaval in the diocese (and the nation), with the impending and overwhelming Civil War, when Charleston and nearby Columbia were significant urban centers and therefore targets for military action. But because of the records maintained when the community was under the care of the more formal institution, we do have traces of the *people* who practiced, like a woman known by the name Hetty, a shortened version of Henrietta, who served at St. James in passing on the faith in 1850.

## Henrietta: Elder of St. James

We know that Henrietta was among those who served this Catholic community on the frontier because in 1850 she is listed as the sponsor in the baptism of five-week-old Mary Priscilla. The role of sponsor, or godparent, was one that required Hetty be recognized as a Catholic "in good standing," so we have evidence of Hetty's recognizable piety, practice, and leadership. This conferral of symbolic capital surrounds our reconstructed portrait of Henrietta as a named leader in the Catholic community. We can imagine her as an elder in the Catholic Church of St. James, taking on the role of godparent in passing on the faith and commitment to the next generation: spiritually, relationally, physically. As Kresbach describes: "The godparent would accept guardianship, if necessary, as well as a commitment to the child's emotional, physical, and religious well-being."[27] Situated in the Catholic community at the Crossroads, Hetty is especially connected to Francis and Lucy, Mary Priscilla's birth parents. With this we can imagine Hetty, Francis, and Lucy leaning on the spiritual capital of Catholic tradition and strengthening their bonds with one another and the social bonds of the church through this ritual expression of baptism that marked them as a new kind of family. A similar pattern of extending spiritual family networks through ritual brings into our view those who celebrated the sacrament just six months prior. Here we extend Hetty's Catholic relations to Carolina Joanna and Edward (who baptized their son Joseph Pompey on February 10, 1850) and the infant's baptismal sponsor Vincent of Paul. A few days later, Carolina Joanna also assumed the leader's role as godparent alongside Vincent of Paul for the baptism welcoming James, the son of Cyrus and Dynah. Already, we have the nucleus of a network of frontier Catholics creating community and drawing on the social and spiritual capital that St. James could provide. The historian Cyprian Davis credits Vincent of Paul with leadership in the years "forgotten" by the diocese, but clearly we can see that Vincent was not alone; Carolina Joanna and Hetty offered community leadership as well.[28] As a woman in the Roman Catholic Church, Hetty did not have the kind of social and symbolic capital of the male priesthood, yet especially when male priests no longer were sent to the community at the Crossroads after 1856, we can envision the community turning to her in order to pass on the faith. The loss of support from the diocese in the form of its economic capital and the symbolic capital of priestly visits *may* have enabled the conditions under which Hetty worked alongside Vincent of Paul and others in maintaining the faith over that stretch of more than forty years.

When we conceive of institutions as "places where people practice," the absence of a church building and of ecclesial representatives no longer marks the absence of the institution. The institution of the Catholic Church was maintained at the Catholic Crossroads even without a church building, as the faithful remnant continued the practices in a network of relation to one another. Baptismal records enable us to reconstruct Hetty as one among the elders of the church, who in the absence of ordained ministers or ecclesial officials carried on the *practices* of the community, consulting with other women like Carolina and Juns Mary and men like Vincent of Paul, helping maintain the faith of the youth like Caroline and Charity (baptized in the 1850s) and bringing their parents—Lucy and Francis, Samuel and Dorcas—more deeply in touch with the traditions of the Catholic faith.

In the absence of priests, we have to imagine *the people who practiced* as the conduits of Catholicism and the institution of the Catholic Church throughout the years of the 1860s and 1870s, as parish records reflect few baptisms in the postwar era.[29] So the congregation that we have on the rolls of baptismal records for 1850 would have been the members of the church going forward. We have to imagine the young people baptized before the fire were the people who sustained the practices of Catholicism: Jenny, Julia, Sarah, Jane Caroline, Isack John, Esther, John Edward, Elizabeth Johanna, Maria, Frederick Joseph, Charity, Benjamin, Joseph Pompey, James, Mary Augusta, Mary Priscilla, Sara, Mary, Michael, Eleanor, Mary Augusta, Joseph, Emiline, Monday, Carolina Abraham, Ben, Julia, Elizabeth, Lucian, Elizabeth, Daniel, Joseph, Hannah, Eliza, Ben, Sully, Sophia, Magdaline, Anne Elizabeth, Gabriel, Frank, Edward, Frank, and Francis Xavier, following in the footsteps of their elders and creating the continuity of practices. Infants baptized in 1850 would have their preteen years under the cloud of the Civil War; in postwar Reconstruction they would be fifteen to twenty years of age. When the Jesuit Fr. Folchi sent his letter to the diocese about the mission in 1875, they would be twenty-five years old, certainly stepping into leadership of the church, and among those Folchi described as "anxious for a priest." And in 1894, when the community was "rediscovered" by Barberich, the infants who had been baptized in 1850 would be nearly fifty years old. Many among this community would have experienced childhood under the yoke of enslavement, and some of those on the original 1850 roll may have been remembered into the twentieth century. As the 1976 "Rough Copy of History of St. James" describes:

> As a result of this situation, members of the congregation assumed some of the functions of keeping the church alive. These persons, who would be known today by the term "catechists," instructed the people, led prayers, probably baptized, and may have even witnessed marriages. The names associated with this function are Vincent Carrol Davis, James Jackson, and Joseph Brown. Charlie Bellinger Davis, Sarah Davis and Viola Dore were involved in teaching, in their stores, in their homes; it is not known, however, to what extent religious instruction was given by them. Since records were not kept during this period, memory must suffice to supply the needed information. But dates melt into one another, and names of many dedicated and faithful people are forgotten. Nevertheless, some of the elders of the congregation guarded the faith and witnessed to it during the time of no priestly care and even after it had been re-established. God alone knows the names of his saints.[30]

While poetic, this is inaccurate to the record keeping we do have. It is not "God alone" who knows the names of the saints, and the "faithful people" need not be forgotten. Plausible reconstruction provides a rich record of those who might have been fostered in the faith by matriarchs like Henrietta of St. James and the children raised from the baptismal fervor of the Bellinger-Pinckney sisters.

In addition to celebrating Henrietta as a foremother in an extraordinary faith at the Catholic Crossroads, records kept by her sister in the faith, Elizabeth Pinckney, give us a bit more of Hetty's relationships and her story. Traces that remain indicate that Hetty had a close bond with someone named Joe and that Hetty's mother was still in the geographical area. Given her work life, we have traces of Hetty even being in proximity to the household of the bishop of the diocese, Patrick Lynch, in Charleston (bishop from 1857 to 1882), who had visited St. James and performed baptisms several years before the fire. While at work in the home of the bishop's sister, Hetty may even have had the occasion to bend Julia Lynch's ear (in 1860) and leverage the social capital of connections to prod ecclesial concern for the Crossroads. Since it is under Lynch's leadership that Folchi sent his 1875 letter and O'Connell published his 1878 history, a sister's nudge might have laid the groundwork for intervention. But we do not know whether Hetty would have had an opportunity to leverage familial employment contacts to inquire of the representative of the institutional church his care or concern for the flock at St. James, especially in the midst of war, in which Bishop Patrick Lynch served as bishop to the Confederacy.[31]

Some of the limits of our knowledge about Hetty among the community of fellow Catholics at St. James are consistent with what we've already encountered in seeking reconstructions through the archives. There are traces of Hetty's presence in the community and the contours of her life as a nineteenth-century Black Catholic leader at St. James, but only very few, and most of them come to us through the writings of her "employer" Elizabeth Perry Bellinger Pinckney.

## Elizabeth: Cofounder of a Renewed St. James

Elizabeth, too, was a Catholic woman who benefited from being on the periphery of the institution. Selecting Catholicism as an adult convert, the marginal location on the frontier enabled her and her sisters to take leadership roles. From the wealthy Bellinger family, it was Elizabeth's relative John Bellinger who served as the personal physician to Bishop John England in Charleston (bishop from 1820 to 1842) and accompanied the bishop during his final days in January 1842.[32] The close relationship between Dr. Bellinger and Bishop England may explain England's influence in the conversion of Elizabeth's sister, Susan Bellinger, who was the first of the sisters to convert in 1839. Later, "Misses Harriet and Sarah Bellinger and their sister, Mrs. Pinckney, of Walterboro, with her husband, the descendant of the distinguished family whose name he bore, were baptized about 1844, and they formed a wealthy and influential body of Catholics."[33] In ecclesial versions of this history, it is Elizabeth Perry Pinckney's extended family that is credited with forging the roots of a multiracial Catholicism at St. James (although the archives help us decenter these White actors and their accomplishments).[34]

Like Henrietta, Elizabeth, Susan, and Sarah were leaders in the fledgling church at St. James. While the "old Irish Catholics" were dying off, the Bellinger-led conversions introduced new families to take their place. Given the infrequency of priestly visits, it was also the Bellinger-Pinckney women who, on several occasions, performed the emergency baptisms in the absence of priests.[35] While serving as sponsor/godparent for the many new members of the faith (both children and adults), the Bellinger-Pinckney women are listed many times, and only once are they alongside lay men as cosponsors. When they are listed as serving as godparents with a lay male member of the community, they are doing so crossing racial lines in seeding the church alongside Vincent of Paul. They are most often listed as the singular lay sponsor alongside the ordained sponsor Fr. O'Neill, and once as cosponsor with the future bishop,

Fr. Patrick Lynch (at an 1852 baptism).[36] The distinctive opportunity for lay Catholic women to stand in such a significant leadership role for the community at St. James may be the result of being on the periphery.

Because of her location in a prominent White family whose archival remains were held in safe keeping, we have more evidence to reconstruct some of Elizabeth's sense of the spiritual resources Catholicism could provide. Writing to her son, Eustace, while he was away at college, she muses about her late conversion as a cautionary tale to the next generation: "How sweet must it be to those fortunate persons, who when meditating on their actions of the past year, feel that they have lived only for God alone. Oh, how deeply do I regret not having served my God in the days of my youth."[37] A future letter echoes a similar sentiment: "Do my precious Son try to be pious and holy now, before you are entrapped by Satan's snares, it is better to devote your youth to the Lord and his blessed Mother than to wait until you are old."[38]

Her attention to youth carrying on the faith aligns with her sponsorship of many infant and youth baptisms. In a sense, Elizabeth is at work reproducing the faith in the form of the children at St. James and in influencing her sons while they are away at college. Encouraging her son to access the spiritual capital made available at their Catholic college in New York City, she writes, "I hope when you next write you will be able to say that you have gone to your duty and partaken of that Heavenly Bread which is the only true support on which a poor miserable fallen sinner can lean."[39] In Elizabeth's Catholic piety, the material encounter with the Eucharist was a particular conduit for a relationship with the divine and source of spiritual grounding. This framing of encounter through sacramental practices of the consecrated body and blood of Christ (made possible uniquely through the ministrations of ordained priests) expands our understanding of how a lack of access to priestly care for Catholic communities on the frontier would be felt in a particular way. Priestly care did not convey merely the social or symbolic capital of the expansion of Catholic institution; priests provided also a means for the spiritual capital of access to the God who was resident in the body and blood at the Eucharistic table. The poverty that a lack of spiritual access on the frontier-periphery could create is seen in comparison to when Elizabeth writes from a visit to the center in Charleston, with enthusiasm for the access to spiritual capital the location would afford.

> What a blessing it is to be able to go to Mass whenever I please, and partake of the Holy communion and that great happiness I have just partaken of. Thank God. Oh! How ardently do I wish that you as well as my other dear children felt that great necessity of approaching the Holy Altar. . . .

> I have just returned from high Mass, and heard touching sermon preached on the Immaculate Conception of the Blessed Virgin by Dr. Lynch. And Oh! How I prayed to her to take my own dear Eustace for her own child to guard and guide him through this world of sin and suffering until he will have arrived safely in the Garden of rest.[40]

While less available in her home location, Elizabeth's bankroll of economic capital would enable her to partake of the spiritual nourishment she sought both on her trips to Charleston and at the churches in Walterboro and at the Catholic Crossroads of St James. And even in 1852, when the in-town church of St. Philip's was already fully established, Elizabeth seeks the spiritual capital available at the now predominantly Black Catholic parish: "I expect to go down with Mr. Carr to St. James', and hope to be allowed to partake of the blessed Sacrament."[41] It is as if the spiritual capital of the Eucharist is drawing this converted Catholic to Charleston, Walterboro, and the Catholic Crossroads, demonstrating the centrality of the Eucharist in her practice.

Yet we cannot lose sight that this spiritual seeking and drawing did not stand apart from an economy of enslavement. The economics of enslavement would never have released her so far that she was not aware of the death dealing that surrounded her sanctuary. By the 1850s, Charleston was the epicenter of the domestic slave trade, with more than forty slave markets in a four-block radius, an entangled geography of wealthy families, ecclesial institutions, and business practices that relied on shackles, chains, and "jails" for other human beings. When Elizabeth escaped to the city "for a change of air" and access to the sacraments, she was surrounded by and sustained within an economy of enslavement from which most of her Black Catholic sisters and brothers had little escape.

## Elizabeth and Henrietta: Sisters in the Faith

What we see in the story of Elizabeth Perry Bellinger Pinckney is a nineteenth-century Catholic White woman on the periphery of her church (as convert, on the frontier, as a woman) but whose sources of capital enabled her to move to locations of the center (in the city, as a catechist/cosponsor). Hetty moved also through Catholic systems and stepped into the role of leader at St. James on the frontier. At this point, it is necessary to place Elizabeth's story more closely in relation to Hetty's, because at the same time that they were bound in faith at the Catholic Crossroads, they were also bound in an economy of enslavement. While Hetty shared some of the features of Catholic womanhood with Elizabeth (in access to leadership, given the lack of priests on frontier, and moving through Catholic networks from frontier to center), Hetty experienced her Catholic womanhood in likely very different ways. Because although historical sources can tell us of a close companionship between Hetty and Elizabeth—both serving as sponsors to the fledgling St. James, both moving in circles of relationship with the priests and bishops of the Diocese of Charleston, maintaining their relationship with each other for well over ten years—theirs was an unequal relationship of nineteenth-century Roman Catholic women of St. James. A letter from Elizabeth to her son in 1854 captures this for us, as she writes in closing:

> Tell all of my servants howdye for me. . . . I suppose that if I do not name them separately they will think that I did not mean them. Therefore I will begin with Hannah, Polly, Louisa, Leah, Rose, Benjy, and Margaret, and Nancy when you see her. Tell Hetty that Joe is quite well and sends much love to her.[42]

In this salutation, Hetty appears to be among the close companions of Mrs. Elizabeth Perry Bellinger Pinckney, alongside other enslaved women who may have been companions to Elizabeth for decades. It is in the ecclesial record of the baptismal registry that we have confirmation of her status in their relationship. June 2, 1850, the sacramental record names as "S[acramental] Sp[onsor]. Hetty slave of Mrs. E.P."[43]

The archival records of Mrs. Elizabeth Perry Bellinger Pinckney not only afford insight into a frontier-convert-White-elite-female-Catholicism; they also provide a snapshot of White Catholic women who held humans in bondage using their resources to support the Catholic Church. The names Hannah and Polly are the same names given to women who appear on Elizabeth's 1827 prenuptial agreement. If they are the same women cited in the 1854 letter, they would have been Elizabeth's unpaid companions for more than twenty years. Since the time of her marriage, Elizabeth had been an independent slaver by virtue of her inheritance and had acquired more legal ownership from her husband, who left his human property to her upon his death in 1847. On the 1850 US Federal Census—Slave Schedules, Elizabeth Pinckney is listed as the owner of thirty-seven persons.[44] The 1850 census also indicates that her unmarried sister, Sarah Bellinger, resided with her and that together they were the legal owners of eighty-two human beings.[45] Elizabeth had already been dependent upon the purchase and sale of human beings for more than twenty years when she helped found St. James the Greater, and her sisters and extended family were among the wealthiest planters in South Carolina.[46] Her sons also were propelled to their positions as Catholic students in New York City still legally attached to the persons they held as property and whose work funded their foray into the systems of Catholic education.[47]

Nancy Stockton analyzes the Catholicity of women in the slaveholding Carolinas to propose that in addition to the desire to "fit in" with the slaveholding gentry, the fundamental hierarchical and patriarchal nature of Catholic ecclesiology was a crucial feature of Catholic slaveholding theology. Stockton describes the "double-yoked bond between slavery and female subordination: Side by side they pulled the wagon of patriarchy, both systems existing in service to it."[48] Southern White women's commitment to the supremacy of the plantation patriarch secured their subordination and the subordination of others under them. But Catholic southern women also had the ecclesial subordination of the laity to further cement the logic of hierarchy and the naturalness of slavery. While Stockton's analysis may help us in understanding the social and ecclesial realities for many White Catholic slaveholding women, it seems as though Elizabeth and Hetty subverted at least some of this paradigm. Yes, the institutional church was patriarchal, but the reproduction of the faith at St. James through female leadership offers some element of challenge. Yes, women's subordination to husbands was expected, but in the absence of a husband, Elizabeth seems to have thrown off that yoke, at least in some respects. And, yes, legally Hetty was in a subordinate position to Elizabeth, but the practices established at St. James and in the Pinckney home provide intriguing openings to consider otherwise possibilities.

Connecting the salutation from the 1854 letter to later writings, we learn more about Hetty's relationships in the affection that Joe sends to her through Elizabeth and her son Charles, who has returned to the family home after graduating from college.[49] Hetty remains at the Pinckney home with Charles, while Joe is with Elizabeth at Edgefield (one hundred miles away). The same salutation and conveyance of care across the distance (written in an 1854 letter) is repeated six years later, when Hetty moves with another son and Elizabeth writes to him: "Tell Hetty that Joe is quite well and that I heard from her Mother and she was well also."[50] Here, Hetty is working in Charleston with Eustace, and Joe remains at the Pinckney family home; that Hetty's mother is nearby expands our portrait of Henrietta and her closest relationships.

From these brief flashes of recognition in Elizabeth's letters, we learn some minimal contours of Hetty's life as an enslaved Catholic woman. Her role at St. James provided an opportunity to help found a fledgling Catholic church on the frontier, and her decades-long work for Elizabeth reveals another dimension of Hetty's life. In the exchanges of Elizabeth's letters, we meet Hetty as a woman in a long-term relationship with Joe and also that Hetty seems to have avoided the trauma of permanent dislocation from her mother. Any more of the close relationships that sustained Henrietta are lost to the limits of the sources.[51] We don't know whether Hetty had children of her own and, if so, what losses to her own children she may have experienced as she performed surrogate roles for Elizabeth: "These performances perpetrated a form of commodification specific to women by requiring them to direct their maternal energies toward their oppressors, often at the expense of their own children."[52] Whether or not Hetty had to forsake roles to her own children while serving in a surrogate role standing in for Elizabeth toward Elizabeth's children, the letters show us ways Hetty does perform roles as Elizabeth's surrogate. When Elizabeth is away from the Walterboro home (writing from Edgefield), she conveys to her son Charles greetings to the women who serve as her surrogates to him, keeping home in her absence. When Elizabeth sends the similar greeting "Tell Hetty that Joe is well" to Eustace in Charleston, Hetty stands again in a place that Elizabeth as mother-in-law might have played when Hetty moves with Eustace and his young wife. It is this surrogate and work role that places Hetty in locations of proximity to ecclesial power, as Eustace has married the sister of the bishop in Charleston, their move to Charleston placing the Pinckneys and their bondswomen in physical proximity to ecclesial power.

The close relationship that Hetty serves to Eustace after his marriage to the bishop's sister, Julia Lynch, recommends that we imagine Hetty also among those legally held workers who created the atmosphere of celebration at their wedding. As a family history recounts, when Eustace and Julia returned to the home from their wedding, they were greeted by the merriment of workers held as property by the family.

> A granddaughter, Mrs. Philomena P. Coburn related a romantic story about the welcome given the newly weds on their return home from the wedding trip. The slaves all gathered at the big gate and with clapping and singing they unhitched the horses from the carriage and pulled the carriage along the avenue of oaks to the house where the family awaited the bride and bridegroom.[53]

As Saidiya Hartman reads such a scene, "Such performances cast the slave as contented bondsman and elide the difference between volition and violation."[54]

But Hetty's proximity to elite White Catholics at the center of ecclesial power was not the only privileged position of insight. Surely, her proximity to other enslaved Catholics would have sensitized Hetty to how her coworkers felt about the Pinckney family's plans to relocate to Alabama (a location with more brutal work practices for enslaved workers and more lucrative returns from the hard labor of the cotton fields for enslavers like the Pinckneys).[55]

Would Hetty and Elizabeth both have mourned the possible loss of connection with the Catholic community at St. James? And Hetty's allegiances may have been stretched if she knew of the uprising planned among the enslaved in Walterboro in 1860, when a letter from Anna Lynch, visiting Julia Lynch Pinckney, writes to their brother Bishop Patrick Lynch that "the negroes were to rise in the holidays, & [in] this place, but the plot was discovered a few days beforehand & the leaders taken up. Nine were tried & four in jail to be hung, so it is not safe for Eustace to be away & every body is armed."[56] Did Hetty, Elizabeth, and their Catholic family at St. James have the opportunity to pray for the repose of the souls of those put to death for seeking their freedom? Were members of the ecclesial Catholic family among them? The limits of the archives and the loss of insight into the slaveholding practices of White Catholics and the faith life of enslaved Black Catholics are sharp: Hetty's story gives but glimpses as clues.

## Connected in Catholic Piety: Relics

While Henrietta and Elizabeth are radically disconnected in the differing locations from which they experience the same Catholicism, they are also still connected through their intimate home, work, and church practices. As historians remark of the ecclesial practices of the day: "The Catholic community in Charleston was inclusive, blacks and whites of every status worshiped together in the same edifice, possibly in the same pews. Of course, these communicants never approached mutual, reciprocal equality. . . . However, blacks were deeply immersed in the fabric of the church."[57] From his vantage point in New York City, Archbishop John Hughes indicates that this shared ecclesial space would have been the norm for Catholics in this era; he chronicled that "it would not be uncommon to see the servant and the master kneeling side by side and receiving the holy communion."[58] Indeed, White Bellinger family members in Charleston were witnessing the baptisms of their enslaved workers becoming Black Catholics, but also "166 free females of color presented 398 infants for membership in the church."[59] Indeed, on the baptismal rolls for St. James, several persons are listed as "Free" (while others are listed as "belonging to" members of the Bellinger-Pinckney clan). Like the population growth of Black Catholics on the frontier at St. James, the Black Catholic population grew in Charleston at the same time: In 1846, "the percentage of black baptisms was 50.7 percent, and in 1847, the percentage rose to 59 percent of all baptisms."[60] Our imaginings of the congregations in the Catholic diocese of Charleston, including St. James the Greater, recommend that we not only consider the distinctiveness of this multiracial Catholicism as a minority religion in a dominant White Protestant landscape but also consider it as a multicultural Catholicism infused with the spiritual strivings of West Africa.

When enslaved women helped found the Catholic Church of St. James, we might imagine them weaving a tapestry of deep religiosity across distance. Wherever their cultural location of origin, "Southern bondswomen's religiosity drew on cultural repertoires that extended from the African continent to the African-Indigenous-European cultural milieu of the Americas."[61] Sylvester Johnson aids our imagination with a historical portrait of persons who were enslaved and living in Charleston and whose practices of Catholicism would be embedded in complex lives. Providing a longer view of the multicultural Catholicism that may have been sustained in Charleston, Johnson writes:

> Throughout the seventeenth century . . . African slaves met with a relatively loosely organized system of labor and surveillance that allowed for extensive gatherings in the small urban space of Charleston. There they exchanged news of Atlantic events, met newly arrived Blacks from throughout the Atlantic, pursued romantic liaisons, and planned maroonage or armed resistance to free other slaves. In addition, African slave religion in the region was conditioned by an overwhelming lack of institutional and cultural support for Christian conversion. As a result, the enslaved Africans of South Carolina were able to continue their native religions. The difficult conditions of life in English settlements, for instance, demanded recourse to herbal medicinal practices rooted in West African religious knowledge and ritual. . . . A significant number of those Africans who arrived at the slave-ship port of Charleston brought with them a historically deep tradition of Kongolese Christianity that had thrived in central Africa for almost two centuries.
>
> *Of the approximately 343,878 Africans arriving in the Lowcountry region between 1700 and 1808, almost 30 percent (about 100,000) were from the Kongo and Angola kingdoms.* The long history of Catholicism in this region—particularly as the official Kongolese cult—had established a widespread pattern of Christian conversion. This, of course, did not mean that indigenous Kongolese religion was diminished. As a rule . . . it thrived alongside the expanding influence of the Christian tradition.[62]

Not only in Charleston might the practices of West African religions survive, including an African-inflected Catholic Christianity. Diana Garnett further recommends that we envision the influence of West African heritage on the refounding of St. James the Greater. Garnett describes a link in the very naming of the community at the Catholic Crossroads as "St. James the Greater" and the meaning that identification in the years of diocesan abandonment might convey. As she explains:

> This devotion to St. James' patronage—expressed in their choice to retain that parochial identity nearly half a century after the departure of the whites—could have been rooted in a sense of historic identity, culture, religion, or a combination of all three. The former slaves, whose parents and grandparents had come with their owners from Charleston some twenty or thirty years prior, may have possessed African-Catholic traditions that predated conversion under their masters. These Afro-Catholic roots would have traveled to Charleston and the South Carolina Lowcountry following the arrival of Catholic slaves of Kongolese and Santo Domingan descent during the eighteenth and nineteenth centuries.[63]
>
> Thousands of slaves with West African origins flooded into the South during these centuries, carrying with them distinct Afro-Catholic cultural customs and beliefs that dated to the 1400s. One notable such custom was the special affinity Kongolese Catholics held for St. James the Greater (also known as St. James Major). St. James was traditionally the patron saint of Kongo, and his feast day, July 25, was Kongo's national holiday. Likewise, St. James still holds a place of special veneration in Haiti and the Dominican Republic (both formerly constituting the island of Santo Domingo), where Catholic West African slaves arrived in vast numbers during the colonial period. Several names on the gravestones in St. James' cemetery that postdate the presence of white parishioners indicate French or Spanish origin, despite the Anglo heritage of the founding whites.[64]

It's possible, then, that when Elizabeth Perry Bellinger Pinckney was considering the best spiritual "fit" in her search toward conversion, the influence of her enslaved companions moved her in the direction of a faith filled with sacramental presence and their own transplanted and maintained Catholicity. Perhaps Hetty, Carolina Joanna, and Vincent of Paul influenced Elizabeth's decision to convert as much as her wealthy cousin and enthusiastic sisters.

When we return to the shared religiosity of Hetty and Elizabeth, we might imagine them drawn together in a Catholic Eucharistic piety, such as the one reflected in Elizabeth's letters. But given the paucity of priests and difficulty of accessing this form of spiritual capital, we also see Elizabeth tap into alternative Catholic resources popular in her day, that of capital residing in relics. As Elizabeth writes to her son describing Catholicism's material cultural practices, she recounts: "I have just received a Relic of an unknown Saint and a small bit of crimson silk which has touched the precious blood of our Divine Redeemer."[65] Placing the meaning of these objects in the wider context, Johnson helps interpret them: "Throughout Western Christendom, in fact, the bodily remains of saints and martyrs and pieces of the cross used to execute Jesus evidenced the degree to which Christianity was in great measure a material religion, one whose devotees invested physical objects with meanings and power that afforded access to immanent, immediate, and unmediated religious experience."[66] Scholars can describe for us the ways in which Elizabeth's use of relics may have functioned relative to a wider Catholic practice, but how might they have functioned as a bond between her and her companions? In one of the locations on one of the days that no priest was in sight, might Elizabeth, Susan, and Sarah have joined with Hetty and Carolina Johanna in a women's prayer group, with these relics at the center? If they did, what might Hetty and Carolina have brought to the exchange?

If Hetty or Carolina traced their roots to West African religiosity, they might have approached the material object with the sacred sense of the fetish tradition from their ancestral home. Describing the "fetish," Johnson writes: "As a central element of religion in West Central Africa . . . its fundamental significance lay with its constitution at the intersection of spirit and matter."[67] Emergent from constellations of exchange in economic capital, the material object of "the fetish" served as a reminder of the bond of exchange in trading promises. Johnson explains that the power of the material object (the "fetish") "was conceived as ontological and as bearing the capacity to guard fidelity to a vow and to inflict injury, disease, or death on any party violating the oath. . . . The larger context for the fetish idea, then, was not strictly commercial but was more comprehensive. It functioned as part of a grander social economy of exchange broadly conceived, establishing a mechanism of trust and obligation."[68] Sacred objects in the religions of West Africa aligned with sacramentality of a Catholic tradition, possibly in the African context of Kongo, possibly in the African American context of St. James. Relics from an unknown saint and the material object of crimson silk passed around the prayer circle might have enabled the expression of being bound together in a new spiritual family. The religious objects express what some scholars assert as "religion's" original meaning: *religio*, to bind. The fetish may have reminded these women of Christ's promise, since accompanying the relic, Elizabeth's letter describes an icon created by her daughter, which presented "a picture of death in the coffin, sent by your dear Sister Ria, the picture was drawn by herself and the design well executed. No one can behold it without its making a strong impression on their mind, that it is the Symbol of what they too must assuredly realize very soon."[69] Even as the relics seal a promise between those whose hands it passes through, it simultaneously conveys a promise distinctive to the Christian belief in the Redeemer's crimson blood conquering death. The fetish marks a promise and seals an exchange. The faithful dedicates her life through the relic to the Redeemer, with the promise of life eternal in exchange. Such access to a horizon of life beyond this one would be a distinctive benefit of spiritual capital deeply embedded in the streams of both Euro-American Catholicism and African Catholicism.

In the precarity of life and health, we can see in her letters that the relic assured Elizabeth of the more that was yet to come. "My health is better than I have any right to expect, thank God, but I feel at times very weary and bothered too. But you know this is not my resting place."[70] Were Elizabeth to pass the relics into Hetty's hand, invoking a final resting place, Hetty might have closely connected this sentiment with the spiritual geography of the Church at St. James. Garnett describes:

> Another significance of the possible Catholic West African origins of the St. James blacks lies in the African spiritual traditions that value the natural landscape as space elemental to daily spirituality. West Africans commonly believed that nature—especially, forests and bodies of water—hosted the spirits of their deceased ancestors, who played an active and powerful role in the lives of their living descendants. Land served as a continued habitation for the dead who were really not "dead" in the traditional European sense of the word, but rather were alive and participating in the lives and wellbeing of their descendants. Catholic Hill during the nineteenth century could hardly have been a more ideal landscape for this tradition, surrounded by dense woods and swampland as it was. These traditional African beliefs could explain the outstanding tenacity of the St. James blacks in holding to their parish roots, despite the long absence of any church buildings or clerical guidance. The rural seclusion of the parish would have insulated these African customs from outside influences, until Daniel Berberich arrived in 1892.[71]

In the between time of a Catholic life integrated into a future horizon with Christ, the promise sealed by the relics might provide capital to sustain a life amid real suffering. One of the characteristics of spiritual capital is precisely its use as a resource to sustain in times of challenge. When life experience exhibits the discomfiting realities of illness and loss that might lead to a sense of unmooring or dissolution, spiritual capital provides the horizon for integrating such disorienting realities. Elizabeth's letters are replete with such disintegrating realities of loss and threats to life and health. In turning to her Catholicity as a resource in times of difficulty, Elizabeth was not alone. In fact, scholars characterize key features of Catholic piety in her day as an element that enabled persons to deal with the difficulties of their lives and the sufferings they encountered.

> The Catholic Jesus of the mid-nineteenth century was a suffering Jesus, the Jesus of the Passion more than Jesus the teacher or the risen Lord. The usefulness of suffering, the conviction that it served as part of human redemption, sustained a range of devotions associated with the Catholic revival, one reason for their enormous popularity in Ireland and Germany immediately after the famine and economic distress of the 1840s.[72]

The transatlantic connections with Catholic piety in suffering would have found a certain home in the sufferings endured and reflected in the health conditions of the Carolina frontier. In each and every letter to her sons and extended family, Elizabeth recounts the devastating health crises that could not always be remedied with wealth and status. "Rupture of a blood vessel,"[73] "cholera afflictions,"[74] "yellow fever,"[75] "inflammation of the Eyes,"[76] blindness, loved ones who are "pale and sickly"[77] and afflicted by "typhus fever"[78]—all regular reports to her sons amid updates on which of her extended family was traveling, visiting, or enjoying the "jollifications" of a wedding. A piety embedded amid bodies in decay opens up to a spirituality of both finitude and a God who transcends it. In reading the correspondence of this mother to her sons at college, one gets the sense that the space of the sanctuary afforded Elizabeth an escape from the human condition in its frailty. An escape to the solitude of an interior life in the silence of a sanctuary away from social climbing and economic woes, Elizabeth's piety sustained her through her own failing health. "I know it must be the will of God, therefore, I submit willingly."[79]

Not merely the flight from but also the embrace of the frailty of the human condition in nineteenth-century America could be an avenue for spirituality, as Elizabeth takes great joy and religious consolation in the professed life of her daughter as a Sister of Charity, celebrating Maria's commitment as "a handmaid of the Lord" even when Ria's health is failing. The mother takes her daughter's failing health as a sign of blessedness:

> She does not look well, but that is <u>nothing</u>. I feel comforted, when I look upon her meager and broken down person, and know that it is caused by close attention to her Father's business. Would that all of mine were following her example. She is indeed one of those wise

> virgins who keeps her Lamp always burning, so that when the Bride Groom comes she will be ready. I can with truth say that amid my numerous trials and difficulties, I have been always able to turn my thoughts to that dear child of mine and find a bright spot to rest my eye upon. For this all praise be to Almighty God.[80]

In the broad horizon of a God who integrates all in a final resting place, the disintegrative realities of suffering could serve a higher purpose. Trials, difficulties, and suffering itself could be framed as a sort of penance toward the higher aim.

Yet this spiritualizing of her own suffering might have negatively affected her awareness of the suffering of those around her. The same Catholics who relied on the bodily exertion of their enslaved workers "also found it difficult to distinguish the suffering endured by slaves from other forms of human agony."[81] While Elizabeth suffered from health afflictions she could not relieve, her enslaved workers may have been suffering from inflictions she herself could have relieved. While the bodies-at-work in Elizabeth's home and plantation afforded her the means to retreat to a spiritual space that transcends death, her spiritual strivings simultaneously ignored the death dealing of the practices of enslavement from which she benefited. The suffering of the enslaved was not reflected in any of the letters retained in the archives.

But the suffering of Black Catholics whom the law named as Elizabeth's property was certainly real and distinct from the sufferings that Elizabeth herself endured. Their arrival to the home of Elizabeth in 1826 physically placed some of the workers legally bound to her in the rice fields along the Ashepoo River, where their legs, knee deep in frigid waters, exposed them to alligators and cholera, and their backs were put into digging and redigging canals that pushed fresh water into the fields of the Carolina Lowcountry, their arms winnowing the stalks, transmuting human limbs into the profit of that year's harvest.[82] There was no end to the work, because the profit gained from a season's work was expended on the upkeep of the plantation. "Most lowcountry plantation owners were always one or two crops in debt to their city dwelling factors."[83] Elizabeth's family of origin had been profiting from unpaid labor for many generations, and the network of the Bellingers' agricultural wealth extended back to the original landgrave Edmund Bellinger in the seventeenth century. The work undertaken by Elizabeth's dotal property joined the work already in progress on the plantation of her husband, William Cotesworth Pinckney MD. The Pinckneys' generational wealth spanned back to the original land grant of Thomas Pinckney,[84] and the investment in human property was kept safe constitutionally in part by a Pinckney family member's introducing the Fugitive Slave Clause in 1793.[85] After her husband died, Elizabeth shared her residence in Walterboro with her sister, Sarah Bellinger, who is listed on the 1850 census as the owner of nearly fifty human beings. The sisters joined the resources of the enslaved to secure White Catholic wealth in the precarity of single motherhood and single spinsterhood, Elizabeth also sharing the care of the plantation and raising Pinckney nieces, aiding her mother-in-law in this task (as did Fortune, whom the Pinckneys rented out for profit).[86] The fluctuating fortunes in the rice field and single women in a patriarchal world were insured by a much broader span of enslaved lives.

Elizabeth and Henrietta were bound together in a lifetime of work, caring for home and family in the absence of Elizabeth's husband. Hetty and Lizzy shared in the cultivation of the next generation of Catholics on the Carolina frontier as leaders in the congregation of St. James the Greater. The meeting at St. James may have been a place where African Catholic traditions invited Elizabeth's conversion to Catholicism and sustained them both with the spiritual resources of Eucharist, prayer, relics, and the promise of salvation beyond suffering. But this interracial and intercultural meeting in the context of a Catholic congregational practice failed both Elizabeth and Hetty in a most profound way. For while their Catholic resting place may have enticed them to a world beyond suffering, their living Catholicism in nineteenth-century America only added to the suffering that Hetty and her Black Catholic companions would experience.

## An Institutional Church That Bound and Betrayed Them

Elizabeth and Henrietta worked side by side in forming and fostering the fledgling Catholic Church on the Carolina frontier. As sponsors to the next generation of Catholics at St. James the Greater, they both infused the faith-life of a community that would sustain the institution in the absence of both priest and church building. As fellow Catholics, they might have both turned to the Eucharist and the celebration of the Mass as resources for integrating the questions of meaning, joy, and suffering in their lives. As fellow Catholics, they may have come to the material presence of the relics as another location over which to bond. And yet, as fellow Catholics, they both were failed by a religious institution that did not sufficiently enable them to create human relationships of mutuality. For despite the many interpretations of the relationship between Hetty and Elizabeth that we might conjure, none can erase the depth of evil that the institution of slavery created as the condition of their encounter as fellow human beings and fellow Catholics. The guardians of the symbolic capital of their shared Catholic tradition did little to mitigate that human evil and much to perpetuate its inhumane practices. One location of church sustained Hetty and Elizabeth; another location of church betrayed them.

While Bishop John England is credited with providing the resources for the Black Catholic community that will become St. James, England missed the opportunity to align American Catholic practices with the call for the abolition of slavery put forward by Pope Gregory in 1839. In fact, it appears that all the American bishops willfully interpreted Gregory's denouncement of the slave trade as a condemnation of others' sins but not their own. Instead, England became a spokesperson for the American bishops who received Gregory's condemnation of the slave trade at the 1840 Council in Baltimore and responded with a complex historical, biblical, and theological argument that distinguished the condemnation of the slave *trade* across the Atlantic from the perpetuation of the use and sale of enslaved persons in the United States. Bishop John England was so impassioned in his defense of slavery as a domestic practice that he used the platform of the first US Catholic newspaper, his own *United States Catholic Miscellany,* to advance and extend the argument to the US secretary of state, John Forsyth. The articles written by England ran as a multiletter series published on the front page of the *Miscellany* for sixteen weeks, from October 3, 1840, to April 3, 1841. Sixteen front-page articles of substantive length reveal a prelate of the Catholic faith mobilizing an enormous amount of resources—the time it takes to write such complex articles and the years of learning that went into honing his craft, the symbolic capital of biblical interpretation and church teaching, the capital it required to produce and distribute the paper itself—all of the capital of an institution leveraged in defense of the system of enslavement.

Disturbingly, the *United States Catholic Miscellany* reran the arguments over the years to come, mobilizing Catholic identity to protect inhumanity, defending an antiabolition position with the use of the Bible, Catholic tradition, northern and southern Catholic Bishops, *and* the highest level of Catholic moral reasoning published and promoted within the United States (Archbishop Francis Patrick Kenrick's 1841 *Theologia Moralis*). The December 1843 effort reiterated what had earlier been published. I quote it at length for the detail and depth of the argument, condensed from sixteen letters to a single editorial. Note how the 1843 *Miscellany* reveals a Catholic groundswell of response to Gregory that the new bishop, Ignatius Reynolds, now seeks to quell:

> We understand that considerable attention has been exciteded [*sic*] by a document going the rounds of the papers under the title of a "Bull of Pope Gregory XVI against slavery." And several inquiries are made as to the meaning of the document and the truth of the charge that the

Catholics have concealed or suppressed it in the United States for the last four years.

On recurring to our own files we find that the document itself, not a *Bull* but an APOSTOLIC LETTER, was published in the Miscellany of March 14th, 1840, and that our late lamented Bishop, in his first two letters to the Hon. *John Forsyth*, then secretary of State, published like wise in the Miscellany, Oct 31 and Oct 10th 1840, full explained its true meaning. . . .

As to the meaning of the Apostolic Letter, we can see no room for doubt. His Holiness speaks of reducing Indians, Negroes and such others, into slavery; of assisting those who engage in that inhuman traffic, and through desire of gain and to foster their trade, go so far as to excite quarrels and wars among them in their native country. . . . In one word, he condemns what our own laws condemn as felony—the slave trade. Domestic Slavery as it exists in the Southern States and in other parts of the Christian world, he does not condemn. This is evident from the tenor of the Apostolic Letter itself, from the declarations made concerning it in Rome, and from the fact that at the fourth provincial Council of Baltimore, in which the majority of Bishops were from the Slaveholding States, it was accepted without any one's thinking it interfered at all with our domestic polity. We apprehend there is a vast difference between the slave Trade and Domestic slavery. . . .

There is no danger, no possibility on our own principles, that Catholic theology should ever be tinctured with the fanaticism of abolition. Catholics may and do differ in regard to slavery, and other points of human policy, when considered as ethical or political questions. But our Theology is fixed, and it must be the same now as it was for first eight or nine centuries of Christianity. During that period, as Bishop England has ably shown in his series of *Letters to the Hon. John Forsyth*, the Church (Let XVI) by the admonitions of her earliest and holiest pastors; by the decrees of her councils made on a variety of occasions; by her synodical condemnation of those who under pretext of religion, would teach the slave to despise her master; by her sanction and support of those laws by which the civil power sought to preserve the rights of the owner; by her own acquiring such property, by deeds of gift or of sale, for the cultivation of her lands, the maintenance of her clergy, the benefit of her monasteries, of their hospitals of her orphans, and of her other works of Charity, repeatedly and evidently testified that she *[the church] regarded the possession of slave property as fully compatible with the doctrines of the Gospel*: and this whilst she denounced the pirate who made incursions to reduce into bondage those who were free and unoffending, and regarded with just execration the men who fitted out ships and hired others to engage in the inhuman traffic. In Catholic Theology the question is a settled one, and no one would be recognized as a Catholic who would utter the expressions we have heard from the lips of American Abolitionists, who called themselves protestants: "If the Bible allows slavery, it should be amended." "The Christianity of the nineteenth century should as far excel the Christianity of the Early Church, as that did the old Jewish law" &c.

The line of conduct prescribed especially to the Catholic Clergy is laid down by the venerable and learned Bishop of Philadelphia [Francis Kenrick] in his standard work, *Theologia Moralis*, Vol. I, Tract. V, Cap VI and Tract VII, cap IV. From the first cited chapter we translate the following paragraph.

37. But what is to be thought of the domestic servitude which exists in most of the southern and western states, where the posterity of those who were brought from Africa still remain in slavery? It is indeed to be regretted that in the present fullness of liberty in which all glory, there should be so many slaves, and that to guard against their movements, it has been necessary to pass laws prohibiting their education, and in some places greatly restricting their exercise of religion. Nevertheless since such is the state of things, nothing should be attempted against the laws, nor anything be done or said that would make them bear their yoke unwillingly. But the prudence and the charity of the sacred Ministers should appear in their effecting that the slaves, imbued with Christian morals, render service to their masters, venerating God, the supreme master of all; and that the Masters be just and kind, and by their humanity and care for their salvation, endeavor to mitigate the condition of their slaves. The Apostles have left us these rules; which if any one should neglect and through a feeling of humanity endeavor to overturn the entire established order, he would in most cases but aggravate the condition of the slaves. The Pope, in the before mentioned constitution, omitted not to lay this before us. "For the Apostles, inspired by the Holy Ghost, taught slaves to obey their temporal masters, as they would Christ himself and to do the will of God cheerfully; and they also gave a precept to the masters to act kindly towards their slaves, to give them what is just and reasonable, and to refrain from threatening them, knowing that the Lord of both is in heaven, and that with Him there is no acceptation of persons."[87]

What we see in this lengthy refutation of abolition is the theological reasoning that scripture enjoins on Christians a love of neighbor *within* the unjust and inhumane system of slavery and the insistence that this love does not require changes to the structure of the institution itself. As further proof, the tradition of Catholic practice that relied on enslavement and Catholic institutions participating in the sale and purchase of human beings testifies to the compatibility of Catholicism and slavery.

Contemporary responses to historical documentation such as this defending the evils of an institution of White supremacy and anti-Blackness often advance the defense that our forebears were products of their time or that we cannot judge the past by the values of the present. What's important to recognize here is that the full range of efforts of abolitionism, an expansive movement throughout US history and culminating powerfully in the nineteenth century, was itself a product of its time. Abolition efforts demonstrate to us that the values of the nineteenth century *included* the refusal of slavery and the revisioning of a fuller humanity without unpaid labor. Immediate emancipation and a reworking of the labor system as goals of the abolition movement were among the productive values of the time. It was precisely because abolition efforts were successfully mobilizing resources and leveraging capital to advance this social, political, and economic transformation that the American bishops felt it necessary to mobilize the resources of the Catholic Church to counter those values and the very currents *of their time*. A close reading of Reynolds's editorial, in fact, reveals also that there were Catholic readers inquiring about the possibility of abolition. But the bishops sought to end the debate. John McGreevy captures the result: "In the United States, Catholics calculated that social stability outweighed any benefit to be gained from immediate emancipation."[88] Adapting McGreevy's terminology, White American Catholics calculated that social stability through the structures and systems of White supremacy and anti-Blackness outweighed any benefit to be gained from changing the structures and systems that enabled White Catholics to enslave, torture, and steal wages from Black Catholics.

It was not only church leaders in Charleston and the South who refused to embrace the value of full humanity for all Catholics, preferring instead the system of White supremacy. McGreevy summarizes: "Studies of membership lists for American abolitionist organizations in the 1830s find few Catholics, and not one prominent American Catholic urged immediate emancipation before the Civil War."[89] Such a failure of imagination impoverished the spiritual and social capital being offered by the Catholic Church throughout the nineteenth century (and beyond), as the spiritual and social capital of American Catholicism was used instead to manufacture inhumanity. As we see in the

1843 defense published in the Charleston diocesan newspaper, this manufactured symbolic capital ran all the way through American Catholic production, including the highly recognized symbolic capital of American Catholic institutions of higher learning and theological training. It's important to note that the prelates, priests, and theologians of the nineteenth century advanced an argument that their proslavery stance was in accordance with the long tradition of the Catholic Christian church, Reynolds's short excerpt an example of themes mobilized to support this argument. But it's also crucial to recognize the way that the precepts and pronouncements of the global Catholic Church would be interpreted specifically with the view of the American context in mind.

For example, in the seminary and university setting of American Catholic theological education, the tradition of following theological manuals as the grounding for passing on the faith was current in this era. The crucial passage from Kenrick's *Theologia Moralis* cited in the *Miscellany* was central among the arguments American Catholic moral theologians might put forward.[90] Kenrick could widely disseminate his ideas through the moral manual *Theologia Moralis,* in which seminarians and students across the vast network of Catholic educational institutions might read that "slaves, informed by Christian morals, might show service to their masters, venerating always God, the supreme Master of us all; so that in turn the masters might show themselves gentle and even-handed and might lighten the condition of their slaves with humanity and with zeal for their salvation."[91] But Kenrick was adapting the moral tradition he had received with applications specifically designed for the American context. American Catholic guardians of the symbolic capital of "sacred knowledge" were mobilizing specific interpretations of scripture and tradition to speak to their day, while other American Christians were mobilizing an interpretation of the same scripture for liberating practices. When we recognize institutions as people who practice, we can trace the agency and actors who make theological ideas work in the world. It is not the "Christian scripture" that speaks; it is a wide variety of Christian interpreters who make the scriptures speak.

Although their church betrayed both Henrietta and Elizabeth in failing to provide them with the spiritual resources to enter into full relationship with each other, it did not fail them in the same way. In fact, the church as an ecclesial institution as well as an educational institution served them in wildly different ways. We can even say that through the systems of the institutional Catholic Church, its symbolic capital of theological argumentation and its social capital of networked relationships, the Catholic Church facilitated the transfer of capital that might have been otherwise acquired by Black Catholics throughout their lives directly to White Catholics instead. The 1843 editorial in the *United States Catholic Miscellany* provides a gut-wrenching example of this in noting that the scriptural warrant that the enslaved should serve slave master with Christian love could have beneficial economic effects for slavers. Bishop Reynolds's editorial concludes by commenting on the *economic* benefits of the Catholic interpretation of the scriptural message:

> How strictly this instruction [for slaver and enslaved] is complied with, and how beneficial are its effects, is known to every one who has any knowledge of the character of Catholic slaves. They are every where distinguished as a body for orderly habits and fidelity to their masters; so much so that in Maryland, where they are numerous, their value is 20 or 25 per cent above that of others.[92]

White Catholics who received a particular interpretation of scripture from the guardians of symbolic capital would also benefit economically from putting this interpretive application into practice, when the purchase and sale of Black Catholics is included in the economy of theological interpretation. As White Catholics received an interpretation of scripture that supported the purchase and sale of human beings, the personal, economic capital that White Catholics reaped from the illicit sale of Black Catholics could then be transferred back into the ecclesial and educational institutions of the Catholic Church. This was a generational inheritance: The sons of slavers would be sent for Catholic education and the process repeated. Once again, the Spirit and Breath of enslaved Black Catholics were being mobilized for the benefit of White Catholics. But in this era, our scope can recognize that this was an interstate commerce of ideas fueling the interstate transfer of slaving wealth.

This was precisely the situation when Elizabeth and Henrietta were tending to a flock of future Black Catholics at St. James the Greater. For at the same time, Elizabeth was reaping the economic benefits of an economy of enslavement and sending her sons to be educated at the Catholic college of St. John's Fordham in New York City. And Elizabeth was not alone: Many among the most prominent Catholic slavers of the South were propelling their sons through Catholic education at St. John's. Indeed, the list in the 1852 catalogue of this northern institution offers clear evidence of the resources of the lives and breath of Black Catholics being transferred through tuition payments. The sons of the wealthiest slavers are found in St. John's enrollment. From Walterboro: Charles, William, and Eustace Pinckney (the latter future son-in-law to Confederate Bishop Lynch), along with Patrick Maloney; from Columbia/Barnwell: John and William Bellinger and Edward Bradley; from Charleston: Amos Bellinger (son of Bishop England's personal physician), Lucius Northrop, and John and Edward O'Neill. This short list alone names sons of families who combined were the legal owners of more than two hundred persons in the Charleston diocese, quite likely two hundred enslaved Catholics.[93] Wealthy, slaveholding Catholics in the South supported not only the Catholic Church in Charleston but also in the North by infusing the struggling institution of St. John's Fordham with full-tuition-paying students—each sufficiently endowed to pay not only the $200 annual tuition but to bring with him the requisite "three suits . . . three pairs of shoes . . . a silver spoon and silver drinking cup, marked with his name."[94]

In Colleton County, South Carolina, before the boys' entrance to college, the region experienced a "rice boom," grounded in "the exploitation of intelligent & experienced slave labor arriving from the west coast of Africa with many agricultural skills & methods."[95] Expertise crafted by ancestors on the African continent supported the growth of White wealth, which would be transferred to tuition at St. John's Fordham. Yet the extraction of the ancestors' labor from living bodies, doing physical work and applying expert skill, not only cultivated the "Carolina Gold Rice" that would be sold for tuition payment; the efforts of the ancestors also released the bodies of the Pinckney sons to acquire skills in theological education. While Black Catholics worked the rice fields in cultivating the Pinckney family wealth, their lifeblood provided not only the means of money as a resource to send Pinckney sons to attend St. John's Fordham; it also accorded the boys the time they needed to do so. As Mary Pinckney Jones explains, Pinckney women ran the household and hired male overseers to run the plantation, and enslaved workers did the work, leaving male Pinckneys not much to do—so in addition to the traditional recreations of cockfighting, horseracing, and hunting, they went to school.[96]

While on the home front it was enslaved Catholics who made possible the Pinckney boys' freedom for education, it was the network of Catholic institutions that provided a location for that education. Although still in its infancy, the steadily growing network of Catholic schools in the United States was already expanding to establish institutions of higher education beyond Georgetown. Charleston Catholics may have known of the opportunity in New York City precisely because the Catholic Church was already a *network* of institutions. Charleston Catholics not only participated in the spiritual capital of Mass attendance, sacramental life, and prayer; they also entered into the sociopolitical capital of networks of relationships that might mobilize legislation in their favor. The Catholic Church provided an informational network not only through social networks and sermons but also through newspapers and other publications that shaped a common outlook on the religious, social, and political realities of the day. It is through this networked reality that the Catholic young men in the slaving economy of Charleston and beyond might have imagined the opportunities that awaited them in other parts of the nation.

For example, in the 1840 *United States Catholic Miscellany*, young Catholics might read of the intellectual affairs not only of Georgetown's commencement but also of possibilities emergent at St. John's Rosehill, just outside of New York City: "The large population of Catholics in this city may now look forward with the most pleasing anticipation to the spiritual aid they are destined to receive" in the seminary that is to be founded there.[97] They might have read in this ecclesial newspaper not only of the struggles of Irish Catholics and Catholics in England but also of the mission efforts around the globe *and* of the efforts of Bishop John Hughes to serve young men just like them in New York City. Networked messaging drawn from the New York Catholic paper was reprinted prominently for Charleston Catholics, who became part of the efforts the bishop would undertake. Just one year later, Charleston boys might read the lead article on the front page to learn that the archbishop's "New College" would be opening later in the fall. This announcement was published as the lead article on February 20, 1841, in the same layout location where readers had come to expect the series of letters to Secretary of State Forsyth, which had held that place since October 1840. From such a placement, families might infer that the new college would align with southern interests and would similarly be opposed to freedom for enslaved Catholics.

The young men of Charleston and their families might have had their interests piqued in the possibilities of schooling in New York City when they recognized the names of their hometown sons, Alex Allemong and James Brennan of Charleston, celebrated at St. John's College's "First Annual Exhibition" and graduation. It is clear that Charleston Catholics felt connected to this institution and its very first class of students, at a time when the economic and educational future of the institution was uncertain. Amid the celebration of their Catholic brethren, a cohort of the boys from Charleston might have eagerly read: "The location of the college, as no doubt a large portion of our readers know, is at once beautiful and romantic, well calculated to impress upon the minds of the young students a deep love for all that is sublime in nature."[98] A feast for the mind and for the soul was promised through the Catholic media.

Should the Charleston Catholics have wondered what the northern Catholics in New York City were thinking about their slaveholding economy, they surely would have been relieved if they heard echoes of Archbishop Hughes's theological stance through their institutional networks. And later, Charleston Catholics did not need to simply infer this antiabolition position when they read in the *Miscellany* in 1854 the sermon of New York City's Archbishop John

Hughes. The model of patriarchal care of women, children, and the enslaved was a Catholic theological anthropology that crossed the Mason-Dixon Line, as Archbishop John Hughes preached in New York City a hierarchy of power rooted in the divine. Reporting on a recent visit to a Catholic Cuban plantation, Hughes preached:

> In fact, all power on earth is of God; and whether that be of the sovereign or the rulers, or whether it be that of the father of the family, whether it be that of the owner of slaves, or that of the masters of those who are temporarily placed in that position by their own voluntary act, there is throughout all this an extension of the pastorship of God, and it is that it may be employed for His glory that we find it thus distributed among men. Then, if men have this authority over others, whether it be over children, or slaves, or servants, they have power, and that power is from God; and because it is from God it is to be respected, on the principle of conscience, by those who are subject to it.[99]

For Archbishop Hughes, a combination of hierarchy and defense of property as *theological* building blocks made the benevolent dictatorship of Catholic slaveholding households an extension of the ecclesial household. The overarching theme of this benevolent dictatorship was soteriological, rooted in an understanding of Catholic Christianity as the premier source of salvation and the "one true faith," in which slavers had a key role to play. In the words of Archbishop Hughes:

> Seized in their own country, where they lived in ignorance of God—and transported from it, how glorious is the privilege of the master who, in that position, might introduce them to a knowledge of their real dignity, as the redeemed creatures of our common heavenly Father! While we all know that this condition of slavery is an evil, yet it is not an absolute and unmitigated evil; and even if it were any thing more than what it is—a comparative evil—there is one thing, that it is infinitely better than the condition in which this people would have been, had they not been seized to gratify the avarice and cupidity of the white man.[100]

The extended network of Catholic institutions, of church and school, mobilized a similar theological messaging, a symbolic capital in defense of White Catholic slaveholding.

It was in seminaries and Catholic educational institutions like St. John's Fordham that the manuals of the moral tradition defending slavery would be read and studied most intimately. And when new interpretations came on the scene, they would be studied as well. As an early-twentieth-century journal reports:

> For many years, the Sabetti's *Compendium Theologiae Moralis* has been a favorite text-book with American students of theology. It took, in most cases, the place of Archbishop Kenrick's admirable manuals. . . . Gury's manual, in use by the Jesuits and Redemptorists, was accordingly adapted to American conditions, and replaced gradually the scholarly work of Kenrick in the other missionary seminaries.[101]

The multiple copies of Gury's manual purchased for the St. John's library (in 1850, 1853, 1857, 1858, 1860, and 1862) give witness to the flavor of theological training they might receive, especially after the college came under the leadership of the Jesuits in 1846. Gury also incorporated into his manual the interpretations readymade for slaveholding Catholicism. In standard question-and-answer format, his manual queried: Can a man have dominion over another man? To which Gury reasoned the possibility that a person could alienate themselves from their own work and thus could become another's possession, even forever. While Gury named that civil law in many places had outlawed slavery, his manual put forward that slavery itself did not absolutely conflict with natural law.[102]

When the Jesuits chose to mobilize the capital to purchase Gury's text simultaneous to their using their capital to take out an advertisement in Charleston's *Catholic Miscellany* to actively recruit students from South Carolina's slaveholding families, they were mobilizing social, economic, and symbolic capital across a wide network of Catholic institutions, the spiritual capital of scripture, tradition, and theological studies making this work possible. The practice of hermeneutics—reading the text of scripture or any text through a particular lens—helps us recognize the variability of Catholic thought and practice and identify the leverage by which slavery could be made salvific.

As the Jesuits at St. John's Fordham advanced Gury's pattern of thought through their purchase of multiple copies of his text and the availability of his reasoning in their library, they formed the student body of the next generation of Catholics with *Butler's Catechism* (as announced in the college curriculum published in the yearly catalogue).[103] When the boys from slaving families arrived on campus, *Butler's Catechism* could easily be read through the lens of their slaving commitments. *Butler's Catechism* becomes then a guidebook of ecclesial reproduction that helped young men at St. John's Fordham navigate what it meant to be Catholic slavers. They would have been reminded of the duty to those under their care (Catechism from Lesson 17 on the Commandments) but could also take refuge in the *Catechism*'s conferral of power when the fourth commandment is translated as the rule "to love, honour and obey parents and superiors" and glossed further with the help of Paul, who is quoted: "Let every soul be subject to higher powers; for there is no power but from God: and those that are, ordained of God. Therefore he that resisteth the power, resisteth the ordinance of God" (Romans xiii.1).[104] Affirming that the power they enjoyed as young slave drivers derived from God, they might also be banking that the Catholics enslaved to them had also been duly instructed in the "the chief duties of servants . . . to their masters," which the catechism described this way: "To be obedient, respectful and faithful to them; to be diligent in their work and services, and not to suffer their masters to be injured in their property by any person."[105] The boys would be crafted to lean into the learning in the faith and to recognize those who broke the commandments, when what was forbidden by the fourth commandment: "all contempt, stubbornness, ill-will and disobedience to parents and superiors."[106]

But the catechism that served as a guidebook for reproducing the church may have also helped Henrietta and other enslaved Catholics navigate what it meant to seek the otherwise possibilities enabled by the "Creator God, sovereign Lord of Heaven and Earth" who had made them, because the Catechism set out responsibilities or "duties of masters to their servants" that included "to lead them to God . . . to see that they be exact in their religious duties."[107] This would include the requirement that Catholic slavers not only provide baptism and cultivation in the Catholic faith, as we have seen at St. James, but also that on days of the Sabbath, everyone would be bound by the third commandment and granted a freedom from "all unnecessary servile work; and whatever may hinder the due observance of the Lord's day" as outlined by the Council of Trent.[108] Knowing this religious requirement of their enslavers, it may have been some among Henrietta's fellow Catholics who joined the planning when the enslaved in Walterboro "were to rise in the holidays" in December 1860. And even though "the plot was discovered a few days beforehand . . . [and] Nine were tried & [by December 27] four in jail to be hung,"[109] we know from this correspondence that the holidays as holy days were opportunities for new life among the enslaved, who capitalized on the catechetical requirements of the faith to make space for life outside the oversight of their Catholic and Christian enslavers.

When Elizabeth Perry Bellinger Pinckney's sons enrolled at St. John's Fordham, we might imagine her sharing the salvific possibilities of her role as "slave master" for those enslaved by her. Throughout her letters, the practical care of her human property intertwines with her spiritual self-care, and her son, in a course on Catholic moral theology at St. John's, would have practical experience to weave into his reading of Gury's text in the library and *Butler's Catechism* in the classroom. Elizabeth writes,

> I visited the plantation . . . I have employed Mr. Jakes Sanders to manage for me this year. Your horses and dog are quite hearty, also your boy Thomas. I expect to go down with Mr. Carr to St. James', and hope to be allowed to partake of the blessed Sacrament. (Walterborough, January 8, 1852)[110]

> My crop they say looks well. Your horses are well, your mare has lost her colt. Black Thomas and Bruser are well also. (June 20, 1852)[111]

> I have lost three negroes on the plantation with the same fever, vix, Premier, Merida and Bess, all were children. My plantation is almost gone to ruin for want of a good manager. My crop is a lost one. I expect to get Your Uncle to manage for me this year and I am looking out for a driver in this place. (December 18, 1852)[112]

The precarious state of the new college at Fordham and the precarious state of the plantation were cause for concern on both sides of the Pinckney–St. John's relationship. A year earlier, J. Marshall, treasurer at the Jesuit-run institution, wrote to Mrs. Elizabeth Perry Pinckney in hopes of collecting missing tuition. He confessed the institution's inability to advance any more money for the Pinckney sons, even though it "would be painful to us, as we have for them both affection and interests which they so well deserve."[113] Drawn from her resources made possible by the Black Catholics whom she enslaved, Elizabeth must have paid the Jesuits what was due, since Charles graduated with honors in 1852, and Eustace returned that year in the fall to continue his studies. But concerns continue to plague their relationship, as Elizabeth writes in October: "We have had a miserable harvest this season much of my rice has been totally ruined. You can tell the Treasurer not to be uneasy and have a little patience and he will eventually be paid."[114] An economy of enslavement supported White slaveholding Catholics, and their capital was distributed throughout slavery-defending institutions of Catholic church and school. Despite the precarity of the plantation's cash flow, the Jesuits continued to reap the benefits of a slave economy, actively recruiting students from slaveholding families with the "Prospectus of St. John's College" placed among the advertisements in Charleston's *Catholic Miscellany* in 1854.[115]

But while Elizabeth took advantage of the ecclesial-educational network of the Catholic Church, none of Henrietta's extended biological family would have had any such opportunity. Learning classical languages and becoming steeped in scriptures was leisure activity for the Catholic Pinckney boys while other Catholics worked to sustain the family physically and economically. The theological education provided to the sons of St. John's Fordham in New York City was made possible financially and practically by the work of enslaved daughters and sons in fields of the family plantation near the Ashepoo River and thirty miles away in the home at Walterboro. Reciprocally, Catholic education of the day made theologically defensible the system of enslavement that provided the resources for Pinkney sons to be so released from their bodily toil. In the network of Catholic education as instantiated in the North, the Pinckney-Bellingers of South Carolina might be far from the Crossroads of a southern slaveholding Catholicism, but their right to hold fellow Catholics as legal property would not be challenged by their northern theological education. The public exchange between Bishop Patrick Lynch of the Charleston Confederacy and Archbishop Hughes in New York City demonstrates clearly the interstate network of Catholicism that provided for a commerce of ideas and the flow of capital within an economy of enslavement.[116] Even as late as 1861, New York's Archbishop Hughes reasoned that "the constitution of this country, the laws of the State, regard his title to his slaves as not less legitimate than his title to the land."[117] And therefore, "where slaves have been introduced into a country, she [the church] does not require of her members that they shall be restored to their primitive condition which would be often times worse than the one in which they are placed."[118]

## Henrietta and Elizabeth in the Wider Net of Enslavement and the Catholic Church

In the precarities of health and fortune, Elizabeth Perry Bellinger Pinckney's letters reveal an overarching trust in the work of God to make things well. But like the institutional story of which she is a part, this spirituality of escape and inscape obscures the backs and breath that made the endurance of precarity possible. In her letters, Elizabeth joins the two sources of salvation: the health and heartiness of enslaved workers and the hope and hospitality of spiritual escape. The well-being of crops and human property align for the future of the family, as others' lives are manipulated for the benefit of Elizabeth, her sons, and the institutions they will support:

> The rice at my place is fine, the harvest is nearly over, the provision crop will last the next year. Thomas looks well, and has grown much, I mean your boy, and Brauser looks fat and healthy. Your mare and three colts are all healthy. Disliking to part husband and wife, I exchanged

> Backus with Billy for Mary, and gave him two-hundred and fifty dollars for the little boy for his fathers sake.[119]

The normalcy with which Elizabeth narrates the purchase and trade of human beings indicates that the trade in human beings was simply a part of her landscape and livelihood, patterned into the world in which she moved. Elizabeth may also be providing evidence of historians' proposal that Catholic practices of slavery included the directive to maintain family systems, especially in keeping together husband and wife. But the ease with which she seems to communicate the purchase of a child remains shocking when her family is named as "distinguished" in the annals of Catholic history. It is not only Elizabeth who could reconcile ownership of human beings with her Catholic piety but a theologically produced defense of the practice that set her soul at ease. While her enslaved property worked the fields to provide the economic resources to survive, Elizabeth used the metaphor of harvest to encourage the spiritual growth of her son: "May the Son of Justice with all his splendor shine forth upon thy labours, producing in the Autumn a fruitful harvest."[120] There appears to be nothing in their Catholicism, South or North, that would mirror back to Elizabeth the irony of this metaphor. It was Black Catholics of her ecclesial family whose labor and harvest was under conditions of grave injustice.

While Elizabeth's sons were sent to a northern Catholic institution, it did not influence their practices of slaveholding and slave trading: The Pinckneys were a slavery-saturated family up to the point when they were legally required to relinquish their human property. By 1852, William had already left St. John's Fordham and set out to make his own fortune in the slave markets of Alabama. In 1852, Eustace returned to Walterboro, but he is also engaged in expanding the family business over the next ten years, with the possibilities of moving the family to a more lucrative practice in Alabama in the 1860s. This reengagement with the profitability of the slave system was not apart from their Catholic identity cultivated at St. John's. For Eustace, that was far from it; he had married into the family of Rev. Dr. Patrick Lynch, who would become bishop of Charleston and subsequently bishop of the Confederacy. Eustace's sister also married into the Lynch family. So the Catholic education at a New York institution neither mitigated nor interrupted the family practices of slavery; in fact, it seems to have strengthened the ties with a slavery-supporting church and its social capital.

After schooling in New York City, both Catholic sons of Elizabeth went to serve the cause of the Confederacy as soldiers in the Civil War. Elizabeth died in 1865; in 1866, Eustace was the last to leave the Catholic Crossroads:

> After 1865 and the end of the Confederate War, some of the Catholic planters of Walterboro, who had lost heavily in the last months of the war, moved elsewhere. Fran Smith, in *The Island Packet,* wrote that "Eustace Bellinger Pinckney, a Civil War physician in the Confederate Army, paid the taxes on the 300 acres of Calhoun Plantation and moved his family from Walterboro to the Colleton River side of what is now called Pinckney Colony in 1866," near Hilton Head.[121]

No record of Hetty's whereabouts after the war have yet been found.

## Reading Catholicism through the Lens of an Economy of Enslavement

In her *Dancing with God: The Trinity from a Womanist Perspective,* Karen Baker-Fletcher reminds us of the complexity of Black Christians emerging from this history. She writes that "those who are African Americans and connect with [the] violence perpetrated by many so-called Christians, yet remain 'Christian,' find themselves in paradox."[122] So, too, do those who are White Americans and connect with the violence perpetrated by many White Catholics yet remain Catholic. If we theologize a God from whom all power comes and a Spirit who dances in our relationality, the exploitative relationality of a slave economy tests the limits of our theological thinking. Reluctant to assign a positive value to Elizabeth Perry Pinckney's spirituality, with Baker-Fletcher I ask, "Is there a place where God is not present?"[123] And I wrestle with the theology of Kelly Brown Douglas, who advances a position directly: "Within the black faith tradition forged in the invisible institution of slavery, the freedom of God means that there is a profound difference between God and those who would make chattel of black bodies. God was not with the slaveholders."[124] Once we start listening to the voices of the ancestors, the complexities of pressing questions come through in the exploitative relationality of a slave economy, making it difficult to pin down where divinity is, and is not, at work in the world.

An extended account of the Pinckney family history serves to illuminate this reality, where White Christian women play a complex role in the economy of enslavement as narrator, interpreter, and actor; as death dealer and healer; dispenser of the family fortune and founder of faith communities among the enslaved, inhabiting a multiplicity of places in the economy of enslavement. Mary Claire Pinckney Jones relays the stories told to her by Eustace's son (her grandfather) about what happened when he and his brothers were away in New York attending Fordham. She recounts:

> The Ashepoo plantation went down quickly and severely following the death of his grandfather, Dr. Cotesworth Pinckney, in 1847 for the supposed lack of male management. To bear this out, John Edward told me a story of great charitable proportions but of poor business practices. He told of how it was a practice—hopefully limited—to turn out old and worn out slaves from the plantations into the woods to die. Rebecca D'Oyley and her daughter-in-law [Elizabeth Perry Bellinger Pinckney, Dr. William Cotesworth Pinckney's surviving wife] made it a habit to give refuge to these poor unfortunate creatures. In Uncle Edward's words "a noble cause but not necessarily in the best interest of well-run plantations." These non-productive slaves had to be fed, clothed, and housed. I like this story very much, although it probably meant the eventual loss of the plantations.[125]

The many-sidedness of an exploitative relationality is captured in Elizabeth's descendent reflecting on her family history. She recognizes that the family wealth is rooted in an economy that disposed of human beings inhumanely, simultaneously mourning this inhumane practice and the loss of family wealth that addressing it would bring. The inhumanity of enslavement came at a cost, and the redress necessarily comes at a cost as well. In this episode, ultimately, this descendant reconciles the loss of the family's wealth and successful plantation ownership as a happy story, one that she likes "very much," considering the humanity her White female forebears exhibited in the face of certain death for the Black elders whom they enslaved.

But Pinckney-Jones continues and draws us more deeply into the evil economics of enslavement. She writes:

> On the other side of the coin is the story told to us by the present day manager of an Ashepoo plantation. He related the name "Pinckney" is still held in disrepute by the elderly blacks of the community as stories still circulate about a slave mill on Pinckney lands where slaves were bred solely for the purpose of sale.[126]

If the Pinckneys were harvesting children for sale, wrested from their mothers' wombs, they too were benefiting from the deepest inhumanity of the slave economy—not uncommon among Catholic slaveholders in our history.[127] And if St. John's Fordham received tuition payment transferred through the Pinckney hands from the sale of human beings, we too, as an institution, have blood in our buildings.

Pinckney Jones captures the desire for White innocence that permeates the White Christian response to the reality of slavery's inhumanity, as her report continues: "This latter story is certainly in conflict with other information. In reviewing correspondence, recorded wills and other documents which show the great respect and love for slaves, the latter story is hard to believe."[128] Through a White racial frame whose foundation is the presumption of goodness and morality, it is hard for White Christians to believe that our ancestors maintained the hardness of heart that an economy of enslavement required. White Christians gravitate toward those aspects of history that can be read as White Christian kindness. Coming to terms with a Catholic theological sensibility that could be reconciled with enslavement may be aided by a recognition that the exploitative relationality of slavery took many and diverse forms. As we've seen, some among the enslaved were servants Elizabeth greeted with affection and shared in the church-building activity at St. James. But others among the enslaved in the Pinckney holdings were "Negroes" who would be "carried on" by Eustace to Alabama to enhance the family production at a time when exploitative labor practices included the torture of workers to increase each day's cotton yield.[129] White Christian relationships to enslaved Christians took many and diverse forms, yet however complex those relationships were, the truth telling must include the ways White Christians benefited from the diminishment of Black Christians. We must situate any Bellinger-Pinckney acts of kindness in the broader structural perspective of familial, ecclesial, and state institutions that betray the realities of White supremacy and enhance White capital.

But we also must embrace the Pinckneys as part of the St. John's Fordham family and engage in our own reckoning as an institution. In 1841, St. John's was founded by an American bishop who himself had acquired benefits in overseeing enslaved workers as a pathway for his ecclesial education.[130] This bishop/archbishop defended the rights of White Catholics to own Black Catholics and inhumanely to divert economic benefits from Black Catholic lives and labors into the hands of White Catholics and the White Catholic institutions of church and school. The northern bishop was part of the creation of the Catholic network North and South, and he maintained close relationships with southern bishops, including the bishop to the Confederacy. When the Jesuits took over administration of the New York City school in 1846, they did not dismantle but rather capitalized on the close relationships through which the Catholic network recruited slaveholding students to support the Jesuits' educational endeavor.

The story of Elizabeth Perry Bellinger Pinckney, her sons, and her companion, Henrietta of St. James, is just one of the many stories of a White Catholic slaveholding family at a northern slavery-accommodating Catholic institution. It is the complex story of this White Catholic slaveholding family contributing to the foundations of a Black Catholic community at St. James the Greater. And it is a story that does not yet have an ending.

> The demands of the slave on the present have everything to do with making good the promise of abolition, and this entails much more than the end of property in slaves. It requires the reconstruction of society, which is the only way to honor our debt to the dead. This is the intimacy of our age with theirs—an unfinished struggle. To what end does one conjure the ghost of slavery, if not to incite the hopes of transforming the present? Given this, I refuse to believe that the slave's most capacious political claims or wildest imaginings are for back wages or debt relief. There are too many lives at peril to recycle the forms of appeal that, at best, have delivered the limited emancipation against which we now struggle.[131]

# 4

# Institutional Networks and Nation Building

*Collaborating with the State through Systems of Education*

Illicit gains from the sins of White supremacy have flowed through Catholic institutions of church and school. From the ecclesiology of the preceding chapter, we've come to a place where we are able to ask critical questions about the Catholic Church as an institution in the dynamic realities of the US history of White supremacies. Through the story of St. James (Colleton County, South Carolina) we met Henrietta and Elizabeth, who drew us in to the complexity and complicity of the Catholic Church in an economy of enslavement. Their lives, their relationship, their histories on the frontier of the church in mid-nineteenth-century South Carolina allowed us to pose the crucial ecclesiological questions: Did the church betray them? Or did the church sustain them? Within the structures and systems of White supremacy and the tragedy and trauma of American chattel slavery, the answer is both. The church as institution, as storehouse of capital, withdrew its support from Black Catholics and infused the social and symbolic worlds of White Catholic slavers. The church as institution, as places of practice, however, sustained both White and Black Catholics—at times sustaining them simultaneously and in the same place. The recognition of this complexity and complicity allows us to put forward new notions of institutions and new ecclesiological proposals about the institution of the church. That is, that it exhibits and expresses *both* the reality of entanglement in the sin of White supremacy *and* the "otherwise possibility" of lives of resistance to the sin of White supremacy. This allows us to ask the question of how *our* instantiation of the church today is performing these roles in the present.

Further, in the imagined possibilities of African traditional religious practices infusing the prayer practices of Henrietta and Elizabeth we can consider what Sandra Schneiders describes as a porosity in spirituality, including those sustained within the institution of the Catholic Church. This porosity signals that practices within the tradition of Catholicism are blended with practices originating with other traditions and forms of religiosity. Persons blend what they find to sustain them from the many rich resources of human being in the world, and we might envision these as diverse encounters with God. The ecclesiology of such spiritual practices, then, is an ecclesiology of internal diversity and hybridity: Within Catholic institutions, persons are sustained by identifiably "Catholic" practices along with many and diverse spiritual resources. The complexity of historical evidence enables us to hope for the otherwise possibilities of our own day: that the institutions of the Catholic Church in America might be incorporating new resources to become locations of antiracist practices drawn from the many cultures and religions of the globe, even if they are not yet.

The examination of St. James the Greater on the frontier simultaneously opened an awareness of the ways in which the gain from the sins of chattel slavery not only benefited individual slaving families but was infused into the network of Catholic institutions of church and school. Monies derived from the illicit practices of enslaved labor (including the possibilities of harvesting human lives) provided economic capital for generations of White students to attend Catholic schools across an emergent institutional network, including those in the North. At the same time, ideas generated in these institutions of higher learning manufactured the logic of slaveholding as compatible with Catholic commitments. By disseminating these ideas, the Catholic media promoted practices by which White Catholics withheld economic capital from enslaved workers, which White Catholics could then dedicate instead to building churches. Furthermore, Catholic media networks promulgated such ideas widely, and it was through the media that Catholics could identify landing places for slaveholding capital throughout the national network, sending children to Catholic schools, purchasing Catholic books, and donating to a wide range of projects of Catholic expansion. In turn, the same media systems would name these White Catholic slavers as "good benefactors" for an expanding church, passing this symbolic capital along to us today and erasing the deep involvement in the sins of an economy of enslavement. The expansive scope of a network of institutions of school and church asks us to see the ways in which responsibility and reparation for the sins of White supremacy are spread widely across our nation and intimately within Catholic configurations.

This chapter capitalizes on the trajectory of our study, which asks us to see the Catholic Church at work in both parish and school in a networked configuration of institutions that continued to prioritize White well-being. Just as our ancestors in the faith built up the Jesuit Catholic institution of Georgetown as expressions of both church and school, and just as our ancestors in the faith built up the institutions of St. John's Fordham and St. James the Greater as expressions of both church and school, so too the examination of this chapter will consider both church and school as we press the "frontier" of the Catholic Church further in the era of an expanding nation. As I tell this story of Catholic institutions in the drama of American White supremacy in new locations, I'll draw key threads forward from out of the periods already discussed. That is, the nineteenth-century expansion to the American "frontier" of the Midwest and the Plains is an extension of the establishment of the US Catholic Church in earlier periods and on the East Coast.

This chapter will follow the tendril-trajectories of Catholic institutions as they help create an American nation across the full landscape of what will become the United States. Here, we hold onto the backdrop of the church as an ecclesiological institution conveying spiritual and social capital, but we will distinctly pursue the church as an educational institution conveying not only spiritual and social capital but the symbolic capital of recognition. Students earning degrees in Catholic institutions were shaped also in the state's recognizable aim of "educated citizens." As Catholic educational institutions advanced the interests of the state, they were intimate partners in the project of settler colonialism, the means by which White European-heritage Americans came to see themselves as the rightful heirs of this land. As Santiago Slabodsky describes, the settler-colonial project included "the construction of an alternative society in that location in a way that makes the colonizer invert the understanding of him-/herself as an invader and think of him-/herself as a native, deeming the native as a foreigner."[1] So powerful was the inversion of invader as native in this era of struggle that immigrant Catholics wrestled to secure a position in the nation amid other White settlers who excluded them. The latter named themselves (Protestant Euro-heritage persons) as Native Americans. The "nativist" controversies witnesses both Slabodsky's insight *and* reflects to our present the practices by which White Euro-heritage Christians (including Catholics) understand *themselves* to be the populations most native to the land.

And like the purposes to which history was put in earlier chapters, this chapter also asks: What forms of coloniality still lurk within our Catholic educational systems? Our colonial history should provide a lens through which to seek out and address a remnant coloniality in patterns of thought, knowledge, and recognition today. As Slabodsky presents:

> Coloniality describes a subtle and pernicious reality. It refers, and here I use Walter Mignolo's term, to the patterns of domination that were developed during colonial times and that continue to reproduce themselves beyond formal colonialism. In other words, it is the construction of racial hierarchies set in the sixteenth century that helped to define, for example, blackness by its "lack."[2]

Knowledge systems borrowed from Europe and taking root in the United States constructed a portrait of non-European and non-Christian peoples as "foreign" to the plan God put forward for humanity and as fundamentally lacking some key characteristics of what it means to be human. By virtue of that lack, those named less than fully human (still conveyed in the "non" of "non-Christian" and "non-European") were restricted within or barred from the body politic.

As we will see in this chapter, not only "blackness" but also indigeneity was defined by its lack. Here we can see systems of White Catholic education participating in what sociologists name as our nation's "racial project," constructing racial categories of "other-than-White" by descriptors that measure persons in relation to European-heritage notions of progress and mastery.[3] Simultaneous to producing knowledge systems that categorized non-White peoples according to their "lack," White Catholic educators aimed to bring these same persons into a White project of supremacy *through* the systems of education. Education, then, becomes a dual-edged sword, with opportunities to access capital (in all its forms) but with the colonizers' aims dictating the parameters of "knowledge" and driving toward mastery. To address our inheritance in colonizing institutions, we may be encouraged to consider what decolonizing our curriculum and practices might mean. Can institutional resources be leveraged for the reparation of past breaches but without once again absorbing Indigenous peoples and peoples of African descent into White projects of coloniality?

What we will also witness in this history is that when a capital-rich institution like the Catholic Church is expressed through systems of coloniality and the hierarchy of humanity it presumes, the results have included the unequal distribution of Catholic capital in its many forms. The symbolic capital that comes with the recognition of where one fits in a social landscape, pressed through the sieve of White supremacy, creates recognition for those who have been racialized as "White" and misrecognition for those racialized as Black, Native, Indigenous, Asian, Latinx, and other categorizations in the race matrix. The social capital conveyed through networks of Catholicism has maintained the people power of White Catholics in decision-making and leadership locations. And the economic capital of resources distributed among the "faithful" for manifesting the Gospel in each age has been unequally distributed to the benefit of White Catholics as well. Such an unequal distribution of capital can be traced through distinct case studies that take us across the nation in a landscape of the emergent Catholic network. Following the methodology of Maria Yellow Horse Brave Heart, the narration of unequal distribution of capital, and the analysis of the theo-logic that made this inequity possible *might* bring forward the transformed institutions of church and school as locations for the redistribution of capital for a more equitable world. Knowing this history, each of us can ask how do *we* leverage our locations within institutions in the project of redistributing capital, creating transformed institutions in the service of creating a transformed world?

## Institution of the Church and Its Mission to Black Catholics in Baltimore

We return our study to the origins of Catholicism in the US landscape. As the nation settled, so too did the church settle into the institutions of the nation, benefiting from the systems put in place for land ownership, wealth building, citizenship, and city planning. It was the former Jesuit John Carroll who was assigned as the first bishop to the first Catholic diocese of a new republic in 1789 on land acquired to establish a Catholic presence not only on plantations (as examined with Maryland Jesuits in Chapter 2) but also in the city. Although a minority Christian denomination in a landscape of Protestants, there were capital-rich Catholics interested in participating in the American project, as the previous chapters have demonstrated. So identifiably Catholic was the location of Maryland in an emerging nation that Catholics fleeing toward safer spaces from the revolutions taking place in other parts of the world found their way to this political geography through the social capital of the church. Thus, when Toussaint L'Ouverture led the first successful revolution of formerly enslaved peoples on the island of Saint-Domingue (what is present-day Haiti), White and Black Catholics with the social and economic means to flee that instability made the emerging nation of the United States their destination (recognizing, of course, that this choice meant that they were not actively supporting the revolution of the enslaved). The historian Shannen Dee Williams describes:

> During the rebellion, thousands of free and enslaved Saint-Domingue residents and others from neighboring islands fled to the United States, with many settling in port cities, including Baltimore, New Orleans, New York, Philadelphia, Richmond, Norfolk, Charleston, Mobile and Savannah. The humanitarian crisis that resulted from the influx of

> mostly French-speaking refugees, who were overwhelmingly Catholic, and the refusal of most white Church leaders to extend equitable resources to the Black faithful prompted Black Catholics to take the lead in providing essential services to these displaced communities.[4]

As the Haitian Revolution raged from 1791 to 1804, numerous Catholics found Baltimore their home: Black and White Catholics, English speaking and Francophone. It was thus in a racially, religiously, and politically dynamic Baltimore that the Oblate Sisters of Providence, the "first successful Roman Catholic sisterhood in the world established by women of African descent," was born.[5]

One among those Catholics who fled unrest in the Caribbean and found refuge in the network of the Catholic Church in Baltimore was Elizabeth Lange, one of the four foundresses of the Oblate Sisters of Providence (OSP). Her parents before her were "refugees who fled to Cuba from the revolution taking place in their native Saint Domingue."[6] As first stop on their migration, they found refuge on another island where enslavement still structured the economy and interests. In the early 1800s, Lange's family left Cuba and relocated to Baltimore. Her family was among the many French-speaking Catholics of means who could begin a new life.[7] Yet as Diane Batts Morrow explains: "In the late eighteenth and early nineteenth centuries, white Baltimoreans, in sharp contrast to their reception of the white San Domingan refugees, had received the black Francophone immigrants from the Caribbean inhospitably."[8] Thus, Lange was compelled by the plight of fellow immigrants to offer support to children by establishing a school in her home for the education of Haitian immigrants. Lange's status as a free woman of color, a woman from a family of some means, provided sites of capital to undertake the endeavor, albeit within a racial project of American White supremacy. The social capital of Lange's Catholicism saw her invited to further the work of the church in the mutually beneficial project of embedding her school in the network of the Catholic Church when she was invited by James Joubert to expand her project. Now not only would Lange be shaping students in the cultural capital of education, but she and her companions would be shaped in the spiritual capital of the Catholic tradition as professed women religious. "Joubert helped Lange, [Maria] Balas, and another Saint Dominguan woman, Rose Boegue, secure a separate house to relocate their school and begin their novitiate in June 1828."[9] Once Lange committed to this work, her embeddedness in *Catholic* networks provided leverage for its expansion. As the OSPs describe their history:

> Father James Hector Nicholas Joubert, SS, a Sulpician priest discovered it was difficult for the Haitian refugee children to master their

> religious studies because they were unable to read. He heard of two devout religious Caribbean women who were already conducting a school for black children in their home in Baltimore. In 1828 those two women, Elizabeth Lange (later Mother Mary Lange) and Maria Balas accepted his proposal to start a sisterhood with the primary mission of teaching and caring for African American children.[10]

While we can celebrate their commitment to care for Black children, it is crucial to see that the necessity of this alternative schooling for *some* of the Catholic Haitian immigrants must be read through a national-institutional lens as embedded in the systems of White supremacy. That is, we must see that education *was already available* for some children. Established in 1782, it took Baltimore just forty years to develop a system of public schools, a service alongside those of housing, health, and public works. But this public school system was denied to children of color, even those whose free parents contributed through the payment of taxes. The religiously motivated, Catholic-identified school for Black children founded by the OSPs under Joubert's patronage was filling a systemic gap created by a nation structured by White supremacy. Free Black women expressed their faith by engaging the struggle to educate amid the structures and systems of White supremacy.

Joining Elizabeth Lange in this project of filling the gaps of education left by a White supremacist state was another free woman of color, the "nineteen-year-old Almaide Maxis Duchemin, the US-born daughter of a Saint Dominguan émigré nurse and a British major, whom Lange and Balas had raised and educated."[11] Almaide Maxis Duchemin will become Theresa Maxis in her adoption into the family of the Oblate Sisters of Providence, and Theresa's story also has roots in the revolution of enslaved people in Haiti. Her mother, Mary, worked in the home of a White family who had fled the uprisings in Saint-Domingue in 1793. Historians describe Mary as a "biracial San Domingan (Haitian),"[12] and the location of service within the Duchemin family indicates Mary's dependent condition. By contrast, Theresa's father was an English visitor to the Duchemin household, which historians posit may be further evidence of her mother's unfree condition: "Bright-skinned and blue-eyed [Theresa] was the illegitimate child of a white British father and a biracial San Domingan (Haitian) mother."[13] While Theresa too was a free woman of color, she was less "free" than others given her status of dependence on the Duchemin family:

> Born of unwed parents and of mixed racial lineage into a society that held both conditions in contempt, she nevertheless received a rearing and education far superior to most women of her time, attributed to the kindness of her adoptive family, the Duchemins. Through them

> she was immersed in the French language, culture and heritage. These resources were pivotal in the development of her life and provided her with the key to open doors otherwise closed to her.[14]

This description shines a light on the different forms of capital persons might possess. "Unwed parents" and "mixed race" were qualities that withheld from Theresa the recognition that is the currency of cultural (symbolic) capital. Within the culture, parenting systems other than those religiously and state sanctioned withheld recognition of full personhood, misrecognizing such persons like Theresa's unwed mother as "lower than" on a hierarchy of humanity. Nevertheless, access to education and the resources of cultural capital through her adoptive family equipped Theresa with other forms of capital to overcome such misrecognition. Individuals are heirs to different forms of capital, through the institutions that are the storehouses that make this capital available: institutions of the state, the family, religion, and education.

In considering the institution of professed religious life with the OSPs, the third established order of Catholic women religious in the United States, we might pause to expand the analysis of how diverse kinds of capital flow through institutions of the state, family, religion, and education. Recall that the state directed capital to White citizens through the systems of education, and it was the church that stepped in to fill the gap left when those citizens and others deemed "non-White" were left out. The racialized distribution of government capital saw the church dedicating its resources to address needs unmet by the state. Such charity was crucial to meeting educational needs but enabled the structures of state injustice to remain intact. Systems of the family empowered these foundresses of the OSPs in different ways: Lange with family wealth (in a family configuration recognized by the state), Maxis with a family unrecognized by church or state, moved through systems with capital derived from her adoptive family. But when historians name Theresa as "bright-skinned and blue-eyed," they indicate the symbolic capital of Whiteness, which she was able to leverage despite what she lacked in material resources. Williams explains: "Consensual interracial intimacy and the rampant sexual abuse of Black women and girls produced hundreds of thousands of African-descended people whose skin color and hair texture enabled them to move across society's manufactured racial boundaries and access the privileges and protections of whiteness during slavery's reign."[15]

In the pairing of Maxis and Lange in the work of the OSPs as an arm of the institution of the church, Theresa was more White, but in her indebtedness to the Duchemins, perhaps less free; Lange, a woman of means but unable to access the symbolic capital of Whiteness, yet came to be enriched by the symbolic capital of church leadership as Mother Mary Lange. The two were among the originating four members of the first Black Catholic order of women religious in the United States, but both remained on the periphery of an institutional church ordered toward Whiteness. As marginalized members *in* a White-centered church, nevertheless Lange, Maxis, and other OSPs could leverage the capital *of* a White-centered church for the benefit of dedicating capital to the empowerment of children of color left out of a White supremacist state. The access to capital and leveraging of capital is multifaceted and complex, once again revealing a church that could be participating in the sins of White supremacy yet that also could be used to mitigate its effects.

In the era of their companionship in Baltimore, Theresa Maxis and Mother Mary Lange together worked as representatives of a church that devalued them as they tried to care for a community made marginal by US systems of White supremacy.[16] The Oblate Sisters of Providence, in leveraging the capital of the Catholic Church toward the most marginalized, filled a need created by White supremacist culture in Maryland, not only addressing a structural "lack" in the systems of education but also in the system of health care. In 1832, when a cholera epidemic hit the city, access to clean streets, clean water, adequate housing, health care, and hospitals was directed to Baltimore's White citizens. The Oblates ministered to those left out of state systems of care amid the crisis. Furthermore, "From the late 1820s the state of Maryland increasingly adopted the text and tenor of the racial ideologies of the states in the Deep South, even as it imposed more intrusive restrictions on its free black residents."[17] When Maryland's White citizens (among them notably White Catholics) responded to the uprising of enslaved people led by Nat Turner (in Virginia in 1831) by limiting the movement of free people of color, they included the parameter that African Americans could no longer hold religious meetings without a White minister present. So when the OSPs served the spiritual needs of the Black Catholic community, hosting gatherings in their chapel from 1837 forward, they were filling a spiritual need under the supervision of White Catholic priests. But oversight by White priests was nothing new to Black Catholics, since the White-serving church in America had long since refused to accept Black Catholic men into seminary training. As Morrow concludes, "Maryland legislators utilized legal proscription, forcible expulsion, threat of enslavement, and voluntary colonization to marginalize free black people and to render them social, legal, and political anomalies within the state."[18] While made up of free women of color, the OSPs moved unfreely through systems of the state. Yet with the networks of social capital enhanced by the symbolic capital of recognition as women religious, they did manage to leverage resources of the Catholic Church to serve Baltimore's Black Catholic community from

1828 onward (through a crucial period of 1843–1847, when they experienced a stretch of "clerical neglect" perhaps not unlike the longer period we witnessed at St. James the Greater).[19]

The story of the Oblate Sisters of Providence as free women of color advancing the work of the Catholic educational system takes a turn in 1845 when the congregation splits at the invitation of White clerics (of the Redemptorist order) to expand the Catholic mission to the nation's frontier. Extending the work geographically with ecclesial systems by establishing new institutions in the Midwest, the OSPs, America's first African-descended order of women religious, helped found new institutions of Catholic education. The opportunity for expansion of the church at this time was directly related to state systems of land acquisitions in the early nineteenth century and governed by structures of White supremacy.[20] Only some of the OSPs would be selected to undertake this mission.

## Expanding to a New Frontier

When some members of the nation's first African American congregation of women religious set out to expand the church in what is now the Midwest of our nation (but then was the "frontier"), they were aided both by systems of religion (driven by a theology of mission) and by the power and capital of the state. From a mission perspective, the nineteenth-century Sisters were heeding the "apostolic command" rooted in a biblical directive to "go and make disciples of all nations" (Matthew 28:19). Such an American mission was first announced by Pope Alexander VI in 1493 when he blessed the activity of Christopher Columbus in expanding Christendom through the papal bull *Inter caetera.* Propelled by the third-century aphorism "no salvation outside the Church," pope and people alike approached the project of shaping generations in Catholic spiritual, social, and cultural forms. The spiritual project of "mission" fueled the economic and political project of settler colonialism. In their enthusiasm for the Gospel and their willingness to enter the "wilderness" of the frontier, we might imagine that the women religious shaped in the congregation of the Oblate Sisters of Providence read their work as the next chapter in this expansive mission.

The Sisters were also aided by the generations of legislation from 1493 to 1823 that directed ownership of the land firmly into the hands of White Christians. Assessing the lifeways of Indigenous nations as contrary to God's directive that humans master the earth (revealed to Christians of this period in the biblical design of Genesis 1:28), legislators reasoned that Indigenous peoples had forfeited any right of ownership (since their seminomadic lifestyles kept them only lightly enforcing their rule on the land).[21] From this interpretive vantage point, God ordained that Christian nations claim their rightful place. Just as Pope Alexander VI decreed in 1493, legislators in the new nation echoed the call to Christians to bring to the land "civilization, science and true religion."[22] For White settler-colonists, those who were blessed and carrying out God's wishes were those who related to the earth and its creatures in a particular way: an individual mastery in "subduing" and "dominating" the land that leads toward "progress."[23] It was in this way that "the colonizer invert[ed] the understanding of him-/herself as an invader and [thought] of him-/herself as a native, deeming the native as a foreigner."[24]

Indigenous rights to the land and ancestral lifeways were reasoned away with the aid of the theological concept of the Creator's design. This interpretive pattern came to legal expression in the 1823 Supreme Court decision of *Johnson v. M'Intosh*, which ruled in favor of the White Christian nation's right to ownership through discovery superseding Indigenous peoples' right to occupancy. The theology underwriting the law was captured powerfully in the sentiment of Thomas Hart Benton on the floor of the US Senate in 1846. As elected officials debated another forcible acquisition, this time in the Oregon Territory, Benton proposed, "It would seem that the White race alone received the divine command to subdue and replenish the earth."[25] Across the many projects of settler colonialism, the fundamental assessment that Indigenous peoples were not "subduing the earth" meant that the nation therefore had a divine right to the land and a sacred duty to seize it. By this, White Christians carried out God's sacred plan.

Under the patronage of White Redemptorists, the formerly (African American) Oblate Sisters of Providence expanded their work on an expanding frontier. Not only scripture and legislation but also the government's military arm further secured the Christian salvific project of settlement. The way for them to arrive in this "wilderness" had already been paved by the military power that went before them. Here, it is Zebulon Pike that reflects back to us what may have been the encounter, noting in his diary from the military expedition to the headwaters of the Mississippi that the native peoples "appeared anxious to avoid the Americans," as Americans were considered (in Pike's words) "a vindictive, ferocious and warlike people."[26] And yet, he continues: "Although these impressions seem to have been made with evil intentions toward us, they will have contrary effect when the Indians find our conduct toward them to be magnanimous and just: reverence will then be joined with fear, in estimating the American character."[27] The dual facets of reverence joined with fear were supported by a national ideology asserting that God had destined the United States to become a Christian nation, and it was backed by the military arm of the nation to make it so. In the same era that sees the cementing of the War of 1812 (recall Harry Mahoney's encounter in Maryland from Chapter 2), military structures and systems to protect White settlers were put in place throughout the Midwest (Fort Osage, MO, 1808; Fort Snelling, MN, built 1819–1825; Fort Atkins, IA, 1840, Fort Wilkins, MI, 1844; Fort Collins, CO, 1864). Thinking with the lens of institutions, the military served as another arm of the state at work for the benefit of White Christian settler-colonists.

Understanding itself to have subdued the earth in the military conquest, the state was determined to subdue native peoples by bringing them in to the project of the nation, specifically through education. In this practice, nineteenth-century Catholics continued a project started when the first American Catholic bishop, John Carroll, wrote to his president, George Washington, that conversion to Christianity would facilitate the alignment of Indigenous peoples to state interests, writing that for "Indian tribes [that had] received formerly some instruction in the principles and duties of Christianity . . . a strong attachment was formed in their minds towards the nation."[28] Just under thirty years later, the 1819 "civilization fund" in Congress dedicated resources to bringing Indigenous peoples into a more settled, Euro-American way of life, and forms of Christian mission and Christian missionary education were key features in that national project. When the Redemptorist mission to the Winnebago at Sault Ste. Marie was established, it took root within the networks previously laid down by the Jesuits and other Catholic missions that had created institutions to support White settlers. Traders and shipping companies, government representatives of the military, and specially designated Whites who served as "Indian agents," hoteliers, and settlers formed a network within which Christian missions and schools could be found. As the Catholic Church expanded to the Midwest, it carried with it the longer history of the church and its mission to the Native peoples of the land. Yet while educators had reasoned that Indigenous peoples were teachable, Bishop Peter Paul Lefevere complained that "to give the Indians a full classical education [was] doing him more harm than good."[29] At the same time, priests of Lefevere's diocese were being advised to establish schools in their mission so that in their report to the government they could "show the visible superiority of Catholicism to get a proper share of the $7000 guaranteed by the treaty for the instruction of the savages."[30]

When women religious formed in the congregation of Baltimore agreed to help in the expansion of the church to the Midwest, the wider racial project of assessing native peoples as less than White and Whiteness as superior in culture, religion, and practice was already in the air. They left the endeavor of educating Black children in a White supremacist nation and stepped out into the frontier, where some arms of the church were dedicated to the project of ministering to Indigenous peoples. But the educational task to which the original OSPs were called by the Redemptorists on the frontlines of an expanding nation was to neither of these racialized populations; rather, their mission was to the White frontier settlers of Michigan. The state had paved the way for Theresa Maxis to found a new order (Sisters, Servants of the Immaculate Heart of Mary [IHM]), as she stepped into the role of educating White settlers within Catholic institutions.[31] But her ability to do so was still framed by White supremacist gate keeping and illumines for us the plasticity of racial projects. In a letter from 1859 looking back on the founding of the IHM mission in Monroe in 1845, Bishop Lefevere (of Detroit) writes to Bishop James Wood (in Philadelphia) and describes those Oblates who had been invited to extend the mission as "much whiter than any other of the Sisters."[32] Indeed, the fair-skinned and blue-eyed Theresa, although racialized as a woman of color in Baltimore through her mother's line, was sufficiently categorizable as "White" by phenotypical measures to accompany the White Catholic Redemptorists in the mission. Her companion, Sister Ann Constance, similarly followed from the African American community of the Oblate Sisters of Providence, capitalizing on her Whiteness. But a third sister who was to join them "received word from Sister Therese not to come as her color was too dark."[33] As Morrow comments, "Duchemin (Theresa) and Schaaf (Ann Constance), both light-skinned mulattoes, passed for white in their new religious community, the Sisters, Servants of the Immaculate Heart of Mary in Michigan."[34] The story of Theresa Maxis divesting of Blackness[35] and capitalizing on Whiteness asks us to see the institution of the Catholic Church involved in the institutions of education in many different ways in this era. Leaving behind the mission to educate children who had been sorted into the category "Black," Theresa abandons the project that filled a gap in a White supremacist education system by which children of color—even free children of color—were denied access to the institutions of the state. Traveling to the mission outposts of the Midwest (1845), she also did not participate directly in the educational project of church-facilitated work with Indigenous peoples, which was also a feature of the church's participation in the assimilationist projects of the state. What she represents is the alignment of the church with the interests of White settler-colonists in the mid-nineteenth-century phase of a nation's expansion from East to West.

We might pause to consider two different expressions of the institution of the Catholic Church in two different locations through the experiences of two founding members of the Oblate Sisters of Providence, now embedded within the Oblate Sisters in Baltimore, Maryland, and the newly founded Sisters, Servants of the Immaculate Heart of Mary in Monroe, Michigan. Knowing what we do about the history of struggle for Black Catholics setting up schools in Baltimore and ministering to the sick there, we might experience in a complex way the description of the *Monroe Journal* (Michigan, 1845) and the institution Theresa would step into. Describing the school on the frontier for the purposes of White recruitment, the newspaper reports: "This Institution. . . . is situated in the most beautiful and healthy part of the city, opposite the Catholic Church. . . . The diet is good, wholesome and abundant; spacious grounds afford the pupils the facility of pleasant walks and bodily exercises."[36] The symbolic capital of Whiteness afforded Theresa and Ann Constance the opportunity to be part of the Catholic Church expressed in this location of health, tranquility, and education. Meanwhile, back in Baltimore, Theresa's Sisters in the Oblates struggled: "By 1846 there were only eight students in the school who paid tuition. The order asked permission from the Bishop to beg on the streets in order to help support the convent."[37]

Just pause and envision the same Oblate Sisters in such different locations: some enjoying a facility of spacious grounds and pleasant walks in Michigan, others begging on the streets of Baltimore, both endeavoring to pursue the church's mission. One community engaging the material benefits of Whiteness, the other denied these material resources. Theresa and Ann Constance, in becoming White, could access a different lifestyle and real benefits to their overall health and well-being.

While we might recognize the differential support the Sisters received from the same institution of the Catholic Church distributing its resources in unequal ways, the mission of educating White girls on the frontier still lacked the necessary funds for complete success. While their OSP Sisters in Baltimore were begging on the streets to support their mission, historians recount a different kind of begging trip that Fr. Gillet was undertaking to raise funds for the school in Monroe:

> A Mission given by Father Gillet in New Orleans during the Lent of 1847, proved providential, supplying the nucleus of the building fund ($525.00 and thirteen large boxes of furniture): this was shortly afterwards increased very materially by the settlement of Sister M. Alphonsine's estate (the Godfroy-Smyth estate.)[38]

We would need to explore more fully the source of resources passed through the Godfroy-Smyth estate, but we know that New Orleans in 1847 is rooted firmly, deeply, and expansively in an economy of enslavement. A refrain we might have come to expect in our examination of Catholic institutions is simply: *Where did the money come from, and where did it go?* While Catholic Sisters who had been racially sorted into the category "Black" ministered to Black Catholics by begging in the streets of Baltimore, their sister Catholics who had been racially sorted into the category "White" ministered to White Catholics by tapping into a slave economy, extracting capital from the lives and labors of Black Catholics. It is a special kind of sin that hides the many ways the Catholic Church reaped the benefits from an economy of enslavement. It will take a special kind of grace to face White supremacy in the capital inheritance of our education system.

## High-Profile Catholics in a Nation's Racial Project

It was an ideology of White Christian supremacy that marched "progress" across the land, establishing industry and cities and White civilization. Backed by the military arm of a White Christian nation, White industry, White wealth, and White well-being could be secured, even as wealth building and well-being were denied people of color. This was a racial project, to be sure, but it was simultaneously a theological project. In the religio-racial project of White Christian supremacy, the essentialized characteristics of "religion" were attendant with imagined features of "race." These ideological and theological imaginings of peoples racialized into the categories of White, Black, and Indian fueled frontier missions that built up White settler Catholics and contributed to the ongoing struggles of Indigenous peoples and Black Americans.

Frontier territories were sites for the accumulation of White wealth and the establishment of White Catholic institutions, but northern locations could also be the last stop on a journey to freedom for the formerly enslaved who had self-emancipated. Our historical reckoning should include a willingness to ask the question of whether the resources of the institutions of the Catholic Church were mobilized to support the freedom struggle under the yoke of enslavement in its many forms. Were frontier White Catholics crafted with the spiritual capital to sustain the struggle for freedom by mobilizing their resources to support the formerly enslaved? Historians can tell us, for example, that Michigan was a crucial location for a network that leveraged resources to aid formerly enslaved persons through the Underground Railroad. In fact, just a day's journey from where the IHMs settled in Monroe, we have evidence of the solidaristic practice of the people of Marshall, Michigan, who protected the Crosswhite family when slavers from Kentucky brought vigilante "justice" to return the Crosswhites under the legal guarantee of the Fugitive Slave Law (1846). Further archival investigation is required, however, to know whether Catholics in Michigan supported or were threatened by these networks. Given the national Catholic narrative of state's rights and "law and order" promoted in Catholic media originating from the East Coast, it is difficult to imagine the church taking a stance other than the protection of White interests to protect White "property." But deeper investigation and our historical truth telling may also present us with otherwise possibilities fueled by the Catholic faith.

While the military power, legal system, and educational infrastructure of the state prioritized White well-being, Black Christians could leverage their locations within some of these systems to assert their full humanity. Take Minnesota as a case in point that illuminates cross-country connections to Baltimore and a criss-cross extending from Missouri to New York. The work of the historian Christopher Lehman reveals how travel via the new technology of steamboat (in 1854) quickly made Minnesota ready for tourism, joining White Christian industry, with White Christian church and school building, White Christian military presence, and now White Christian recreation. While Minnesota eventually emerged as a free state within the Union in 1858, Lehman asks us to feel the presence of slaveholding wealth and investment in the infrastructure in order to see that the naming Minnesota as a "free state" isn't a clear and straightforward story; it is, rather, a story of struggle.[39] Even though eventually settling as a free state, the Minnesota Territory allowed the presence of enslaved persons with their captors and named them as "property," in deference to the laws governing their state of origin. Here, enslaved people leveraged the priority of a state's right to define the law in order to argue their freedom. So when White vacationers traveled to Minnesota, enslaved persons accompanying their enslaver on holiday, for example Eliza Winston, could use the court system to petition for their freedom.[40] Or when enslaved persons moved through the geography of free and unfree territories as part of the movement of White people in the military network of the states, enslaved Christians like Harriet and Etheldred Scott could leverage their residence at Fort Snelling (Minnesota), situated as it was within a landscape of freedom, to override the laws their home state of Missouri. But in the complex configuration of movement between free and unfree, White interests were also leveraged in the courts. Even the state granting freedom to enslaved persons could be overturned by a White supremacist nation. Consider the shifting reality of Harriet and Etheldred: "The Scotts' case was based on the fact that they lived as enslaved people in free territory at Fort Snelling and other places, and therefore should be granted their freedom. The Scotts lost their initial trial, but they appealed the decision and were granted their freedom in January 1850."[41] Stepping into the possibilities that laws governing a free state might afford them, the Scotts employed the court system to gain their freedom. Yet in a litigious nation bent on protecting White property, the case could be overturned: "Irene Emerson appealed the verdict, and the case was sent to the Missouri Supreme Court in 1852 where the Scotts lost."[42] Given the pace of the court system and the machinations of White interests, when the Scotts moved to appeal the 1852 loss, Emerson protected her investment:

> Irene Emerson transferred ownership of the Scotts to her brother, John Sanford [*sic*], who lived in New York. Because the case then involved residents of two different states (Missouri and New York), there was precedent to have it tried in a federal court. The Scotts filed suit in the Missouri federal court in 1853, and after losing the following year appealed the decision to the US Supreme Court in February 1856.[43]

In this short paragraph, we have witnessed an eight-year struggle by Black Christians Harriet and Etheldred Scott to find freedom in a White supremacist state. Here we can see once again an agonistic legal system pitting rights of property over rights of personhood. But the struggle reveals something more: While enslaved people were governed by the laws of the state of origin, enslavers were not, since the White Sandford resided in a state that barred the ownership of human beings (New York), yet he could still "own" human property in the slave state of Missouri. Kicked up into the highest court of the land, it was a Catholic judge who would speak on behalf of a racist nation. "A devout Catholic and an active member of the Baltimore Cathedral congregation," it was Roger Taney's job to interpret what the Constitution had to say in what came to be known as the *Dred Scott* case.[44]

What we see in the practices of law parallel interestingly with the practices of interpreting scripture, that is, the text of the Constitution is presented to the reader, and the reader makes meaning within the symbolic capital of a shared community in order render the text "legible."[45] Given the shifting sense of the meaning of words in context, the "text" is never straightforward but must be interpreted in order to draw out its meaning. Such was the letter of the law in relation to the freedom of those bound in slavery when entering territories and states that disallowed the practice of holding in bondage other human beings. It is clear that some within the US legislative system interpreted the law to afford enslaved persons the right to argue their changed status when residing in a "free state." This was the interpretation activated by Scott for himself, his wife, and his two daughters, bringing suit to court over his treatment by John A. Sandford. Sandford, a citizen of the state of New York (a free state), claimed ownership of the Scott family in Missouri (a state that defended the maintenance of humans as property). But in the struggle for racial justice in our nation's history, no single interpretation of the moral law or the law of the land was ever fully settled. When the case was raised to the nation's Supreme Court, the court was split, and their agonistic deliberations were published as dissenting opinions. But Taney wrote for the decision of the Supreme Court that denied Scott his citizenship and therefore his freedom. Taney's bottom line: "The Constitution of the United States recognizes slaves as property, and pledges the Federal Government to protect it."[46] Taney based his ruling opinion on the ideology of White supremacy, which he claimed that all the White people of Europe (and therefore also in America) had agreed upon. He reveals to us the "racial project" that had been manufactured by philosophers (like Immanuel Kant), anthropologists, botanists, and those involved in "race science," and he concludes that enslaved persons

> had for more than a century before been regarded as beings of an inferior order, and altogether unfit to associate with the white race, either in social or political relations; and so far inferior, that they had no rights which the white man was bound to respect; and that the negro might justly and lawfully be reduced to slavery for his benefit. He was bought and sold, and treated as an ordinary article of merchandise and traffic, whenever a profit could be made by it. This opinion was at that time fixed and universal in the civilized portion of the white race. It was regarded as an axiom in morals as well as in politics, which no one thought of disputing, or supposed to be open to dispute; and men in every grade and position in society daily and habitually acted upon it in their private pursuits, as well as in matters of public concern; without doubting for a moment the correctness of this opinion.[47]

Taney erases any of the struggle that we can see among the American people, the colonists, philosophers, and theologians of the United States and Europe and conveys what he assesses to be the majority opinion of White people, carrying on a tradition of considering enslaved people "so far inferior, that they had no rights which the white man was bound to respect." Rendering Black persons as "property," the White Catholic Taney allowed White supremacy to be read as "fixed and universal in the civilized portion of the white race."[48] Taney is mobilizing White Enlightenment thought that supposes the possibility that the universal, "civilized," and White race forms the united frame of final decision making.

While Americans are often enticed to believe that our history reflects a "separation of church and state," this has hardly been the case in the practice of law throughout US history. Indeed, scholars draw attention to the fact that Taney seems to have read the Constitution through a hermeneutical lens aligned with the position of the wider American Catholic Church. Morrow writes: "Taney's legal position on slavery coincided with the position assumed by the Roman Catholic Church: both accepted the fact of the institution of slavery, but both decried the abuses and atrocities inherent in the system."[49] The close reading of the American bishops' defense of the practices of enslavement we encountered in the previous chapter helps us see the missed opportunity the Catholic Church had in the ongoing struggle for a racial justice that would affirm the full humanity of enslaved Catholics, indeed the full humanity of all people. While the church was ministering to enslaved persons, it was not aimed at fundamentally dismantling the systems of enslavement. In Taney's decision, the Catholic Church missed an opportunity—an otherwise possibility—to inform positively the state. Perhaps this could have been the case had the Catholic Church in Baltimore been structured differently or had Taney experienced a more robust encounter with the successful work of the Oblate Sisters of Providence.[50] Or, even if he had known of the plasticity of racial projects (when the Catholic IHM Sisters moved from "Black" to "White"). Instead, Taney's Supreme Court decision aimed at cementing Blackness in such a way that the material benefits granted and withheld were locked into place. White Americans like John Sandford and Irene Emerson and literally countless others would receive the benefit of claiming the profits of their "property" while Black Americans like Etheldred and Harriett Scott would lose another dimension of their personhood in the loss of their freedom.

In Patrick Carey's analysis, Taney's position emerged from a deeper root cause in a Catholicism that bifurcated the sacred and the profane, arguing "a fundamental separation . . . of the temporal and spiritual orders of existence."[51] Such a position held that the church should speak on matters "spiritual" but should not touch the structural or systems of "the profane." In Taney's work, we see the replication of a Catholic position we've encountered in the letters of the slaveholding Bishop John England to Secretary of State John Forsyth, in Bishop Reynolds's 1843 editorial, and Bishop Kendrick's *Theologia Moralis* (examined in chapter 3). We might sense that Taney faithfully conveyed what he and countless other Catholics had received as symbolic capital in the preaching each week, in Catholic systems of education, or in the Catholic media. Bishop Reynolds synthesized this for us, arguing that "nothing should be attempted against the laws," that "the Apostles, inspired by the Holy Ghost, taught slaves to obey their temporal masters," and that the Lord of both slaver and enslaved "is in Heaven," and "with Him there is no acceptation of persons."[52] Such a position was reflected in Taney's reasoning and later reported in the Catholic media: "Our clergy and press have been true to their mission. Our priests in the North, whatever their private opinions about slavery have not desecrated their pulpits by slavery harangues. Our clergy in the South, who have a true appreciation of the facts, preach to the slaves' obedience, and to the masters' clemency."[53] In our truth telling, we can see that high-profile

Catholics contributed their anti-Blackness to a US racial project. With analysis, we can see how this rested on a bifurcation of the sacred and profane and on the status quo of systems that directed benefits to White Christians.

Here we might pause to consider how the words of symbolic capital in preaching, teaching, and writing create worlds of material and social capital when informing US law. If we are still wondering how theological ideas create symbolic capital that affects material reality (that is, how words create worlds), it is traceable from symbolic capital to social capital of people power and the experience of that power among those who legislated the structure of our worlds. Capital in its many forms flows through institutions governed by education and religion and through to the institutions of the state and its legal system in just this way.

Yet the witness of Orestes Brownson pushes back to remind us that it could have been otherwise, for Brownson argued with both Taney and the US Catholic bishops that history is one and that the Catholic faith requires a "synthetic theology of life." This led Brownson into the high-profile location of Catholic media mounting an opposition to slavery. As Patrick Carey reports, Brownson's counterposition to the spiritualization of the realm of the church was to see

> natural and supernatural, nature and grace, reason and faith, earth and heaven, are not antagonistic forces, to be reconciled only by the suppression of the one or the other, but really parts of a dialectical whole, which, to the eye that can take in the whole in all its parts, and all the parts in the whole, in which they are integrated, would appear perfectly consistent with each other, living the same life in God, and directed by him to one and the same end.[54]

Brownson published not only his antislavery vision, but publicly wrangled with high-profile clerics, denouncing their defenses of the institution of slavery. It is only through this public wrestling, conveyed in the Catholic press, that we come to see clearly the complicity of even northern archbishops like John Hughes of New York in making theological peace with the evils of enslavement for the benefit of White Catholics.[55] Simultaneously, the Catholic press of the mid-nineteenth century reveals to us the ways in which the church encompassed White people on differing sides of the economy of enslavement. The idea of an "otherwise possibility" embedded in the history we pursue comes forward from this consideration of Brownson. What if more Catholics had been persuaded by the integralist position Brownson advanced, where the spiritual formed an integrated whole with the social, historical, and political? What road not taken in Catholic political practice is revealed when Brownson reasons that God directs the church *in the world* to the fullness of life together?

Taney's rendering of the Supreme Court decision and Brownson's public engagement with high-profile Catholics reveals the struggle at the heart of Catholic participation in the US racial project during an era of enslavement. It reveals also that the US racial project was not only Black and White but that legislation, military force, religion, and education were simultaneously sorting some people into the category of "Black" and others into the category of "Indian." The US racial project of the mid-nineteenth century constructed these categories of "other than White" in different ways, while maintaining a hierarchy of racial ordering with White at the "top." White supremacy looked differently when inflicted on diversely racialized people, but nevertheless, it was still always for the benefit of those categorized as White. Note Taney's assessment of those he has racialized as Black: They were "so far inferior" and "altogether unfit to associate with the white race." Commenting within the *Dred Scott* decision, by contrast Indian subjects *could* become citizens. Taney writes that Indian tribes "within the limits of the U.S. [were] under subjection to the white race," albeit with the hopes for assimilation. Because of this assimilationist goal, it was "necessary" (Taney reasoned) "to regard them in a state of pupilage." Conveying the sentiment set out in *Johnson v. M'Intosh* (1823), Taney continued:

> Many of these political communities were situated in territories to which the white race claimed the ultimate right of dominion. But that claim was acknowledged to be subject to the right of the Indians to occupy it as long as they thought proper. . . . It is true that the course of events has brought the Indian tribes within the limits of the United States under subjection to the white race; and it has been found necessary, for their sake as well as our own, to regard them as in a state of pupilage, and to legislate to a certain extent over them and the territory they occupy. But they may, without doubt, like the subjects of any other foreign Government, be naturalized by the authority of Congress and become citizens of a State, and of the United States.[56]

Taney is thus both reflecting *and* shaping America's racial project in an economy of enslavement, whereby the decision he rendered regarding the possibilities of citizenship for African-descended people within the United States (which were denied) simultaneously revealed that there were possibilities of citizenship for Indigenous people within the United States. While African-descended people were racialized as "property," those categorized as "Indian" were destined for "pupilage." Such pupilage was necessary from the view of coloniality so that the White nation could hold the reins in determining how best to deal with human life upon the land. The efforts of the state to render the people into "civilized citizens" were aggressively pursued.

## "Saving the Man": The Salvific Project of Indian Education

With the further enrichment of US land holdings through newly confiscated geographies acquired through the military aggression of the war with the United States of Mexico (1846–1848), structures and systems were put in place to incorporate and populate this land through the institutions of American society. White Americans benefited in fundamental ways from this era's dispossession. In 1851, Congress legislated the control and containment of Indigenous nations with the Indian Appropriations Act, which created the nation's reservation system, parceling land and moving Indigenous nations to locations with newly drawn boundaries. Through the decades-long projects of allotment to tribal nations and to individuals within them, the US government claimed the "surplus" for furthering US interests. In 1862, the Homestead Act enabled White citizen-settlers to claim ownership of a share of this land (facilitating wealth building through land ownership), and that same year Congress established the system of land-grant universities through the Morrill Act. Legally, methodically, and piece by piece, a White Christian nation built up its (White) citizens on the foundational premise of White Christian ownership of the land and the superiority of White culture and religion.

In the era of nation building and expansion, the War Department and industry were conjoined, and church ministers could be acting very much as instruments of the state. After Congress legislated on the Oregon Territory in 1848, it was the military arm of the US government that paved the way for the railway, which itself was the project of the US government securing settler access to the area.[57] As Cyril Van der Donckt described in the settlement of the United States in relation to Indigenous nations in the Northwest, "In 1869, the Government assigned a military officer as agent to each agency [what we might call 'mission' or 'tribal nation']. In 1870, Congress passed an Act substituting as agents the ministers of the various religious denominations."[58] Priding themselves on their expert knowledge, the Jesuits disseminated the idea of Indigenous people's teachability through various academic, ecclesial, and missionary publications.[59] But the teachability of native peoples would require a distancing from the inherent qualities that adhered to them as a race and would require the rejection of Indigenous lifeways to more perfectly pursue God's plan. In 1877, Augustus Thebaud SJ, a former St John's Fordham president, explained in the widely disseminated *The Month and Catholic Review*:

> A sufficient study of the Red Indian will prove that he was not only a pagan, when the first Catholic missionaries came—not only a degraded savage, but in appearance totally unfit for a *settled* life, either as an agriculturalist, a fisherman, or even as a hunter, the wildest of all the pursuits of inferior tribes. . . . Now, before a pagan can become a thorough Christian he must be made to a certain extent at least, a man of steady habits.[60]

Steady habits and a settled life were necessary ingredients for the mastery reflective of those who would become thoroughly Christian.

The drive toward "settlement" had devastating effects on the practice of native lifeways, but it brought positive benefits for White citizens of the nation. When *Johnson v. M'Intosh* decided that Indigenous peoples had ever only had a "right to occupancy" but invading Christian nations' "right of discovery" granted them ownership, economic benefits of title to land remained in White hands.[61] With the 1862 Homestead Act (and subsequent reiterations) and the 1887 Dawes/Allotment Act, US territorial expansion came to advantage White settlers when Indigenous peoples were forced to conform to the ideal of individual ownership of land. As described by the US Department of the Interior:

> After [native] families claimed their allotments, any remaining tribal lands were declared "surplus" land. These lands were then sold off to non-native settlers. Additional legislation like the Homestead Acts further encouraged white settlement of the West, and with that settlement came calls for assimilation. Many settlers viewed native practices as barbaric and primitive, seeing assimilation as the only option for coexistence.[62]

With enforced lifeways of individual ownership, the federal project turned to cultivate in Indigenous peoples the mastery it would take to survive.

No project became more central to the state's aim of incorporation and assimilation than the system of education. Willie James Jennings places this work in the racial project of the day when he describes how "master formation meant entrance into the racial paterfamilias through which indigenes would enter the European world of civilization and citizenship and thereby enter their humanity."[63] The project of Catholic and Jesuit education was situated in the matrix of mastery in a threefold way. First, White Catholic and Jesuit institutions were among those that benefited from the acquisition of formerly native lands in the nineteenth century.[64] Second, White Catholic and Jesuit thinkers produced "knowledge" about Indigenous peoples through their proximity in missionary and educational settings. And third, White Catholic and Jesuit institutions acquired benefits through their practices of educating native children. While participation in the US project of assimilation brought benefits to Catholic institutions of school and church, it was a mixed inheritance of benefits and deficits for Indigenous people.

Throughout the nineteenth century, Catholics and Jesuits drew resources for their theological mission from the state, as mission schools were subsidized by the US government from 1810 to 1917.[65] Catholics competed with other Christian denominations for government sponsorship by setting up schools on their missions. It was not until the 1860s that the government established its own federal school system for Native Americans and "in 1879 opened the first off-reservation Indian boarding school, Carlisle Indian School in Carlisle, Pennsylvania."[66] The founder of Carlisle, Brigadier General Richard Henry Pratt, had developed a way to "successfully" extract Indigenous men from the compromising influence of native culture in his experimental prisoner-of-war camp transporting Apache warriors from defeat on the southern plains to his regimented camp in Florida. Pratt's model, tested on prisoners of war, became the template for the Indian school for Indigenous youth set up in the former Carlisle Barracks.[67] As an indication of the initial and ongoing resistance to the program, Pratt reports the response of Chief Spotted Tail (Brulé Sioux), who indicts the values promoted in such a system. When asked to send his young people, Spotted Tail responded:

> The white people are all thieves and liars. We do not want our children to learn such things. The white man is very smart. He knew that there was gold in the Black Hills and he made us agree to give up all that country and now a great many white people are there getting out the gold. . . . We are not going to give any children to learn such ways.[68]

The mastery of deception and extraction from the land for personal gain had been well exhibited by White settlers. In response, Pratt did not deny Spotted Tail's accusations of White settlers and the US government but argued that Indigenous people would have been better equipped to navigate such deceptions had they been educated in White ways.[69] This is the double-edgedness of White-centered education in a White supremacist state. Over the next eighty years, Indigenous parents would wrestle with the benefits and liabilities that the US system of education could provide, and they would determine variously whether or not to participate, whether by agreement, coercion, or force.[70]

To equip Indigenous peoples to become "useful citizens"[71] and to cultivate the mastery that would "save the man," Pratt's program required the geographical removal of young people from their family-tribal network, a military regimen, an educational curriculum in English, and physical labor.[72] Because even government-run schools included a curriculum of Christian education, many of the schools were overseen by Christian denominations. Catholic orders also pursued their own educational projects modeled on Pratt's program, some even intending to "rival Carlisle," as John Mullan, director of the Bureau of Catholic Indian Missions described the Jesuit-run St. Ignatius in 1885. In Mullan's words: "We want St. Ignatius in the future to be a model mechanical and industrial boarding school to which Congress and the U.S. Indian Department may be able to point as a type and a pattern to be followed by all other Indian schools in the states and territories."[73]

The Jesuits had long been pursuing a program in which their schools would be recognizable as model institutions, as reflected in St. Ignatius's *Ratio studiorum*, developed in 1599 and revised in 1832. As Gerald McKevitt describes, Jesuit pedagogy of the day reflected

> a high priority on a pupil's early mental and moral formation, the typical Jesuit *collegium* comprised two departments, the first of which was roughly equivalent to the modern high school and the second to collegiate studies. . . . The ideal scholar exhibited *eloquentia perfecta*, or articulate wisdom. . . . To achieve this lofty end, the preferred course of studies centered on the humanities, especially classical Greek and Latin, the natural sciences, philosophy, and, to a lesser degree, theology.[74]

Yet while this vision of education propelled Jesuit schooling for White students across the United States during this era (in many cases on land recently transferred from Indigenous nations), the model of *ratio studiorum* and *eloquentia perfecta* was withheld from native youth. Instead Jesuit and Catholic schools formed Indigenous children into the labor class of a hierarchically ordered society. As Lorenzo Palladino SJ reported, in the late nineteenth and into the twentieth century:

> The training of the Indian should be industrial: for after religion, next in importance as a factor of Indian civilization, must be placed manual labor. This is all the more true, because our Indians have a deep aversion to real labor; and as lack of industrial activity is what actually causes their uncivilized condition in the material sense, it is likewise what perpetuates it. Consequently, it is impossible to civilize them, except by forming them to habits of industry and useful toil.[75]

For Palladino, manual labor was a necessary first step toward civilization that incorporated a mastery over the self in the process of the mastery of industry.

The internal conflict of Jesuit Catholic schools serving Indigenous students and White with very different curricular aims is evidenced in the history of Gonzaga University, founded in 1887. It is also a case study in the foundations laid by military, industry, settler colonialism, and the church. As the Jesuit missions to Indigenous nations expanded across the Plains, Fr. Joseph Cataldo "wanted to build a school for the tribes they were serving and decided to look around the area of Spokane Falls because [in Cataldo's words] 'that would be a central point for our Missions where we could build a large school for Indian children, or even for white, if many should come to the country.'"[76] In fact, a White, Christian government made it not only possible but profitable for White settlers to come to the Pacific Northwest. Some among those White families who claimed land in what would become Washington State had built their family wealth within an economy of enslavement. Money from the government supported the White industry of the railroads,[77] and settlers also were supported by a government transfer of lands from Indigenous nations, as the 1862 Homestead Act provided the transfer of title at low cost for those who would help build the nation (at this time Chinese workers and African Americans would have been excluded from these purchases, as they were not citizens). The Department of the Interior sold land to the Great Northern Railroad at $2.50 acre, and in 1881 Fr. Cataldo purchased 320 acres from Great Northern Railroad. Here both the government and industry afforded ecclesial educational opportunities for the Jesuit Catholic school system. While the government supported the move of White settlers through these systems, in the same year (1881) the government, through President Rutherford B. Hayes, established the Spokane Indian Reservation (154,602 acres known as Chief Lot's reservation).

> Soon after Cataldo's purchase, the settlers in Spokane Falls wrote to Fr. Cataldo asking him to build them a college that would attract students from all parts of the west, even as far away as California. James Glover, sometimes called the Father of Spokane, gathered fifteen other settlers and sent Cataldo another letter, pledging $2,650 to help build a college. . . . The bishop for the Washington territory was also urging Fr. Cataldo to build a college in Spokane Falls.[78]

Note the leveraging of wealth from the slaving family of James Glover, born in Port Tobacco, Maryland (near the Jesuit plantations of Chapter 1), who moved to Catholic-rich locations like St. Louis and Kentucky, through the military to Minnesota, and ultimately directed his capital to the Pacific

Northwest.[79] Our Catholic institutions are once again recognized as embedded in these criss-crossing systems of White supremacy. Under the leadership of Cataldo, the college was built, and the Jesuit never lost sight of his original vision of inviting Indigenous students to join the educational endeavor. But when the college opened in 1887 and Cataldo attempted to enroll students from the surrounding tribes, the native students were denied entrance. The structures and systems of government, the military, education, industry, and the church had been formulated to serve White Christians exclusively. And when Gonzaga developed its own form of military training on campus, it was clear whose interests would be protected in this church-run undertaking.

Although Catholics and Jesuits had established schools across the nation for the education of young people, the majority of these institutions remained White serving and the education of Indigenous youth crafted as a separate project. This was a case of "separate and unequal" when we consider the content of the curriculum and the structure of the setting developed to serve Indian youth. A theological assessment was already in place by which the education of tribal nations required the separation from Indigenous lifeways, which were seen as a compromising and degrading influence for the salvific mission of a Christian education. By the 1890s, "nearly three-fourths of appropriations" from the government were being directed to Catholic-run Indian schools.[80] In the beginning of the twentieth century, the Jesuit-educated Ignatius Horstmann, as bishop of Cleveland, concluded that "all who have investigated the Catholic schools admit that the Catholic plan for the civilization of the Indians is the only practical one."[81] Boarding schools could either be located on the reservation (to serve as a model for the wider conversion of the tribe) or off-reservation, drawing children from many different tribes and often at a great distance from their homes. In either of these cases, the Catholic-run educational mission directed toward Indigenous children was premised on the necessity of separation from what was profane in order to inculcate students in the sacred mission of a salvific civilizing. Here we see again a nineteenth-century pattern of the church involving itself with what is "sacred" and distancing itself from what it considered "profane." In Palladino's description of the necessity of this division, the Catholic education of Indigenous youth can be seen: "We say emphatically, the red man of the mountains is still too much a savage for anyone to entertain even the faintest hope of civilizing him by means of a day school. . . . How can you civilize these savage beings, except you withdraw them from the blighting influences that encompass them on every side?"[82] The compromising influences of a profane home culture continued to be a threat to full conversion, and separation from home in the boarding school continued to be the norm into the twentieth century.[83]

In the many years of Christian mission and Christian education, the drive of "mastery" would continue to be regulated by White Christians, who assessed one's standing before God according to the measure of White Christianity. No form of self-mastery by Indigenous peoples could be positively assessed unless it conformed to the mastery of the White masters. The limits of Indigenous mastery and the supremacy of White ways of relating to God were disseminated through Catholic publications like the *Indian Sentinel*. In 1910, the Jesuit J. B. Carroll reflected on not only the supremacy of White ways but on the foolishness of the Piëgan Indians, who tried to employ those ways outside the control of the White master:

> For, because they know a little of the ways of the white man, they think themselves wise, and in their conceit they are satisfied with themselves, imagining that their ways are as good for Indians as white people's ways are for white people. They use the education borrowed from white people to strengthen their position in barbarism, and if they can read and write a little . . . no white man need tell them anything. Many of them seem to have some respect for Christianity and civilization, but they think that their old heathen customs are just as good as civilized customs, and even more venerable.[84]

Not content to advance his argument on the basis of culture or educational attainment, Carroll drives his point home *theologically*:

> Now the religion of the Piëgan Indians is devil-worship, clearly so; for although they will tell white people that they pray to God, yet we know that they pray to the sun, to the earth, to the rocks, and a host of other unintelligent creatures, to which they attribute divine power. God condemns such worship.[85]

In Carroll's reasoning, White people knew better than Indians about Indian practices because White people have a superior understanding of what God desires. A similar theological pattern of bringing Indigenous peoples to a better relationship with God was expressed in the very last edition of the *Indian Sentinel*, published in 1962, which announced its purpose as "to bring God nearer to the Indians and to bring the Indians nearer to God."[86] In an imaginary that relied on a distinction between the sacred and the profane, White ways of knowing and relating to God continued to reside on the side of the sacred, and Indigenous practices were placed in the profane (or demonic).

## White Supremacies in the Mission to Indian and Black Catholics

The establishment of Catholic Indian boarding schools that followed the state project of educating Indigenous children illuminates the patterns and practices of the Catholic Church, which was a multiracial institution but simultaneously prioritized Whiteness. Pressing further, we can also see the patterns of the Catholic Church's distribution of capital that named ecclesial efforts toward both Indigenous and Black Catholics under the category of "mission." Such symbolic capital designated *some* among the Catholic Church's ecclesial stations properly "church" and other of the ecclesial stations merely "missions." The consistent rendering of a White Catholic Church distributing its capital in racist ways, insofar as the patterns elevated White Catholics and left at a disadvantage Black and Indigenous Catholics, is a key to an analysis that might inform our revisiting of history with the purpose of transforming institutions.

While in some places the Catholic Church stepped in to fill a gap in White supremacist society by providing resources for church and school, in the late nineteenth and early twentieth century the work of the church in Black and Indian missions rested on individual financial commitment and less on institutional support. Here, an individual might use the systems and structures of the church as network to distribute resources the church itself had failed to dedicate. Such is the story of Katharine Drexel, heiress to an investment fortune, who used her expansive inheritance as a Catholic woman to fund a variety of projects aimed at evangelization in North America. According to Amanda Bresie, "The Drexel family financed the bulk of the Catholic Indian missions in the late nineteenth century."[87] Working closely with the Bureau of Catholic Indian Missions, "established in 1874 to lobby the government on behalf of Catholic mission interests," Drexel mobilized individual family wealth through the systems of religion and state.[88] "Between 1895 and 1928, Drexel estimated that she supplied almost $6,000,000 to the Indian missions for buildings, maintenance, and subsidies, not counting funds for the SBS [Sisters of the Blessed Sacrament for Indians and Colored People, founded by Drexel] schools."[89] It was Drexel's Sisters who provided religious education for students at government boarding schools like Carlisle, collaborating with the state in pursuing the Catholic religious mission.[90]

At the same time, it was an infusion of capital from Mother Katharine Drexel that sustained many Black Catholic parishes, like St. James the Greater in Colleton County, South Carolina (whose story we studied in Chapter 3). In the archives of the Sisters of the Blessed Sacrament are found letters sent by Fr. Barberich both requesting funds and thanking Mother Katherine for her consistent economic support for the mission at St. James the Greater. The fate of the Catholic school at St. James the Greater is further embedded in the structures and systems of a White supremacist state simultaneously in a double-bind of a White supremacist church. As Shannen Dee Williams reports, the state continued to prioritize White students. "South Carolina spent over four times more educating a white child than a Black child, and only about 12 percent of the state's African American youth aged fourteen to seventeen were enrolled in a secondary school in 1933."[91] This made St. James the Greater's educational program and success of utmost importance in its landscape and historical context. Letters from the archives indicate that Drexel lent her support in from 1901 to 1955. Yet missions dependent on individual donations reveal again an institutional Catholic Church embedded in the ideologies, structures, and systems of White supremacy. For just as easily as individual decisions could be made to dedicate personal resources to "mission" projects, they could be cut off. As letters in the archives reveal: "June 1, 1955 *The death of Reverend Mother M Katherine Drexel on March 3, 1955 necessitated an end to many donations among which they would have to include that to Catholic Cross Roads.*"[92] Still a "mission" on the "frontier" of the diocese of Charleston, more than one hundred years after it was founded it was still not fully sustained by the diocese. Instead, St. James the Greater relied on the private wealth of its benefactress Drexel to pay salaries for the education of Black children and upkeep of buildings, a benefaction that could easily be withdrawn.

Drexel's benevolence and benefaction toward the education and mission for those racialized as "Indian" and "Black" reflects again a church that could be simultaneously working to alleviate the structural inequalities of a White supremacist state yet also participating in its ideologies and exclusions. For even while Drexel dedicated funds to these educational causes, her congregation of women religious refused admittance for those racialized as "other than White." Williams chronicles how Drexel's Sisters of the Blessed Sacrament

> formally voted against admitting African Americans and Native Americans to their ranks. An entry from the SBS annals from 1896 recounted the 1893 decision, citing "the strong racial feeling now existing in this country with respect to the Indian and Colored Races," "social prejudice" among potential white recruits, [and] "the innate sensitiveness of both Indians and Colored."[93]

Here we see a White Catholic racial project at work. The White Sisters of Drexel's SBS recognized the prejudice of White Catholics and how hurtful this prejudice might be to women racialized as "Indian" or "Black." Seeing these racist patterns in White Catholic women, SBS administrators chose to protect those prejudices and imagine racial disharmony because of the "overly sensitive" response of potential Black or Indigenous Sisters. Instead of denouncing said patterns of White supremacy, responsibility for potential disharmony was placed on Black and Brown Sisters as having maladjusted sensitivities owing to their race. This is racialization at work: the creation of racial categories with innate characteristics by which resources could be distributed or withheld. It was a refusal of social and spiritual capital by which a White-only community of women religious was defended; it was this White-serving body that determined the distribution of Drexel's White wealth to missions in Catholic educational endeavors.

In advancing its agenda of state-recognized Catholic education, the church could also be caught not only in the interpersonal racism of White supremacy but also in the racist systemic structures that advanced White interests. At this structural level Williams again is instructive as she describes the network of Catholic schools in the post–World War I era:

> Although the Catholic Church, which operated the nation's largest independent school system, had fiercely resisted earlier secular attempts to regulate its educational facilities, ecclesiastical authorities largely reversed their stance in the postwar years. Believing that state approval would elevate the standards of Catholic education and bolster the Church's expansion projects, Church leaders embraced the national campaign for accreditation. As a result, the higher education of sisters—on whose under-paid labor the Catholic educational system depended—became a top priority for Church school boards and the leadership councils of teaching sisterhoods. However, white clerical demands that all Catholic teachers become state certified posed a seemingly insurmountable challenge for the Black teaching sisterhoods. Church mandates and canon law dictated that all Catholics be educated in Catholic schools. Yet most US Catholic colleges, universities, and normal institutes systematically excluded African Americans from admission on the basis of race. As a consequence the Black teaching sisterhoods had to secure the higher training of their members and the accreditation of their schools with minimal support from their church.[94]

What this chapter in our study reveals is that the institution of the Catholic Church not only drew capital from the land of Indigenous peoples and unpaid labor of peoples of African descent but that it distributed its capital in the late nineteenth and throughout the twentieth century in a racially biased—indeed, racist—way. Williams concludes: "The Catholic Church's financial support of its Black schools always paled in comparison to its support of its white institutions."[95] The differential experience of those educated in Indian schools reveals another demonstration of the way a multiracial church distributed its capital in unequal ways.

## What "Salvation" Looked Like: Twentieth-Century Boarding Schools

In the analysis of Willie James Jennings, the outlook of White Christians was that the Western education system was "crucial for reforming native inhabitants away from what [the] self-sufficient white man perceived as their infantile and hopelessly tribal ways of life that undermined their sense of intellectual independence and individualism."[96] Following Jennings, education for Indigenous youth was not an entirely different project than that for White youth, because "White self-sufficient masculinity is the quintessential image of an educated person, an image deeply embedded in the collective psyche of Western education and theological education."[97] But the assessment of Indigenous lifeways as "infantile" and culture getting in the way of the project of Christian education was distinctive. The structure of the boarding school, *as boarding*, was premised on the necessity of a divine disconnection from cultural practices, which would be replaced by a setting saturated with the effects of Catholic life. As survivors report from the experience at boarding schools in the northern Plains region, the regimented schedule of military precision was punctuated by enforced liturgical and prayer practices throughout the day:

> We were put in schools. The first school we were put in was a Catholic [school] called St. Junipero Serra. . . . It was all regimented. Everything was militarized. (Tommy Davis)[98]

> We had to march everywhere. It was something that you had to do. . . . They were very strict and very disciplined and they wanted everything their way, and if they didn't get it you got disciplined. . . . In the morning . . . no matter how small you were you fixed your bed, got yourself together. We went to church, then we went and ate breakfast. . . . We went to lunch, and then had a little Mass, a little prayer session in the afternoon. And then at night we'd have supper and went to church. I was constantly kneeling and my knees are sore, I mean, I've had a lot of problems with my knees since. I don't remember any games I played. I did a lot of prayer. I don't remember a favorite subject or happy memory. Nothing was fun. ("Josephine")[99]

> We had to march everywhere, like one two, one two. We were done at school at about four o'clock. We marched back to the dorm, and then we got ready to go to Mass, again. Lunchtime, too, we went to Mass before we went to lunch. (Roger White Owl)[100]

A militarized Catholic environment overseen by men and women religious was the structure into which Native children were ushered. In this context, interviewees often recall the physical punishment and punitive abuse at the hands of priests and nuns, from straps employed by priests on young boys to solitary confinement and the physical punishment of kneeling on broom handles for boys and girls.[101] As one survivor pointedly remarks on the religiosity of physical punishment: "But that Catholic thing was, the nuns were mean."[102] As a stock character in Catholic cultural lore, "the mean-ass nun,"[103] is familiar, indicating a widespread experience and therefore responsibility for such patterns of behavior, which invites further analysis and explanation for all Catholic educational institutions of this era. But in the context of the boarding school, children had no recourse for support from outside family members and the comfort and care they might provide.[104]

To create the conditions where separation from family was nearly total, White educators at Catholic boarding schools followed the model of the "outing program" instituted at Carlisle. Seeing Indigenous cultures as a problem, instead of returning home during school breaks, boarding schools sent Indigenous children to White homes for the summer, holidays, and other breaks. In this project, White Christian families could participate in the education and assimilation of Indigenous children.[105] This model "encouraged students to enter the homes of a white American middle class and like a sponge, soak up their values. Simultaneously, they were expected to dedicate hours of labor to surrogate families while strategically being separated from their own relatives and kin."[106] While native youth experienced a deficit in the extended isolation from family and culture through the outing program, White families could experience a benefit from the cheap labor the young people would perform.

The benefit directed to White Christians replayed on the boarding school campus as well, where labor formed a substantive part of the curriculum. When White students in Jesuit institutions might be studying Latin, Greek, philosophy, and theology, Jesuit-run schools for Indians included woodworking and shoemaking.[107] As Anselm Weber OFM reported in the wider network of Catholic Indian schools:

> In the way of industrial work the girls are taught plain sewing, dressmaking, cutting and fitting, blanket weaving, laundry work, and domestic science. The boys are taught farming and gardening; at times

> they take a turn at masonry and carpentry and assist in the laundry and the bakery. As in all Indian schools, half of the time is devoted to class work, the other half to industrial work.[108]

Indian students in other Catholic boarding schools recall stringing rosaries and creating complex beadwork artifacts that would be included in letters soliciting donations. Stuffing envelopes and "selling" their stories became part of the requirements for those who attended the school. Labor at boarding schools included also the work to be done in running the schools. Mary Ann Cavanaugh describes: "There's fourteen sisters taking care of about four hundred kids. So the kids, just like in the history of all these boarding schools, kids did the work."[109] Students were put to work for the upkeep of the physical grounds in custodial work and agriculture and for making items that could be exchanged for a profit.[110]

The liturgy and labor of the boarding schools formed a regimented context to cultivate "good Catholic students." But the saturation of new ways of being at the militarized boarding school was not merely the taking on of a new Catholic culture; it was the simultaneous and violently enforced rejection of students' culture of origin. The geographical practice of moving children from home life to the institutional setting, designed to remove youth from the influence of native lifeways and wisdoms, was exacerbated by policies that kept children even from their siblings at the school. Upon arrival at age five, "Josephine" recalls, "Then they immediately separated me from my brother. I saw him once in a great while, like on Christmas."[111] It is not surprising the number of survivors who recall, as young people, the sound of sobs and crying filling the halls of dorm and school.[112]

In the setting of separation from the tribe and family members on campus, young people were mixed into settings of multiple tribal affiliations and were punished for speaking in their native tongue, which might have provided some sites of connection. Tommy Davis recalls students having their mouths washed out with soap for speaking Cree and concludes that through these and other practices, "their Indianism was beaten out of them."[113] The federal government's English-only policy could be strengthened with the symbolic division of sacred and profane, naming speech in Indigenous tongue as "the devil's language."[114]

Through the military regimen that monitored every movement and punished infractions, students were taught forms of self-mastery and self-control as an isolating program. What was sacred and to be revered and emulated were the masters of control—the adult (or young adult) Christians on site. What was to be avoided as profane (or denounced as demonic) was all that was associated with tribal lifeways: culture, language, and religion. Separation of the boarding school was premised on the defiling nature of Indigenous culture and religion. Nothing demarcated the categorical separation of the sacred and profane more than the ritual "washing" survivors report from the memories of arrival at the boarding school compound. Welcomed to campus with the indignities of having their hair cut or shaved, their heads treated with harsh chemicals, and their bodies scoured, this widespread practice marked Indigenous life as dangerous and "dirty" and forced students into a militarized lifestyle of transformation.[115] Stuck in a place "where they also felt looked down upon as Indians," many students resorted to flight: "When loneliness or tensions inevitably surfaced, the typical response of Indian students was to abandon school, usually for the security of family and tribe."[116] Running away to the security of home, family, and tribe points to conditions in which young people felt they had exhausted their resources for response in the condition of separation and inculcation in systems of White supremacy.

For those who stayed or were forced to return, the pattern of separation and divinization of the dominating culture created the structure for abusive actions that brought them harm. While the pattern of Catholic adults perpetrating acts of physical and emotional abuse on children has been widespread in American Catholic culture, using fear and harm as part of the cultivation of a Catholic ethos, children within the boarding school system would not have had recourse to other adults to mitigate these patterns of violence. The combination of supremacy (of adult Catholics) and separation created a dangerous dynamic for native children. Such a pattern, wrapped up in sacred symbolisms, created lifelong trauma, as Demus McDonald / Makah Wammi Omni recounts from his time at St. Michael's Indian Mission boarding school:

> They had a big nun, Sister Forest, tall sister, mean [laughter]. Coming down the line, she would point to the floor and say, "Pray." So the little boys would get on their knees, and they would pray. And when she came to me, because I could barely speak English that first day of school, I didn't know Hail Mary or Our Father and all that, so I started praying in Dakota, the way I'd hear my grandma pray. When I started praying in Dakota, that sister grabbed my ear and twisted it, stood me up. And Father had an office up there; she marched me to him . . . they put a ruler on the floor in the corner, and that's where I had to kneel on the ruler, straight up like that with my hands in front of my face. . . . That went on for I don't know how long. Finally they sent me back to bed. I still speak Dakota at home, but to this day when I'm

> asked to pray in public I say no. Too many painful memories of this priest grabbing my hair and neck.[117]

Male and female adult Catholics collaborated in the disorienting dehumanization that structured children's lives at boarding schools. We can note similar patterns of separation from Indigenous networks and the supremacy of White Christian ways infusing the recollections of abuse from three children at St. Joseph's Indian School, run by the Congregation of the Priests of the Sacred Heart.

> I remember having to serve the priest wine, but never in the wine hall. I remember being brought to the priest's room, but I never really remembered leaving . . . I was six years old. . . .
>
> The memories of sexual abuse are deep inside of me. It wasn't like it happened just once; it was almost every day. . . . If I start to remember things that happened when I was small I try to do something else to get it out of my head. . . . I never told the doctors about the priests sexually abusing me. *I was too ashamed. What would they think about me because I'm Indian.* I should have stopped that priest. ("Josephine," age five to thirteen while attending)[118]

> I was the littlest one in the school. They'd call me out of school and the nun would say, "*Father wants to see you,*" and I'd say, "No, I don't want to go," and I was told, "You have to go." They'd pull my pants down and fondle me. There was no one I could tell, couldn't tell the nuns. I still haven't told anyone. . . . I often blame myself; I should have been more aggressive. ("Julia," age five to ten while attending)[119]

> The sexual abuse would happen late at night when all of us were sleeping or were supposed to be sleeping. *The Brothers would come in and they would take somebody out.* When the kids would come back they would be crying. They didn't want to be touched and they were always scared. No one ever talked about it. (Roger White Owl)[120]

The elevation and separation of male Catholic religious, built on longstanding patterns of the elevation and separation of White Catholic ways, created the conditions for abuse. The survivors cited here do not point to the practices of grooming that other survivors of sexual abuse report, but the strategy of separation and supremacy of White Christian adults could provide the backdrop for diverse forms of manipulation and abuse. The more than one hundred lawsuits advanced in South Dakota alone demonstrate that these patterns and practices were not limited to only some of the boarding schools.[121] Catholic authority figures had been valorized for their "mastery" and made sacred in their separation, providing the structure for isolation and abuse.

The persistent structure of separation and supremacy followed the students beyond the limits of the campus, where the symbolic capital of "Catholic" created a protective barrier that hid abuse. Phil St. John recounts the pain of abuse shared by his brothers and the haunting presence of Catholic Christian supremacy in the exchange with his mother when she asks: "Why didn't you tell us?" and his brother responds: "'Mom, you never would have believed us anyway. . . . You're a Catholic and Catholics don't do that.' So all the things that happened to us, the bad things, half of it I think my parents didn't really believe."[122] The strength of symbolic capital that adheres to Catholic Christianity as a site of truth and goodness created the conditions not only of systems of supremacy within the schools themselves but overshadowed the wider context for believing the victims of abuse.

We might note also the unreasonable expectations of agency self-reported by children who were abused—for example, when "Josephine," in attendance at ages five through thirteen, voices in her interview, "I should have stopped that priest." And "Julia," ages five through ten, when she blames herself, "I should have been more aggressive." Truth telling and releasing the pain will require analysis to ensure that guilt rests with the abusers and the institutional systems that made these harms possible. White Catholic practices must face the reality of memory, trauma, and survival if we are to support our siblings in the release of pain.

In the opening chapter of this book, I proposed the spiraling steps of Maria Yellow Horse Brave Heart in the journey of releasing the pain of historic trauma. Brave Heart's methodology was created in her work with Indigenous communities healing from harms like those perpetrated by White Catholic settler colonialism and the abusive experience of Catholic boarding schools. But when we recognize "Catholic" as a multiracial, multicultural institution, we might envision the possibilities for Catholics across racialized divisions participating in this work together. The essential first step of truth telling about history is a history of ancestors who were White Catholic perpetrators of violence and ancestors who were Indigenous Catholic victims of violence. How might this work of truth telling, access to the archives and institutional records, and hearing one another's story be a project of healing historic trauma not only of our nation but embedded within our community of faith? How might our truth telling about this history also reveal a complexity in the spiritual sources that sustained survivors?

## Grace of the Grandmothers

The analysis of our truth telling about this history (Brave Heart's second step) helps us see patterns of practice reflected in this era's instantiation of Catholic institutions: a fundamental division between the sacred and the profane. In the elevation of Catholic lifeways as "sacred" and denigration of indigenous lifeways as "profane" or demonic, students were forced and coerced to reject all that bound them to the safety and security of the home. Yet some survivors report the connections to their home culture and religion as a saving grace. "Genevive" was in second and third grade when she experienced the abuse at St. Joseph's, and she describes a trauma that followed her into adulthood, reflecting: "I'm very connected to the spiritual. That's how I survived."[123] Tommy Davis, punished for speaking his native language, illuminates the healing accessed through Indigenous lifeways: "I make songs because I have the language [speaking Chippewa] the Creator gave us to use. . . . I always thought I got more understanding and more spirituality out of my Indian ways."[124] Davis concludes: "I don't know what the Creator did for me, but I mean, he wouldn't let them break my spirit, no matter what."[125]

Like Demus McDonald/Makah Wammi Omni, for Eugene Hale, it was the women elders of the community who forged this saving connection, repeating in his interview the role his grandmother's mother played:

> My great-grandmother . . . she taught me how to pray. She would pray in Dakota, and I would say the same word that she does and try to remember it.
>
> My great-grandma, she taught me how to pray. She told me about the Sun Dance and the sweat lodge and she told me at that time, she said, "When you become a man," she said, "you can do that, but," she said, "You've got to do it from your heart." So I did. I had it in my mind when I went to the Catholic school there.[126]

Other resources can provide a fuller narrative of the sustaining practices of Indigenous lifeways woven into Catholic students' sense of identity and survival, for those survivors who chose to adopt both. It was (and is) an extraordinary practice to bridge the two worlds and two religious wisdoms.[127] And for many survivors of abuse in Catholic boarding schools, we have the grandmothers to thank for providing the sustaining spiritual connection.

In the writing of the Jesuits, Indigenous lifeways and Indigenous religiosity were the foundation that needed to be dismantled. It was the "old women" who kept up the foolish traditions, so removal from the tribal network would ensure their replacement. As Pietro Paolo Pandro described of the St. Xavier mission in 1887:

> These children are severed away from their lodges and brought to school where they will lose their tracts of Indian mythology and foolish traditions that the old women are telling to their children during the cold nights of winter, and in the mountain breeze in summer, filling up their brains with wild imaginations and stories. So the very fact of having the children out of their lodges is a great step towards civilization and religion.[128]

But survivors recall being rooted deeply in the native traditions and linguistic paths to the divine *conveyed* through female elders. It was not a demonic deterrence in the Indian traditions the women were telling to children, but a saving grace: "I survived because I'm Dakota."[129]

## Conclusion

In the one hundred years of nineteenth-century nation building, the Catholic Church expanded across the nation in the creation of a network of educational institutions alongside parishes and missions. In ministering to a multiracial collective, the church set up nonetheless internal structures that gave highest priority to Whiteness. The designation of "missions" to Black and Indian communities in distinction from established parishes, the differences in curriculum that might be developed in the different school settings, and the unequal distribution of the many forms of capital (social, symbolic, economic) are some among the many ways in which the church failed to enact the fullness of its mission to *all* peoples. In this historical frame, where education systems aligned with coloniality, participation in White Catholic educational institutions could be a double-edged sword.

The exploration of this chapter has brought us through a wide-ranging network of Catholic institutions in coloniality. Recall Slobodsky's frame of analysis whereby "coloniality" indicates those practices of domination developed during colonial times that persist as patterns identifiable within institutions. These patterns of domination were attendant with a racial hierarchy by which resources were unequally distributed. In the telling of this chapter's history, we can glance back at the patterns laid out in the structures of 1830s Baltimore, in which the Catholic Church in its institutions of school and parish centered White interests yet simultaneously leveraged resources for Black Catholics denied access to White-serving institutions. A White-serving church on the East Coast of a nation laid down patterns of thought in which the church was attentive to the spiritual needs of the souls of Black folks but refused to dismantle those systems enslaving their bodies. A multiracial church that created separate and unequal systems saw the church functioning in multiple ways in Baltimore, in South Carolina, in Michigan, and in Minnesota. Providing Catholic education for Black and Indian youth, the church nevertheless advanced a White supremacist agenda in the differential resources allocated and in the differential locations from which these resources derived, the status of "mission" persisting and revealing a White supremacy project. The church could solicit its donations for people of color but could just as easily restrict the flow of funds. The church could also communicate its White supremacist ideologies—elevating White Euro-Christian heritage for the salvation of souls—and the damaging distinctions of "sacred" and "profane."

Such is the truth telling of this era of history. And Maria Yellow Horse Brave Heart's spiraling method invites us to extract from that history an analysis so that we might see patterns and practices laid down in earlier eras still residing in our institutions today. From the foregoing histories, let me propose sites of analysis by asking a few simple questions: Do our institutions continue in the practice of elevating "Christian" (or "Catholic") above all else and in the process deny a divine presence to what is named "profane" or "secular"? Do we trade in the symbolic capital that elevates Christian *and* Whiteness in our messaging—in recruitment tools and sermons, in curriculum design and administrative appointments? Do our institutions elevate a hermeneutic of White-centered knowledge in education that might continue to inform White-protecting laws?

As educational institutions in the Catholic Christian tradition, the purpose of recognizing these patterns from out of history involves identifying ourselves as inheritors of the institutions and as gatekeepers in sustaining or transforming them. The purpose of recounting the history of this chapter is precisely to be afforded the resources of analysis by which we might unearth the continued coloniality of our Catholic institutions and leverage our locations for change. As educational institutions, we have access to control of knowledge production and opportunities for producing both counternarratives and critical hermeneutics. To move our multiracial institutional network to the antiracism of transformed institutions, we might move from question to action with some of the following considerations specific to our particular locations.

First, do we know our history and the actors in our institutions who leveraged White supremacist ideologies to create the cultural capital, symbolic capital, and economic capital that is passed down to us in our institutions today? If we can identify actors in our history producing the narrative of White Christian supremacy and mobilizing the inheritance of a slave economy toward White-serving ends, we might be able to capitalize on that inheritance by redirecting resources toward cultural, symbolic, and economic capital for change.

Second, can we recognize patterns of demarcation of "sacred" and "profane" that continue to elevate White Christian ways above others? If we can identify actors in our history producing the narrative of White Christian supremacy in a way that demonizes and devalues the cultural and religious traditions of the globe, we might be able to take responsibility for that pattern and redirect resources toward learning from and with the great diversity of religious and cultural traditions.

Third, do our educational institutions critically understand our involvement in nation building and the systems of the military? If we can identify actors and actions in our institutional history through which our faith-based institution came to acquire benefits made possible by the state-sanctioned violence of the military, we might be critically aware of the ways our institution *still* gathers resources from its participation in structures and systems designed to kill.

And fourth, can we identify practices of elevation and abuse in our institution's past and work to be agents of change in our institution's present? In this query we might recognize the many locations that we inhabit within the Jesuit, Catholic, and Christian institutions of our nation. Are we located within Catholic schools—and can we work to dismantle practices of supremacy in the curriculum and in admissions and financing in our school's culture? Are we located within Catholic parishes—and can we work to dismantle practices of supremacy in preaching, in outreach, and in collaboration across congregational and religious lines? How do we participate in the wider Catholic practices of funding enterprises that either maintain or resist White Christian supremacy's status quo?

The critical history of this chapter is designed and directed toward transformation. Telling the truth about our institutional inheritance moves us through Brave Heart's steps and yields analysis and release toward transformed institutions. But this history also paused to consider the "otherwise possibilities" of Catholic history. Evidence of what might have been is another potent resource for imagining the possibilities of our future. So, in a place like St. James the Greater, where Black Catholicism could thrive; and in the pursuit of school settings among the Oblate Sisters of Providence; and in the renewal of Indigenous knowledge evident at contemporary Catholic Indian schools, we have witness to the otherwise possibility of a God who works in history. So although we must wrestle with the history of our institutions in their prioritizing of Whiteness, we might also lean into the God of continual surprises who might help us leverage instead the variety of Catholic resources—economic, symbolic, and spiritual—in order to become a more truly multiracial, multicultural church.

# 5 Leveraging Capital

## *Church Institutions for Change in the Twentieth Century*

In the preceding chapters, we've witnessed Catholic institutions of church and school participating in White supremacist culture in numerous ways. The institution of the Catholic Church participated in the ideology of exceptionalism of a White state, in its project of national expansion via settler colonialism, by which Indigenous peoples were dispossessed of their land throughout the nineteenth century. Catholic educational institutions served the state purposes of absorbing Indigenous peoples through the erasure of their lifeways and cultures by processing them through curriculums of European heritage and Christian sensibilities. In this era, the institutions of the Catholic Church simultaneously drew to themselves the resources of Indigenous land and the creative effort of African-descended laborers for the expansion of a White-centered church. Practicing diverse expressions of "separate and unequal," the Catholic Church unevenly distributed multiple forms of capital, withholding significant benefits from Indigenous Catholics and Black Catholics. Naming such congregations as "missions," the Catholic Church relied on individual donations and the charity of benefactors (like Katharine Drexel) to fuel the institutional efforts of both church and school. The separate and unequal education accessed by Indigenous Catholic and Black Catholic youth was a double-edged opportunity, as it provided locations of access into the systems of White Catholicism in a White-centric nation, yet it was premised upon distancing from Indigenous lifeways and values as well as African-centered ones. Recognizing this double-edgedness of Catholic institutions in the past (extracting resources from Black and Indigenous peoples yet unequally distributing its capital and cultivating Black and Indigenous youth in White-centric Catholic culture) might provide a lens of analysis to consider patterns that persist today. Are our Catholic educational institutions still maintaining the priority of White ways of being and knowing, cultivated as "mastery" and descended from White Eurocentric patterns of "knowledge"? If we can identify the continuing of nineteenth-century colonizing practices even in our twenty-first-century Catholicisms, we are in a position to name and to change the institutions in which we are found. Disrupting our heritage as White-serving institutions, we might step into the "otherwise possibilities" that were roads not taken in our history.

To imagine our present as well as our past as containing within them the "otherwise possibilities" announced by the Spirit provides a more nimble movement of our theology and our ecclesiology for today. That Indigenous children were sustained by the grace of the grandmothers in keeping language and spirituality alive in their lives, as resources *against* the onslaught of White supremacy culture and Christocentrism, speaks forth an otherwise possibility embedded within the history of Catholic boarding schools. That St. James the Greater thrived as a Black Catholic church and school in South Carolina cultivating a unique Black Catholic culture, eluding some of the controlling grasp of White-centric Catholicisms, recalls for us the work of God in the world, providing the grace and Spirit of sustenance *despite* the Catholic Church's White supremacy culture. That the archives at Georgetown might hold for us the witness to the work of the Spirit sustaining our enslaved ancestors points to possibilities beyond a White-centered history of Catholicism. Indeed, Catholic and Christian institutions have been *both* repositories of capital for transformation *and* storehouses of illicit wealth from the sins of White supremacy. There was no single way of being Catholic, just as there was no single way of being human in any of the eras of our study thus far.

Therefore, it may not be helpful to think of people, or institutions, as "products of their time," as if there were only one way of being in any given time. Too often the critique of truth telling about inhumanities in history leans into the charge of "anachronism"—judging a different time by the values of our present time. But to suggest we can't assess the practices of the past and find them disturbing leads us into a corner that simply dismisses past injustice as if conditioned by insurmountable structures that made inhumanity necessary. And yet in perhaps every era throughout human history and most certainly throughout every era of the history of the United States of America, there has never been one way of being "in the time" that produced a singular "product." White Catholic bishops mobilized resources to defend the practices of slavery from the pulpit and in print, but questions raised by Catholics in their letters to the editor of the *United States Catholic Miscellany* (to which the bishop felt it necessary to respond) demonstrate that there were Catholics who questioned these practices. While the White-identified IHM Theresa Maxis traveled to serve White settlers in the Midwest, her OSP sisters remained in Baltimore, and both groups reflected the commitments of Catholic women religious. An infusion from the White capital of Katharine Drexel enabling the Black and Indian "missions" to thrive (while withholding access to her community of women religious) is a complex reality that reminds us that our histories do not come in black and white but in the many shades and hues of complicity and complexity. Given the evidence of internal diversity, it is more helpful to frame each period as agonistic—a struggle to bring to light the differing commitments to distinctive ways of being human, some of which we judge by our times to be capaciously life giving and others of which we judge otherwise. We need to be able to level judgment on the past in order to leverage the assessment to our own time and to see the options available for our being human—even options we have not yet considered. To view history and engage in our truth telling through the lens of the agonistic, the lens of struggle, opens up our imaginations to see the great variety of actors and the great variety of options for our being human—in their time and in our own.[1]

## Considering Agonistic Institutions

In place of thinking about institutions as products of their time, I'd rather think of them as sites of agonistic practice. "Agonistic" is related to "antagonistic," but it's not the same. With antagonistic, difference comes together in a way that is hostile and in opposition. But if we trace "agonistic" to its etymological roots, we might consider the way it comes with a range of meanings from the Greek. "The root of *agonist* is the Greek noun, *agôn* which originally meant a group of people brought together, a gathering, an assembly."[2] Ruth Russo notes that the word in its ancient context "connotes competition and contention," but sometimes such activities were situated in the midst of festival. A word used to describe the coming together of people at festival that might include contest breathes a little more room into the kind of struggle that my use of agonistic intends. Yes, we are in contest, but it does not necessarily convey a battle to the death, but perhaps a more loosely held relationship of bodies in balance. Here, I capitalize on the way that contemporary scientists have come to adopt this term when they talk about receptors at the molecular level. Scientists discovered that what they thought were *antagonistic* reactions were not as oppositional as that word connotes. Russo writes: "As the understanding of a drug's action at a receptor becomes more and more refined, the boundary between *agonist* and *antagonist* gets blurred; all neurotransmitters and drugs are just contenders at the molecular *agôn*, binding with more or less affinity, exerting more or less physiological response."[3] Russo embraces the poetic flexibility of the term "agonist" as a way that scientists can provide different conceptualizations for productively different models. So too with my use of "agonistic" to describe the functioning of members of the body politic as contenders in the social and institutional arena.

"Agonistic" can describe also the contenders in the struggle of bodies in balance within the body of Christ. Like the encounter of receptors and the push and pull of places where it is difficult to discern precisely antagonist and protagonist, the biological processes of organisms include an agonistic struggle to work into the necessary balance required for functioning. To press this use of the term further, "agonistic" asks us to see a set of relationships among bodies that shift and move toward proper functioning of the social body, a functioning that might lead to flourishing but also a deadly malfunctioning when the flourishing of one part of the social body, within the body politic, is at the expense of another part of the same body. Think of Paul as an early Christian leader using the metaphor of body parts to describe the ecclesial body of Christ (Romans 12:5 or 1 Corinthians 12:12–25). Yes, we are struggling to coordinate our activity together, but we are struggling *together.*

I use the term "agonistic" to try to capture the push and pull of different bodies as they are living and working together. Sure, sometimes the agonistic can still be a struggle that has a feel of hostility, but a struggle can also be a struggling together to find just the right balance of bodies that are different but that are working together. So even with the people I love, the people who are closest to me, I'm always in a struggle to meet their needs, to meet my needs, and to meet those needs we have in common. In other writings, I have used the term "a calculus of concern" to describe the never-ending agonism of life by which I struggle to meet my needs, the needs of my children, my partner, my students, my professional commitments, and more.[4] And also in the social sphere, with persons with whom I fundamentally disagree, their actions and my response will have consequences on both of our lives. So when we're thinking about diversity as a project or practice of involving people who are different, we might lean into the idea of the agonistic—but it doesn't have to be a hostile wrangling; it could be a cooperative or negotiated struggle to find the right kind of balance. I think this is what human social life actually looks like and what the church actually has been.

As we move into another chapter of our nation's history read through the institutions of church and school, we might consider the activities of Catholics within new locations with the agonistic as our guide. The church has never been one thing or a singular institution. As we engage in the truth telling about our institutions, we might see more fully the great range of options that were available (yet not taken) in the past, and those that were taken might be investigated for the fruitfulness of their witness to our agonistic practices today.

Such an agonistic lens on institutional histories in the United States can be fruitful for many reasons. From one angle, it helps us see that our institutional history—indeed, our national history—is not a singular story but one with many facets and many actors in the push and pull of our living together. Thus both the story that "things were bad but now they are better" or "let's get back to the good old days" are both fictitious narratives that mask the realities of good and bad intertwined in each era of our nation's life and our institutional lives. The push and pull of actors on differing sides of the agonistic struggle for survival and for mutual flourishing ask us to consider our national and our institutional histories from the vantage points of different actors within that history. There is no one trajectory of history, and there are no singular actors of history, but (with an agonistic consideration) we as human beings exist in the push and pull, the struggle for survival and for flourishing, always and everywhere alongside others, both the human and the nonhuman world.

An *institutional* lens, added to this, then reminds us that within our institutional histories there are not merely bad actors and good guys but complex positionalities in which agents and receptors, receptors and agents, agonists, antagonists, and protagonists interact and move and shift and give life to the living reality of our institutions. The complex actors include those who were written out: women in a patriarchal church, Black Catholics in a White-centered world, enslaved and enslaver, native grandmothers whose memories church leaders aimed to erase, and the children (including Catholics) who carried these memories. When we commit ourselves to an agonistic lens on our institutional history, we can ask questions about erasures, about whose lives mattered, and about which persons were sacrificed within the corporate life of the institution. As we write these stories back into our history, they open up for us the roads not taken and our futures that could be otherwise.

While the agonistic tends toward an external conflict between two parties in our national history or two agents in our institutional history, the struggle may also be an internal one, as a single actor moves into the different institutional and social spaces. Henrietta of St. James, featured in Chapter 3, may have struggled in the complex life of agent and enslaved, of companion and "property," of marginal in a marginalized "mission" but central to the livingness of the community, of struggling with loyalties to church hierarchy in support of the enslavers and church members struggling for self-emancipation. Theresa Maxis, too, as she shifted identity from Black identified to White passing, may have been seeking for herself what she saw as the best way to pursue the path of proclaiming the Gospel. The agonistic may enable us, as we will see in this chapter, to see the multiplicity of identifications in a figure like James Bouchard, who struggled as an Indigenous man in a White supremacist church but who leveraged his positionality to buy into that supremacy. Or it may allow us to understand better the experience of Indigenous Catholics like those who remain connected to the institution even after experiencing harm at the hands of a church they continue to love. Our own positionality in an agonistic history—of church, school, institution, and nation—provides an accounting that invites a move back into the history to reveal even more dimensions of institutions on competing sides of the struggle. It might also open the door for Christian readers to consider again the story of Jesus as one of struggle and our positionality within that story as ever shifting.

We return to our history with a final chapter situated in a West Coast Catholicism, in a multiracial church, in the agonism of workers' rights. Entering this landscape, we witness again a church on many sides of the struggle. And we consider the present possibilities of a church poised to be a vehicle for change in *our* world. We will see in this narrative how the social and symbolic capital of the Catholic tradition can sustain the struggle for workers' rights.

## Shifting Identity along the Way of the Cross

> Friday, April 8 (Good Friday): Cortland to Freeport There will be 14 stops to symbolize the stations of the cross, and a rally and passion play at the Freeport Sportsmen's Club at 7:00 p.m.
>
> Saturday, April 9: Freeport to West Sacramento, after a joint Catholic, Protestant, and Jewish prayer service at 8 a.m. In West Sacramento, the pilgrims will go to Our Lady of Grace School, at Jefferson and Linden. A rally at 6:30.
>
> Sunday, April 10 (Easter): 8:30 a.m.—Easter Mass and service (Grace School, Jefferson & Linden); 11:00—Start of the last march; 1:15—Arrival at the bridge, and entry into SACRAMENTO; 1:45—Rally on the steps of the Capitol; 3:45—Procession to Our Lady of Guadalupe Church, 7th and T streets for the lighting of the eternal flame and Benediction by the bishop; 4:00 Gran fiesta, with music, dancing, merrymaking (South Side Park across from the church).[5]

Stations of the Cross are a deeply Catholic way of entering into the symbolic capital of the story of the Crucified One. They are part of the ritual enacted as a community of faith around the globe, walking through the last days of Jesus's life in history and anticipating the Easter promise. As one steps into the episodes on the way, you are invited to consider yourself among the crowd at a crucifixion (a brutally violent form of execution directed toward the criminal behavior of those who would disrupt the power and peace of the ancient Roman Empire). Jesus, who was misrecognized as disposable by the state, has, over two thousand years, become the locus of symbolic capital for those who are bound by his witness. The cross as symbol of this state-sanctioned torture is a reminder, a witness, to God's presence at work in the world in the most desperate places. Walking the steps of condemnation, humiliation, and death, in the Stations of the Cross Christians travel deeply through time to walk the way of the Lord, willing to place themselves in the position of suffering, shifting their positionality of alignment from being with those who followed and carried Jesus to standing at the foot of the cross where the penitent stands convicted. As the follower stands at the foot of the cross and the being-crucified-Jesus cries out "forgive them they know not what they do," the follower seeks the mercy of God for all the ways *we* are the crucifiers. Christians, then, by walking the way of the cross, are called to be relievers (and even receivers) of violence as we too walk in the way of justice, but we are also those who too often walk in the way of benefiting from violence, so we also are receivers of the condemnation that it is we who put to death the one who would be our savior.

As pilgrims trace the steps of the redeemer, they understand themselves to be reliving the way and seeking the necessary transformative redemption out of our ways of violence and suffering and through to the otherwise possibility of new life. At the beginning of the earliest Gospel, according to the community gathered around the Markan storyteller, Jesus opens his way with the invitation, the requirement, to repent and Believe in the Good News that there are Otherwise Possibilities, other ways of being in the world, new life beyond the structures and systems of violence. "The kingdom of God has come near, repent, and believe in the good news" (Mark 1:15, NRSVUE). In the particular version of the stations that open this section, we meet up with the pilgrimage of the United Farm Workers on their journey toward transformed working conditions for those who feed the nation. In incorporating practices of pilgrimage and penance into the struggle against structures and systems of White supremacy, César Chávez recognized the shifting identities of the oppressed. Assessing the need for repentance of our various practices of harm, not even the oppressed farm workers were exempt from being victim in one location but potential victimizer in others. Like them, we don't hold a single subject location; we also experience agonistic struggles with(in) our own personhood. The pilgrims gathered with the UFW across denominational and religious lines and arrived at the sanctuary of Our Lady of Grace, receiving good news for the journey ahead. The Mass of celebration on Easter morning anticipates the fullness of new life promised by the One who has been named *God.* Music, dancing, and merrymaking may not be the expected response to the ongoing and lifelong struggle against systems and structures of violence enacted in the Stations. Indeed, the struggle has not ended, but shouts of celebration enact and foretell the possibilities to come.

The Stations of the Cross and Pilgrimage from Cortland to Sacramento walked the way of suffering from the White supremacy that had created unsafe and unjust conditions for Asian and Latinx workers in the mid-twentieth century, just as White supremacy had created inhumane and unjust conditions for Indigenous peoples and persons racialized as Black in previous centuries.[6] As we have seen in the preceding chapters, through the structures and systems of White supremacy, institutions of church and school partnered with the state to become conduits of capital designed for the well-being of White Christians. The church helped create the conditions of White supremacy even as it endeavored to mission to the Original Peoples of this land and the African-descended peoples forcibly building the nation. In our preceding investigations, we've seen a church at odds with itself in serving White interests but also in becoming a location in which those suffering under the weight of White supremacy could access capital for both survival and thriving. The church in America, then, is an institution that *both* served Catholics as a multiracial community and betrayed us. Had the church not been a White-serving institution, had it not been wedded to an ideology of White Christian supremacy, perhaps it could have been the "already" foretaste of a glorious Kingdom in which peoples of all hues and cultures made manifest the promise of a common dominion of justice and love among humanity. As Bryan Massingale has imagined, the promise of salvation is one that knows no racialized distinctions, but the Kingdom on earth has been clearly bound by them. Indeed, Massingale describes the celebration of the Mass as a "dress rehearsal for the Kingdom, because in the Reign of God everyone will not look like you, pray like you, sing like you, or think like you. You are here to celebrate a new identity, your true identity, one that is not based on race or color. Here, at last, you see *all* of your sisters and brothers."[7] The practices of White priority and Christian supremacy woven into the history of the Catholic Church in America have made us little prepared for the banquet to come.

But the story of grace in the face of White supremacy precisely is a story of celebration amid struggle, one conveyed in the announcement and invitation of the United Farm Workers in 1966. As the announcement reveals, the various forms of capital embedded in Catholic institutions could be mobilized as graced locations to structure the struggle: Our Lady of Grace School and Our Lady of Guadalupe Church are institutional locations to hold the holiness of the gathered assembly. Celebrating the "already" and "not yet" of the Kingdom of God, the grand fiesta celebration does not mark a final turning away from White supremacy and the alignment of the church once and for all on the side of those who bear its scars, but it does witness the in-breaking of a Spirit that supports the struggle.

The story of the United Farm Workers movement is the story of a multiracial, multireligious movement in which the church stood on both sides of the agonistic struggle and saw Catholic actors themselves shifting locations. What we see in the announcement of the UFW Easter pilgrimage is the leveraging of capital for real and lasting change. Gathering together, the people power of social capital expanded the power of the movement across many lines, enlisting persons with diverse forms of cultural capital to lift up the struggle for others to witness it. The symbolic capital of the Catholic, Christian, and religious traditions joined together to speak forth the importance of this movement, and the capital of physical space for gathering made much of this possible. Ultimately, these forms of capital were leveraged in order to ensure that conditions for accessing economic capital and the humane working conditions that might build wealth were made real. All of these various forms of capital were shifted by persons drawing deeply from the spiritual capital of the Catholic Christian tradition as sustenance for the journey. The story of the UFW is a story in which we might see the power and otherwise possibilities of a church amid the structures and systems of White supremacy in America.

In every era, we have seen the church as a conduit of capital that flowed *both* in the direction of establishing and maintaining White supremacies *and* mobilizing resources for resistance. That Nelly expanded her repertoire with spiritual capital in her role as sacristan and Nancy found a grounding to collect the economic capital needed to set Sophia free are both examples of a complex institution that was both liberating and enslaving (as we encountered in Chapter 2). So, too, the enslaving and liberating church on the South Carolina frontier that both Henrietta and Elizabeth called home (explored in our third chapter). In the systems of church-based education examined in Chapter 4, we've seen the double-edged complexity of institutions that could simultaneously be resources for elevation and liberation while also tools for domestication in the systems of coloniality. This double-edgedness, this complexity (which is sometimes duplicity), remains as the Catholic Church in the United States continues to be an institution(s) of simultaneous liberation from White supremacy and protector of White interests. The culmination of this chapter will visit again the church as a capital-rich institution that can manifest both liberation and oppression in the witness of the United Farm Workers movement, and like our forebears in the faith, we will ask again where the balance of capital in the Catholic Church will be spent and how *we* will be a contributing factor.

## Reading History as Theology

> If humanity, each person, is the living temple of God, we meet God in our encounter with others; we encounter God in the commitment to the historical process of humankind.[8]

> Salvation—the communion of human beings with God and among themselves—orients, transforms, and guides history to its fulfillment. . . . The history of salvation is the very heart of human history . . . the salvific action of God underlies all human existence.[9]

The question of the church's role in the world, in the nation, in our moment is not only interesting historically, socially, or politically; it is also important theologically. From the analysis put forth by Gustavo Gutierrez and cited earlier, we are asked to consider whether Christian faith requires that we see not two histories, one sacred and one profane, but one history, in which the Divine works in time and space. This is the unfolding of "incarnation": that the Supreme Reality that is Creator of All so desires the fullness of expressions of life in the created world, that the divine inhabits the world as human. For Gutierrez and other Christian theologians, this possibility has been confirmed in the witness of the Creator coming near to us in the person and presence of the Jew Jesus, in the first century, under Roman occupation. Casting that affirmation backward in time, Gutierrez reads the biblical text to affirm that the Mystery that created order from chaos (imagined in the Genesis account) began the saving trajectory of God at work in the world, calling the prophets and the people to union with the Divine. This salvific calling is revealed as human in the person of Jesus Christ, who makes God manifest and enacts salvific presence to heal a broken world.

Such a liberationist approach to the intersection of faith and history has been embraced by many within twenty-first-century Catholic institutions. We see ourselves participating in that sacred history, in a faith that does justice, applying critical thought toward addressing some among the world's most pressing problems. Indeed, leveraging the resources of knowledge and the various forms of capital has been a liberationist embrace for Jesuit and Catholic schools since Gutierrez's mid-twentieth-century insight.

But as the preceding chapters have demonstrated, as institutions that embrace the idea that humanity partners with God in the salvific work of history, we must be critically alert to those places in our own history that have brought destruction rather than salvation. Importantly, the *claim* of bringing salvation crucially harmed Indigenous peoples in the history of the Americas (through a salvific logic of mastery over the land and its inhabitants) and the lives and histories of African peoples and people of African descent (through a logic that saving souls was the highest priority, even it if meant doing so through the soul-crushing systems of enslavement). Believing that one has a monopoly on God's work in the world has brought damaging practices in our institutional histories.

At the same time, our earlier investigations have tried to show ways in which people of diverse faiths accessed a saving power in the midst of Christian-induced suffering. African-descended peoples drew on African practices (both Indigenous and Islamic) and blended them with new Christian forms witnessing the work of grace among enslaved peoples. So, too, when Indigenous children found solace and salvation in the grace of the grandmothers and the wisdom they passed along through prayer in native tongues and the sacredness of Native American practices. When looking for the saving graces in US history that bore persons through the sins of White supremacy and White Christian supremacy, we open up to a theology of religions that takes as evidence of God's work outside the Christian tradition the grace it takes to face White Christian supremacy. Through the classic Christian categories of sin and grace, we might not only consider grace at work through the many religious and spiritual traditions of the world but also come to terms with a Christian church that is simultaneously graced and sinful. This chapter pursues a theology of cultural and religious expression that witnesses to the divine at work in history in the ongoing and extended struggles *against* White Christian supremacy. It once again demonstrates the Catholic tradition as made up of institutions that convey the simultaneity of oppression and liberation within their walls—and invites us to think further about leveraging the capital of institutions in the direction of liberation and leveraging the great range of spiritual capital that might be found in the faith and wisdom traditions of the world.

## Excluding Asian Populations: How State and Religious Power Collude

In order to move into the twentieth century and examine multiracial movements against the sins of White supremacy and the role of the church as structure and support within this story, identifying some elements of the historical back story is in order. We pick up, in a sense, where we left off in the last chapter, at the overlapping era of the late nineteenth century and through the twentieth century. By the mid-nineteenth century, the outline of the land that today we call the United States of America had only recently taken shape, with the 1803 Louisiana purchase, 1848 annex of land from the Mexican–American War, and the extension of the effort to wrest land from Indigenous nations (Indian allotment continued in the 1880s and 1890s, with a move toward the sovereignty of tribal nations only in the 1930s). This expansion pushed the boundaries of the nation westward and now required bodies to help master the land, settling it for the benefit of the colonizer nation. Land that had formerly belonged to Spanish-speaking residents of the United States of Mexico now fell under the domain of the English-speaking United States of America extending its reach westward. To build the land within the project of the nation, the US government actively recruited workers from around the globe. In the late 1800s, an estimated ten million immigrants came from Europe, nearly one million from Latin America, and quarter of a million from Asia.[10]

In the early phase of this late-nineteenth-century growth from Asia, labor recruiters in China promoted the opportunities in America with the promise that Americans "want the Chinaman to come."[11] As Erika Lee explains, "Industrialization and the growth of American capitalism created an insatiable desire for labor in the United States."[12] Lee describes how the Chinese workers "were heavily recruited by foreign labor agents. . . . It started with the search for workers to build the Central Pacific Railroad in the 1860s. The recruitment of Chinese laborers grew even more after regular transpacific steamship service between Hong Kong, Shanghai, and San Francisco was established in 1867."[13]

International businesses based in the United States profited from the flow of labor from various parts of Asia, and many Asian workers found difficult and low-paying jobs as miners and railway workers and in factories and fisheries. Immigration and the recruitment of laborers played an important role in an expanding state. Lee describes how the media presented this influx of labor: "In 1869, the *Daily Alta California* praised the role that Chinese immigrants were playing in developing the state's economy. 'The Chinamen are ploughmen, laundrymen, placer miners, woolen spinners and weavers, domestic servants, cigar makers, shoemakers, and railroad builders to the great benefit of the State.'"[14] Note briefly how symbolic capital is conferred on Chinese immigrants as their work contributes to the nation and their efforts are "to the great benefit of the State." Leland Stanford, president of the Central Pacific Railroad, had already similarly, on the national level, reported on the utility of this group of workers, in the report of the secretary of the interior (1865): "As a class they are quiet, peaceable, patient, industrious and economical—ready and apt to learn all the different kinds of work required in railroad building, they soon become as efficient as white laborers. More prudent and economical, they are contented with less wages."[15]

Here we see how corporations might contribute to the dynamic nineteenth-century racial project where "White" indicates a grouping (a "race") of laborers who excelled in efficiency but who are constructed as less prudent in their spending than the "class" (or "race") of Asian workers. Further consider how this construction of inherent characteristics attendant to "the races" ultimately benefits the growing of capital by the owners of the railway systems. If the Chinese workers are by nature, as a "race," more thrifty, then White Christian American owners of industry can content themselves in paying them less wages. The symbolic capital of racialization has always been deeply entwined with the distribution of economic capital.

The development of the technology of the railway in this era not only built the infrastructure of transportation but also served to convey distinctive elements of America's religio-racial project, and even still with a Christendom mentality. When immigrants from around the globe were invited to help settle and build America's newly acquired land in the West, White Christians took on a new understanding of their role in God's design. In the popular press, images of White preachers surrounded by Chinese workers aboard a steamship announced to the nation that the work of Christianizing was being done.[16] The systems laid down by industry that capitalized on trade with Eastern nations to build wealth for White American industry were also conduits for Christian missionary activity. But not all White American Christians welcomed the Chinese into the fold or into the nation. The benefits that Asian workers could bring with the efforts of their industry were not valued by those White Catholics in America who saw themselves in a "natural" competition with Asian immigrants. The Irish who immigrated to America at this same time vied for the symbolic capital of being "recognized" by the state as worthy of citizenship. The church in this dynamic could be a powerful ally in supporting some immigrants and denying others. While the model-minority status of "hard worker" served the interests of White industrialists, a wider racial project debated whether Chinese immigrants were capable of assimilating into a White Christian nation. When the railroads were completed (on which the Chinese laborers represented 90 percent of the workforce), the workers joined the variety of immigrants and migrants in the cities on the nation's West Coast in the late-nineteenth-century project of nation building. But White supremacy and Christian supremacist ideologies targeted workers who traveled from Asia to America in the mix of labor competition of American capitalism. At this time, immigrants from Ireland were also relocating to the various opportunities in the United States, and capitalism's drives created new opportunities for racialized categorizations of workers to be placed in competition. A wider racial project emerged that named the 5 percent of the immigrant population as "Chinese" and "foreign," while the 63 percent of the foreign-born immigrants from the United Kingdom, Ireland, and Germany were somehow *less* "foreign." And the Catholic Church had a hand in the debates that capture the dynamic of this moment.

As workers racialized as "Asian" enter into the religio-racial landscape of an expanding America, they are not only competing with White workers, like the Irish (similarly competing for recognition); they also are entering into a landscape already woven through with strands of the agonistic religio-racial project that preceded them. Spanish, Indigenous, French, Asian, Irish, and African-descended peoples (among others) created a dynamic location for Catholic identity and institutions to emerge. A new racial project was also to emerge where religion took center stage, built upon a foundational religious project in which "church" aided in the project of assimilating those who had been racialized into the categories of White, Black, and Indian.

In this period—when a White Catholic Church is intensely pursuing mission to the Indigenous people in the West and the institutionalizing church is building churches and schools on the California coast—the Jesuits claim their first Indigenous priest: James Bouchard. His mother, Marie Elizabeth Bouchard, had moved with her family from France to New Spain during the turn of the nineteenth century and settled in territory claimed by Mexico that would be claimed by the United States to become Texas. At age seven, Marie's parents were killed in a conflict between settler Spaniards and the Indigenous tribe of the Comanches. Marie was adopted by a Comanche family and raised with the given name Monotawan. As a young woman, Monotawan married a Delaware chief, Kistalwa, and to Monotawan and Kistalwa was born a son, who was given the name Watomika ("Swift Foot").

Looking back as an adult, Watomika credited his French-Comanche mother with "inculcat[ing] on his youthful mind ideas of the grandeur; power, and goodness of the Great Spirit, to impress upon his heart a profound reverence & love to so Great a Being."[17] Watomika remembers himself to have been a particularly theologically precocious young boy, drawing young and old to him as he conveyed what he had learned from his mother. Monotawan also passed along to her son the stress on caution that was becoming a component of Indigenous knowledge (reflected by Chief Spotted Tail from Chapter 4). His mother warned him "to regard the religion of the pale-faces as an invention for deceiving & destroying the red men & for taking away their best lands."[18] Watomika grew into a young man with an understanding and respect for Delaware culture and lifeways, narrating in his recollection not only the hunt and the battle but also the possibility of the human-divine encounter and the guardianship of the Great Spirit in the many aspects of Delaware life.[19]

These recollections offer only traces in his autobiography of the motivations that made Watomika willing, as a young man, to travel with a visiting Presbyterian missionary and to attend Mariotta College (Ohio) to learn "the GREAT MEDICINE of the White Man."[20] And in Watomika's own remembrance, after "a long & fearfully contested battle, sacrificed all that was near & dear to his heart, in order to follow J- C- in his holy Society."[21] Thus, Watomika journeys to become James Bouchard SJ, transforming from Delaware to Presbyterian to a Catholic and Jesuit faith.

As nation building proceeded on the West Coast, so too did church building, with both parishes and schools. Although Catholic education was excelling as an arm of the state (as we have seen in the previous chapter), in the struggle for survival Catholics also bemoaned their necessary financial contribution *to* the state and winced under the system of taxation. Here the symbolic capital of Christian discourse could be used to generate the capital necessary for institutions to thrive in the wider landscape of the nation. At the same time that the Catholic Church sought funds from the state to carry out the education and missionization of Indigenous peoples (explored in the previous chapter), the church was also required to pay into the state to create institutions of learning and mission for White Americans. It was clear that some Catholics preferred the former.

In the racializing dynamic of historical production, Bouchard becomes an "eloquent Indian," a fiery preacher and dynamic speaker drawing on and disseminating the symbolic and social capital of one ordained to speak on behalf of the church.[22] As an 1890 biographer describes, the symbolic capital leveraged by Bouchard was directed quite often at building the economic capital needed by a church struggling on the frontier.

> He was fond of lecturing too and applications to lecture came to him from all quarters. He lectured now for the benefit of newly built churches burdened with a load of undebtedness [*sic*]; now for convent schools and colleges, to enable poor sisters to contribute their share of taxation to the inexorable tax-collector, for the privilege of imparting gratuitously a moral and religious education to poor children, now for the relief of abandoned orphans, or famished cities or destitute populations. Wheresoever charity needed a zealous advocate to plead her cause and to touch men's hearts and reach their purses—Fr. Bouchard's voice was not silent.[23]

Consider here how symbolic capital and economic capital intertwine. In his various speaking engagements, Bouchard could leverage Catholic symbolic capital to generate economic capital to support the Catholic institutions of newly built churches and convent schools. These institutions, in turn, would generate social, cultural, and economic capital for those who attended. Proceeds from Bouchard's leveraging of symbolic capital might also be used to provide economic and spiritual capital to accompany those in need.

And yet, this race-evasive description of *who* Bouchard's preaching helped invites deeper investigation. James Bouchard was not only the Jesuit's first ordained man of Indigenous inheritance; he also inherited the alliance with White Christian supremacies that flowed through Catholic institutions. One particular event is noteworthy in capturing the work of the church in a multiracial nation and the commitments to White well-being it might betray. On February 22, 1873, the San Francisco *Catholic Guardian* publicized an upcoming event:

> It is a shame that the state should tax the buildings in which 1500 to 2000 children are educated gratuitously; but we hope to see a generous response to Fr. Bouchard's efforts to relieve them of this burden. . . . Let, therefore, every friend of Christian education, every lover of justice, every-one who would lighten the burden which bears so heavy on these noble, self-sacrificing women, make this occasion of doing good, and purchase one ticket, or more, to this lecture. Every little helps—many drops make the sea. The subject is an interesting one, and the well-known ability of the lecturer is a warrant that it will be well-handled. . . . If you want to be entertained, instructed and pleased, go (Tickets, one dollar).[24]

On this particular evening, when the Catholic Church in San Francisco hoped to raise funds for the convent school run by the Roman Catholic Sisters of the Presentation, Bouchard would be debating a topic of interest to a wider public: Should the Asian workers who built up the nation through their industry now be welcomed as citizens?

Given Bouchard's heritage as the son of Indigenous parents whose people had been the target of colonial efforts, we might desire that Bouchard's fiery oration mount some critical position with respect to those who had been racialized as White. This expectation becomes all the more potent given the messaging about White ways that Bouchard's mother imparted to him. Indeed, by birth and by heritage, Bouchard had been devalued in the systems of Catholic and Jesuit identity because of his Indigenous roots. But, the double-edgedness of

Catholic institutions meant that he could rise through a White supremacist society by succeeding in the Catholic seminary system.[25] With his roots in Kansas among the Delaware Indians, Bouchard entered the Jesuit novitiate at Florissant, Missouri, in 1847, when the Jesuits still employed enslaved labor there. Moving westward through the systems of the church, Bouchard leveraged his position as a Catholic priest to align with White interests on the question of granting citizenship to the many Asian workers who had worked to build up the new land of the nation.

On the evening of February 25, 1873, Bouchard would contribute to the era's racial project, entering the public debate on the worthiness of Chinese workers to be considered for citizenship (the gateway to all rights and privileges). While others in the area were arguing that Christians should double down on their commitment to Christianization, in the belief that it would facilitate assimilation, Bouchard took a different tack. In the racialized categorizations of the debate, Bouchard answered the headlining question, "Chinaman or White Man, Which?" with the following religio-racial response:

> It is the white race we want. The white man, the head of all his kind in bone and muscle, in pluck and in endurance, in intellect, a head and shoulder above all the other races; a man, even in the natural order, more or less governed by sentiments, of honor and the obligations of honesty and, in accordance with the principles of Christianity and controlled by Christian morality in his every-day life.[26]

Aligned with the racist projects of White academics and the Christian supremacies of theologians, Bouchard stood at odds with his own heritage and in alignment with a Catholic Christian system that pushed him in the direction of White supremacy. Perhaps the strength of "knowledge" produced in Jesuit education systems enabled Bouchard to argue in this way. His elevation of White Christian ways included the denigration of the Chinese as an "inferior race" and was replete with demonizing characterizations and stereotypes. In this event, the symbolic capital of an educated Jesuit orator mobilized the spiritual capital of Catholic tradition from the physical space of St. Francis Catholic Church to secure the economic capital for a Catholic educational institution to pay the taxes due to the state. Somewhere near three thousand dollars was collected to save the Catholic sisters' endeavor, at the expense of the Chinese, the targets of Bouchard's oration and political mobilization.[27]

Lest we think of Bouchard's anti-Asian sentiment as a benign supremacy, we must situate his 1873 public speech, citation in newspapers, and publication of the pamphlet that disseminated the event within a broader landscape of anti-Asian violence across the West. In the years preceding and following the anti-Chinese legislation, waves of White violence targeted Asian workers in Los Angeles (1871); Denver (1880); Tacoma (1885); Rock Springs, Wyoming (1885); and Bellingham, Washington (1907).[28] Through the lens of White supremacy, we can connect this anti-Asian violence to the wave of White terror during the Red Summer of 1919, in which White supremacists swept through Black communities in Tulsa, Texas, Georgia, Chicago, and Washington, DC, with deadly anti-Blackness. And six years later, thirty thousand members of the KKK were granted permission to march in Washington, DC. We cannot afford to imagine that Bouchard and other Christians spoke words of hate without consequence: Symbolic capital has material outcomes of violence.[29] From the soft power of coercion to White Christian ways to the hard power of violence against people of color, the race riots of this era point to the evil of White production and calculation. While a White nation that saw illicitly gained benefits (like land and wealth) as gifts from a gracious God, White mob violence destroyed homes and drove workers from their jobs, denying Black and Asian Americans access to these same benefits. The symbolic capital produced by church and school could incite violence, and that violence took from Asian Americans and Black Americans the economic capital they had worked hard to secure.

White Christian mob violence toward persons shaped by Chinese religious traditions and racialized as "pagan" was accompanied by White Christian structural violence in the form of laws determined to keep Asian immigrants in a second-class status and finally to restrict immigration from China altogether. The absence of Christian identity (and the symbolic capital it carried) proved to be pivotal in both soft and hard forms of White supremacist violence, and the Asians in America who persevered were put in a precarious position.

Bouchard witnesses a nineteenth-century multiracial Catholic Church leaning into White supremacy and alerts us to the possibilities of a multiracial church today bearing the imprints of White supremacy culture. The history of Catholic and Jesuit institutions of church and school offering evidence of the embrace of White supremacy in this era and this geographical location continues to be an important place from which to wrestle with the multidimensionality of this struggle. As we have moved into the geographical expansion of the United States of America westward to the coast of California, we can situate our stories in the ongoing dynamic explored in the previous chapters—both in relation to Indigenous nations and people of African descent. That is, the institutions we inhabit today bear the scars of this violent supremacy in our history.

The University of San Francisco offers a glimpse of this struggling on the part of historians to reconcile our mission in teaching for justice and our history of injustice. Alan Ziajka, university historian emeritus of the University of San Francisco, published in 2022 an example of historians' wrestling and our invitation to wrestle as well. Recognizing the Jesuit embeddedness in colonizing efforts (first on the part of Spain, then with setter colonialism in the nineteenth century), Ziajka demonstrates a struggle with the dual-edgedness of our Jesuit and Catholic heritage. After reckoning with USF's alignment with the state power of a genocidal governor who served on the board of trustees, the history softens to wrestle invisibly with the racialized project of Jesuit education. Ziajka describes:

> Almost all the students at St. Ignatius College, during its first decades, were first- or second-generation Irish or Italian Catholics, a partial reflection of the [White settler] population of San Francisco. An analysis of the list of St. Ignatius College students from 1855 to 1905 reveals no students that appear to be Native Americans. Students were recruited from the [White] immigrant communities in and around San Francisco, and from the [White] mining communities in the gold fields of Northern California. One of the school's prime recruiters was Fr. James Bouchard, who had a French mother and a Delaware Native American father. Fr. Bouchard was also an outstanding public speaker who filled the pews of St. Ignatius Church with his homilies.[30]

Ziajka offers three insights for our discussion of agonism today. First, the White supremacist Bouchard remains celebrated as the first Native American Jesuit, erasing his supremacist ideology. Second, wrestling with our past can continue to be race evasive, as it is only my editorial revision that names the portion of the immigrant community served by St. Ignatius as White. And third, many historians and others must continue to tell our stories, stories that resist the romanticization of White history and the erasure of Others. As we attempt to do this work at our own institutions, we might learn from the challenges across the network of Catholic and Jesuit institutions and support one another from afar. We might be reminded of the countless histories and stories of hidden supremacies that have been told over generations and how ongoing and challenging this work will be to tell new histories.

We can pause at this place in our history to again connect with the orienting framework provided by Maria Yellow Horse Brave Heart. Recall her spiraling method of truth telling about our past that might lead to transformed institutions of our present. As we engage with the historians' tools to uncover our institutional past through the lens of racial justice, we remain attuned to the ghosts our histories create. For example, Ziajka's elevation of Bouchard without the attendant anti-Chinese content creates Chinese workers as ghosts within USF's institutional history, violently written out by Bouchard's fiery rhetoric. By insisting on race-specific narratives that note when our institutions have been White serving, we might witness the absent-presences of those our story writes out. These phantoms of modernity's violence witness to us a something-to-be-done.

*What* is to be done in this instance seems to include writing race back into our institutional histories. Such a move would help us with Brave Heart's second step of analysis, as we understand the history of our institutions as having been White serving. This enables us to interrogate practices today that continue to invisibly center White actors and erase the excluded. Brave Heart's insistence on truth telling about our histories invites us to ask if we *can* tell our institutional histories of White-serving schools and parishes in such a way as to honor the complex complicity in structures of domination this entailed. Can those more complex histories help interrogate whether our Catholic institutions remain White serving even today?

In the example of Bouchard, and undoubtedly countless others, we might find patterns in the diverse location of this era's violence as a lens to consider our truth telling. The symbolic capital of Catholic thought conveyed in preaching, lectures, media, and publications and the social capital of Catholic networks housed in the built capital of Catholic institutions created a death-dealing network that denied the fullness of life, and even life itself, to those who fell outside the scope of White Catholic concerns. (I write this on the anniversary of Rosewood, Florida, and wonder about the Christian capital mobilized in the destruction of that Black community in 1923.) Recognizing the absent-presences of those violently excluded from Catholic concerns alerts us to a something-to-be-done in *our* day. As we read our past as a cautionary tale, we might also look to our institutional past for otherwise possibilities. And as we move to the witness of the United Farm Workers, a more complicated portrait of the location of the church emerges.

## Weaving a History of Latinx Americans

As we are weaving the threads of diversely racialized groups in the history of America and its ecclesial systems and structures of White supremacy, we return to the crucial phase of coloniality and empire when the United States of America claimed land from the United States of Mexico (1848). But the wider scope of Catholic Christian presence and the alignment of American Catholicism with White interests are helpfully situated in a longer view in order to recognize the church entangled in an agonistic struggle in the web of White supremacies in this particular geography. Timothy Matovina provides a starting point for this longer view:

> In 1598, eight Franciscans and other members of the Juan de Oñate expedition crossed into present-day El Paso, Texas, and established the initial Catholic foundations in the region. Two and a half centuries later, the war between the United States and Mexico (1846–1849) resulted in Mexico's loss of nearly half of its territory: the present-day states of Texas, Nevada, California, Utah and parts of New Mexico, Arizona, Colorado and Wyoming.[31]

Matovina helps us see the longer history of the Catholic Church in the American West as a Spanish colonial enterprise, which takes a new turn when it meets with the Anglo-US settler-colonial project. Readers situated in the West might want to pause and locate their particular institutional heritage within this moment, while those of us situated in other locations in the United States might want to pause to ask what our educational institutions have passed on to us about this Catholic history. In the unfolding and deepening engagement with the historic trauma of White supremacy, we might need to retell our US history and our ecclesial history to recognize the vast geographical area that was populated by Indigenous nations and persons colonized by Spanish-speaking Catholic Christians who had claimed independence from Spain in 1821. When White American Christians sought to incorporate the land and the people into the United States of America in the nineteenth century, a new form of coloniality was constituted. Recall Slabodsky's insight that the settler-colonial project includes "the construction of an alternative society in that location in a way that makes the colonizer invert the understanding of him-/herself as an invader and think of him-/herself as a native, deeming the native as a foreigner."[32] Here, the English-speaking White Christians claimed the position of native owner of the land by extending the systems of the American state and employing them to White advantage. Although Spanish-speaking Christians who were formerly citizens of the United States of Mexico were granted citizenship in the new colonizing nation of the United States of America, they were at a disadvantage when Anglo settlers arrived and brought a court system that adjudicated land claims in the language of the colonizer. Matovina recounts how "conquered Mexicans resisted the U.S. takeover in various ways."[33] For example:

> Native Texan José Antonio Navarro made various legislative attempts to protect the ancestral lands of Mexican Texans. While his fellow

> lawmakers did not enact any of his land-claim proposals, at the 1845 Texas Constitutional Convention Navarro was able to prevent passage of an "odious" and "ridiculous" law that restricted suffrage to the "free white population."[34]

Navarro's need to stand in the way of White supremacist legislation reveals that there were those seeking to cement its advantages. Among them, in the early phase of Anglo settlers to the Southwest, were East Coast and Southern Catholics who could make their way to take advantage of new opportunities for wealth building that settler options afforded. Thus, settler colonialism continued in a new phase, as the East Coast trajectory of westward expansion made connections between Catholicisms in the East and Catholicisms in the West. Families like those in slaver economies sending their sons to northern institutions also pursued wealth-acquiring opportunities in Texas and California. Keep in mind that the White population often comprised Christian transplants from US states deeply dependent upon and capitalizing on the enslavement of fellow Christians, as families like the Bellinger-Pinckneys, who founded the Catholic Church in South Carolina, were expanding their holdings to Texas locations at this time.

To examine here just one trace of how the network of East Coast Catholic institutions expanded to these far-reaching locations, we might ask how a now priceless Cristóbal de Villalpando painting (created in Mexico in 1683) was "given to Jesuits shortly after Fordham's founding (circa 1860)."[35] While the territorial United States had only recently arrived in West Coast locations, Catholic and Jesuit institutions were already a functioning network there. Just as East Coast Jesuits made connections with a slaving economy to build wealth for their institutions, they simultaneously drew resources from "begging trips" to Mexico and formerly Mexican territories.

While some elite Mexican, and now Mexican-American, young men could access new sites of capital through systems of White US Catholic education, Mexican-Americans in the West and Southwest continued to struggle against systems of White supremacy of US settler colonialism, at times with little support from the institutional church. In this particular racial project, phenotypic and religious categorizations were made even more complicated, given the linguistic and cultural distinctions among Catholics of this area. Matovina recounts another example of institutional abandonment (paralleling the OSPs in Baltimore and St. James the Greater in South Carolina), where the White Anglo-heritage American Catholic Church did little to mobilize resources in defense of Catholics who had been linguistically and culturally racialized as other than White:

> At Nacogdoches in east Texas, near the Louisiana border, where Spanish-speaking Catholics first established a settlement in 1716, Anglo-American ascendance led to ethnic tensions and outbreaks of violence with Mexican Catholics. The local pastor, Father José Antonio Díaz de Léon, died mysteriously in 1834, probably at the hands of an Anglo-American assassin. Subsequently Anglo-Americans expelled or killed numerous Mexican-descent residents and burned the local Catholic house of worship to the ground. No resident priest replaced Father Díaz de Léon until 1847. But in the thirteen years the local community was without a priest they continued to conduct Sunday services on their own and organized rituals for feast days and funerals, gathering in private homes after their parish church was destroyed.[36]

During those thirteen years of institutional abandonment, Spanish-speaking Catholics could be the target of the White supremacist violence that accompanied the structural violence of a loss of land and loss of power. This episode repeats the pattern of the US Catholic Church in this era decidedly abandoning its missions and reserving its support for Anglo-White congregations. The African American Oblate Sisters of Providence in Baltimore recount an abandonment in the years 1843 to 1847. From 1856 to 1897, St. James the Greater Black Catholic Church in Colleton County, South Carolina, survived forty years without a priest or institutional support. And here, at the border of Texas and Louisiana, the church withdrew its support for thirteen years (1834–1847). Nevertheless, each Catholic community persisted. We can see here a renewed ecclesiological analysis that "the church" works on both an individual and an institutional level. While individual Catholic priests may have advocated for Black (Fr. Joubert in Baltimore, 1830s), Indigenous (Fr. Cataldo in Spokane, 1880s), or Mexican-descended Catholics (Fr. de Leon in Texas, 1830s), the institutional church prioritized those who had been racialized as White.

As new waves of Catholics expand the US church to the West and encounter Western Catholicisms shaped by Mexican and Latin American roots, we can begin to tell a new story of an agonistic institution in the swirl of White supremacy. The admixture of agonism, differentials of power, and the sin of White supremacy all within the same institution purporting to follow in the saving power of Jesus invites us into a closely textured investigation of the many ways Catholicism was expressed—even in the same location. European-transplant priests extending American Catholicism to the West might have brought with them a distinctive ethnocentrism, like that exhibited by the first bishop to Los Angeles (c. 1859), Thaddeus Amat. Jeffrey Burns describes:

> Bishop Amat disapproved of the spiritual practices of Mexican Californians. According to historian Michael Engh, Amat "envisioned a local Catholic community, Roman in orientation, uniform in expression, and obedient to him in its actions." He attempted to Romanize and Americanize his new diocese, Engh contends, by standardizing ritual and strengthening discipline by subscribing "to measures adopted in Baltimore [by the national hierarchy] and confirmed in Rome."[37]

As we've seen in the long view of US history, the Catholic Church acquired the capital of land on which to build its institutions by way of legislation, structures, and systems of White supremacy. In the eras of nation building, the church served as an arm of settler colonialism and as a White institution reaped the illicit benefits of White supremacy in the taking of land from Indigenous nations and the erasure of their culture. When, in 1821 Mexico became independent from Spain, transitions in the Catholic missions in California made way for new material configurations as "the era of the great land grant ranchos began as *Californio* elite established the vast estates that dominated California life."[38] In West Coast Catholicism, where our story now takes place, the church would come to decide where it stood in relation to Mexican-American, Black American, and Indigenous peoples. Did God reside on the side of the dispossessed and oppressed, or would the People of God be found among the oppressors? This question becomes more complex as the United States moves beyond the bounds of the continent and expands as a global empire. We will return to this question after setting the scene with another thread of Asian-American experience.

## The Church in the American Empire

Having reached the end of the land mass that was named by Indigenous nations as Turtle Island, the insatiable desires of an American empire fueled by capitalism, mastery, and progress burst the bonds of geography and, having conquered the inhabitants of the continental land mass, catapulted themselves beyond the seas to further conquest and colonization. Eying key locations for national security and economic productivity, the Spanish-American War fought in the Caribbean opened a space for the temporary US acquisition of the Philippines. American colonization of the Philippines laid the migration routes for another chapter of the Asian-American story we are following on the West Coast.

> On June 12, 1898, the Philippines declared a short-lived independence from Spain. The contest for imperial expansion by two significant colonial powers led to the beginning of the Spanish-American War later

that year on Philippine soil. Despite bitter resistance by Filipinos, William Howard Taft, the subsequent 27th president of the United States, became the first governor general of the Philippines on July 4, 1901. In claiming wardship of the archipelago of over 7,000 islands, the United States would Anglicize the name to *The Philippines*. The Philippines' and the United States' histories and fates fused.[39]

Through a new project of colonization in the opening of the twentieth century, children in the Philippines were educated in an American-based system, forming deep cultural connections, with the result that many immigrated to the United States when they grew into adulthood. With intimate political, economic, and cultural ties between the United States and the Philippines, migration flowed as the harvest of empire.[40] "In the 1920s and 1930s [Filipino workers] arrived in the United States full of hope. They were, after all, American nationals."[41] And yet, status as "nationals" was not the same as "citizen." Juanita Lott explains: "Although the Philippines was a colony of the United States at this time, Filipinos could not become naturalized citizens. State anti-miscegenation laws abounded. Filipinos could not be property owners."[42] Erika Lee describes:

> With the colonization of the Philippines came the need to incorporate Filipinos into the United States in some way. Citizenship was out of the question. Filipinos were described in racial terms as uncivilized savages, brutal rapists, and even dogs and monkeys. At best, they were characterized as children in need of (U.S.) guidance. As the young lawyer William Howard Taft, chairman of the U.S. commission that established the colonial government and future U.S. president explained, Filipinos were "little brown brothers" who would need "fifty or one hundred years" of close supervision "to develop anything resembling Anglo-Saxon political principles and skills."[43]

Note here how the project of American White supremacy once again racializes those categorized as "Other" in a project of tutelage toward mastery. In patterns similar to those enacted upon peoples of nations Indigenous to the Americas, peoples of nations colonized in the twentieth century were racialized as "uncivilized," "savage," and lacking the skills and sensibilities available in White Christian America. Lee continues:

> The United States' role in the Philippines was characterized by President William McKinley as one of "benevolent assimilation." The United States would educate, civilize, and uplift Filipinos so that they could one day rule themselves. And Filipinos were considered "U.S.

> Nationals," an unequal legal classification that granted Filipinos "ward" status (like Native Americans) without citizenship rights.[44]

In the dynamic racial project of US White supremacy, Filipinos were racialized via categories similar to Indigenous (as "wards" in need of civilizing influence). Their cultural origins in Spanish colonialism rendered them close also to Mexican-Americans, and their Catholic identity did little to challenge the White supremacist ideologies into which they stepped as the latest wave of immigrants to the United States.

Like the Chinese before them, Filipino workers were recruited by American business interests. As Lott describes, the first generation of Filipino immigrants was distinctive in its gendered composition:

> It was a mobile population of young, primarily single males from the barrios and farms of the Ilocos and Visayan regions of the Philippines. They were recruited as contract workers and manual laborers initially for the Hawaiian sugar and pineapple fields and subsequently for the Alaskan canneries and California agriculture. The 1910 census enumerated 2,767 Filipinos, of whom 90% were male. . . . Females made up only 1 out of every 10 Filipinos. By 1930, the census enumerated 108,424 Filipinos. . . . Between 1920 and 1929, 31,092 Filipinos were admitted to the state of California alone.[45]

The capitalist competition that pitted White workers against their racialized Others was exacerbated in the national catastrophe of the Great Depression. Shortly thereafter, the wave of White violence was turned now against Filipinos, as evidenced in Watsonville, California, in 1930.[46]

## Neighborhoods as Sites of Struggle

As the nation struggled to recover from the fallout of the stock market crash in 1929, legislative efforts to rebuild the country once again set White priorities for relief, assistance, and future stability. New Deal legislation put in protections for workers (with minimum wage laws, legal rights, and social security) while also laying out new opportunities for wealth building and security through homeownership. These key legislative efforts to protect human well-being and flourishing had their own racialized expression. Just as land rights had prioritized White Americans since the founding of the nation, the United States built legislation upon this historical foundation with access to housing and the wealth building that would accompany it. Depression-era legislation made available government resources for home ownership, but the system of mortgage lending was structured by a racial hierarchy determining which families would receive this government assistance. It was White families that received the government sponsorship necessary to invest in the long-term wealth generation that homeownership brings. The government support of homeownership for European-descended/White families was not only a handout to help with the immediate need of housing; it was also an investment in White families that would help create generational wealth.[47]

Snapshots from *McMichael's Appraising Manual* (the real estate handbook in use from the 1930s through the 1960s) remind us of the endurance of the Enlightenment-era racial hierarchy that constructed "the races" of humanity with "White" on top. In the 1931 edition, appraisers were advised to consider the impact of racial categorizations on land values. The query then posed was, simply, "Are there undesirable racial elements in the neighborhood, and, if so, are they likely to expand in a way that may injure the property?"[48] Within a decade, real estate appraising expanded into a national system of evaluations. By 1944, the work of the University of Chicago economist Homer Hoyt was incorporated into the appraisers' manual to reflect a sliding scale of humanity, accounted by race in relation to real estate. Admitting that these classifications may be "scientifically misleading from a standpoint of inherent racial characteristics," the manual offered a "ranking of races" to be used "with respect to their beneficial [or detrimental] effect on land values." The listing was as follows:

1. English, Germans, Scotch, Irish, Scandinavians
2. North Italians
3. Bohemians or Czechs
4. Poles
5. Lithuanians
6. Greeks.
7. Russians, Jews (lower class)
8. South Italians
9. Negroes
10. Mexicans[49]

As we see on the scale, White Euro-heritage categorizations rise to the top of the list. The more positive the rating, the more easily individuals and families could access the financing of mortgage lending necessary to become homeowners. With homeownership came many other benefits of a system set up to enhance well-being: the infrastructure of roads, clean water, and garbage collection; the systems of schools and churches and town councils; access to transportation and recreation. Sifted through the sieve of White supremacy, the Federal Housing Administration facilitated another chapter in the nation's prioritizing of White well-being. For Asian-Americans, Latinx Americans, African-descended people, and Indigenous nations, the systems and structures of White supremacy made necessary strategies of coexistence, survival, and ultimately solidarity. As promised in the opening of this chapter, we have arrived at an era in which Catholic farm workers open up for us the otherwise possibility of interracial solidarity.

We enter the story of an agonistic Catholic Church in a complex racial project of the twentieth century by following the life of Dolores Huerta. Born in 1930, Huerta was the daughter inheriting the Mexican-American lineage of those whom the border crossed in the US acquisition of land following the Mexican–American War. "Her mother, Alicia Chávez, descended from several generations of Hispanos in New Mexico. Her father, Juan Fernández, was the son of Mexican immigrants."[50] Her mother's line would have been granted citizenship with the US acquisition of the land, while her father would have had to struggle for such state recognition. As a child, Huerta moved from New Mexico to California, and we might imagine her single mother struggling for access to the various forms of well-being, as she "worked in the canneries and as a waitress until she owned and operated a restaurant and later acquired a hotel."[51]

In the search for affordable housing for her young family, Huerta's mother settled in a neighborhood created by the many racialized families who had been shut out of access to other locations because of the White supremacist structures of a US housing system.[52] "The agricultural community [of Stockton, California] was made up of Mexican, Filipino, African-American, Japanese and Chinese working families."[53] As Stacy Sowards describes the backdrop for Huerta's story, she also recognizes the racialized agonism that formed the fabric of Stockton life:

> The Chinese laborers were not allowed to become US citizens or to work in most other industries, so they did not have many options for earning a living: "Growers, in other words, learned how to recruit a workforce too powerless to give them much trouble—a workforce of impoverished new immigrants, noncitizens, and people of color" (Ganz, 2009, p. 24). As Natalia Molina argues, rising capitalistic labor markets created more opportunities for low-end employment of non-white and noncitizens: "capitalism needs race and gender to create endless new forms of seemingly natural divisions that allow exploitation to take place" (Molina, 2014, p. 10).[54]

Into this agonistic landscape, Huerta grew to recognize the advantages afforded to White land and business owners resulting from legislative decisions that disadvantaged the variously racialized workers. "Growers were not held accountable for workers' treatment because the legislation that regulated minimum wage, unemployment insurance, and the right to organize pointedly excluded agricultural labor."[55] Both Huerta's own Mexican-American community and Asian farm workers were excluded. As Juanita Tamayo Lott describes: "The socioeconomic status of [Filipinos in America] in the period between 1941 and 1959 was still primarily lower income and lower occupation. Over half of the Filipino labor force (58%) were farmworkers and domestics. Roughly one third (32%) worked in restaurants and hotels."[56]

Let's pause to survey the scene structurally: White land owners claimed cultural and economic capital from a judicial system that granted land rights in their favor. Legislation prioritized wealth-building access to government-sponsored home ownership for White Euro-heritage families. US political interests laid down networks of connection to the Philippines and funneled both Filipino-American and Mexican-American peoples into the same low-wage work and service locations. Farm work and domestic work were excluded from the National Labor Relations Board's protections of the New Deal era. In a system structured to segregate them into low-paying jobs and neighborhoods denied economic investment, Filipino-Americans and Mexican-Americans now faced the same systems of White supremacy that had practiced the art of deception on Black Americans and the peoples of Indigenous nations.

Even before the stock market crash, Filipino workers had already responded to the developing structures skewed to White advantage. While lacking the economic capital of White American business owners and short on the cultural capital that would afford them "recognition" as citizens, nevertheless as agricultural workers they recognized the power of the people in the social capital that might disrupt unjust practices. As Lee describes: "In 1928, the Stockton-area Anak ng Bukid, or Children of the Farm, became the first formal Filipino American labor organization. The first Filipino strike occurred in Watsonville in 1930."[57] Is it any surprise that White violence descended in *this* location of Filipino activism in Watsonville? But the Filipino farm workers persisted. "Over the next six years, there were more than twenty Filipino labor disputes throughout the San Joaquin and Imperial Valleys, and by the mid-1930s there were seven different unions. One of them was the Filipino Labor Union, the FLU, formed by D.L. Marcuelo, a Stockton businessman, in 1933. It soon had 4,000 members."[58] In the struggle for economic capital, in the absence of cultural capital, Filipino farm workers recognized the people power of social capital.

Mexican-American communities were similarly organizing in their neighborhoods. Sowards describes how "women, through *mutualistas*, sought to help their neighbors; they worked within their communities in a public way, although their labor generally remained invisible outside the barrio."[59] While these families were precisely those restricted by the social capital of Whiteness, their networks of sharing space created opportunities to leverage their resources of knowledge and availability through relationships with neighbors. For Huerta, the people power of mutual aid created a foundation for understanding the people power of union organizing. "We were organizing from 1962 to 1965, and we had done services with those workers so they could have faith in what we were doing."[60] From out of the communities of mutualistas Huerta also began labor organizing by tapping into the people power of social capital, mobilizing what capital her community had, in contrast to the economic capital in the hands of White growers and agribusiness working for the benefit of White owners.

Filipino-American and Mexican-American farm workers were organizing against structures and systems designed for White advantage at the same time and in the same geographical location. But when legislative, social, and cultural capital was also located on the side of White supremacist culture, those who had been sorted into racial categories other than White could be manipulatively pitted against one another in the struggle against the system. Alex Fabros, who grew up among the farm workers, recalls the strategic racial animosity stoked by White growers:

> The growers liked to play off the races, or the ethnic groups. You could always break a strike. If the Mexicans are striking, you call in the Filipinos, you pay them a nickel more. Course then when the Filipinos strike, then the Mexicans are going to cross over and they're going to scab our strike, they're going to make the money. So no one ever really wins.[61]

It is perhaps little surprise that when Filipino farm workers struggled in resistance to White grower-owner discriminations and oppressions, White power strategically mobilized the project of racialization to disrupt the Spirit of people power at work in the world.

In the California fields, a multiracial crucified class was preparing to rise despite the efforts of interpersonal and structural White supremacies. Recall that in the hierarchy of the mortgage lending manual, Mexican-Americans were assigned the lowest location, but since Filipinos were prohibited from owning any property in California, their position was even more precarious. Many of the Mexican laborers may have been temporary workers, continuing the project of the US government's Bracero program, which had legalized their presence. In a US racial project that both created categories of "the races" to sort people into and then granted or withheld benefits on the basis of one's racial categorization, growers banked on racialized divisions to increase White profits.

But the power of the Spirit opening again an otherwise possibility offers a new witness. In this landscape we remember:

> Filipino farm workers were offered lower wages than Mexican farm workers, even after struggling for years to receive the same pay. As the leader of the Agricultural Workers Organizing Committee (AWOC), Larry Itliong called a meeting to propose a strike. On the evening of September 7, 1965, AWOC members voted to strike. On the following day, over 2,000 Filipino farm workers and members of the AWOC marched off the vineyards in what would become the beginning of the Delano Grape Strike.
>
> Both Larry Itliong and César Chávez knew growers historically pitted the races against each other to break strikes and defeat unions. So Larry approached César, asking the Latino members of his National Farm Workers Association (NFWA) to join the grape walkouts. César was not yet ready to join a major farm strike. As César, Dolores Huerta, and other leaders of the Latino union debated the issue, César's wife Helen settled the matter by asking, "Are we a union or not?" On September 16, 1965, Mexican Independence Day, NFWA members cast a unanimous vote to join the Filipinos' picket lines during a meeting at Our Lady of Guadalupe Catholic Church Hall.[62]

The historic vote that joined Filipino and Mexican-American farm workers, taking place in the built environment of the Catholic Church, under the patronage of Mary, Mother of God–Mother of Jesus, made visible as the Virgin of Guadalupe, opens a new line of inquiry for our story.

## Catholic Social Capital

An analysis of the racialized dynamic of the agricultural workers joining in solidarity to resist agribusiness practices that would dehumanize them and keep them from the wealth building of work reveals the dynamic of capital in its many forms. The economic capital of the growers was accompanied by the social capital of power in the systems of legislation and policing; the limited economic and cultural capital of the Filipino-American and Mexican-American farm workers was supplemented by the social capital of solidarity. It is at this point that we can expand to consider the symbolic and spiritual capital of the Catholic Church. As the Filipino-American organizer Philip Vera Cruz reminds, "You have to remember that when the grape strike started in 1965, about 95 percent of the Filipinos and Mexican farmworkers in the Delano area were Catholics."[63] As the workers elevated their people-power campaign to the necessary stoppage of the strike, the spiritual capital of Catholicism was used to sustain their struggle.

But in Delano in the 1960s, the Catholic Church served not only Filipino and Mexican American farm workers but White growers as well. Vera Cruz reflects on the agonistic community of Catholicism: "The Slavonian [*sic*], Italian, Irish and other Catholic growers usually attended St. Mary's Church, praying for more bountiful harvests and profits, for the expansion of their ranches. It wasn't surprising they believed God favored their prayers because in a few short years many of these farmers became millionaires."[64] Because many of the growers/owners were also Catholic, their interests were at times protected by the social and symbolic capital of the church. "When the grape strike started, the bishop of Fresno was a supporter of the rich growers. The actions and statements he made were in accord with the priests in Delano who at that time were anti-union."[65] Dolores Huerta concurs: "When the strike broke out the priests were all related to the growers and they were telling people to break the strike and go back to work."[66] The priests had no economic power over the striking workers; they were but one link in a network of social capital that could not require the workers seeking justice to cease their struggle. But the priestly representatives of the Catholic faith held a significant cache of symbolic capital. That is, the community and the institution over time had deposited "value" into the position and figure of the priest, as leader of the faith community and as exemplar of God's design. Their aligning with the wealthy interests helps us recognize how social, economic, and cultural/symbolic capital intertwine. Since "the church" instantiates in parishes and schools, it is perhaps unsurprising that Huerta also reports, "Once I moved to Delano I put my kids in Catholic school too. But once the strike broke out [the nun] actually asked me to take the kids out of school. . . . The growers all had their kids there because the growers are Catholic."[67] Recognizing the networks of Catholic institutions provides a view of the many places the church might grant or withhold its capital.

Reading the scriptural text through the lens of wealth and bounty, Vera Cruz suggests that the bountiful harvest that would bring growers greater wealth was identified as a gift from God. But that wealth was not put into the hands of those who worked the fields. In the agonistic struggle for survival and thriving, White ownership gathered to themselves the fruits of the field, and the church, it seemed, aligned with their hoarding. What otherwise possibility might have been announced with a lectionary rotation that proclaimed,

"Listen! The wages of the laborers who mowed your fields, which you kept back by fraud, cry out, and the cries of the harvesters have reached the ears of the Lord of hosts" (James 5:4). Here we return to our earlier question: If "we meet God in our encounter with others,"[68] did God reside on the side of the oppressed while the People of God sided with the oppressor? Throughout our history, in the agonistic institution of the Catholic Church, cultural, symbolic, and economic capital align with White interests. But the institution of the Catholic Church is not only its ranked and recognized members; Catholic institutions are also recognizable in the Catholic places of practice.

From the beginning of the strike through the years of struggle that followed, Chávez, Huerta, Itliong, and Vera Cruz, bound by their common struggle and shared Catholicism, despite having been racialized and pitted against one another for the growers' interests, capitalized instead on the people power of solidarity across difference. From out of two distinct initiatives and racialized into separate unions, the Filipino-American and the Mexican-American farm workers joined to become *united* farm workers. And like the Jesus Movement of the first century, this sociality and solidarity was contagious for many Catholics across the nation. "In 1965, César Chávez and Dolores Huerta launched a major strike against grape growers that pitted Catholic farmworkers against Catholic growers. Ordinary Catholics across the country rallied to their support."[69] As Igna Kim describes: "The boycott connected middle-class families in big cities with poor farm worker families in the California vineyards. Millions stopped eating grapes."[70] Even while the power of White government could once again mobilize the military to secure their interests (sending grapes to US troops aggressively mobilizing in Vietnam), the power of the people grew.[71] Precisely because the Catholic Church had created a network of institutions stretching from the East Coast to the West, now Catholic farm workers could mobilize through these networks to reach American Catholics across the nation. Networks included the people power of social capital and institutions like parishes, seminaries, and Catholic media. And the struggle bore fruit: "The signing of the contract between [Lionel] Steinberg and the UFW [in 1969] was truly a breakthrough, a historic landmark in the negotiations for table grape contracts, and it only came about because of the tremendous support which came from the churches."[72]

A sense of the faithful rallying with striking workers by withholding economic capital through boycotts rippled through the Catholic community and gives evidence of the struggle *within* the institution and the many locations in which Catholics are found. As the UFW struggle continued, the symbolic location of priests and nuns that once served as sites of resistance to the plight of the worker now was leveraged in support. Catholic people power swelled further:

> In the San Francisco Bay Area, around eight hundred priests supported and were actively involved in the UFW's boycott of non-union grapes. The nationwide boycott would have never been as successful as it was without the support of literally thousands of priests, nuns, and other church-affiliated people.[73]

Changed leadership and nationwide mobilizing led to transformations in the Church and in the workers' struggle, initiating "years of strong church support for the farmworkers."[74]

> The next bishop of Fresno, Bishop Manning, visited Delano and expressed concern and desire to listen to the farmworkers' problems with the growers. His successor was Bishop Hugh A. Donohoe who had been helping to resolve farmworkers' problems even before the strike had begun. He even left two priests, Fathers Mark Day and David Duran, to work full-time with the union.[75]

The local mobilization in California expanded across the nation as farm workers, priests, and seminarians mobilized together, the church providing the built environment for housing boycott organizers and activists. This was a growing movement in a long struggle for justice. Huerta recalls:

> When we signed the first grape contract we got the bishop of Los Angeles supportive. By the time we finished the boycott after several years the bishop of Los Angeles was supporting us. For the second grape boycott the Church really went all out. They supported the boycott, they opened all the seminaries all across the country where farm workers could stay at. . . . We had a committee of the bishops that was very involved in the boycott including Bishop Roger Mahony. The bishop was later on the ALRB (Agriculture Labor Relations Board).[76]

The Catholic Church as an institution was on both sides of the struggle for worker justice and the repair of business practices for racial justice. And the creative agitation and agonistic struggle for bodies in balance allowed the people power of social capital to influence the symbolic power of church leadership throughout the many years of the farm workers' struggle. But with the weaving of the social and symbolic capital of the Catholic Church we can read the historical record not only as a political crusade but as a spiritual one as well—one in which the resources of the Catholic Church in the built environment, in people power, and in symbolic capital gives witness to the deeper resource of *spiritual capital*.

## Spirituality of the Strike

The symbolic capital that Catholic identity might offer as a site of solidarity among Filipino-American and Mexican-American farm workers is evident when the independent unions joined together in the United Farm Workers, with the Virgin of Guadalupe offering refuge as a symbol of their struggle. Originally manifest as the patron of Indigenous people and then patron of Mexico (tracing back to Juan Diego in 1531), Mary manifest as Guadalupe expands her patronage to the *united* farm workers. In an iconic photo, the flag of the Virgin of Guadalupe is lifted alongside the American flag and the UFW flag with the Aztec eagle design. But the Virgin was not merely a convenient symbol to forge a Catholic solidarity as a symbol of God's care for Indigenous people in a White and Eurocentric church. The presence of the Virgin gives witness to the power of spiritual capital to ground the struggle for racial justice.

Recall our discussion of spiritual capital in the struggle of enslaved and formerly enslaved Catholics at St. James the Greater Church in South Carolina. The horizon of the "spiritual" places practices in the widest possible framework of meaning, engaging "personal integration through self-transcendence and toward the horizon of ultimate concern."[77] The artist Sister Corita Kent elevated the farm workers' struggle using her printmaking with "an increasingly political edge" to support the UFW.[78] Chávez featured on a print of Kent's design, with the text of Christian witness announced: "In the vineyards where the grapes of wrath are stored the poorest of the poor began an epic struggle against the masters of the land. Here is the violent and engrossing story."[79] For the striking farm workers, the struggle was not just for wealth building but for the survival rooted in safe conditions for their work and just wages for their toil. Grounding the activity in a vision of a God who works in history, Kent linked the farm workers to scriptural witness and opens up to the wider spiritual capital of Latinx and Filipino Catholicisms. Growing up Catholic, with a special devotion to St. Francis Xavier ("about helping others and doing good for other people"), the Virgin of Guadalupe, and Santo Niño de Atocha, Dolores Huerta speaks not only of core values she drew from religion but holy-day celebrations and youth group, as well as being sustained by ritual practices into her adult/political work, lighting candles at the cathedral when lobbying for social change.[80]

As an otherwise possibility, that is, the opening of the richness of Catholic symbolic capital, Catholic social capital, and Catholic spiritual capital, the 1966

Grape Strike March presents for us the anticipation of Catholic institutional transformation in our future. The symbolic and spiritual capital of the Catholic tradition helped elevate the farm workers' struggle to national consciousness. Gathering as a collective, the people power of the farm workers and allies engaged in a 250-mile march from Delano (where the farm workers were organizing) to Sacramento, the state capital and site for structural change through legislation. This march and mobilizing was not just a performative expression of people power. As Robert Chao Romero describes: "Unknown to many, however, Chávez fashioned his famous march from the Central Valley to Sacramento as a penitential pilgrimage, or 'peregrinacion.' . . . Chávez viewed the Sacramento march in terms of this Mexican, Catholic spiritual tradition."[81] Chávez framed this in a way that grounded the work in the spiritual capital of repentance, reflecting "public penance for the sins of the strikers, their own personal sins as well [as] their yielding perhaps to feelings of hatred and revenge in the strike itself. They hoped by the march to set themselves at peace with the Lord, so that the justice of their cause will be purified of all lesser motivation."[82]

As Huerta recalls, while Chávez and other leaders arrived at the decision for a march during a retreat of discernment, Chávez himself was drawn through the witness of Gandhi and the salt marches of the 1930s (demonstrating already the interfaith opportunities available in practice). At the same time, many of the farm workers were understandably resistant to "penance" on their part. As Huerta recalls, the workers asked, "Why should we be penitent, the growers are the ones that are oppressing us, they're the ones that that are abusing us."[83] Turning the theme of penitence on all sides of the struggle, Chávez mobilized a deep spiritual involvement in the work of justice. There is no location in the agonistic struggle that is free from some element of the human condition in sin, and Chávez's insistence on the spirituality of penance in the work of justice seems to acknowledge that. Reflecting on the 250-mile mobilization, Huerta continues, "We actually did the march during Lent, and we ended the march on Easter Sunday, so the whole theme of penitence was very much a part of the march, it was a very spiritual march."[84]

It is in this context of the Lenten march that the Stations of the Cross, which we encountered earlier in this chapter, were enacted. In the temporal space of the Triduum we not only stand witness to the "summit of the liturgical year"[85] and the unfolding of pilgrimage among the farm workers and those who would support them but quite possibly the unfolding of the very heart of the Catholic Christian faith in the person of Jesus and the witness of the Paschal Mystery. For in the events leading to Easter, Christians tell the story of a God who comes near *in* humanity and a faith that culminates in the giving over of life for the well-being of others. In the Stations of the Cross, the penitent moves slowly, agonizingly, through episodes in the final day of Jesus's historical life. Having been convicted of agitation against the state, the law and order of first-century Rome enacted the brutal execution of crucifixion. Elaborately portrayed in the Christian witness of the Gospels, Jesus pauses to meet the many agents in the agonistic struggle: his executioners, his companions, his mother, the stranger, the crowds. In reenacting the stations, the penitent shifts location to ask: Where am I situated in this epic struggle for life against principalities and powers, against structures and systems that kill? In inviting the farm workers to penance, Chávez recognized the shifting identities of victim and victimizer and the hope of redemption for all.

In the three days that closed the pilgrimage, demonstrators/penitents marched forward from Freeport to West Sacramento on the day designed as that liminal location of Holy Saturday. Defeated in death on a cross, the community surrounding Jesus receives his broken body and gives it over to the tomb. Holy Saturday is the empty fullness of waiting to see what will come after death and defeat. In the ongoing struggle for racial justice in America, Holy Saturday stands as the perpetual space of the crushed, defeated, dying, dead. The life of the One who came that all may have life ends on the structure of state-sanctioned torture. The crucified One reveals the crucified class of all whom the state-sponsored and religiously affiliated have put to death in the long history of America's White supremacy.[86] In the tomb of Holy Saturday, we do not know how this will end. Indeed, it appears that death does deal a final word.

Cautiously, fearfully, Easter breaks on Sunday morning and pilgrims flood the park by evening with a grand fiesta, music, and merrymaking. For even though no business is done on Sundays, and even though no new laws will be enacted for change today, the activism that foretells the joy of the resurrection steps into celebration in the expectation of God's promise of new life. The long history of the Catholic Church in America is a slow struggle with the realities of White supremacy, but in this place the people shout forth an otherwise possibility infused with Easter joy.

The repetition of the Stations of the Cross embedded with the fiesta's joy of the resurrection reminds us that the story of Scripture has no ending. Salvation has only broken in, and Christians are called to ever replay the story as the struggle continues. For the gains won in the 1966 campaign did not represent the final defeat of injustice; they were significant but only steps in a long, ongoing, agonistic struggle. The struggle continued, and spiritual capital was needed for the long haul. Undeterred by the pace in which the moral arc of the universe bends toward justice, Chávez drew on the spiritual capital across religious lines to continue the movement. "Again following the example of Gandhi, César announced in February 1968, he was fasting to rededicate the movement to nonviolence. He went without food for 25 days, only drinking water. It was an act of penitence for those who advocated violence and a way of taking responsibility as leader of his movement."[87] Simultaneously interfaith and deeply Catholic, the movement drew many to its witness through the penitential rite of fasting in the form of a hunger strike. Chávez's witness and the wider movement surrounding him drew strength from a range of spiritual practices: "A Catholic mass was said daily near where César was fasting in a tiny windowless room of an adobe-walled gas station at the Forty Acres, the UFW headquarters outside Delano. Hundreds, then thousands, came."[88] In the Rev. Dr. Martin Luther King's *Letter from Birmingham City Jail*, the activist reflects on the necessity of grounding the work of racial justice not only in community, advocacy, and nonviolent activism but also in prayer. Chávez, too, demonstrates the necessity of spiritual capital to ground the long struggle for racial justice.

At the same time that community, spiritual capital, and celebration are woven together as sustenance for the journey of antiracism, the willingness to give of and give over one's life is also made visible in these leaders for change. During the February–March 1968 fast/hunger strike, Rev. Dr. Martin Luther King "wrote César, expressing admiration and solidarity."[89] In April 1968, King was assassinated. At the March 10, 1968, Mass that broke the fast, Senator Robert Kennedy was there among the thousands of supporters and strikers. By June, Kennedy had also been murdered. In the agonistic struggle for life and well-being, the reality of giving over one's life is not a metaphor but a truth. The witness of King, Kennedy, Chávez , Huerta, Itliong, Vera Cruz, and countless others asks us where we stand in the witness of *our* lives to the possibilities of a new life to come. "Unless a grain of wheat falls to the earth . . . it remains just a single grain, but if it dies it bears much fruit" (John 12:24–26). This ancient metaphor might structure our consideration of what the struggle against powers and principalities requires. Our ancestors also provide patterns to consider.

## White Following

In 1965, Itliong, Chávez , Vera Cruz, Huerta, and countless others began the strike for worker justice; the year 1966 saw the pilgrimage of 250 miles and 1968 saw Chávez's hunger strike. And still the struggle continued over many years and across the nation, and a wider nation of Catholics stepped up. As Vera Cruz describes, "I could list literally thousands of other church-affiliated persons who, in one capacity or another, have assisted the farmworkers movement over the years."[90] Some among those church-affiliated persons were high profile, like Dorothy Day, who "with her pen and with her presence"[91] brought the witness to a wider Catholic readership.

In the February/March 1973 issue of Day's *Catholic Worker*, we can see the way in which the work of spiritual, social, and symbolic capital from the farm workers in California spread across the nation in boycotts and marches. Like the pilgrimage of 1966, this era's ongoing struggle gave witness to the joy of an "otherwise possibility" that Day shared with her readers from her vantage point in New York City.

> It was a thrilling sight last month to stand on the steps of the Cathedral of St. John the Divine and to see the parade of the United Farm Workers coming up the steps—beautiful, dark, sturdy, men, women and children, dressed in those clothes in which they work in the fields, flags flying with the Mexican Indian eagle black against the red of their banners, led by César Chávez and Mrs. Martin Luther King. . . .
>
> I had enjoyed every minute of the evening before—a fiesta held in the hall of the great old Paulist Church . . . a party to greet the busload and caravan of ten cars which had made its zig-zag way across the country from California. It was a pilgrimage to encourage the workers in various cities to continue the boycott of iceberg lettuce. . . .
>
> A fiesta meant a feasting, and everyone, hundreds served themselves from the buffet tables. They sang . . . and radiated a spirit of joy as they sat on chairs, benches and the floor. . . .
>
> Dolores Huerta, one of the vice presidents of the Union, spoke first. She is the mother of eight children who sits with the agribusinessmen, the growers, in conference over contracts for better wages, decent living conditions—all the most elemental needs of man. . . .
>
> When they marched into the Paulist Church hall the crowded hall resounded with song, especially the triumphant song "We Shall Overcome." They have overcome so much in this long continuing struggle for justice.
>
> Dolores spoke, César spoke, and others, but it was briefly. It was a fiesta, after all, and everyone wanted to talk to each other.[92]

Day describes for her readership and for us, the celebration in community, the joy in good company, and the spirituality of the struggle against the structures and systems of White supremacy.

We can pause to note the agnostic flow through Catholic media becoming now a resource for a more racially and economically just world. As we've witnessed in our study, outlets like the *Catholic Miscellany* and the *Catholic Month and Review* could be locations where White interests were advertised and contested within an economy of enslavement. When the *Indian Sentinel* announced Catholic missions to Indigenous nations, the wider Catholic public could be brought on board to provide resources that served the educational mission that advanced state interests. The UFW had their own newsletter to disseminate information, and through the coverage of the *Catholic Worker* Day's messaging could reach countless White Catholics.[93] The systems of Catholic communication can and have been used in the racial project of each era of our study, inviting the question of how they are being used today.

The participation of Day, Kennedy, and countless White Catholics in the struggle for justice for Filipino-American and Mexican-American farm workers opens the space for another possibility we might lift up and name as "White following." That is, the strategy in the struggle for racial justice where White-identified Catholics and other Christians "show up" and follow the lead of Latinx, Filipino, Black, and Indigenous leaders in the struggles against the structures and systems of White supremacy. As Huerta recalls, "Robert [Kennedy] didn't come to us and tell us what was good for us. He came to us and asked us two questions. All he said was, 'What do you want? And how can I help?' That's why we loved him."[94] Kennedy here stands as an example of White Catholic social, ecclesial, and political capital that stretched from the East Coast to the West. Kennedy, in the most prominent White Catholic family in the nation, brother of the first Catholic president, stood ready to receive direction from the striking workers. For today's Catholics who have been racialized as White and sorted into the categories of benefit accruing symbolic, social, and economic capital, the practice that he manifests is the capacity to leverage White locations with two questions: *What do you want? How can I help?* Prioritizing the practice of *following* invites the questions of where we stand, whom we know, and what sort of relationships we are embedded in that facilitate this practice. Where might we leverage our social capital toward creating networks of solidarity and transformation? Where might we open the spaces of our built environment to witness Catholic resources being leveraged for social action? Where might we live into locations where we are dispossessed of our power, following the footsteps of One who placed as central the concern for those who were struggling under the weight of the world?

The witness of the UFW was a witness to multiracial solidarities infused with the resources of the Catholic tradition, but it was *also* a joy-filled struggle that broke the bonds of institutional identity into a multireligious expression as well. Recall the Stations of the Cross, in which the story of the Savior in the Struggle provided the framework for pilgrimage, healing, and celebration. But precisely in this witness we see the multireligious participants in the public event. This witness of the power of symbolic and social capital is captured in the announcement of a "joint Catholic, Protestant, and Jewish prayer service." And Vera Cruz reports:

> There were many other church people or groups besides the Catholic Church that supported in one way or another the farmworkers. The Migrant Ministry, which was under the directorship of Chris Hartmire, was the first church organization to give active support and financial backing to the NFWA's decision to merge with AWOC. Representatives of the American Jewish Congress and rabbis came to Delano and discussed with us the ideas of a kibbutz-style community organization, which was very appealing to César. In helping to work out the UFW's jurisdictional quarrels with the Teamsters, the committee that brought the two feuding parties together consisted of a Protestant minister, a priest, and a rabbi who was the chairman.[95]

White following, White Catholic following, is a posture that leverages locations across racial and religious lines, asking the question of where *we* can be situated in the struggle and the joy that breaks in through solidarities, where we meet the God who draws near to us across religious and racialized lines.

## Mobilizing Capital in the Struggle for Racial Justice

In truth telling about Catholic institutions of church and school, we have, in the history we've been exploring, evidence of widespread accommodation to and advancement of White supremacy culture. In such a culture, material gains for White Catholics were secured against the well-being of people racialized into the categories of Black, Indigenous, Asian, and Latinx and locatable in religious categories beyond Christian. But the more complex witness of the United Farm Workers invites an additional lens on this history. For, in this twentieth-century movement toward economic justice for farm workers who had been racialized as Asian and Latinx, we recognize a multireligious, multiracial movement in which the church stood on both sides. Without erasing the locations in which the church mobilized its capital for the continued interests of White power(s), the UFW invites us into a history to be leveraged for the present work of institutionalizing racial justice. Because in this moment, the church (understood as the many and diverse people who practiced their Catholicism) *did* mobilize its capital for the sake of a better world. And the otherwise possibility of rights and protections for those who feed the nation were made part of a nation's values. As a lifelong activist, Dolores Huerta looked back and guides us forward:

> We have to remind people what the labor movement has brought us: minimum wage, Social Security, workers' compensation, safety standards on the job. Labor unions created the middle class of our society. This is the only way in our society that we can redistribute the wealth.[96]
>
> So we also kind of have to come together. We have all of these segregated movements. The environmental movement is over there, civil rights movement over here, women's movement over here, the workers are over there. We have got to bring all these together, and we need to do that.[97]

Throughout the many years that the UFW struggled to transform legislation and secure rights and well-being for the people who feed the nation, the institution of the Catholic Church delivered not only the capital of built environment and symbolic and social capital but spiritual capital as well. Huerta asks us to look forward and to step into that otherwise possibility again.

The reality of racial injustice and White supremacy in our nation's history and in our church history is a terrible reality to face. Looking squarely into the current of White supremacist ideologies running through Catholic institutions of church and school, we might become paralyzed by the weight of truth telling. But as we look into that blinding reality, we might also peer deeply into our complicity in structures and systems that continue to deal death while protecting White life. The weight of truth telling about the sins of White supremacy is a terrible burden to bear, but we each must carry our portion of that weight in the struggle to shift it toward an otherwise possibility. And in carrying the weight and in shifting the weight of the world, we become Jesus followers with the work that we do. As Huerta reflected, "That was what Christ was about, feeding the poor. All of Christ's life was about that."[98] And Chávez, too weak to speak at the end of his fast, had someone convey his words, "It is my deepest belief that only by giving our lives do we find life. I am convinced that the truest act of courage, the strongest act of manliness, is to sacrifice ourselves for others in a totally nonviolent struggle for justice. To be a man is to suffer for others. God help us to be men."[99] As Christian institutions in the twenty-first century, do we have a conviction about what kind of human Christ calls us to be? And with Chávez, might we question whether we have the strength enough to suffer? But with their witness, we might tap into Christian spiritual capital, aligned with the multiracial, multireligious opportunities to step into and create the otherwise possibilities of a more just world.

The witness of the United Farm Workers, as a multiracial movement that found solidarity and spirituality in the work of justice, invites us once again to reconsider the role of the church in the world. Past conceptualization envisioned a church dedicated to the "sacred" in contrast to the "profane" that structures our everyday lives. But Gustavo Gutierrez's liberationist witness proposes that history is one and that the transformation of history is part and parcel of the in-breaking of salvation among us. As we reclaim a multiracial history of ancestors and activists who promoted human well-being, we restore to the communion of saints a richer portrait of the work of God in the world. And as we tell the story of the United Farm Workers as a collective that grounded itself deeply in the spiritual capital of the Catholic tradition and expanded the project to incorporate people of diverse faiths, we become witness to a multiracial and multireligious Catholic history. I name this historic moment as part of church history first so that our elders become ancestors written into our story of the faith and not ghosts written out of it and, further, so that their witness of solidarity and struggle across religious and racialized lines might be embraced as our inheritance. That we might step into the story of what the farm workers reveal to us—the otherwise possibility of a truly multiracial and multireligious Catholic tradition willing to stand collected *against* the principalities and powers of White supremacy in our midst. With these ancestors and elders as our guides, we might also mobilize the various forms of capital toward transforming and transformative Catholic institutions for the world.

# 6

# Confronting a Culture of White Supremacy

*Spiritual Strength for Mobilizing Capital*

## Recognizing a Culture of Racism

Duke Kwon and Gregory Thompson ask American Christians to see racism not simply in personal acts of discrimination (although that is foundational) but also in the structured separation that is the reality of segregation for our schools, our churches, and our neighborhoods. But they do not stop there. They call attention to the ways in which structures and systems are embedded in institutions as sites that perpetuate segregation and personal discriminations. On institutionalized racism, they write: "The same prejudices and estrangement that mark our individual and relational lives are encoded—often invisibly—in the institutions that shape our common life."[1] As each of these patterns of racism builds upon the others, personal, social, and institutionalized racism form the fabric of American life to the point where Kwon and Thompson simply state that "racism is fundamental to American culture."[2] This painful reality of the air we breathe and the water in which we swim, choking the breath of life and drowning our humanity, is recognized as the location from which twenty-first-century Christians live the faith. Summarizing, Kwon and Thompson present:

> Taken together, these claims indicate a belief that American racism is not simply personal prejudice, a relational division, or a specific institutional injustice, but something much more profound. Specifically, *racism is an entire culture—a comprehensive way of being and doing that is embedded in our structures of meaning, morality, language, and*

*memory and expressed in our patterns of individual, social, and institutional behavior.*[3]

Working through the reality Kwon and Thompson describe with a group of twenty-first-century undergraduate students, the reaction to this analysis was compelling. The affective response saw them naming themselves as "disappointed" and "disgusted"; they were "angry," "ashamed," but also "unsurprised." Some within the multiracial classroom expressed "embarrassment"; some were "worried," but some were "reassured," perhaps because they felt "seen." Among these young adults, some were "shook," some were "shocked," some were "sad." They were "surprised" and "not surprised," "frustrated," and "scared." At least one person was "relieved" that others could see what they had seen and perhaps experienced. As people in an American society that is a culture of racism, we come to this shared historic trauma from a wide range of locations; we carry the trauma as victims and as perpetrators, as descendants of past harms but also as the ancestors of future generations. We recognize all of these affective responses, but the one that is placed centrally on the table in this chapter is the feeling of being "stuck."[4] If racism and White supremacy is our cultural heritage, if it flows through our structures of meaning and seeps into the very corners of our institutions, what is the prognosis of possibility for our "undoing" what has been done? How do we bear fruit from the truth telling of history and analysis of the reality of White supremacy, in order to release the pain (and the gain) and recreate transformed institutions?

To move the needle on an American culture of racism and White supremacy, Kwon and Thompson offer an analysis that names the history of racism and White supremacy in America through the category of "theft." The theft of life and labor from enslaved Africans and African-descended peoples is an example we have seen throughout our examination in this book. And it is through the theft of life and labor that the church in America and its institutions were built. Those who have benefited from such theft, and we as an American culture, must first recognize the transgression that has taken place (the truth telling of history) so that we might begin the process of repentance and repair that is the project of reparations. The theft of land, culture, and religion from Indigenous peoples is a similar project that must be clearly recognized for repair to be enacted. Theft of wages, theft of access to wealth building, theft of the fruits of labor: Each of these names the types of economic theft White people, White institutions, White systems, and White America has dealt not only to African-descended and Indigenous peoples but to those racialized as Asian and Latinx as well.[5] The truth telling of history developed in the pages of this book takes economic theft as a central reality from which White Christian America must repent and repair.

But Kwon and Thompson also incorporate forms of theft that accompanied this economic project. The very project of racialization, where European Enlightenment patterns of thought assigned essential characteristics inherent to "the races," was a form of theft of identity. When the project characterized Asian peoples as more "thrifty" and therefore content with lower wages, it was project of wage theft that drew its justification from the project of the theft of truth and identity, with a White racial narrative dictating the qualities of the race for the benefit of White industry. The racial project that assessed Indigenous peoples and Filipinos as "uncivilized" in relation to White standards of mastery and progress was a project that included a theft of identity. The project of religio-racialization characterizing the people of Africa and the Americas as "pagan" and therefore in need of White Christian salvation was also a theft of identity, and further it was a theft of the sacred by which White European-descended Christians laid claim to a monopoly on salvation, cutting peoples off from the life-giving contact with the divine that originated in untold locations around the globe.

When our cultural, institutional, and personal narratives erase these racial projects of White supremacy, they also engage in a theft of history. As Kwon and Thompson explain: "White supremacy also stole the truth about history. It could hardly be otherwise. White supremacy, after all, was not simply an anthropological account but a cultural order, a world. As a world, it required an account of itself that could render this world believable."[6] It is precisely in the service of rendering the world of White supremacy "believable" and simultaneously invisible that the project of cultural racism created and perpetuated an account of history through *romanticization*. While Kwon and Thompson importantly point to patterns of romanticization in history telling about the Founding Fathers and the "honorable war" between the states, it is crucial to see how ecclesial history is conveyed with its own form of romanticization.[7] When Catholic Church histories celebrate the expansion of Christendom, the proliferation of the Gospel to all nations and peoples, the missionizing of "pagan" peoples, and the buildup of ecclesial institutions that harbor the sins of White supremacy; when all of this is told as the unfolding of God's plan for America; and when the sins of American Christian White supremacy are erased, *romanticization* is the means by which White Christians continue to mask ideologies of White *Christian* supremacy. Simultaneously, when ecclesial histories and institutional storytelling romanticize the past and do not recognize those who struggled beneath the weight of White supremacy, it engages what

Kwon and Thompson see as *erasure*. "This erasure, this 'willed forgetting,' reveals something deeply important about the nature of American racism: its aim was not fundamentally to hate African Americans [Indigenous peoples, Asians in America and Latinx peoples]; its aim was to *not see* them. Its aim was to render invisible their humanity and its claims upon White Americans."[8] Analyzing these patterns in our ecclesial and institutional histories, the rationale for truth telling finally and firmly comes into view. We dig up the past, we retell the painful histories of White supremacy and its toll on bodies racialized into the categories of other-than-White, in order to *see* reality clearly and in order to *own* the illicit benefits from the sins of White supremacy that reside in our institutions. The grace of the ghosts aids us in this task.

Recognizing and naming, as twin practices that address the theft of identity, humanity, and history are but two elements of a multifaceted approach that addresses White supremacy as fundamentally a practice of theft. The history of White Christian supremacy in America was also a theft of power: personal power as well as political power. Here, an understanding of institutions as conveyors of social and symbolic capital is the layer of our investigation we can activate in this analysis. By withholding full membership from church and school, Catholic Christian institutions withheld access to the social power that comes by way of our human networks. At the same time, by narrating church history and Gospel concerns through a White racial frame, the symbolic capital of God's care for humanity was contained within and funneled through White social, material, and political interests. Similarly, the symbolic capital of recognition within systems of education, when tuned into White history, White actors, and White concerns, confers symbolic capital—glory, honor, credit, praise, fame—onto White persons past and present.[9]

These facets of theft of identity, history and power were also propelled by, substantiated through, and concomitant with the theft of wealth, which is the fundamental theft of America's foundations in stolen land and stolen labor. In centering the experience of African Americans in relation to this theft, Kwon and Thompson name this as the theft of extraction, whereby "enslaved human beings *were* wealth" for White Americans, as enslaved human beings created wealth for White Americans and for White Catholic and Christian institutions.[10] Importantly, this original extraction sustained by the systems of White supremacy continued in forms of exclusion (what Kwon and Thompson name "obstruction") that kept wealth in White hands. The Homestead Act of 1862 allowed stolen land to be sold for a profit to those who would cultivate it for mastery within the United States, but enslaved persons and those who were denied the cultural capital of "citizen" were excluded. The legal systems of dedicating government funds in the form of mortgages for home ownership but were distributed unequally according to a racial hierarchy manifest in the mortgage-lending manual also kept wealth building in White hands. The legal systems by which agricultural workers and domestic workers were kept out of the minimum wage and social security systems landed in a distinctive way on African Americans and Asian and Latinx agricultural workers, as we have seen in the example of the United Farm Workers. Similarly, through legal systems, White-serving institutions of Catholic education barred access to wealth building in the denial of admission. Capitalizing on legal protections for faith-based institutions relative to admissions policies, our education system undertook forms of theft and obstruction with lasting consequences.

When we analyze the structures, systems, and institutions of White supremacy through the productive category of "theft," Kwon and Thompson open up for us a world of repair, restitution, and reparation to account for the theft of identity, theft of history, theft of personal power, theft of political power, and theft of wealth. These come in the form of returning what has been stolen through rich reserves of social capital, symbolic capital, economic capital, and spiritual capital.

The aim of this chapter is to move from the truth telling and analysis of our study toward action by which we become unstuck from the structures and systems of White supremacy and recreate transformed institutions. "In the Christian tradition, we use the language of confession to acknowledge as sin the wrongs committed against one another and God. Confession requires telling the truth. . . . We [need] to come to terms with our historical legacy in order to develop a vision of a more equitable and inclusive way of life together."[11] Once we have the diagnosis of a culture of racism rooted in theft, we can move toward undoing White supremacy through specific actions of repair.

## Christian Reparations in the Struggle of the Nation

Our institutions are filled with illicit gains from the sins of White supremacy. Constructed as they were to serve White people exclusively, historically White-serving institutions of church and school so often met the needs of people racialized as White through the direct exploitation of peoples racialized as Black and Indigenous and the exclusion of those sorted into the categories of Asian and Latinx, as well. The history recounted in this book has asked us to engage in the necessary truth telling and analysis that might lead toward the release of our national pain that is the thorn of White supremacy in the side of solidarity. The truth telling of this history is essential to our work as a nation to undo the structures and systems by which so much has been stolen from those in America who have been racialized into categories other-than-White.

But it is precisely at this moment, when a greater number of people of color and the insights of critical theory on race (rooted in the critical theorization begun in the 1930s) have been centered in many spheres of our academic work, precisely at a time in our history when a critical engagement of this history has become mainstream, that the struggle for racial justice continues. For it is precisely at this moment that the theoretical frame of critical race theory that we have been adopting in this book and that is essential for helping us see the sins of White supremacy has been targeted as un-American and unfit for the mastery of education. In more and more states across the United States, legislation is being put forward by White Christian legislators to withhold state funding from any institution—K–12 as well as colleges and universities—that would employ critical race theory or, in the language of the Iowa state legislature, teach "specific defined concepts." Among these forbidden concepts are those that name "the United States of America . . . [as] fundamentally or systemically racist."[12] In essence, the law now denies us the opportunity to see reality clearly and recognize the structures, systems, and institutions that make up a nation steeped in the culture of racism. As an evolving racial project, readers might want to pause and access online the most recent legislation passed in the many states of our nation, possibly including their own.[13]

Considering our role in this era's struggle over curriculum, religiously affiliated schools might be exempt from the constricting, obfuscating, and romanticizing versions of history that such legislation will govern. But we have seen in our examination of history both the tightrope negotiation of church and state and the state as a potential funding source for religious institutions of education. Today, in many states, religiously affiliated schools can receive some form of government funding.[14] And in 2022, the Supreme Court issued a ruling that requires that states "fund private religious schools if they fund any other private schools, even if those religious schools would use public funds for religious instruction and worship."[15] Access to funding is a double-edged sword that might also lead to restrictions on curriculum. Anticipating the Supreme Court decision, Thomas Reese recommended that "those who support government funding of religious schools should focus on programs that are the least controversial and most secular."[16] But in the tangled agonism of church commitments and state interests, Catholic institutions might head the opposite way, taking a theological path that insists on naming our past sins of White supremacy in the confession that is crucial to religious instruction in the faith. Catholic educators, administrators, families, and congregations can mobilize around the practice of truth telling and analysis of the United States as a culture of racism as foundational to Catholic practices of loving God and loving neighbor. Truth telling about history is essential to the structure of our worship when we open with a penitential rite seeking forgiveness in the expression of a general confession of sinfulness. Accounting for our sins is a practice of the faith, and thus antiracism work is essential to our deeply held religious beliefs. Catholic institutions of church and school, in practices of education and practices of prayer, must become leaders in a twenty-first-century liberation theology that insists that God works for the care of all humans, for the care of all creation, *in* history and in the struggle for racial justice, with a particular concern for the most marginalized. Will Catholic institutions be able to resist the pull of economic gain? And will we embrace or discard the liberating curriculum of God's care for all humanity and the theological requirement of truth in the face of our own participation in sin? Catholic institutions of church and school have a new and compelling need to take responsibility for our past failures as historically White-serving institutions fueling the sins of White supremacy in our nation and to step up into the truth telling of history as a theological commitment and as a way that God might work in the coming kingdom of our nation's salvation.

As Catholic institutions of church and school seek to be locations where White supremacy is dismantled so that solidarity across lines of racialized divisions can create the world anew, these same institutions must reckon with their realities as storehouses of illicitly gained capital. We must also reject the historic patterns of church and school as White serving. As the stories of St. James the Greater, the Sisters, Servants of the Immaculate Heart of Mary, the Oblate Sisters of Providence, and Catholic-run Indian boarding schools have shown, the church as an institution takes many forms and distributes its resources in unequal ways. The inequality of dedicating resources to the flourishing of those who had been racialized as White and of withholding resources that might have enhanced the flourishing of those who had been racialized as Black, Indian, Latinx, and Asian is a deep wound in our multiracial Catholic history, and its scars of separation remain with us today. Instead of a church that witnessed the in-breaking of a coming kingdom where all God's children dwell together, the church participated in the death-dealing divisions of racial categorizing that holds our bodies in trauma even today.

At the same time, our Catholic institutions are storehouses of diverse stories that offer counterwitnesses to possibilities in these places. As the stories of Sucky/Susannah and Henrietta/Hetty have witnessed in Chapters 2 and 3, Black Catholics enslaved by the church gave some of themselves to the creation of institutions of parish and university. We remember their labor poured into institutions that served White interests. But we simultaneously recall the grace that sustained them to withhold their labor and direct it instead to the flourishing of their companions. Sucky withheld her emotional labor toward the priest who abused her; Henrietta reserved some among her efforts to dedicate to the Black Catholic Church of St. James the Greater. The multiplicity of action and activity buried in the histories of our institutions might be drawn out more fully to guide us in the tasks that lie ahead.

Here, the witness also of Dolores Huerta alongside Larry Itliong and César Chavez, together leading a movement that could invite Catholics who had been racialized as White and received the benefits of Whiteness—like Robert Kennedy and Dorothy Day—reminds us of the ongoing struggle for flourishing, which is always a multifaceted story. The church in the midst of the struggle of the United Farm Workers was a shifting entity that *both* stood in the way of flourishing for Latinx and Filipino workers as victims of financial violence (lending advantage to wealthy growers) *and* stood alongside those who confronted the growers to adopt more humane and humanizing practices, which returned people to their place of dignified work. Precisely because the church has claimed to be "all things to all people" it is necessary to analyze and understand the ways in which the church aligned itself with White flourishing and served White interests.[17] We simultaneously recount the ways Catholics stepped into the otherwise possibilities of struggling for legislation that might bring forward a transformed world.

We arrive in this chapter at our present where those readers among us who are part of Catholic institutions of church and school might ask ourselves the question of whom *our* practices serve. Because so many of our institutions were created as historically White serving and exploited Black, Indigenous, Asian, and Latinx peoples across each era of our nation's history, those of us who reap benefits from these institutions have a specific investigation to undertake. To interrogate and to understand past practices within our institutions has at least three aims. The first is to reckon with the benefits passed on to us from out of these injustices: to know them and to name them as rooted in evil. The second aim of interrogating past practices is to ask whether the pull of these patterns remains today in White-centered interests. And the third aim is to return what has been stolen. Dwelling in the depths of these realities is work we must undertake together, and this is holy work. It is a sacred calling to faith-fully recognize our saturation in sin and to seek together salvation. As Christians we are called to bring forth a better world, even with our feet mired in a world fully compromised by evil.

But even as our world is fully compromised, utterly saturated in sin, it is still a grace-filled wonder where the divine meets us at every turn. The celebrative *fiesta* among the farm workers on Easter morning, the sanctuary sanctified by Nelly even in her enslaved condition, the generationally transformative witness of Henrietta as she promised to shepherd Mary Priscilla in the next generation of the faith. It is the faith of the Catholic and Christian tradition that God meets us in our humanity, even in its evil, even in its failing. In the struggle is something worth celebrating—the anticipatory joy of the resurrection. In the work that is the work of redemption today there is joy in-breaking in our coming together and transforming what has separated us. Gustavo Gutierrez witnessed to the transformation of the world in history as the work of God's salvation among us: "Salvation—totally and freely given by God, the communion of human beings with God and among themselves—is the inner force and the fullness of this movement of human self-generation initiated by the work of creation."[18]

In the history of White supremacies examined in this book, we recognize the path of racialization as a practice that fundamentally separated us from one another. The work of healing is the work of communion among human beings, which mediates our communion with God. Such a witness to the possibilities of our companionship and communion wraps our work within a salvific project. Gutierrez continues: "Consequently, when we assert that humanity fulfills itself by continuing the work of creation by means of its labor, we are saying that it places itself, by this very fact, within an all-embracing salvific process. To work, to transform this world, is to become a [hu]man and to build the human community; it is to save."[19] In our work today we celebrate that an otherwise possibility fueled by the inexhaustible Spirit is available. As we mount our struggle and the difficult work that lies before us, we anticipate the in-breaking of a transformed future in our midst.

The celebration that is to come will not arrive without giving up and giving over the hold on the benefits that White supremacies have delivered. Here we are invited into the kenotic rhythm of the earth and redemption, witnessed in the teaching remembered of the one who walked among the agricultural families in the Galilee under Roman occupation: "Unless a grain of wheat falls into the earth and dies, it remains just a single grain, but if it dies it bears much fruit" (John 12:24, NRSVUE). This kenotic truth must also be borne in the lifeways and halls of Christian institutions, especially historically White-serving institutions who come to recognize that what they have been holding onto was stolen from the lives and labors of others. How might Christian institutions take seriously the heart of the Gospel, that only by losing one's life do we save it?

The proposal that follows invites members of Christian institutions, both church and school, to release the illicit gain of capital through practices that leverage the resources of institutions for the transformation of the world. Given the structural and structuring reality of the sin of White supremacy, we might ask at every level of our institutional life: *Whom does this decision serve? Whom does this practice benefit?* And if we find that those decisions and those practices disproportionately result in benefits to people who have been sorted into the category of "White" and historically received benefits from the sins of White supremacy, we might recognize those White-serving practices as rooted in the racism of our world. At every level of our institutional lives we ask: Whom does that messaging—of sermon or institutional identity—serve? Whom does that curriculum serve? Whom does that admissions policy serve? Who benefits from the resources of our institution? Color-evasive practices that do not interrogate the racialized makeup of the beneficiaries of our actions fundamentally perpetuate an unjust status quo, where American institutions were built for the purpose and succeeded in directing benefits to those who had been racialized as White. Institutions are places where people practice particular ways of being human; as Christians recognizing the sin-saturated state of our institutions, might we be recognizably identifiable as *kenotic Christians* willing to leverage our resources for a different world? If our answer is "yes, we seek to be Christian institutions in the kenotic pattern of Christ," what is it we must do?

Returning to Maria Yellow Horse Brave Heart's cycle of addressing historical trauma, we are reminded of practices that deepen in a spiral of transforming institutions: Know our histories, understand/analyze our histories, release the gain, transform our practices. Attending to her structural process on a personal level, we do what we can in the places we are already found. The People's Institute for Survival and Beyond names this self-reflexive practice as identifying where *we* stand as gatekeepers *within* institutions. As the People's Institute describes: "Persons who work in institutions often function as gatekeepers to ensure that the institution perpetuates itself. The gatekeeper becomes an agent of institutional transformation by operating with anti-racist values and networking with those who share those values to maintain accountability in the community."[20] If the call of the Christian is toward the kenosis that brings new life, those of us who are embedded in historically White-serving institutions are gatekeepers who might aim to ensure that the institution not simply perpetuate itself but transform itself. Because the natural inclination of institutions is to perpetuate themselves, this work of transformation will be countercultural and may be painful. But that is where Christian institutions might lean into the multifaceted reality of our locations and seek the *spiritual* capital that can be found there.

Bringing together Brave Heart's analysis with the theorizing of Kwon and Thompson, we might render the spiraling process of transforming institutions anew. Brave Heart begins with the essential task of truth telling, and Kwon and Thompson provide the proposal that this project would return stolen histories and stolen identities, erase the erasure of peoples, and restore the humanity and agency of those who have been rendered absent-presences. Truth telling would move the ghosts from their haunting location into the full portrait of the ancestors of our institutions. Brave Heart's second step by which we understand this history through analysis would allow us to reap the insights of the graced ghosts by recognizing stolen wealth, stolen identity, stolen history, and stolen power. For those institutions that have *benefited* from the historical trauma of a culture of White supremacy, Brave Heart's third step is translated to insist that we must release the gain and return what has been stolen. Thereby, the otherwise possibility of transformed institutions might emerge: institutions in which we move forward together with shared history, shared identity, shared power, *and* shared wealth.

In what follows in this chapter, we will pursue the combined analysis of Brave Heart and Kwon and Thompson to propose followable steps for Catholic institutions of church and school to be partners in the project of repair and transformation. We will use the framework thus constructed to ask how our institutions create shared history, shared identity, shared power, and shared wealth to atone for the sins of White supremacy. Looking at examples from institutions that have engaged in this work helps us brainstorm for our own projects of repair. But the heart of the project in this chapter will be to recognize how difficult this work is and to commit to its unfolding by grounding deeply in the spiritual capital available to us from the many examples of our Catholic tradition.

## Christian Institutions and the Resources of Capital

The Catholic Church in the United States is a capital-rich institution on many levels. It is an identifiably organized network of persons with the people power of social capital. It is home to the symbolic capital of recognition as "religious" and an effective network of "education"—two of the key systems that organize societies. Those who participate and those who matriculate are often enhanced by participation in these locations of the institution. Those who participate might also tap into the spiritual capital conveyed by a tradition that provides an ultimate horizon of meaning to ground the changeable fortunes of human lives. Access to spiritual, social, and symbolic capital is facilitated by the Catholic Church as a network of church and school that holds resources of economic capital to support its work. But if the US Catholic Church was built on the illicit gains from stolen land and stolen labor (as Chapters 2, 3, and 4 have demonstrated) and if the American Catholic Church unequally distributed its capital (as Chapters 2 through 5 have shown), then a mobilization of capital to address the inheritance from the sins of White supremacy seems to be in order.

## Capital to Repair the Theft of History

When Kwon and Thompson name the form of thievery that is the "theft of history," they are drawing attention to the kinds of histories that trade in romanticization and erasure. Romanticization names the White-centered histories that elevate White actors (even those with supremacist expressions) and simultaneously engage in the erasure of White harms and of those who have been harmed by the actions of these White actors. The believable history of White supremacist institutions of church and school is still recounted in our institutional histories. Our built environments of church and school that display portraits and bear the names of persons known to have advanced White supremacist aims are evidence of the power of a White racial frame that presumes the innocence and moral character of White actors. The history of educational institutions that derived funding from an economy of enslavement but offer nothing in the official institution-selling narrative to suggest this trades in the simultaneous romanticization and erasure that protects historically White-serving institutions from the truth telling necessary to engage the process of healing. The first step of reparation follows Maria Yellow Horse Brave Heart's starting point: To tell the truth about our histories begins by knowing our histories.

Do you know the history of the institutions—of church and school—in which you reside? For those established during and sustained through the 1920s through the 1960s, what benefits were accrued through the racist lending of the era of redlining? For those established before 1865, do you know their indebtedness to an economy of enslavement? And for all our institutions, what benefits were gained "by purchase or by conquest" when land was transferred/stolen from Indigenous peoples?

To repair the theft of history, we must engage in the project of truth telling about our institutions and tell our histories anew. Who were the people of color whose life and work went into the creation of our historically White-serving institutions? By what means have our institutions been transformed in the direction of racial justice? For all the landmark "firsts" in our student body or our faculty, who were the many excluded by racist practices of hiring and admissions? How do we tell a more complex history that honors our past and proclaims a commitment to a different future?

Many institutions of higher education have begun the project of revisiting history so as to engage it more complexly. One of the earliest was undertaken by Brown University, and a robust engaging of history can be found in the work of Craig Steven Wilder in *Ebony and Ivy: Race, Slavery, and the Troubled History of America's Universities*. Since the Brown Report and the publication of Wilder's work, many other institutions have engaged in the project of learning histories erased and restoring complexity. "In 2003, Brown University, which is named for a family of slave traders, convened a committee to study the issue and recommend an official response, and since then, more than 30 other schools have followed suit."[21] Although Brown's self-study was begun more than two decades ago, and although historians have for a long time known about the Jesuit practices of owning humans and employing enslaved labor, Catholic and Jesuit systems were not publicly engaging our histories until a 2016 *New York Times* front-page story featured Georgetown's 1838 sale. Over the last twenty years, institutions of higher learning have entered into the stage of healing that begins with truth telling about their histories. And new histories have emerged as the fruit of this labor: Harvard University's ongoing work, William and Mary, Princeton, the University of Virginia, and the entire undertaking of the consortium of Universities Studying Slavery. In the Jesuit network, Georgetown's ongoing work and the work of the Jesuits across the United States are evidence of the embrace of this project of facing our history.[22] And a wider Catholic network, with projects at, for example, De Paul University in Chicago, see the list growing. Associations of women religious, like the Loretto Sisters and the Sisters of Charity, are similarly engaged in the difficult revisiting of history by which we might restore our ancestors to their more full location as participants in our institutional histories.[23] In 2022, Kelly Schmidt provided an accounting of the many and diverse locations of Catholic institutional reckoning, including colleges and universities, Catholic secondary schools, religious orders, and dioceses, identifying real possibilities for the creation of consortia to continue this work.[24] There are many hands and hearts at work in the project of Brave Heart's first step: truth telling about our histories.

Considering this first step and moving toward the second in transformative analysis, Jody Allen queries, "How do academic institutions evaluate their histories?" and responds:

> They have to be thorough. Do not give up the hunt for information. There is always more to be found. They have to be willing to be tough on themselves. They have to be deliberate. They have to fully commit

and that means providing adequate staffing, funds, and time. Institutions have to be willing to make their findings public; if not, you are wasting your time. No one alive today is responsible for anything that happened in the past. No one can control the past, but we are responsible for the present and the future. When you know better, you must do better.

Steps to consider:

1. Acknowledge that there is a story that hasn't been told.
2. Find your constituencies and listen to them; talk to them, involve them.
3. Make a plan based on what you've learned.
4. Take action.
5. Evaluate.
6. Start over.[25]

Recognizing the widespread sharing in the illicit gains of past harms within church institutions invites the collaborative efforts of individuals across the network to tell truth about the institution's history and engage together the analysis of its patterns. For Catholic and Jesuit institutions, this collaboration might be more fully enacted when we recognize the networked reality of Catholic and Jesuit institutions past and present. Catholic media systems disseminated "knowledge" that was produced in ecclesial and educational Catholic and Jesuit locations. Actors who perpetrated harms in one location moved through networks with their influence. The illicit gains in one part of the network regularly were transferred to other locations in the network. Because of our networked histories, our networks today should be resources for our shared work. Organizations like the Association of Catholic Colleges and Universities and the Association of Jesuit Colleges and Universities might collaborate across institutions to recognize the shared responsibility in our networks of the past and to share the responsibility in our networks in the present.

A lens that sees Catholic institutions as networked also asks us to consider the histories of parishes and other Catholic institutions alongside schools in retelling past practices of harm and understanding which of their underlying patterns might persist today. The work being undertaken by Catholic educational institutions will need to be linked also to work to be done at the diocese and parish levels, asking each Catholic parishioner the question *where did our money come from?* not only in relation to an economy of enslavement but also in relation to the key moments of wealth building that stem from land acquired from Indigenous nations and homeownership withheld during the era of redlining. Perhaps the witness of the state of New York, in returning one thousand acres of forest to the original Onondaga nation, or Stony Point Presbyterian Church, which signed over the title to its land and church to form a new partnership as the Sweetwater Cultural Center in Stony Point, New York, can serve as otherwise possibilities that might lead Catholic institutions forward. The Jesuits returning land to the Rosebud Sioux Tribe shows the steps that might be possible.[26] Leveraging our cultural capital toward community land trust and ownership for those dispossessed by White supremacy could be a project our Catholic and Jesuit institutions might undertake across the nation.

Among the roadblocks to interrogating our histories will inevitably be the allure of romanticized identities we can sell to alumni donors, future students, and ourselves. Romanticized identities once again place profits over people, centering White interests to remain undisturbed by the sins of White supremacy. And yet it is precisely here that we dig deep in our faith and double down on the theological awareness that the human condition is always compromised by sin and ever striving toward a fuller expression of our humanity. What would it look like if our Catholic colleges and universities took the lead in promoting identities that grapple with the insights of Critical Race Theory precisely when the education systems of the state are mounting their refusals? What would it look like if our network of Catholic institutions became known for our willingness to address and account for the sins of White supremacy?

But just as the struggle is external to our institutions as it ripples across our nation, the struggle is also internal: Members of our institutions may actively resist such liberatory truth telling. One key location where this has already become an issue is with those who control the narrative through access to archives. Recall our insights from the opening of our study, that archival retrieval forms a critical location for telling new histories, ones that account for erasures. Martha Sandweiss reports on the productivity of archival access in Princeton's project of truth telling. When members of the committee asked, "What might we be able to find by digging into the University Archives for a semester? The project grew from there. And our research is now publicly available on a website that includes the work of some 40 contributors, 1000 pages of text, and more than 400 digitized primary source documents, along with dynamic maps and videos."[27]

But researchers regularly report the resistance on the part of gatekeepers of the archives to disclose the contents that might serve us in this endeavor. Even now, as Jesuit and Catholic institutions are called by grace into the truth telling that confesses our demonic histories, many among these same institutions are not only willfully ignoring the past (what Kwon and Thompson recognize is a willful "unseeing") but also *willfully withholding* access to the past by denying access to the archives. As a Catholic and Jesuit community across the United States, we must encourage one another in the releasing of holds on archival materials that will enable this work, and partnering with organizations like the National Native American Boarding School Healing Coalition will further our work.[28]

The fear-based refusal to illuminate past sins feeds into resistance to the fearfully powerful collaboration of beneficiaries and descendants. To resist patterns of fear-based practices of erasure, we might orient ourselves across our lines of difference to encounter both the deficits of the denial of race-based benefits and the accumulation of unearned privilege as currents within our institutional communities today. We as a multiracial church are *both* the inheritors of unearned privilege from the sins of White supremacy and the inheritors of a promissory note from the denial of access in the past. What would it look like if we saw the work of repair mobilizing both sites and locations from which to do the work of repair in our relationships and in our institutions? The differential inheritance from a racialized church—in both parish and school—is an embarrassing confrontation with the failures of our common tradition. But our common humanity, and the potential of our common faith, and from a Catholic theological perspective our common future and love of the Creator we share in common *should* be sufficient to begin to bridge the fault lines of past failures. The leadership of descendent communities among some of the projects of repair at Georgetown is witness to the possibilities that come forth when we follow the ancient call to love God and neighbor, or, as Gutierrez has written, to love God through love of neighbor. Although face-to-face confession of the sins of our unequal inheritance may be difficult, we hold that the Creator of us all calls us into speaking that common truth. "Healing will not take place in silence."[29]

Such a willingness to speak our truths of injustice received as inheritance could have as its goal the fuller picture of a God at work in the world. Reclaiming a shared genealogy of our spiritual ancestors, we can witness together the strength of the Spirit at work in resistance and survival. Grace in the face of White supremacy is a witness among the communion of saints that might be a grace to sustain our work—whether our inheritance has been of unjust deficit or unjust benefits, together we tap into that grace of the Spirit to address White supremacies today.

## Returning Stolen Identity

In addition to material exploitations that brought economic capital to institutions, the institutions of the church fueled the believability of lies about racialized people through the production of cultural and symbolic capital. When pastors and preachers, educators and researchers produced false "knowledge" of peoples they were racializing as Black, Asian, Indigenous, or Latinx, they fueled the engines that engaged in the thievery of identity for countless human beings. As Kwon and Thompson describe, "White supremacy stole the truth about the identity of African Americans"[30] and, in similar projects, stole the truth about the identity of Native Americans, Latinx peoples, and Asians in America. Through "knowledge" that situated the great range of humanity into racial categories that served to create White Christians on the top of a hierarchy of humanity, educators and preachers "stole the truth" about persons thus racialized with White supremacist aims and "replaced it with lies."[31] In theological perspective, "the social identity assigned by the order of White supremacy was a powerful theft of the truth of [peoples'] inherent dignity."[32] The ethicist emilie townes names this as the cultural production of evil, and for institutions that participated in this production of evil-knowledge systems, we might have a special directive to leverage our educational and ecclesial resources to restore new knowledge.[33]

The cultural production of evil took up residence in a unique way within educational institutions, and the production of race-"knowledge" is among the components of history with which institutions are reckoning. The Harvard Report, for example, identifies its institutional complicity in intellectual production and "race science" through prominent scholars creating knowledge systems of harm for people of African descent, both in the era of enslavement and subsequently in fields like eugenics.[34] What might a similar query unearth in our educational institutions? In the institutions where you reside—of church and school—what was the symbolic capital of theological ideas about peoples racialized as Indian, Black, Latinx, and Asian preached from your pulpits or produced as "knowledge" in your libraries, classrooms, or publications supported by scholars and priests of your institution? How do we account for this history and recognize the positive impact it produced for the institution and the simultaneous negative impact it had on those racialized as other-than-White and other-than-Christian by the "knowledge" produced in our institution?

A leader in this work in the Catholic-Jesuit network, Georgetown offers models of truth and healing, facing history, and working with descendants. Their report "also recommended infusing Georgetown's curriculum with information about our history and advocated for research and teaching around this history."[35] Here we see the effects of Brave Heart's spiraling steps as history gives way to analysis, which in turn gives way to transformations within our institutions, which return to truth telling to deepen the analysis and institutional transformations. The uncovering of history and the restoring of identity will be long-term, ongoing work.

Truth telling in the project of re-membering history serves as the lever for opening the project of restoring stolen identities, but acknowledgment of past harms is insufficient for the more robust project that is repair. Although an inherent requirement of our work will be to recognize the lives stolen through the project of White supremacy, the accompanying project must also commit to replacing any deficit narratives of the abused with the strength narrative of resistance. But traditions of White-centering knowledge systems are hardly equipped with the tools necessary for the truth telling of history to witness anew the strength and self-definition of peoples who have withstood the assaults of White supremacy. In historically White-serving educational institutions, such alternative truth telling will invite all of the disciplines into the interrogation of White-centering work and the expansion of knowledge that centers instead persons who had been racialized as Black, Indigenous, Latinx, and Asian. This will require changes in hiring and changes in admissions so that our institutions can authentically restore the living heritages of peoples who have been erased from our institutional consideration under the structures and systems of White supremacy. No longer serving a colonizing project of bringing people racialized as "Other" into White systems of knowledge, our admissions, hiring, and curriculum might be decolonized. It will require White-heritage locations that have enacted White supremacies to recognize patterns of sinfulness and seek to become White followers in an identity of discipleship, shared power, and shared leadership.

For Catholic ecclesial institutions, this project invites us to consider the deep roots of diversity *within* our Catholic community. Elevating this diversity, we might return with a commitment to witness how White-serving institutions convey the value of Whiteness in centering of White, European-heritage cultures. Instead, Catholic institutions that continue to pass on romanticized versions of history can move toward centering the faith-lives of Catholics of color in the collective memories conveyed through curriculum and liturgical spaces. What have been the marks of grace, the gifts of the Spirit infusing the resistance among African-descended Catholics? How have Indigenous, Latinx, and Asian Catholics created a multiracial, multiethnic, multicultural church? In this, White Catholic institutions will once again become demonstrations of White following insofar as Black Catholic institutions have long centered Black history.[36] For Catholic educational institutions, this project expands into curriculum. To what extent does the educational curriculum in Catholic K–12 schools, colleges, and universities continue to prioritize White cultural systems of knowledge inherited from Europe and even from European-colonizing systems of knowledge, control, and mastery? In locations that actively erased cultures and languages, a specific curriculum of restoration might be envisioned across the network of Catholic schools. For example, in Catholic boarding schools, there was a punishment linked to speaking English. As one survivor reports:

> I don't remember what the punishment was but it was almost like you didn't want to speak that language, your Native language, your Indian language as it was called then, because it was punitive and almost shamed for having to speak that language. There was a time when I think there was a lot of denial in the culture, not only in the culture, but denial. A deeper feeling was a denial of who I was as a person.[37]

We might ask whether Catholic schools across the nation denied children their personhood in speaking the various languages of the globe. Restoring original languages, like at Mahpiya Luta (former Red Cloud Indian School), points in a direction within our reach as educational institutions, returning stolen identities through our curricula.[38] Similarly, the liturgical expressions that restore the rich diversity of language and culture might be prioritized. The restoration of cultures and the restoration of multireligious heritage can also be a project of repair for the deep denial of the personhood of persons made marginal by institutional past practices. For educational institutions, this is work we have been prepared to undertake in the very wisdom and learning of our missions. For liturgical spaces, we might be host to the witness of divine encounter in its many forms.

As Catholic institutions become locations for the restoration of what were and remain stolen identities, this will also require a deeper wrestling with Catholic-Christian *theological* supremacies that express God's priority and preference for Christian traditions. As we've seen throughout this book, one of the key features of stolen identity in the project of colonization across the nation was the theft of identity and the theft of spiritual capital in the advancement of a theology/ideology and practice of Christian hegemony. From the fifteenth through the twentieth centuries, Indigenous peoples were systematically denied their ancestral access to the divine through the structures and systems of Christian theologies that deemed them "pagan" or "devilish." Christian theologies of supremacy attempted to steal identities and access to the divine for 12 million enslaved Africans, forced from their homeland and held captive to an enforced Christianity in America that sent into hiding African traditional practices and Islamic expressions. It was precisely because of Christian hegemony and the ideologies of Christian exclusivism and supremacy that countless Asian workers were refused the benefit of citizenship and entry into the body politic. Christian hegemony and Christian supremacy were the beating heart of the project of White supremacy as it marched across the land, creating the illusion of a "White Christian nation" in its wake.

The heritage of White Christian supremacy makes it especially difficult for White Christian schools and churches to break free from the supremacies embedded in the faith. Several generations of Christian theologians have tried to address the theological maneuvers available to us as we navigate our heritage and our future in theologies of religion and interfaith studies. At this point, it is reasonable to say that the study and engagement of the wide variety of religious traditions of the globe and, in a special way, those that sustained peoples against the tide of White Christian supremacy can be part of the project of repair. Curricula and commitments to interfaith learning will advance, then, as a potential project for restoring stolen identities and stolen sources of access to the divine. In the context of parish ministries, coming to know and work alongside our neighbors of diverse faiths can also be seen as a project of repair, dismantling also the structures and systems of segregation that Kwon and Thompson name as a byproduct of generations of racism in America. Interfaith becomes a site of antiracism efforts.

The theft of identity took many forms in the long history of the US racial project. Our institutions can step into a future racial project by mobilizing the capital needed to change what we teach, how we teach, how we pray, and how we gather. The project of return for the theft of identity will also include the transformation of campus cultures from their heritage as predominantly White-serving institutions to the multicultural, multiracial embrace of our full humanity. The return for the theft of identity is also a transformation of the identity of our institutions. It will require White-heritage locations that enact White supremacies to recognize patterns of sinfulness and seek to become White followers in an identity of discipleship, shared power, and shared leadership. "It is impossible to end racism while at the same time continuing the systems of white privilege that for centuries have maintained the churches [and schools] as segregated white institutions."[39]

## Return of Stolen Power

White-serving institutions have tended also to be governed by European-heritage culture and persons racialized as White. In light of the historical segregations that have been bequeathed to us in our churches, Joseph Barndt has pursued an analysis of reshaping congregations toward shared culture and shared leadership in ways that might be steps in the progress of returning stolen power. The comprehensiveness of his program lends itself to study by White congregations seeking to transform communal worship settings and can be applied to our educational institutions as well. The bottom line is that it is not just a matter of outreach but of changing institutions from the inside. As an antiracist ecclesial activist, Barndt concludes:

> The institutionalized racism in the church that we are seeking to change was created over a period of five hundred years. During those five hundred years, within the church there evolved carefully designed racist ecclesiastical structures and processes of decision making, the training of white clergy and other white leaders, the creation of racist programs of worship, education, and other services, and the shaping of racist policies and practices, cultural styles, and values—all intentionally in the context of a mission and purpose to exclusively serve white Christians. Not only does this need to be undone and redone, but a new anti-racist leadership and membership in the church needs to learn about and accept these changes and then live with them long enough until they are as natural as the previous way of life.[40]

Catholic and Christian institutions of higher education that have been and continue to be historically White serving might take cues from Barndt's proposal, where leadership, governance, admissions and aid, hiring, hospitality, shared power, refusal of White-centric institutional identity, and the practice of White following are enacted at all levels and locations of our institutions and our networks.

## Return of Stolen Wealth

Culture change, power sharing, and curricular adjustments are necessary interventions in the transformation of historically White-serving institutions. And each of these invites deeper consideration of the illicit wealth that might be recognized as the foundational sin on which the histories of our institutions sit. That is, the very capital that was gained through racist projects might now fund antiracism within our institutions.

> In September 2019, [Virginia Theological Seminary] announced the creation of an endowment dedicated to the payment of reparations, and the intent to research, uncover, and recognize Black people who labored on-campus during slavery, Reconstruction, and segregation under Jim Crow laws. The endowment is a part of the Seminary's commitment to recognizing its participation in oppression in the past and commitment to healing and making amends in the future.

> Additional funds have been allocated to support the work of Black congregations that have historical ties to the Seminary; to create programs that promote justice and inclusion; and to elevate the work and voices of Black alumni and clergy within The Episcopal Church.[41]

Georgetown University and the Jesuits of the Maryland Province have made financial commitments as part of the project of repair, but still very few institutions have been willing to step into the financial dimension of reparation. The possibility of returning wealth stolen from the lives and labors of enslaved persons and the probability of returning wealth stolen in the form of land from Indigenous nations are among the stumbling blocks for many institutions to even begin the project of repair.

The depths of the debt and the complexity of the complicity render many of us paralyzed to imagine a possibility other than that of retaining the wealth stored up in our institutions. But this undertaking should be a holy task, an otherwise possibility that hears a divine call to repair what has been broken, to return what has been stolen. To engage in an accounting of our institutional history is but a first step toward what might be a very long road of repair, but our unwillingness to even ask the questions, to even imagine what it might look like to return land or pay reparations, is a fundamental hardness of heart and protection of property in a stand-your-ground culture that once again places profitability over personhood.

More than thirty years ago, in 1989, Representative John Conyers introduced legislation that would form a commission to begin the process of research and study toward creating a national plan for reparations for African Americans. For more than three decades, the US legislative body has revisited and refused this initiative. In recent years, however, the reintroduction of HR 40 has gained momentum in Congress, with the possibility of a future study on the horizon. Embedded in the text of the legislation is the recognition by lawmakers that truth telling about our national past is the necessary first step. The bill envisions an audit of "the direct benefits to societal institutions, public and private, including higher education, corporations, religious and associational" (HR 40, Section 2.b (6)).[42] When we see on the horizon a national audit requiring that we consider the direct benefit to our religious and educational institutions that came at the expense of African Americans, and when we couple that with the analysis that these same institutions benefited from the exploitation and exclusion of peoples racialized into the various categories of our nation's racial project, why would we not get our houses in order, encouraged by the grace of our ghosts?

Because the road is long and the journey difficult, we will need strength, sustenance, and the spiritual capital to endure the next stage in the unfolding story of redemption. As scholars in the field of religion, Kwon and Thompson offer biblical foundations from the Hebrew Bible and the New Testament as paths to pursue in our twenty-first-century work. In addition to those scriptural warrants, we might turn to the cloud of witnesses and the communion of saints in the practices of our ancestors to journey with them in the next phase of resistance and struggle against the sin of White supremacy.

## Spiritual Capital: Sources for the Struggle against the Sin of White Supremacy

Throughout this history of institutionalized White supremacy and the United States as a culture of racism, those who were racialized as Black, Indian, Asian, or Latinx within America's racial project found resources to survive and to withstand the assault on their person, on their dignity, and on their humanity as it was leveled by White persons and a White supremacist culture. Often denied economic capital, people identified alternative forms of capital for the project of survival. The people power of social networks and the symbolic capital of self-affirmations are crucial. But it is the spiritual capital that intrigues me as a theologian. For we too might find sources and strategies for survival in our troubled times and sustenance for our fight against White supremacy if we pattern ourselves on the strategies they discovered and employed. The research of this book suggests that people racialized into the categories of Black, Indigenous, Latinx, and Asian found resources to situate the assault and theft of White supremacy within a wider horizon in order to *resist* it. In the field of theology, situating the everyday in the long view of our lives is named as one's "spirituality." Recalling Sandra Schneiders's definition, spirituality is "the experience of consciously striving to integrate one's life in terms not of isolation and self-absorption but of self-transcendence toward the ultimate value one perceives."[43] In so defining, Schneiders elevates spirituality as a project by which persons seek "personal integration through self-transcendence and toward the horizon of ultimate concern."[44] Spirituality, measured in the acts of integrating our everyday lives into the horizon of ultimacy, provides the web of meaning in which we move and into which we fall when faced with the inevitable meaninglessness or frequent despair that confronts us in the project of our human existence within a culture of dehumanization.

In what follows, we return to the witness of the ancestors, the grace of the ghosts, and find interpretive practices, assets for truth telling, patterns of redemption, and commitments to self-care in the joy of a community of struggle. Let them lead us from our history into a transformed future.

## A Hermeneutic Posture

As Shawn Copeland and others have demonstrated, many women and men who were enslaved found the symbols, stories, songs, and shouts of the Christian tradition to be life-giving in the face of the attempt to impose meaninglessness through systems of White supremacy. Copeland asks us to see how through the depths of their faith practices of prayer and witness "enslaved people negotiated this ontological and metaphysical assault by audaciously asserting their essential humanness in the face of dehumanizing conditions by choosing transcendence."[45] An African American hermeneutic attuned to the liberating God of Exodus and the liberating love of a cosuffering Jesus provided a powerful and sustaining web by which persons were held in the cradle of a creative God concerned for their life and well-being. Paul Dunbar's "Ante-Bellum" sermon, Harriet Jacobs's biblically framed redemption of her children, Harriet Tubman patterning her practices on God's emissary Moses, Phyllis Wheatley echoing the vengeance of the liberating God in Isaiah, Sojourner Truth leaning into her mother's God of love and care and compassion. Each of these provides evidence that a hermeneutic posture toward Christian tradition can be sustaining. The sustaining spirituality of Christian tradition is in strong evidence in the breakaway life of the African Methodist Episcopal tradition of Black churches and the subsequent expansion of Black Christian and Black Catholic spaces in which to meet in community the God who loves humanity and who in a particular way bears a deep concern for the oppressed. In the words of James Cone, "In Christ, God enters human affairs and takes sides with the oppressed."[46] The vibrant realities of Black Christians reflect back to us the story and song and shout that could convey to enslaved peoples the love of a Creator repulsed by the evils of enslavement. The African American hermeneutic of a God of liberation and love, and even a God of vengeance toward the oppressor, formed the fabric of "spiritual capital" that enslaved Christians mobilized as a resource in the context of a social world of White supremacy denying them the symbolic capital of recognition and the economic capital of payment for their work. The spiritual capital of the Christian tradition did real work, providing a framework to integrate the everydayness of assaults on Black bodies in resistance. As we continue our work as Catholic Christian institutions, how will we ground deeply in the spiritual capital afforded by the witness of an African American hermeneutic toward Christian scripture?

Such a hermeneutic simultaneously recognizes that the Christian witness to the God who saves and sustains is not only found in our sacred texts. Those forced into servitude and the trauma of the Middle Passage were already held in the hands of God, if by God we mean the Creator of all that is. Peoples enslaved by White Christians already knew God in the hollows of their hearts and the hollers of their shouts, in the prayerful resonance of recitation of the Qur'an, in the Catholicism they inhabited in the Kongo, in the ancestral traditions of the Spirit/spirits among whom they dwelt in Africa. Although the argument by White Christians that peoples of Africa were pagan and cursed by God through Ham was mobilized to cement the structures of slavery, our theological understanding must recognize the God at work in all places and peoples and thus contemplate the reality of God journeying alongside African women, men and children as White Christians kidnapped, sold, and killed them.

The inclusion of African Muslim writings from the antebellum era forces us into a transatlantic frame and presses the question: What were the traditions of spiritual capital that sustained the enslaved through the trauma inflicted by White Christians? Held in captivity in Charleston, South Carolina, Omar Ibn Said opens his autobiographical reflection with the words intoned in the opening of the Qur'an: "In the name of God, the merciful, the compassionate. May God bless our Lord Mohammad: Blessed be He in whose hands is the *mulk* [ownership, dominion, 'absolute power through ownership'] and who has power over all things."[47] Just as we envision a God who sustained through African traditional religions to withstand assaults of White Christian supremacy, so too we consider God as revealed through the Prophet Muhammad to have conveyed a life-sustaining hope and affirmation of a God who transcends tragedy and who alone has dominion.

This recognition that God meets us in many ways is a source of strength in the work that lies ahead. Tommy Davis captures this sentiment, recalling, "There-re all kinds of ways you can pray. You never pray the same way. I always start off [speaking Chippewa] . . . I pray like that. I thank the Creator every day."[48] Finding resources in ancestral traditions, "Genevive" explains: "I return to attend the pow wows. There is a beauty in the people that is extraordinary, there is a resilience there, cohesion, and there is a natural inbred sense of the spiritual. I'm very connected to the spiritual. That's how I survived."[49] This insight into the availability of the Spirit of the Creator at work in the world may also give us a new vision as we wrestle with our locations in institutions that have produced harm, even while they convey to us spiritual capital. Davis reflects: "I don't know what the Creator did for me, but I mean, he wouldn't let them break my spirit, no matter what."[50] When survivors of Indian boarding schools dig deeply into their ancestral traditions as a source of strength, they too demonstrate what we have learned from peoples of African descent who withstood the assaults of White Christians: that God finds humanity in many and various ways.

Some boarding school survivors found in the Catholic tradition resources to maintain a Catholic-inflected spiritual practice, while others found a calling to leave Catholic practices behind, and still others somewhere in between. Revealing a common tension for those of us wrestling with our inheritance from a harming institution, Romana Klein conveys: "I'm very much a spiritual person. Religion is meaning less and less to me the older I have become. Currently, I am angry at what the Catholic Church has done to people. I am angry at what the Catholic Church has done to children. Yet I feel torn because that was such a big part of my life."[51] And Roger White Owl concurs, "I was born and baptized Catholic, but I'm not a Catholic. I believe in our Native American spirituality. Its true meaning is the way of our ancestors, so I live that way. I live the way taught to us by the elders and the Old Warrior Society."[52]

Affirming the great variety of ways we might tap into alternative sites of spiritual capital beyond the institutions that have harmed us, our fellow companions in Catholic education also offer insights for deeper, ongoing, and more critical reflection. Thinking through his own relationship with the Christianity conveyed in both family and school, Erich Longie concludes: "I always did believe in what we Dakota call Wakan Tanka, the Great Mystery. . . . I didn't reject Christ's teachings; I rejected Christianity because in my mind it was all hypocritical. . . . I just believe that Wakan Tanka listens to a person who prays if they are sincere and if they really want to change."[53] Given the benefits our institutions have accrued from the sins of White supremacy and given the benefits we have accrued through the sins of White supremacy, Longie's challenging is real: Do we really want to change?

If we do want to see transformed institutions, we must continually seek them. As we've witnessed across the long stretch of American history, the struggle for racial justice and a Catholic stance against White supremacy has been a very long road. At every turn, at every advance we have seen a new setback and a renewed struggle.

## The Assets of Our Ancestors

This means that at every turn in our institutional journey, we will need to return again and again to the truth telling that names the sins of White supremacy in the many aspects of our institutional life. We will need to be willing to tell this truth again and again, and we may need to recall our foremother in the faith, Nelly (whom we met in Chapter 2). She was by the Jesuits' own accounts a remarkable talent, activating brilliance in many spheres of life. An "excellent cook," Nelly was "industrious," keeping house and keeping holy the sacred space of the sanctuary.[54] The Jesuits named these qualities but also put forward their negative assessment: Her only fault was "too long a tongue." Yet our reading of Nelly holds her up for emulation. Her willingness to release the pain of trauma *verbally*, to speak up and speak out, to tell the truth of the Jesuits as they purchased and sold human beings. Nelly's courageous practice might be an asset that encourages us also to tell our truths, even with too long a tongue.

Susannah, too, who over a lifetime with the Jesuits grew up into Grandma Sucky (whom we met in Chapter 2), models a posture to consider as she activates a spiritual self-care. As a young woman, Sucky grounded deeply in the spiritual capital of care as she interrupted the prayer practices of the Jesuit who thought he owned her and experienced harm as she tried to disrupt the self-harm of flagellation. One wonders if young Susannah knew that a temper would be turned on her and risked the extension of care anyway, or one wonders if she was young enough not to have interpreted an act of care as a transgression of "place." But after the Jesuit turned on her, she demonstrates the necessary spiritual capital of self-care, withholding her emotional labor from that relationship. It was as if Sucky lived through the lines of the Gospel: "As you enter the house, greet it. If the house is worthy, let your peace come upon it, but if it is not worthy, let your peace return to you. If anyone will not welcome you or listen to your words, shake off the dust from your feet as you leave that house or town" (Matthew 10:14). Although she was unable to leave the house of the Jesuits, upon experiencing the abuse of her enslaver, she withdrew her peace from his unworthy house, "never to care for him again." Placing Nelly and Sucky in proximity in our recalling them affords an opportunity to imagine the support our ancestors may have given one another in resisting the assaults on their personhood. This support our ancestors bequeath to us.

The spiritual capital of community is also remembered in our ancestors at St. James the Greater, in Colleton County, South Carolina. Having helped build anew the Catholic community in 1850–1852, the thriving church built spiritual capital among enslaved children, women, and men, and this capital seems to have served them when a fire destroyed their sanctuary in 1856. While the institutional church of the diocese of Charleston refused to rebuild, the institution of the church in the practices of the congregation refused to be dissolved. The seeds planted in the prayers and possibilities of a Catholic witness on the world sustained the community through the years of the Civil War, Reconstruction, and eventual reclamation by the diocese. Not only a source of the people power of social capital, the community is also a source of spiritual capital. The power of the Holy Spirit is made available in and through the connective relationships among us; our companions in the journey are the hands and hearts of those who sustain us, who save us. Created for sociality, in sociality we find salvific presence. "If humanity, each person is the living temple of God, we meet God in our encounter with others."[55]

And if we meet God in our encounter with others, then the joy of celebration—a practice of holiness in the UFW tradition—should also be among the sources of spiritual sustenance we tap into for the long road ahead. In the in-breaking of festive joy, companionship, and song, we celebrate the struggle even while it stretches on ahead. And it will be a long road ahead, not only within our world but within ourselves as we shift and move *within* institutions that have benefited from the sins of White supremacy.

## Spiritual Exercises for Deep Reckoning

At this point, it might be helpful to again be reminded that those who have been racialized as White have a distinct temptation to withdraw from this work when it inevitably becomes painful. Some among us have the option of retreating to the safety and security of being surrounded by Whiteness. In fact, we may have what Ignatius of Loyola named as a "disordered affection" toward the benefits of Whiteness. Therefore, in addition to leaning on our ancestors in US institutions, might those of us racialized as White—and those drawing benefits from proximities to Whiteness—lean into our inheritance from a European tradition read now in a new key? What would it look like to engage in the extended practice of Ignatius's *Spiritual Exercises* with the distinct aim of wrestling with Whiteness and coming more fully to terms with our disordered affections toward what we have gained from the sins of White supremacy?

The first week of the *Spiritual Exercises* is expressly directed toward a deep engagement with sin. Ignatius writes: "In the Spiritual Exercises, sins and their malice are understood more intimately, than in the time when one was not so giving himself to interior things. Gaining now more knowledge of and sorrow for them, he will have greater profit and merit than he had before."[56] The *Exercises*' deep consideration of sin and an intimacy with it might benefit all of us who inhabit institutions that have illicitly gained from the sins of White supremacy. Because the sin of White supremacy (in valuing White culture, White forms, and White persons) *can* be a disordered affection of those who themselves have not been categorized as White, this rendering of the *Exercises* could be of value wherever one has been located within the dynamics of our

US racial project.[57] To read the exercises in a new key, it might be helpful to consider Camara Phyllis Jones's definition of institutionalized racism:

> Institutionalized racism is defined as differential access to the goods, services, and opportunities of society by race. Institutionalized racism is normative, sometimes legalized, and often manifests as inherited disadvantage. It is structural, having been codified in our institutions of custom, practice, and law, so there need not be an identifiable perpetrator. Indeed, institutionalized racism is often evident as inaction in the face of need.[58]

When the sins of White supremacy have been codified in our customs, practices, and law, we may not even know that we are participating in a racially ordered reality that creates barriers to access of "goods, services, and opportunities." Because "there need not be an identifiable perpetrator," we also may not recognize when racially unjust systems are directed to our benefit. Era by era, US legislation and social formation built a nation that prioritized White well-being. The very structures and institutions that make up our nation (church, school, law, community) have been created unjustly, *and* the benefits of past expressions of White supremacy have been "stored" within those institutions. Those of us who are located within predominantly White institutions (both White people and people of color) might be acutely interested in undertaking a new form of the *Spiritual Exercises*, to arrive at a twenty-first-century application for understanding more intimately and gaining more sorrow for the sins embedded in *our* institutions, even our Jesuit institutions.

We might think of the *Exercises* as a form of sustenance for the journey of what Maria Yellow Horse Brave Heart has presented in the steps needed to address historical trauma.[59] With Brave Heart, we are asked to recognize that addressing the historical trauma of racism and White supremacy is not an easy fix but a multifaceted, multidimensional process of healing. In a spiraling path, Brave Heart proposes a movement from truth telling and analysis of the historical trauma toward releasing the pain and engaging in transformation for the future. Brave Heart describes healing from trauma, a healing that cannot take place without first naming the trauma that has occurred. And step by step, Brave Heart leads us deeper into the truth telling necessary for transformation. Ignatius of Loyola seemed to have understood a similar need for facing a painful reality before moving toward a transformed one, as the *Spiritual Exercises* invite the seeker into a deep dwelling in the particular and the painful as a process for self-evaluation and self-transformation. How might the deep spirituality of the *Exercises* be an accompaniment for the movement of truth and transformation that our nation needs? What follows is a reimagining and unpacking of the first week of the *Spiritual Exercises* as a way to see the work of racial justice and dismantling White supremacy as the work Christians are called to do in the world.

## Entering into the Spiritual Exercises: Opening Postures toward the First Week

The first week of St. Ignatius's *Spiritual Exercises* invites a pain-filled involvement in the sins we have committed as the foundation for deepening spiritual lives. The twenty-first-century reader may wonder whether Ignatius's sixteenth-century audience had as deep an aversion to investigating sin as our contemporaries do. Given the way sin and guilt have burdened Catholic imaginations to the point of paralysis, as well as the way "sin" has been wielded dangerously in the toolkit of symbolic capital, it makes perfect sense that many of us resist the deep situating of our feet in the self-loathing that talking of sin can produce.[60] But, contemporary readers should take pause in our very resistance to sin saturation with the insight of James Baldwin, who asked White people to see the ways they actively ran from facing their complicity in the sin of racism.[61] In Bryan Massingale's rendering of this sort of sin, the "willful ignorance" of the reality of the depth, breadth, and pervasiveness of White supremacy *and* our cultural, structural, and personal participation in it is a sin that White Christians need to look squarely in the face in order to ground ourselves in the necessary work of addressing, analyzing, and dismantling the racism that has become part of the air we breathe.[62] The first step of the first week is seeing the sin of White supremacy.

Ignatius, then, boldly asks us to enter into a time when "sin and their malice are understood intimately."[63] Attentive to the poetics of Ignatius's invitation, we might pause to consider the intimacy of this sin. How do we name the sin not simply as "racism" but with the greater precision of "White supremacy" to intimately account for the subtle and submerged ideology that persons, cultures, and practices that have been categorized as "White" are of greater value than any others? Where do we need to look inwardly for the intimacy of this pervasive accounting of humanity and human expression? Internalized racism speaks softly, intimately, cultivated close to hearts and minds, and escaping through lips and limbs sometimes nearly imperceptible, sometimes unknowingly. While internalized racism, and even internalized White supremacy, can affect all persons across the categories of "race," there is a special need for those who have been sorted into the category of "White" to interrogate deeply the systems of supremacy that reside internally, precisely because the disordered affection of White supremacy brings real benefits to those of us who have been categorized and racialized as White. When we name White supremacy as a "disordered affection," we might sense the intimacy of attachments that supremacy stirs.[64] The real, material benefits that Whiteness has brought can create barriers for the kind of deep investigation and contemplation that Ignatius envisions the *Exercises* to entail.

The regimen of the *Spiritual Exercises* is a useful measure of the ease with which we might fall into the willful ignorance of our sin of White supremacy. Ignatius describes the formula that the one making the exercises (the exercitant) "should remain for a full hour in each of the five Exercises or contemplations which will be made each day."[65] Over one week, a full thirty-five hours of sustained attention to the disordered affection of White supremacy is recommended. Ignatius's description of the concern raised by "hasty" or "unstable" eagerness to act pairs with this intimate knowledge importantly: The interrogation into the sin of White supremacy is not the guilt-ridden wailing and gnashing of teeth, nor is it the public calling out of every injustice at every turn; it is turning deeply inward to ground with strength and the suitability to each person "the carrying out of what one wishes to promise."[66] Drawing out the length of time dedicated to the exploration of disordered affection serves another function for undertaking the *Exercises*: We are reminded that the transformation of racism is not a quick fix. Given the depth, breadth, and enduring quality of White supremacy as it has sustained structures, systems, thoughts, and practices since the creation of "the races," *undoing* racism must be a similar journey of expansive depth, breadth, and quality if real transformation is to take root.[67]

## The First Week: Spiritual Exercises to Overcome Oneself and to Order One's Life, without Reaching a Decision through Some Disordered Affection

The opening directives of the *Spiritual Exercises* orient the penitent in the practice of an Examination of Conscience. In an imagined twenty-first-century schedule, the first day will be directed toward experiencing the rhythm of the retreat focused on daily disorders. Beginning the day, the retreatants dedicate themselves with a resolve to focus on the sin of White supremacy as "the particular sin or fault he or she wants to correct."[68] White supremacy is understood as being rooted in evaluative thoughts and the categorization of what is "White" as being of highest value; it is also understood as one's retreating to the benefits of Whiteness. Those committing to addressing this sin might begin with the process of cataloguing that Ignatius requires seeking the "grace to recall how often one has fallen into the particular sin or fault, in order to correct it in the future."[69] The first day would be spent calling to mind and chronicling my interpersonal and internalized sins manifest in my thoughts, words, and deeds.[70]

### Day 1 / Preparations and First Exercise

7:00 a.m. Examination of Conscience: resolution to guard against the sin of White supremacy
9:00 a.m. Examination of Conscience: considering the sin of White supremacy in thoughts*
12:00 noon Examen: Review and record failures[71] in thoughts and words*
3:00 p.m. Examination of Conscience: considering the sin of White supremacy in deeds*
7:00 p.m. Examen: List hour by hour a dot for each time he or she fell into the particular sin
*employing memory, understanding, and will

In the imagined schedule for Week 1 of the Exercises, time is set out to directly chronicle the kinds of sins of White supremacy that can be called to mind employing memory, understanding, and will. The essential thrust of Ignatius's work asks the retreatant to become aware of those things that they have known and experienced and bring them back to the surface for deeper consideration. We can retrace our steps, so to speak, and illuminate for ourselves our own faults and failures in our thoughts, words, and deeds. This particular day would benefit significantly from the reimagined Exercises artfully constructed by Patrick Saint-Jean in *The Spiritual Work of Racial Justice*.[72] As his text demonstrates, the use of Week 1 to account for the wide range of expressions in the form of interpersonal and internalized racism could last easily a full week or, indeed, a lifetime. In Saint-Jean's text, the investigation of thoughts, words, and deeds is guided by Ibram Kendi's consideration that "racist ideas make people of color think less of themselves, which makes them more vulnerable to racist ideas. Racist ideas make White people think more of themselves, which further attracts them to racist ideas."[73] Saint-James leads the reader through the encounters with people of other races shadowed by fear, suspicion, and judgment (33) as well as identifying some of the structures that keep racist realities out of view (47). He asks readers to consider when we have failed to see the image of God in our neighbor (56) and points to specifics of thoughts, words, and deeds that benefit from racism and White supremacy (70), encouraging a vision of intentional cross-racial relationships to remain attentive to the impact of our thoughts, words, and deeds (107). The Jesuit parish of St.

Ignatius in San Francisco has similarly developed an online resource to guide practitioners committing themselves to such an investigation.[74] Their Discernment Series provides a wealth of resources—both in reading and through videos—that might aid in the soul-searching retreat we are considering. To address the sins of White supremacy is to reconceive Christ among those who have been crucified by racism and White supremacy and each day to create an exacting account, "hour by hour . . . from the moment of rising to the present examination,"[75] so that at the end of each day, imagining Christ among the crucified, the penitent can ask: *What have I done for Christ? What am I doing for Christ? What ought I to do for Christ?*[76]

At the end of the first day and the morning of the second, the retreatant might rest deeply in the movement of the spirit Ignatius names as "discernment." Am I drawn toward the benefits and gains of Whiteness? Do I experience consolation or desolation in envisioning a multiracial future as the context in which my life takes place? The beauty of the Ignatian spiritual tradition is precisely the long timeframe of examination and the recognition of the affective elements that inform our understandings. Even if we can name White supremacy as "sin," might some retreatants not experience the lure of this evil in the benefits it presents? In the second day of the Week 1, retreatants are invited to name the desired goal of a "growing and intense sorrow and tears for my sins."[77] Some may not experience sorrow for their participation in the sin of White supremacy, and Ignatius recommends that one sets the sorrow for one's sins as precisely a goal for this exercise.

### Day 2 / Second Exercise: A Court Record of My Sins in Inheritance (the Period of My Youth)

7:00 a.m. Resolution to guard against the sin of White supremacy
9:00 a.m. A court record of my sins of inheritance of locality
12:00 noon Examen: Review and record failures
3:00 p.m. A court record of my sins of inheritance in relationships and occupation
7:00 p.m. Examen: Review and record failures in locality, relationships, and occupation

It becomes increasingly interesting to read the *Spiritual Exercises* through the lens of racial justice when we arrive at the second exercise in a week dedicated to enumerating the instances of sin in which we are embedded. For in the first point of focus, the exercitant is asked to create, in Ignatius's words, a "court-record of my sins."[78] More precisely, Ignatius asks the one who would take seriously their sins to look back on their personal history and to consider, "year by year, period by period," very particular elements of their lives. Ignatius asks that the one who would take the record of sin seriously would enumerate details about "the locality or house where I lived . . . the associations I had with others . . . the occupation I was pursuing."[79] This set of directions, focused on geography and habitation, is especially important in the United States, where so much racialized injustice has filtered through the systems of housing and the location of our homes. But it is precisely here that many may not recognize their condition *as* sin. The most fruitful application of Ignatius's invitation to recount our history and the "locality" of our sins of White supremacy requires supplementation precisely because the forms of "institutional" or "structural" sin are invisible to us. Here is a most crucial question when we set out our court record and cultivate our understanding with the analytic frame of the racially unjust legislation directly related to habitation: Do we even know the history in which we are embedded? Our retreat proceeds by offering three "periods" to consider as Ignatius leads us to deepening our engagement.

Consider your life story, period by period, and the place in which the locality of your home was situated. If you are in the United States, your understanding might be structured by an awareness that every inch of America now under the jurisdiction of the United States was land taken from Indigenous nations in the extended project of settler colonialism. In each period of your residence, do you know who the original peoples of that land were? Do you know the conditions under which that land came to be governed by the United States? Was the land taken violently or purchased, and under what terms? Was the transfer of land by treaty, or does the land remain unceded? How does the account of my being wrapped up in the sinfulness of the dispossession of Indigenous peoples find its way onto the "court record" of my sins? The act of land acknowledgment is a form of spiritual exercise that gives witness to the original peoples who inhabited the land, but the questions still must be probed: Do we feel genuine and deep sorrow for that sin sufficient to seek restitution and renewed relationships with the original peoples?[80]

The second major period our histories and our court record must recall is how the "locality or house where I lived" was involved in the nation's sin of slavery as an economic system of White supremacy. While Americans have a shared sense of this as a national reality, it is not clear that all Americans have been asked what relationship *their* locality had in particular to the generations of wealth building from the stolen lives and stolen labor of peoples of African descent. New histories remind us that it is not only locations where legal enslavement endured into the nineteenth century (that is, "the South") but also northern cities with earlier histories *and* economies connected to southern slaveholders' money. Whether in the form of early centuries of slavery in the Northeast, investments from slaveholders in cities "on the frontier" of the Midwest, or the struggle for an expansion of slavery into the West in the new US territories at the close of the Mexican–American War, the history of slavery in the United States and its actual impact on our location is often a point that cannot be brought to memory because we have never been taught this history in the first place. And even though we may know that an economy of enslavement built our nation, do we feel sorrow for this sin in the particular of *our* lives and *our* locations?

One of the reasons many White Americans do not feel sorrow for the sin of slavery is because they see it as someone else's sin, something that happened in the past and for which those of us in the present cannot be held responsible. But Ignatius's composition of place attentive to location renders space and place spiritually relevant. If we benefit from ownership of land acquired unjustly or inhabit "homes" built in an economy of enslavement, are we not the inheritors of the benefits of sin to which we might have a disordered attachment? In contemplating this spiritual geography in a composition of place, we might need to interrogate our disordered attachment to the wealth of gain from stolen land and stolen labor and to monitor the movement of our spirit as we consider the activism of land return and reparations.

A final invitation from Ignatius in the sixteenth century asks us to consider the home in which we reside in relation to the structures of White supremacy in the twentieth century. For this era is most crucial when it comes to the relationship between "home" and "racism." Yet, here again, perhaps many of us were formed in a willful ignorance of the very history that is our inheritance. The locations in which we are now situated across the United States were fundamentally affected by legislation that prioritized home ownership, with the establishment of the Federal Housing Administration (in 1934). Yet the funds that would be dedicated and distributed were informed by a racial hierarchy written into the mortgage-lending manual and used by persons in the real estate industry until well into the 1960s. Practices of the past that distributed government funding for White homeownership but withheld the same funding from families of color became part of the inheritance passed down generationally. If redlining took place in the 1930s and 1940s and the return on investment in homeownership skyrocketed between the 1940s and 1970s, those earlier generations being structured by the sin of White supremacy would have been passed along to me in the location of my inheritance.[81] The online resource "Mapping Inequality" can be a powerful tool in charting this structural sin.[82]

At each step of Ignatius's *Spiritual Exercises*, the penitent is asked to deepen their focus and concern in the court record of their sin that is being built. Week 1, Day 3 asks us to examine our understanding of the benefits we have accrued as we move into the present and, in Ignatius's second point to this exercise, "to ponder these sins, looking at the foulness and evil."[83] We are invited into the record of our sins and *to see them as sins*.

### Day 3 / Third Exercise: A Repetition of the Second Exercise Accompanied by Colloquies

7:00 a.m. Resolution to guard against the sin of White supremacy in my personal sphere
9:00 a.m. A court record of my sins in the present on locality
12:00 noon Examen: Review and record failures in locality
3:00 p.m. A court record of my sins of inheritance in relationships and occupation
7:00 p.m. Examen: Review and record failures; engage failures with colloquies

That this renewed invitation to ponder our sins as foulness and evil comes on Day 3, after the retreatant has already undertaken ten hours of enumerating and considering the court record of their sins, is a particularly potent insight embedded in Ignatius's program. That is, while we may be able to list the sins of our actions and the sins of our inheritance, *do we see them as sinful*? Was the destruction of native cultures and the deceit with which land was taken "foulness and evil"? Is the wealth that accrued through an economy of enslavement saturated in sinfulness? As we ponder the practices of redlining, the dedication of government funds to White wealth building through homeownership, and the withholding of those same funds from people of color, do we name them as "sins"? Our inheritance and our present realities structured by the sin of White supremacy in our locatedness connect directly to the court record of sins that Ignatius asks us to recount also in terms of "relationships" and "occupation." If my locality, my home, was structured in sinful segregations, what forms did my relationships take? What sort of work was being done (in schooling or profession) which, year by year, added to or disrupted the racialized injustice of my personal and family history? The change of heart and mind required to take seriously the sin of White supremacy begins with a willingness to name customs, practices, and law *as* sinful and to recognize the benefits that have accrued or been withheld through them as sin filled as well.

To the apparent aversion that many White Americans seem to have when asked to face the sins of White supremacy, Ignatius's program is an intense journey, ever deepening the requirement of truth telling about our sins. The Third Exercise is relentless in repeating the "court record of my sins" and in dwelling on our sinfulness. But the repetition is not mere self-flagellation or amplification of guilt but a necessary line of questioning for spiritual analysis. If the first expression of this audit of our sinfulness is a form of self-awareness and truth telling, the approach to the same list of specific sins in this repetition could offer a form of analysis toward understanding. Ignatius's *Exercises* presuppose that our embrace of our own sinfulness will require an ever-deepening process, as the Fourth Exercise is a repetition exactly of the movement of the Third. Ignatius enumerates the deepening and complexifying of our understanding of the sin of racism with a threefold aim:

(1) to feel an interior knowledge of my sins, and hatred of them;
(2) to feel the disorder of my actions, so that, hating them, I may correct myself and put myself in order;
(3) to ask knowledge of the world, in order that, hating it, I may put away from me worldly and vain things.[84]

The flow of these exercises in Week 1 invites the contemplation of sinfulness in such a way that the exercitant cannot fail to "see" and is invited to refuse the "willful ignorance" of the structures, systems, and participation in the sins of White supremacy.

Once we have created the court record of our personal sins, we do not need to be paralyzed, for the future weeks of the exercises will ask us to follow a course of action aligned with Christ toward resurrection and always cognizant of our sins. But, before we move on to Weeks 2, 3, and 4 in these modified Exercises of Accountability, we have the chance to deepen our understanding of the court record of our sins by not only considering the homes of our family dwellings but our institutional homes as well.

## Day 4 / Fourth Exercise: A Repetition of the Third, but Focused on Institutions

7:00 a.m. Resolution to guard against the sin of White supremacy in my institution
9:00 a.m. A court record of structural sin in my institutional locality
12:00 noon Examen: Review and record failures in the locality of my institution

3:00 p.m. A court record of structural sin in institutional relationships and occupation

For the purpose of this necessary shift, we might consider a definition of "institutions" as those locations that govern the "customs, practices, and laws" of our society, as Jones's definition of *institutionalized racism* has alerted us. Key institutions include government, religion, and education, so if we are embedded in Jesuit and Catholic institutions and attempting an authentic interrogation of sins in Week 1, the court record of our institutional sins might be especially pertinent. For while the spiritual capital of our Jesuit tradition bequeaths to us the resources of Ignatian spirituality, we must also reckon with the capital residing within Jesuit institutions that is bequeathed to us as the inheritance of racial injustice. Jesuits were among the first Christian missionaries who propelled the projects of settler colonialism, as evidenced in the *Jesuit Relations*, which offer an account of European-Christian encroachment and the logic of Christian supremacy that was its fuel. The deep roots of cultural, linguistic, and religious loss that Native Americans face today were fostered by our Jesuit and Catholic forebears from the sixteenth-century missions through to the twentieth-century boarding schools.[85] In the homes of our Jesuit and Catholic institutions, our academic forebears produced "knowledge" about the shortcomings of Indigenous peoples in their lifeways and beliefs while benefiting from legislation that transferred land from them into the hands of White Christians and White Christian institutions.[86] In both the general sense that all land in the United States was taken from Indigenous peoples and the more specific sense that legislation provided White settler access to more and more opportunities to claim land, the establishment of twenty-one of the twenty-eight Jesuit institutions of the AJCU during the nineteenth century encourages each institution to ask when and how *their* land came into their possession.[87] A similar question can be posed to all 230 Catholic colleges and universities identified by the Association of Catholic Colleges and Universities.[88] And for those readers embedded in Catholic parishes, the list of institutions residing on Indigenous land exponentially increases. Knowledge produced in Jesuit and Catholic academic spaces also forged the symbolic capital for both Jesuit-run and other Catholic, Christian, and governmental boarding schools.[89] In the practice of truth telling that might lead to healing, the Ignatian inspired Exercises of Accountability seem to be a very necessary first step.

The court record of sins of White supremacy, period by period, of our institutional network seems like a necessary endeavor to take seriously the exercises of the first week. Recalling the insight of the historian Shannen Dee Williams, the Catholic Church was the first and largest corporate slaveholder in the Americas, and our Jesuit roots are embedded in this soil.[90] Here, too, we might be overwhelmed with this truth telling, which begins with the buildup of land transferred to the Jesuits in Baltimore through the hands of Catholic bondspeople when James Carroll bequeathed not only his land but also the enslaved workers to the Jesuits. Our truth telling might include not only those named in Carroll's papers (Dick, Tomboy, Jack, Harry, Daniel, Peter, Dicky, Billy, Maria, Mary, Rachel, Davy, Jenny, Dolly, Toby, Adam, Maria, Pedro, Sampson, Rosa, Glascow, Page, and Judith) as the first enslaved Catholics who built our institutions but the countless more who labored in service of church and school in our Catholic, Jesuit network.[91] Might an accounting of the sins of White supremacy include a court record of the specific enslaved Catholics who built *many* institutions but remain unnamed and uncredited?[92] To account for our sins, our institutional homes would need to be audited for the benefits they received during the period of slavery through the structures of sin that built our dwellings and the ways in which money from an economy of enslavement saved our schools, endowed our pursuits, and paid our tuition.

Tracing the same periodization as we did in our personal accounting, we might turn to our institutional histories in the mid-twentieth century, to ask to what extent did Catholic and Jesuit institutions as *White serving and predominantly White* contribute to the assessor's review. As institutions of church and school continue to be stakeholders in our local communities, what are the sins of White supremacy we continue to perpetrate in our localities, our relationships, and our occupations? And which of our institutions were creating "knowledge" about "the races" that might have fed into the assessor's hand? The ideologies and practices, customs, and laws of White supremacy did not drop from the sky. They were cultivated in the institutions of our nation: church and school, family and government. In this, the leading knowledge production of Jesuit education surely had (and has) a role to play. In undertaking twenty-first-century knowledge production and applying our spiritual heritage of the Ignatian exercises, might Jesuit institutions become models alongside other Catholic institutions and Christian institutions, preparing the ground for the work of reparations that might come to fruition as national legislation following House Resolution 40?

The deepening spiral of return to the court record of my sins moves the seeker into ever-deepening saturation in the reality of our sinfulness, like a spiral staircase drawing ever deeper and finally into the Fifth Exercise, which is a Meditation on Hell. Here Ignatius stirs the imagination through the senses to see the huge fires; hear the wailing and blasphemies; smell the smoke and rotting things; taste the bitter flavors of tears, sadness, and the worm of conscience; and touch the burning flames. In the closing of this exercise the exercitant realizes that they are in Hell, with the many textures that entails, but that they are not finally bound in damnation but instead can raise their gratitude to Christ for his pity and salvation.[93]

### Day 5 / The Fifth Exercise: A Meditation on Hell, Using the Imagination

7:00 a.m. Resolution to guard against the sin of White supremacy
9:00 a.m. A meditation on Hell, using the eyes of the imagination, hearing, and stench
12:00 noon Examen: review and record
3:00 p.m. A meditation on Hell, using taste and touch
7:00 p.m. Examen: review and record

The challenge in this meditation on Hell is that too often those who are the beneficiaries of the sins of White supremacy in its institutional form do not experience the results of this sin as "Hell." But the eyes of the imagination might see predominantly White institutions as out of touch with the suffering they are causing and see exclusively White spaces as evidence of deep structures of racism. The ears of the imagination might hear the words of White supremacy woven into White Christian preaching and the White Christian curriculum. The sense of smell lifted up in the imagination might experience the clean air of suburban life and not know that environmental devastation is being breathed into the lungs of children and elders in poor neighborhoods. In our White-benefiting institutions we might taste organic foods and dabble in the cultural cuisines of the world, but are we cognizant of any environmentally racist tolls these practices might reflect? We might touch the forms of wealth that surround us and not know that instead of the wealth of salvation in intercommunion with God and others, we are surrounded by a Hell of our own making within the walls of White supremacy.

There will be time in Week 3 to employ the senses in an imaginative effort to feel the suffering of those who suffer, after Week 2 has invited retreatants to walk in the way of Christ but long before we experience the joy of the resurrection anticipated in Week 4. Those who have moved on through Week 1 of the exercises to the subsequent weeks will know that this journey into the depths of Hell and the salvation of Christ is not the end but only the beginning of a journey that continues through discipleship, death, and resurrection. Experiencing the reality of our sinfulness and the depths of Hell is, in Ignatius's ambulation, only the beginning of the Christian's journey: "For what fills and satisfies the soul consists, not in knowing much, but in our understanding the realities profoundly and in savoring them interiorly."[94] When we savor intimately the understandings of our sins, perhaps the Ignatian spirituality of the Exercises of Accountability might serve the project of truth and transformation our nation requires.

Our exploration in this book has been an exercise in truth telling and analysis pursuant to the goal of releasing the pain of our historic trauma of racism and White supremacy. It has been undertaken for the purpose of creating transformed institutions of school and church. But the road ahead of us is long. Historically White-serving institutions that have received benefits from the sins of White supremacy most often do not see Whiteness of the institution as sin. Enjoying the social capital, cultural capital, and economic capital that accrued from the thievery of racist practices, predominantly White institutions will no doubt be reluctant to "release the gain." But the spiritual capital of the Christian tradition invites us to dwell deeply in the possibilities of new life that emerges from painful reckonings. "Unless a grain of wheat falls into the earth and dies, it remains just a single grain, but if it dies it bears much fruit" (John 12:24, NRSVUE). This kenotic truth must also be borne in the lifeways and halls of Christian institutions, in the embrace of the grace of our ghosts.

## Appendix of Questions for an Examen for Racial Justice

*In Relation to Indigenous Nations*

- Who were the Indigenous people that were the original keepers of the land on which my home (institutional and familial) is located?
- By what means and on what terms was the land transferred from native people into the hands of White settlers?
- When was my institution founded? Did my institution benefit from legislation of the colonial period in the East, the destruction of native cultures in the West, or the acts of legislation in the mid-nineteenth century that transferred lands to White Americans?
- What is my institutional and personal relationship with the Indigenous peoples who were the original keepers of this land and the struggles and lives they continue to build today?
- What is the locality of my home, associations I have with others, and occupation I am pursuing in relation to the Indigenous peoples?

*Era of Enslavement*

- Was my institutional or familial home built with the use of enslaved labor and/or the benefits of an economy of enslavement?
- Do I know the names and stories of those who built my home during this period of our institutional history?
- Has my institution begun the necessary project of reconstructing this history, truth telling about how we benefited from the sins of slavery, and considering paths of redress?
- Year by year, has my institution and my family built associations with African-descended Americans?

*In Every Era*

- Has my institution failed in its association with others and its occupation by structuring its goals as a White-serving institution?
- Did my institution align with the aims of the state in relation to Indigenous peoples?
- Did my institution produce knowledge of peoples of color in ways that ultimately caused them harm, not only African and Indigenous but also Latinx and Asian populations, in an expanding nation?
- Does my institution remain predominantly White and/or a White-serving institution?

*In the Twentieth Century*

- When the Federal Housing Administration employed a racial hierarchy to assess land values, did the home of my family or my institutional home draw a benefit from the mortgage lending that followed?

*Today*

- How does my institution produce knowledge and sacred knowledge about people of color and people of diverse faiths?
- How does my institution take up the task of antiracism and repair to rewire our practices for the full flourishing of all?

*On Relationships*

- Whom do I know?
- Who are my friends?
- Where are the places in my extended family where racial injustice is felt?

- Where are the places in my relationships where racial injustice is left unaddressed?
- How does my institution foster relationships across racial lines and develop cooperation of shared power?

*On Occupation*

- Do I actively seek racial justice in my workplace and in my profession?
- How does my work contribute to racial justice?
- How might my work maintain a racially unjust status quo?
- How could my work be contributing and making deeper the sin of White supremacy?
- What steps are my workplace and my work taking to advance racial justice and dismantle the systems of White supremacy?

# Acknowledgments

The road to the completion of this book has been long, and I would not have been sustained except for the support of amazing companions and essential resources. Funding from a generous, donor-supported "Women, Faith, & Feminism" research grant through the Fordham University Theology Department allowed me to travel to archives I would have never imagined would be so fruitful for my theological work. A Louisville Institute Sabbatical Grant for Researchers (2021–2022) provided the leave during which all of the pieces came together. I am deeply grateful to be shaped by the kinds of institutions that allow me to do this work. This funding and time allowed me to meet some exceptional archivists at the Diocese of Charleston and the University of South Carolina (Columbia). My thanks especially to Melissa Mabry, Brian Fahey, and McKenzie Lemhouse. I also could not have done my work without the many people who contributed to the archival work at Georgetown, with special thanks due to Adam Rothman. My forays into the archives at Fordham continue to be enlivened by the companionship of Vivian Shen and Gabriella DiMeglio, members of my institutional family. And I am indebted to the team at Fordham University Press, and in a special way to John Garza, for helping me share this story with others.

Colleagues at the American Theological Society and the American Academy of Religion provided responses to my work in progress, and dear friends in the New York Catholic Theology Workgroup were around long enough to read two chapters as they were in progress over many years (indeed, these are some very good friends to have found: Roger Haight, Brad Hinze, Paul Lakeland, Elena Procario-Foley, Michele Saracino, and John Thiel). Along the way, two visits to House of Hope Presbyterian Church in St. Paul, Minnesota, helped me meet a live audience interested in this work. The community of World Wisdoms Project in Fort Collins, Colorado, and a visit to Creighton University helped expand my scope and the story I would come to tell. And the Jubilee celebration of the Sisters, Servants of the Immaculate Heart of Mary joined by the Oblate Sisters of Providence was influential in ways I could not have anticipated. The inspirational activism alongside friends in the Northwest Bronx Community and Clergy Coalition served as reminder that another world is possible. My institutional home at Fordham University provided the safe space to test my ideas in a wider public setting, and my institutional family in Fordham's Theology Department provided support and encouragement for the full length of this project. In the final days of the project, I was encouraged by the collegial companionship of Aysha Ames, and I look forward to future truth telling together. My extended family of origin's interest in my work and insights from our own histories has been essential, and sharing the surprises at soul nights with Perri Nunziato, Mary Beth Nunziato, and Anne Stange has been sustaining. Coming home to my immediate family—Michael, Owen, Ella, and Thea—and discussing some of the history I was discovering, and giving me the space to recover from its sadness, has been irreplaceable.

Exploring these histories, I realize there is so much more to be done and that there are, of course, limits to this volume. Methodologically, my work is still shaped in White-centering ways and the privileges attendant to sources from the archives. More work is needed that theologizes with the knowledge passed down from the ancestors through families and unwritten sources. Perhaps this volume is a starting place to recognize that more decolonizing work needs to be done. So I'm grateful to my students, both those who have helped me see the limits of my work and those who are carrying on this work in new ways. I am grateful, in advance, to all the colleagues in Catholic, Jesuit, and Christian-affiliated institutions who might collaborate in this work as well. Finally, a note a gratitude is due to the ancestors, including those who have been ghosts to me. They have left trails to follow toward insights that I would have never arrived at on my own. Through them, God has been at work in my world. I ask their forgiveness for all the things I may have misunderstood.

# Notes

## Introduction

1. Craig Steven Wilder, *Ebony and Ivy: Race, Slavery and the Troubled History of America's Universities* (New York: Bloomsbury, 2013).

2. In this introduction, the reader will notice that I have chosen to capitalize "White," as I will do throughout the book. To do so is an explicit choice to be consistent in capitalizing all racial categorizations. Some practices refuse the capitalization of "White" in order to resist giving White supremacists the place from which to argue the inherent qualities of the "White race" (as superior to other "races"). My conscious choice to capitalize "White" should serve as a reminder to the reader that *all* racial categories are equally functional fictions *and* that those who have been racialized as White accrue benefits (in ways supported by those White supremacist ideologies that disguise the benefits acquired as "inherent" to the supremacy of the White race).

3. Rachel Swarns, *The 272: The Families Who Were Enslaved and Sold to Build the American Catholic Church* (New York: Random House, 2023).

## 1. Truth Telling about Institutions

1. Joy Kang, "Write Their Names," *Georgetown Slavery Archive*, 2021, https://slaveryarchive.georgetown.edu/items/show/516. Kang cites Ana Araujo, "Raising the Dead: Walls of Names as Mnemonic Devices to Commemorate Enslaved People" *Current Anthropology* 61, no. 22 (2020): 328–38.

2. Rachel Swarns offers a fuller account of the family of Harry Mahoney and his descendants in her *The 272: The Families Who Were Enslaved and Sold to Build the American Catholic Church* (New York: Random House, 2023).

3. This understanding of White supremacy derives from Michael Omi and Howard Winant, *Racial Formation in the United States*, 3rd ed. (New York: Routledge, 2014).

4. Swarns, *The* 272, xvii.

5. Maria Yellow Horse Brave Heart et al., "Historical Trauma among Indigenous Peoples of the Americas: Concepts, Research, and Clinical Considerations," *Journal of Psychoactive Drugs* 43, no. 4 (2011): 283.

6. Maria Yellow Horse Brave Heart, "Return to the Sacred Path: Reflections on the Development of Historical Trauma Healing," Indian Health Services, slide 22, https://www.ihs.gov/sites/telebehavioral/themes/responsive2017/display_objects/documents/slides/historicaltrauma/htreturnsacredpath0513.pdf.

7. Duke Kwon and Gregory Thompson, *Reparations: A Christian Call for Repentance and Repair* (Grand Rapids, MI: Brazos, 2021), 78–81. Kwon and Thompson include the theft of history among those forms of thievery for which reparations are due.

8. Kwon and Thompson, *Reparations*, 81, argue that the theft of history derives from a romanticization aimed at the erasure of White violence *and* the erasure of peoples racialized as other-than-White.

9. Rev. Dr. Jeremiah Wright, "Confusing God and Government," sermon delivered April 13, 2003, https://forums.sluggy.com/viewtopic.php?p=315691&sid=4b3e97ace4ee8cee02bd6850e52f50b7. Wright's sermon achieved national recognition as the senator (and future president) Barack Obama was a member of Wright's congregation.

10. Iva E. Carruthers, "Remembrance—toward Righteousness and Reparations," *Ecumenical Review* 72, no. 1 (2020): 6.

11. Carruthers, "Remembrance," 8–9.

12. This is the model of the "Problem Tree" employed by practitioners in social work and other organizational fields as a tool of analysis toward more a complex understanding of the root causes of social problems and social conditions.

13. Qtd. in Seumas Miller, "Social Institutions," *Stanford Encyclopedia of Philosophy, ed.* Edward N. Zalta, Summer 2019 ed., https://plato.stanford.edu/archives/sum2019/entries/social-institutions/.

14. Mark Lewis Taylor, *The Theological and the Political: On the Weight of the World* (Minneapolis, MN: Fortress, 2011), 96.

15. Miller, "Social Institutions."

16. For deepening the analysis of these documents reflecting the sacred scriptures of US civil religion, see Audra Savage, "The Religion of Race: The Supreme Court as Priests of Racial Politics," *Utah Law Review* 2021, no. 3 (2021): 569–628, https://dc.law.utah.edu/cgi/viewcontent.cgi?article=1295&context=ulr.

17. Vefa Saygin Ögütle, "Institution as Mediation between Social Structure and Agency: Toward a Realist Social Ontology of Institutions," *Journal for the Theory of Social Behavior* 51 (2021): 491.

18. Pierre Bourdieu, "Symbolic Capital and Social Classes," *Journal of Classical Sociology* 13, no. 2 (2013): 299.

19. Bourdieu, "Symbolic Capital and Social Classes," 299. Bourdieu writes, "Belief is an adhesion which ignores that it brings into being that to which it adheres; it does not know, or does not want to know, that everything which makes for the intrinsic charm of its object, its charisma, is nothing other than the product of the countless operations of credit and discredit, all equally unconscious of their truth, that are made on the market of symbolic goods and materialized in officially recognized and guaranteed symbols, signs of distinction, tokens of consecration, and certificates of charisma such as titles of nobility or school credentials, objectified marks of respect calling for tokens of respect, pomp, and ceremony, whose effect is to express not only one's social position but also the collective recognition accorded to it by the mere fact of allowing it to make such public display of its importance."

20. I am indebted to Mark Lewis Taylor's discussion of Bourdieu in the former's *The Theological and the Political.*

21. Linn Tonstad, *Queer Theology: Beyond Apologetics* (Eugene, OR: Cascade, 2018), 48–77.

22. Joseph Barndt, *Becoming an Anti-Racist Church: Journeying toward Wholeness* (Minneapolis, MN: Fortress, 2011), 117.

23. Barndt, *Becoming an Anti-Racist Church,* 117.

24. Barndt, *Becoming an Anti-Racist Church,* 27. See also Kwon and Thompson, *Reparations*; and Jamar Tisby, *The Color of Compromise: The Truth about the American Church's Complicity in Racism* (Grand Rapids, MI: Zondervan, 2019).

25. Avery Gordon, *Ghostly Matters: Haunting and the Sociological Imagination* (Minneapolis: University of Minnesota Press, 2008), 25.

26. Gordon, *Ghostly Matters,* 19.

27. Gordon, *Ghostly Matters Ghostly Matters,* 134.

28. Gordon, *Ghostly Matters,* 66, engaging Walter Benjamin.

29. Ashon Crawley, *Blackpentecostal Breath: The Aesthetics of Possibility* (New York: Fordham University Press, 2017).

30. Crawley, *Blackpentecostal Breath,* 6–7.

31. *The Love of the Sacred Heart,* ill. St. Mechtilde, with a foreword by the Lord Bishop of Salford (London: Burns, Oates & Washbourne, Ltd., 1922), 125.

32. Paul Schroeder, "Is the U.S. an Empire?," op-ed following his address to the American Historical Association, *History News Network* (of the Columbian College of Arts and Sciences at the George Washington University), https://historynews network.org/article/1237.

33. Jeorg Rieger, "Christian Theology and Empires," in *Empire and the Christian Tradition,* ed. Kwok Pui-lan, Don Compier, and Jeorg Rieger (Minneapolis, MN: Fortress, 2007), 3

34. Yaakov Ariel, "A Faith Worth Preserving: An Introduction to Judaism," in *Five Voices, Five Faiths: An Interfaith Primer* (Lanham, MD: Rowman & Littlefield, 2005), 23.

35. Richard Horsley, "Jesus and Empire," *Union Seminary Quarterly Review* (January 2005): 55.

36. Horsley, "Jesus and Empire," 56.
37. Horsley, "Jesus and Empire," 56.
38. Horsley, "Jesus and Empire," 63.
39. Horsley, "Jesus and Empire," 73.
40. I am drawing my Christology from Mark Lewis Taylor, *The Executed God: The Way of the Cross in Lockdown America*, rev. and exp. 2nd ed. (Minneapolis, MN: Fortress, 2015).
41. Howard Thurman, *Jesus and the Disinherited* (Boston: Beacon, 1976), 33.
42. Ignacio Ellacuria, "The Crucified People: An Essay in Historical Soteriology," in *Ignacio Ellacuria: Essays on History, Liberation, and Salvation*, ed. Michael E. Lee (Maryknoll, NY: Orbis, 2013), 206–7.
43. Karl Barth, *The Epistle to the Romans*, trans. from the 6th ed. by Edwyn C. Hoskyns (1933; London: Oxford University Press, 1968), 96.
44. A translation error from the original German writing of her *Book of Special Graces* was rendered in Middle English as *The Booke of Gostlye Grace*. See *The Booke of Gostlye Grace of Mechtild of Hakeborn*, ed. Theresa A. Halligan (Toronto: Pontifical Institute of Medieval Studies, 1979).
45. Ellacuria, "The Crucified People," 208.
46. Jean-Luc Nancy, *Corpus*, 79, cited in Taylor, *The Theological and the Political*, 44.
47. Taylor, *The Theological and the Political*, 44, drawing on Nancy, *Corpus*, 47.

## 2. Sucky's Scream: Hearing the Ghosts and Heeding Their Call

1. Matthew O'Hara, "The Supple Whip: Innovation and Tradition in Mexican Catholicism," *American Historical Review*, December 2012, 1373–1401. "Sixteenth-century Spanish mystics, such as John of the Cross and Teresa of Avila, attempted to retreat deeply into the self to escape the mental distractions of the world. Pain, as they understood it, was useful because it could not be communicated to other living things. It muted the din of the external world, and thus advanced one's inward journey" (1392).
2. Maria Yellow Horse Brave Heart et al., "Historical Trauma among Indigenous Peoples of the Americas: Concepts, Research, and Clinical Considerations," *Journal of Psychoactive Drugs* 43, no. 4 (2011): 282–90.
3. The methodology of a "micro-history" is advanced by Adam Rothman, *Beyond Freedom's Reach: A Kidnapping in the Twilight of Slavery* (Cambridge, MA: Harvard University Press, 2015). See also Rachel Swarns, *The 272: The Families Who Were Enslaved and Sold to Build the American Catholic Church* (New York: Random House, 2023).
4. One of the important realizations of our moment of historical reckoning is the way in which historians have known these histories much longer than the broader collective has had an interest in hearing them. For example, the history of Jesuit slaveholding has never been a secret, and historians like Robert Emmett Curran

have been writing their stories for decades, presenting a paper, for example, at the 1980 American Historical Society meeting. Robert Emmett Curran, "'Splendid Poverty': Jesuit Slaveholding in Maryland, 1805–1838," in *Shaping American Catholicism, Maryland and New York, 1805–1915* (Washington, DC: Catholic University of America Press, 2012). See also Thomas Murphy, *Jesuit Slaveholding in Maryland, 1717–1838* (New York: Routledge, 2001).

5. Bryan Massingale, "The Ignatian Witness to Truth in a Climate of Injustice," *Conversations in Jesuit Higher Education*, August 12, 2017, http://www.conversationsmagazine.org/web-features/2017/8/12/the-ignatian-witness-to-truth-in-a-climate-of-injustice.

6. Georgetown Slavery Archive, https://slaveryarchive.georgetown.edu/.

7. On this last note, a special gratitude to Elsa Barraza Mendoza and Adam Rothman of the Georgetown Slavery Archive.

8. Shannen Dee Williams, "Religious Orders Owning Slaves Isn't New—Black Catholics Have Emphasized This History for Years," *America*, August 6, 2019, https://www.americamagazine.org/faith/2019/08/06/religious-orders-owning-slaves-isnt-new-black-catholics-have-emphasized-history.

9. Craig Steven Wilder, *Ebony and Ivy: Race, Slavery, and the Troubled History of America's Universities* (New York: Bloomsbury, 2013).

10. James M. Woods, *A History of the Catholic Church in the American South, 1513–1900* (Gainesville: University Press of Florida, 2011), 112.

11. Woods, *A History of the Catholic Church in the American South*, 133.

12. Edward Baptist's powerful *The Half Has Never Been Told: Slavery and the Making of American Capitalism* (New York: Basic Books, 2014) is structured to account for the ways that enslaved people were reduced to their body parts as mechanisms in the working of capitalist exploitation, counting them, for example, as "hands" to do the work but not as full human beings. Our re-membering is only the first step in reconstructing their humanity.

13. Willie James Jennings, *After Whiteness: An Education in Belonging* (Grand Rapids, MI: Eerdmans, 2020), 32.

14. Maryland Province Archives, "A 'Multiplicity of Deaths': Fr. Mobberly to Fr. Grassi, on a series of deaths that occurred at St. Inigoes, 1812," Georgetown Slavery Archive, https://slaveryarchive.georgetown.edu/items/show/113. Swarns, *The 272*, 26–36, provides a fuller history of the community of St. Inigoes.

15. Maryland State Archives, "St. Inigoes tax assessment, 1804," Georgetown Slavery Archive, https://slaveryarchive.georgetown.edu/items/show/344. The negative assessment of the women's capacities may have been a strategic accounting in order for the Jesuits to pay less in taxes.

16. "A 'Multiplicity of Deaths.'"

17. Br. Joseph Mobberly and Fr. Beschter both identify an aged Sucky as a cook. Mobberly writes of "the cook, who was called Granny Sucky." Joseph P. Mobberly SJ Papers, "Br. Mobberly recounts the whipping of Sucky, an enslaved woman at St. Inigoes, The Mobberly Diaries, Part I, 1820," Georgetown Slavery Archive, https://

slaveryarchive.georgetown.edu/items/show/148. Beschter describes "an old negro woman cook." Maryland Province Archives, "'A Dreadful Whipping': Fr. Beschter to Fr. Leavy on the whipping of a female slave at St. Inigoes, January 7th, 1836," Georgetown Slavery Archive, https://slaveryarchive.georgetown.edu/items/show/103.

18. "A 'Multiplicity of Deaths.'" It is here that Mobberly accounts for her age: "Old Sucky died with old age being 96 years old according to the family record, tho' she often told me she was more than 100."

19. "Br. Mobberly recounts."

20. "Br. Mobberly recounts."

21. "Br. Mobberly recounts."

22. "Br. Mobberly recounts."

23. "'A Dreadful Whipping': Fr. Beschter to Fr. Leavy."

24. "'A Dreadful Whipping': Fr. Beschter to Fr. Leavy."

25. "Br. Mobberly recounts."

26. "Br. Mobberly recounts."

27. "'A Dreadful Whipping': Fr. Beschter to Fr. Leavy."

28. Father Robert Barron, "John Paul II and 'Taking the Discipline,'" *Our Sunday Visitor,* March 15, 2010, https://www.catholiceducation.org/en/controversy/common-misconceptions/john-paul-ii-and-taking-the-discipline.html.

29. M. Shawn Copeland, *Knowing Christ Crucified: The Witness of African American Religious Experience* (Maryknoll, NY: Orbis, 2018), 26.

30. "'A Dreadful Whipping': Fr. Beschter to Fr. Leavy."

31. "Br. Mobberly recounts."

32. Ashon Crawley, *Blackpentecostal Breath: The Aesthetics of Possibility* (New York: Fordham University Press, 2017), 40.

33. Crawley, *Blackpentecostal Breath*, 40, citing Veli-Matti Kärkkäinen, *Pneumatology: The Holy Spirit in Ecumenical, International, and Contextual Perspective* (Grand Rapids, MI: Baker Academic, 2002), 25; and David Hadley Jensen, *The Lord and Giver of Life: Perspectives on Constructive Pneumatology* (Louisville, KY: Westminster John Knox Press, 2008), xv.

34. Crawley, *Blackpentecostal Breath*, 40.

35. "'A Dreadful Whipping': Fr. Beschter to Fr. Leavy."

36. "Br. Mobberly recounts."

37. "Br. Mobberly recounts."

38. Joseph Mobberly, *Treatise on Slavery—Cham* (1 of 2), 32, Georgetown University Manuscripts, Booth Family Center for Special Collections, Washington, DC, http://hdl.handle.net/10822/1060288.

39. Mobberly, *Treatise on Slavery* (1 of 2), 33.

40. Mobberly, *Treatise on Slavery* (1 of 2), 37.

41. Joseph Mobberly, *Treatise on Slavery—Cham* (2 of 2) (1823), 99, http://hdl.handle.net/10822/1060291. Attached to his treatise *On Cham* Mobberly includes an addendum of the divisions of the human race taken from *Goldsmith's Animated Nature* 1, which cites also the racial categorization of Linnaeus; compare also with

the racialized hierarchy Immanuel Kant proffered in J. Kameron Carter, *Race: A Theological Account* (Oxford: Oxford University Press, 2008), 82–96.

42. "Br. Mobberly recounts."

43. Kelly Schmidt culls the archives to demonstrate the regular practice of physical abuse toward enslaved Catholics by their Jesuit Catholic enslavers. Kelly Schmidt, "Sexual Abuse of Enslaved People in the U.S. Catholic Church," paper presented at Taking Responsibility, Gonzaga University, Spokane, WA, April 1, 2022.

44. Joseph P. Mobberly SJ Papers, "'Masters must answer,' *The Mobberly Diaries*, part I, 1820," Georgetown Slavery Archive, https://slaveryarchive.georgetown.edu/items/show/152.

45. Robert Emmett Curran, *Shaping American Catholicism, Maryland and New York, 1805–1915* (Washington, DC: Catholic University of America Press, 2012), 38. Curran cites Mobberly's diary (Mobberly Diary, I:143, Georgetown Library Special Collections [GULSC]) and Jesuit records of Mobberly's removal (Corporation Minutes, April 20, 1820, Archives of the Maryland Province of the Society of Jesus, GULSC; Kenney, "Temporalities," 1820, MPA X-T-I, GULSC).

46. Kelly L. Schmidt, "A National Legacy of Enslavement: An Overview of the Work of the Slavery, History, Memory, and Reconciliation Project," *Journal of Jesuit Studies* 8, no. 1 (2021): 81–107. See also the Jesuits' desire "to *dispose* of the black children of Sarah deceased, now on the farm of Arabia Petrea as soon as possible to humane and Christian masters for the benefit of the Corporation." Maryland Province Archives, "'To Humane and Christian Masters': The Disposal of Sarah's Children, June 1809," Georgetown Slavery Archive, https://slaveryarchive.georgetown.edu/items/show/194.

47. Peter Kenney, 1820 Consultation Report, Archives of the Maryland Province of the Society of Jesus (GTM.000119), Box 38, Folder 15, http://hdl.handle.net/10822/1062955. Kenny's description was reported by Matthew Quallen in Georgetown University's newspaper, *The Hoya*, in 2016. "He observed that Jesuits were whipping women, even pregnant women. He noted as well that in some cases the Jesuits had tied up these women in the parlors of the priest's home to administer whippings. Kenney recommended that this practice, which he called, 'indecorous,' cease." Matthew Quallen, "Beyond the 272 Sold in 1838, Plotting the National Diaspora of Jesuit-Owned Slaves," *The Hoya*, April 30, 2016, http://features.thehoya.com/beyond-the-272-sold-in-1838-plotting-the-national-diaspora-of-jesuit-owned-slaves. This is also discussed in the Jesuit Plantation Project blog, http://jesuitplantationproject.org/s/jpp/page/discipline#fn3.

48. Copeland, *Knowing Christ Crucified*, 81.

49. "'A Dreadful Whipping': Fr. Beschter to Fr. Leavy."

50. "Br. Mobberly recounts."

51. "'A Dreadful Whipping': Fr. Beschter to Fr. Leavy."

52. Archivum Romanum Societatis Iesu, "'As bad as a Priest's Slave': Letter from Fr. Beschter, March 27, 1829," Georgetown Slavery Archive, https://slaveryarchive.georgetown.edu/items/show/469. Emphasis mine.

53. "'A Dreadful Whipping': Fr. Beschter to Fr. Leavy." Ellipses in the original.

54. "'As bad as a Priest's Slave.'"

55. "'A Dreadful Whipping': Fr. Beschter to Fr. Leavy."

56. "'A Dreadful Whipping': Fr. Beschter to Fr. Leavy."

57. "'A Dreadful Whipping': Fr. Beschter to Fr. Leavy."

58. Murphy, 117. Murphy cites, Brother Mobberly's Diary, p. 21 (Special Collections Georgetown University). Emphasis mine.

59. "Br. Mobberly recounts."

60. Murphy, *Jesuit Slaveholding in Maryland*, 117.

61. "'A Dreadful Whipping': Fr. Beschter to Fr. Leavy."

62. "Br. Mobberly recounts."

63. Crawley, *Blackpentecostal Breath*, 24.

64. In walking our way around the relationships between pain and piety in Christian thought, we might consider O'Hara, "The Supple Whip," 1393. Compare also with Allen Greer, *Mohawk Saint: Catherine Tekawitha and the Jesuits* (Oxford: Oxford University Press, 2005); and Copeland, *Knowing Christ Crucified*.

65. Archivum Romanum Societatis Iesu, "Slavery at St. Thomas Manor: Fr. Grivel to Fr. Roothaan, 1831," Georgetown Slavery Archive, https://slaveryarchive.georgetown.edu/items/show/292.

66. Crawley, *Blackpentecostal Breath*, 169, 190, 207, 231–33.

67. Crawley, *Blackpentecostal Breath*, 42.

68. Crawley, *Blackpentecostal Breath*, 52.

69. Crawley, *Blackpentecostal Breath*, 72.

70. Crawley, *Blackpentecostal Breath*, 75.

71. Crawley, *Blackpentecostal Breath*, 184.

72. Kelly Brown Douglas, *Stand Your Ground: Black Bodies and the Justice of God* (Maryknoll, NY: Orbis, 2015), 54.

73. Maryland Province Archives, "'She will not Rule Me": Fr. Steinbacher airs his grievances against the female slaves of Newtown, April, 1848," Georgetown Slavery Archive, https://slaveryarchive.georgetown.edu/items/show/144.

74. Crawley, *Blackpentecostal Breath*, 24.

75. Maryland Province Archives, "'We are in the dark as long as we keep slaves': Br. Joseph Mobberly, S.J. calculates the cost savings from emancipation, February 5, 1815," Georgetown Slavery Archive, https://slaveryarchive.georgetown.edu/items/show/66.

76. Georgetown University Archives, "'Present State of the College,' 1820," Georgetown Slavery Archive, https://slaveryarchive.georgetown.edu/items/show/190.

77. Maryland Province Archives, "'I would be willing to take $450': Fr. Mulledy to Fr. McElroy on pricing slaves, June 12, 1838," Georgetown Slavery Archive, https://slaveryarchive.georgetown.edu/items/show/100. The price assigned to a single human being was roughly the cost of two years of tuition at Georgetown or St. John's Fordham. Jon Reynolds, "Tuition," *Georgetown Magazine*, November/

December 1982, https://library.georgetown.edu/special-collections/archives/essays/tuition.

78. Archivum Romanum Societatis Iesu, "'The unhappy idea of Fr. Thomas F. Mulledy': Letter from Fr. Vespre to Fr. Roothaan, 12 Jan. 1843," Georgetown Slavery Archive, https://slaveryarchive.georgetown.edu/items/show/463.

79. Louis Diggs, "'I know that my Bennett ancestors were slaves to the Jesuits . . .': Interviews with descendants in Maryland from Louis Diggs' Surviving in America," Georgetown Slavery Archive, https://slaveryarchive.georgetown.edu/items/show/60, page 94 of text.

80. Diggs, "'I know that my Bennett ancestors were slaves to the Jesuits,'" 95.

81. The Bennett family's ancestor Harry Mahoney is at the center of the history Swarns recounts in *The* 272.

82. Maryland Province Archives, "Nancy buys her daughter Sophia to set her free, September 19, 1803," Georgetown Slavery Archive, https://slaveryarchive.georgetown.edu/items/show/235.

83. Copeland, *Knowing Christ Crucified*, 42.

84. Copeland, *Knowing Christ Crucified*, 31.

85. Copeland, *Knowing Christ Crucified*, 31.

86. Copeland, *Knowing Christ Crucified*, 35.

87. Maryland Province Archives, "Fr. Francis Neale describes difficulties arranging slave marriages and British pillaging during the War of 1812," Georgetown Slavery Archive, https://slaveryarchive.georgetown.edu/items/show/368.

88. Katie Geneva Cannon, "Transformative Grace," in *Feminist and Womanist Essays in Reformed Dogmatics*, ed. Amy Plantinga Pauw and Serene Jones (Louisville: Westminster John Knox Press, 2006), 139.

89. Diana Hayes, "Faith of Our Mothers: Catholic Womanist God-Talk," in *Uncommon Faithfulness: The Black Catholic Experience*, ed. M. Shawn Copeland (Maryknoll, NY: Orbis, 2009), 130.

90. M. Shawn Copeland, *Enfleshing Freedom: Body, Race, and Being* (Minneapolis: Fortress, 2009), 39, 42.

91. Copeland, *Knowing Christ Crucified*, 40.

92. *Congressional Record*, 20th Congress, 2nd sess. (1829), 176.

93. Howard Thurman, *Jesus and the Disinherited* (1949; Boston: Beacon, 1996), 50–57.

94. Charles Long, Notes from a lecture delivered by Charles H. Long, April 2, 2002, at Virginia Union School of Theology in Richmond, VA, cited in Cannon, "Transformative Grace," 145.

95. Drawn from James Cone, *The Spirituals and the Blues* (1979; Maryknoll, NY: Orbis, 1991), 16.

96. Cannon, "Transformative Grace," 143.

97. Cannon, "Transformative Grace," 142–43.

98. Cannon, "Transformative Grace," 143–44.

99. It is not clear the reason for his frailty, for while this care is enjoined upon him in 1836, he did not die until 1850, at the age of seventy-one. With regard to Nelly, the Georgetown Memory Project proposed that her surname is "most likely Mahoney" and names her with "ID 212." Georgetown Memory Project, "The Lost Jesuit Slaves of Maryland: Searching for 91 People Left Behind in 1838," April 30, 2018, https://www.georgetownmemoryproject.org/wp-content/uploads/Research-Memo-Lost-Jesuit-Slaves.pdf.

100. Maryland Province Archives, "'Belonging to us': Fr. Dzierozynski recommends Nelly as housekeeper for Fr. Lancaster, January 1843," Georgetown Slavery Archive, https://slaveryarchive.georgetown.edu/items/show/139.

101. Maryland Province Archives, "'I have parted from Nelly': Fr. Woodley to Fr. Brocard, September 25, 1850," Georgetown Slavery Archive, https://slaveryarchive.georgetown.edu/items/show/165. Rachel Swarns identifies Nelly as the daughter of Harry Mahoney who had saved the Jesuits' treasury during the War of 1812. Swarns, *The 272*, 150.

102. Maryland Province Archives, "List of enslaved persons remaining on Estate and exchanged, no date—perhaps 1839," Georgetown Slavery Archive, https://slaveryarchive.georgetown.edu/items/show/64. If this is the same Nelly (aged thirty-eight in 1838), the dating of the document might be changed to 1843.

103. Maryland Province Archives, "Distribution of shoes at St. Inigoes, March 1818," Georgetown Slavery Archive, https://slaveryarchive.georgetown.edu/items/show/228.

104. Maryland State Archives, "St. Inigoes Tax Assessment, 1831," Georgetown Slavery Archive, https://slaveryarchive.georgetown.edu/items/show/78.

105. Maryland State Archives, "List of slaves taxed at White Marsh in 1833," Georgetown Slavery Archive, https://slaveryarchive.georgetown.edu/items/show/314.

106. "'Belonging to us.'"

107. Jesuit Plantation Project, "List of people sold by Fr. Thomas Mulledy in 1838," Georgetown Slavery Archive, http://slaveryarchive.georgetown.edu/items/show/9.

108. Maryland Province Archives, "Bill of sale for 56 persons from Thomas Mulledy to Henry Johnson, November 10, 1838," Georgetown Slavery Archive, https://slaveryarchive.georgetown.edu/items/show/12.

109. Maryland Province Archives, "Articles of agreement between Thomas F. Mulledy, of Georgetown, District of Columbia, of one part, and Jesse Beatty and Henry Johnson, of the State of Louisiana, of the other part. 19th June 1838," Georgetown Slavery Archive, https://slaveryarchive.georgetown.edu/items/show/1.

110. "'Belonging to us.'"

111. Kelly L. Schmidt traces the network of relationships and familial ties—both biological and socially constructed—among enslaved Catholics with the Jesuits in the Midwest. Kelly L. Schmidt, "Enslaved Faith Communities in the Jesuits' Missouri Missions," *U.S. Catholic Historian* 37, no. 2 (Spring 2019): 49–81.

112. Melissa Raphael, *The Female Face of God in Auschwitz: A Jewish Feminist Theology of the Holocaust* (London: Routledge, 2003), 86.

113. Linda Naranjo-Huebl, "'Take, Eat': Food Imagery, the Nurturing Ethic, and Christian Identity in *The Wide, Wide World*, *Uncle Tom's Cabin*, and *Incidents in the Life of a Slave Girl*," *Christianity and Literature* 56, no. 4 (Summer 2007): 597.

114. Naranjo-Huebl, "'Take, Eat,'" 601.

115. "Women as Sacristans," *American Ecclesiastical Review* 14, no. 2 (1889): 177, https://babel.hathitrust.org/cgi/pt?id=hvd.ah68l3&view=1up&seq=215.

116. "Women as Sacristans."

117. "Women as Sacristans."

118. National Archives, Fort Worth, TX, "Manifest of the Katherine Jackson, 1838," Georgetown Slavery Archive, https://slaveryarchive.georgetown.edu/items/show/2.

119. "'Belonging to us.'"

120. "'I have parted from Nelly': Fr. Woodley to Fr. Brocard."

121. Swarns, *The* 272, 152.

122. Swarns, *The* 272, 156.

123. Swarns, *The* 272, 182.

124. Mobberly, *Treatise on Slavery* (1 of 2), 35: "at least two fifths of the human family are deficient in parts of intellect, know not how to manage for and take care of themselves." If only the poor around the globe, "these unhappy people had good masters, they would be in a comfortable situation."

125. "Proslavery oration by Rev. James Ryder, SJ, August 30, 1835," Georgetown Slavery Archive, https://slaveryarchive.georgetown.edu/items/show/88.

126. Maryland Province Archives, "Fr. Roothaan, S.J. lays out the conditions for the sale of enslaved persons, 27 December 1836," Georgetown Slavery Archive, https://slaveryarchive.georgetown.edu/items/show/94.

127. Duke Kwon and Gregory Thompson use the category of "theft" in their study of the Christian call for repair in *Reparations: A Christian Call for Repentance and Repair* (Grand Rapids, MI: Brazos, 2021).

128. Kwon and Thompson, *Reparations*, 78.

## 3. The Complexity of a Complicit Church: Henrietta and Elizabeth in a Catholic Network

1. Shannen Dee Williams, "Religious Orders Owning Slaves Isn't New—Black Catholics Have Emphasized This History for Years," *America*, August 6, 2019, https://www.americamagazine.org/faith/2019/08/06/religious-orders-owning-slaves-isnt-new-black-catholics-have-emphasized-history.

2. *St. James the Greater: Catholic Hill, South Carolina, Est. 1826*, pamphlet available at St. James the Greater, Ritter, SC (n.d.), acquired September 29, 2021. The dates indicated on the self-published materials of the congregation demonstrate the flexible quality of "history" and its variability; we will see the dates of rediscovery range from 1875 to 1884 and 1892 before historians finally settle on "rediscovery" marked with 1897. For an overview of St. James the Greater, see "In this Sacred

Place, St. James the Greater Catholic Church," https://www.youtube.com/watch?v=YvsZoWckksI.

3. As Suzanne Krebsbach reports, the Diocese of Charleston included all of South Carolina, North Carolina, and Georgia and was served by only the bishop John England and eleven priests. Suzanne Krebsbach, "Black Catholics in Antebellum Charleston," *South Carolina Historical Magazine* 108, no. 2 (April 2007): 145.

4. "Church of St. James—Colleton," *United States Catholic Miscellany*, May 16, 1840.

5. "Colleton and Beaufort," *United States Catholic Miscellany*, January 9, 1841.

6. The challenges of visiting the Catholic Church on the periphery is conveyed by the historian Jeremiah J. O'Connell when he writes, "I have frequently travelled entire days without having met a human being; despite the extreme culture of the soil, it might have passed as uninhabited, were it not for the crowd of sweltering, half-clad, half-fed negroes, seen now and then in the distance." Jeremiah Joseph O'Connell, *Catholicity in the Carolinas and Georgia: Leaves of its History, 1820–1878* (New York: D. & J. Sadlier & Co., 1879), 181, https://babel.hathitrust.org/cgi/pt?id=mdp.39015068629461&view=1up&seq=11&skin=2021.

7. "Episcopal Visitation," *United States Catholic Miscellany*, April 19, 1845. St. James's histories conveyed in the archives speculate on the forming of the Walterboro congregation: "After the founding families of the St. James Church had mostly died out, several others began to take their place . . . Eustace Bellinger, Sarah, Harriet and Susan Bellinger, Elizabeth Pinckney. . . . Because so many of the slaves were being baptized, they began to outnumber the slave-holders in the congregation. It was about this time that Susan Bellinger donated land in Walterboro for the construction of another church and one might be led to believe that it was for the purpose of segregating the congregation. The land which Susan Bellinger donated was the tract on Hampton Street in Walterboro which was the site of the church there until 1951." Louis (no surname) to Tom (no surname), "Here is a Rough Copy of the History of St. James," June 24, 1976 (II:2, p. 11), Walterboro, St. James, the Greater Mission (Series 142), Files Re: history of St. James, The Greater Mission from the Archives at St. Elizabeth's Convent, Cornwell Heights, PA (2009.02-01-09), Parish Files, Catholic Diocese of Charleston Archives, Charleston, SC.

8. Krebsbach, "Black Catholics in Antebellum Charleston," 145–46.

9. "Colleton," *United States Catholic Miscellany*, January 29, 1848.

10. O'Connell, *Catholicity in the Carolinas and Georgia*, 181. The limits of recognition for women in this frontier church can be noted in the competing histories as to whether it was Susan Bellinger or Sarah Bellinger who donated the land for St. Philips.

11. O'Connell, *Catholicity in the Carolinas and Georgia*, 180–81.

12. "St. James Church Approaching 150th Anniversary," *The Press and Standard*, Thurs. July 3, 1975, 9-A, Newspaper Clippings, 1831–2003 (2009.02-01-07), Parish Files (Series 142), Catholic Diocese of Charleston Archives, Charleston, SC.

13. O'Connell, *Catholicity in the Carolinas and Georgia*, 183. O'Connell served St. James the Greater and knew Pinckney personally. "The venerable and pious Mrs. Pinckney assured the writer that the main cause of the conversion to the true Faith, both of herself and her family, was Bishop England's Catechism, given her by Father Byrne, when she was a little girl, after he had performed a marriage at the church in Colleton" (185).

14. *We Came a Long Way by Faith: Catholic Hill and St. James the Greater Catholic Church*, dir. George Wingard, 2020, https://vimeo.com/415619367.

15. "St. James Church—Walterboro, S.C., Church Records 1839–1854," Digitized Microfiche, Catholic Diocese of Charleston Archives, Charleston, SC. There is a group of infants/youth baptized at the same time but with no parents' names recorded in 1848: Jacob, Valentine, Peter (alias "Cuffey"), Jack, Samuel, Adam, Scipio, Mary, Ann (alias Dinah), Ellen, and Mirida. It is unclear what their situation and status within the community was and no indication is offered for why their parents' names are not listed. J .J. O'Connell is listed as conferring pastor of this sacrament of baptism.

16. Diana Garnett, "National Register Nomination for St. James the Greater Catholic Mission," master's thesis, University of South Carolina, 2015, https://scholar commons.sc.edu/etd/3159.

17. St. Augustine Parish in the Tremé neighborhood of New Orleans claims the status of "first Black Catholic Church in the United States," with a founding in 1841. See https://www.blackpast.org/african-american-history/st-augustine-catholic-church -new-orleans-louisiana-1841/. The flurry of baptisms beginning in 1848 at St. James the Greater raises an interesting question of what it means to be a Black Catholic Church and when St. James can be recognized as one.

18. M. Shawn Copeland, *Knowing Christ Crucified: The Witness of African American Religious Experience* (Maryknoll, NY: Orbis, 2018), 91. Copeland cites Cyprian Davis, *The History of Black Catholics in the United States* (New York: Crossroad, 1990), 209–10.

19. Louis to Tom, "Here is a Rough Copy of History of St. James," II.2, 11.

20. Vefa Saygin Ögütle, "Institution as Mediation between Social Structure and Agency: Toward a Realist Social Ontology of Institutions," *Journal for the Theory of Social Behavior* 51, no. 3 (2021): 491.

21. Ögütle, "Institution as Mediation between Social Structure and Agency," 497.

22. Sandra Schneiders, "Spirituality and the Academy," *Theological Studies* 50 (1989): 681.

23. Sandra Schneiders, "Theology and Spirituality: Strangers, Rivals, or Partners?," *Horizons* 13 (1986): 266, cited in Schneiders, "Spirituality and the Academy," 684.

24. Schneiders, "Spirituality and the Academy," 684.

25. Fr. D. Barberich PSM to Rev. A. Walter PSM, February 4, 1895 [Translation of letter found in Archives of the Generalate of the Pallottine Fathers—Piazza V. Pallotti, 204, Rome, Italy; composed by G. J. Carcich SAC, Provincial, on Letterhead *Pallottine Fathers* dated 21 September 1959], Walterboro, St. James, the Greater

Mission (Series 142), Newspaper Clippings, 1831–2003 (2009.02-01-07), Parish Files (Series 142), Catholic Diocese of Charleston Archives, Charleston, SC. The content and authorial voice of this letter indicates that this is the individual who has been named "Berberich" in other published accounts.

26. Barberich to Walter, 2–3.

27. Krebsbach, "Black Catholics in Antebellum Charleston," 148.

28. Davis, *The History of Black Catholics*, 210.

29. Louis to Tom, "Here is a Rough Copy of the History of St. James," II.1, 10: "The care around there declined so much that baptisms appear to have been held only every other year [locations of baptisms in private homes after church fire]. In 1863, there were 7 baptisms; in 1864, none. In 1865 there were 2 baptisms; in 1866, none; 1867, one; 1868, none; and in 1869, one. From 1870 to 1872, there were no baptisms at all, and in 1873, when activity began to pick up, the five baptisms were held at Eustace Bellinger's place. Four of the five were blacks, and only one had a last name. After that, there were only two baptisms of blacks from the Hill until the community was "rediscovered" by Fr. Daniel Berberich in either 1891 or 1892."

30. Louis to Tom, "Here is a Rough Copy of the History of St. James," II.2, 11.

31. For more on Bishop Patrick Lynch, see David Heisser and Stephen White, *Patrick N. Lynch, 1817–1882: Third Catholic Bishop of Charleston* (Columbia, SC: University of South Carolina Press, 2015). David Heisser, "Bishop Lynch's Civil War Pamphlet on Slavery," *Catholic Historical Review* 84, no. 4 (October 1998): 681–96.

32. O'Connell, *Catholicity in the Carolinas and Georgia*, 84: "Soon after Christmas, and on the commencement of 1842, he took to his bed, never more to rise from it. He lay sick three months under daily attention from Dr. John Bellinger, a distinguished physician, and one of his converts."

33. O'Connell, *Catholicity in the Carolinas and Georgia*, 181.

34. *The History of the Catholic Church in the United States of America* (New York: The Catholic Editing Company, 1914), 135, https://www.google.com/books/edition/The_Catholic_Church_in_the_United_States/KL4YAAAAYAAJ?hl=en&gbpv=1.

35. "St. James Church—Walterboro, S.C., Church Records 1839–1854." See also Elizabeth Perry Bellinger Pinckney to Eustace Pinckney [St. John's College], "My Beloved Son," November 1, 1850, cited in Mary Pinckney Powell, *Back over Home: The Heritage of Pinckneys of Pinckney Colony Bluffton, South Carolina* (Columbia, SC: R. L. Bryan, 1996), 89. Pinckney writes: "James Speights has lost his little son, he intended to get Mr. Carr to baptize it when he came up, and when he found that it was dying he requested sister Susan do it."

36. Note also that while the Bellinger sisters are building the church on the frontier, their cousins, the Bellingers and the Northrups, are supporting the baptisms of Black Catholics in Charleston. Krebsbach, "Black Catholics in Antebellum Charleston," 155.

37. Elizabeth Perry Bellinger Pinckney to Eustace Pinckney [St. John's College Fordham], "A happy New Year to my much loved Son," January 8, 1852, Folder 3,

Pinckney Family Papers, South Caroliniana Library, University of South Carolina, Columbia, SC.

38. Elizabeth Perry Bellinger Pinckney to Eustace Pinckney, "My own dear Son," December 18, 1852, Folder 5, Pinckney Family Papers, South Caroliniana Library, University of South Carolina, Columbia, SC.

39. Elizabeth Perry Bellinger Pinckney to Eustace Pinckney [St. John's College Fordham], "My own dear precious Child," October 3, 1852, Folder 4, Pinckney Family Papers, South Caroliniana Library, University of South Carolina, Columbia, SC.

40. Pinckney, "My own dear Son (1852)." Note how in 1852 Lynch is serving both at St. James and here in Charleston before his elevation to bishop in 1857.

41. Pinckney, "A happy New Year to my much loved Son."

42. Elizabeth Perry Bellinger Pinckney to Charles Pinckney, "To My Beloved Son [from Edgefield]," October 9, 1854, Folder 5, Pinckney Family Papers, South Caroliniana Library, University of South Carolina, Columbia, SC. If this is the same "Hannah" and "Polly" listed in Elizabeth's prenuptial agreement of 1827, these three adult women would have been in relationship for nearly thirty years. Powell, *Back over Home*, 73.

43. "St. James Church—Walterboro, S.C., Church Records 1839–1854."

44. 1850 U.S. Federal Census—Slave Schedules, St. Barth's [Bartholomew's] Parish, Colleton County, South Carolina, #761, column 1, ll. 20–42 (plus one added) "Elizabeth Pinckney" and column 2, ll. 1–14 "Elizabeth Pinckney."

45. 1850 U.S. Federal Census—Slave Schedules, St. Barth's [Bartholomew's] Parish, Colleton County, South Carolina, #759 column 2, ll. 16–42 (plus one added) "Sarah Bellinger" and #761 column 1, ll. 1–19 "Sarah Bellinger." See also 1850 Federal Census, St. Bartholomew's Parish, Colleton County, South Carolina, Real estate 10000, Line Number 23, Dwelling Number 633, Family Number 633, Elizabeth Pinckney household. The census lists Elizabeth Pinckney (41) and Sarah Pinckney (45) along with Elizabeth's children Maria (22), William (20), Charles (18), Augusta (13), Eustace (12), Thomas (10), and Sarah (8); their cousin Guilelmine Youngblood (14) is also listed. Dwelling 632 lists solely Susan Bellinger (71); Dwelling 634 lists Rebecca D['Oyley] Pinckney, Elizabeth's mother-in-law, and an extended family as well. Note the female heads of households in the Pinckney family.

46. Stephanie Jones-Rogers helps us see that Elizabeth was neither alone nor particularly unusual as a White woman who owned human property, White women having been shaped for generations in the practices of the ownership and purchase of human beings. Stephanie Jones-Rogers, *They Were Her Property: White Women as Slave Owners in the American South* (New Haven, CT: Yale University Press, 2019). Elizabeth and her sisters provide a portrait of prominent Catholic women as major slaveholders in this period.

47. In her letters to Eustace at St. John's Fordham, Elizabeth describes the health status of "your boy Thomas." See January 1852 and December 1852 letters.

48. Nancy Stockton, "'I wonder who will think to pray for me when I'm dead?': Elite Catholic Women in Nineteenth-Century South Carolina," master's thesis, The Citadel, 2004, 7.

49. Charles Pinckney was a student at St. John's College from 1848 to 1852.

50. Elizabeth Perry Bellinger Pinckney to Eustace Pinckney, "My Dear Son," August 15, 1860, cited in Powell, *Back over Home*, 107. Eustace is now married to Julia Lynch (sister of Archbishop Patrick Lynch) and residing in Charleston.

51. The slaveholding practices of another Pinckney (cousin of Elizabeth's husband) suggest the possibility of protocols that kept enslaved families together. See Tim Lockley, "The Forming and Fracturing of Families on a South Carolina Rice Plantation, 1812–1865," *History of the Family* 23, no. 1 (2017): 75–89.

52. Alexis Wells-Oghoghomeh, *The Souls of Womenfolk: The Religious Cultures of Enslaved Women in the Lower South* (Chapel Hill: University of North Carolina Press, 2021), 67.

53. Powell, *Back over Home*, 102.

54. Saidiya Hartman, *Scenes of Subjection: Terror, Slavery, and Self-Making in Nineteenth-Century America* (New York: Oxford University Press, 1997), 43.

55. Julia Lynch Pinckney to Anna Lynch, "My dear Sister," January 8, 1860, cited in Powell, *Back over Home*, 103. Julia Pinckney writes: "I could not go down after Eustace came back from Charleston and will not go again until Eustace returns from Alabama. He will carry the Negroes on as soon as the weather clears off and expect him to be absent for about ten days. The old 'Lady' is making every arrangement for moving. I don't think the whole 'State' could keep her back." An 1860 letter describes Elizabeth Pinckney's anticipation of a move to Alabama.

56. Anna Lynch to Bishop Patrick Lynch, "My dear brother [from Walterboro]," December 27, 1860, Charleston Diocesan Archives, Item #13T8, https://lcdl.library.cofc.edu/lcdl/catalog/lcdl:41719.

57. Krebsbach, "Black Catholics in Antebellum Charleston," 153.

58. Archbishop Hughes, "Notes on Slavery," n.d., *Hughes MS*, cited in Rena Mazyck Andrews, "Slavery Views of a Northern Prelate," *Church History* 3, no. 1 (March 1934): 62n15.

59. Krebsbach, "Black Catholics in Antebellum Charleston," 151.

60. Krebsbach, "Black Catholics in Antebellum Charleston," 153.

61. Wells-Oghoghomeh, *The Souls of Womenfolk*, 12.

62. Sylvester A. Johnson, *African American Religions, 1500–2000: Colonialism, Democracy, and Freedom* (Cambridge: Cambridge University Press, 2015), 133. Emphasis mine.

63. Garnett, "National Register Nomination for St. James the Greater Catholic Mission," cites J. D. Lewis, ed., "Green Pond, Walterboro, and Branchville Railroad," South Carolina Railroads, 2012. See also "South Carolina. Charleston," *United States Catholic Miscellany*, January 23, 1831.

64. Garnett, "National Register Nomination for St. James the Greater Catholic Mission," 42–43.

65. Pinckney, "A happy New Year to my much loved Son."

66. Johnson, *African American Religions, 1500–2000*, 80.

67. Johnson, *African American Religions, 1500–2000*, 58.

68. Johnson, *African American Religions, 1500–2000*, 59–60.

69. Pinckney, "A happy New Year to my much loved Son."

70. Pinckney, "A happy New Year to my much loved Son."

71. Garnett, "National Register Nomination for St. James the Greater Catholic Mission," 42–43. "Africans in the Lowcountry maintained traditions about water spirits (basimbi in Ki-Kongo), as derived from the Kongo Kingdom and surrounding regions. They viewed these spirits as an integral part of the natural environment. The indigenous theology of West Central Africa regarded *basimbi* as spirits of nature that occupied or constituted rivers, lakes, and forests. Unlike conventional ancestral spirits, these nature spirits served as spiritual adoptive parents or ancestors to any strange people who entered their territorial domain." Johnson, *African American Religions, 1500–2000*, 134.

72. John McGreevy, "Catholicism and Abolition: A Historical (and Theological) Problem," in *Figures in the Carpet: Finding the Human Person in the American Past*, ed. Wilfred McClay (Grand Rapids, MI: Eerdmans, 2007), 412.

73. Pinckney, "My dear Son (1860)."

74. Elizabeth Perry Bellinger Pinckney to Eustace Pinckney [St. John's College], "My dear Son, [signed May God bless you my ever dear Boy prays your affectionate Mother]" 20 June 1852. Cited in Powell, *Back over Home*, 95.

75. Pinckney, "My own dear precious child."

76. Pinckney, "My dear Son (1852)".

77. Pinckney, "My own dear son."

78. Pinckney, "My own dear son."

79. Pinckney, "My dear Son (1852)."

80. Pinckney, "My own dear Son."

81. McGreevy, "Catholicism and Abolition," 415.

82. The dangers of rice production are chronicled at the Colleton County Museum, Walterboro, SC.

83. Mary Claire Pinckney Jones, *The Pinckneys of Ashepoo* (Lithographed by Furlong Publishing, 1988), 31, South Carolinian Library, Special Collections, University of South Carolina, Columbia, SC.

84. Jones, *The Pinckneys of Ashepoo*, 20. Charles Pinckney, whose plantation is now part of the National Park system in Charleston, South Carolina, was the son of Thomas Pinckney, Eustace Pinckney's great-great-great-grandfather. National Park Service, Charleston, SC. See also Henry Smith, "The Baronies of South Carolina," *South Carolina Historical and Genealogical Magazine* 15, no. 4 (October 1914): 158.

85. Robert Kaczorowski, "The Supreme Court and Congress's Power to Enforce Constitutional Rights: An Overlooked Moral Anomaly," *Fordham Law Review* 73, no. 1, art. 10 (2004): 177n92. Kaczorowski reports that "Senator Henry Wilson of Massachusetts, in his 1872 two volume history of the South asserted that the Fugitive

Slave Clause was inserted in the Constitution at the insistence of General Pinckney, the exponent of that class of slave holders who were in favor of the perpetuity of the slavery of the African race, [who] demanded this provision as a condition precedent to the adoption of the Constitution; and the convention yielded." Citing Henry Wilson, *History of the Rise and Fall of Slave Power in America* 54 (1872). General Pinckney was the cousin of William Cotesworth Pinckney's father.

86. O'Connell, *Catholicity in the Carolinas and Georgia*, 181. "Miss Susan Bellinger joined the Church about 1839, and she led all her servants, for she had many, to embrace the Faith. She was pious, humble, and devoted to her religion, and led a life of unbroken self-denial and prayer."

87. "The Catholic Church—Domestic Slavery, and the Slave Trade," *United States Catholic Miscellany*, December 23, 1843. Emphasis mine.

88. McGreevy, "Catholicism and Abolition," 414.

89. McGreevy, "Catholicism and Abolition," 411.

90. John Francis Maxwell, *Slavery and the Catholic Church: The History of Catholic Teaching Concerning the Moral Legitimacy of the Institution of Slavery* (London: Barry Rose, 1975), 87n170. Maxwell cites many from this period, including J. P. Gury, *Compendium Theologiae Moralis*, 1868, I, n. 539.

91. Archbishop Francis Patrick Kenrick, *Theologia Moralis*, cited in Michael Geelan, "Silent Reply: A Selection of Antebellum American Catholic Opinions Dealing with the Issue of Slavery," master's thesis, University of Dayton, 2007, 31–32.

92. "The Catholic Church—Domestic Slavery, and the Slave Trade," *U.S. Catholic Miscellany.*

93. Numbers collected from 1840 and 1850 census records: Pinckney/D'Oyley (62) Pinckney-Bellingers of Colleton/Walterboro (126); Maloney (9); Bellingers of Barnwell (93); John Bellinger, Charleston (13 in town); Northrop (9); O'Neill (4). The figure of 200 is a placeholder for what is the aggregated slaveholding of these prominent Catholic families, with a few elements that require further detailing. In-town censuses in locations like Charleston may not include enslaved persons on family-owned plantations in a different location. In addition, Catholic slaving families from Savannah, New Orleans, and the Caribbean can be added to this number.

94. *A Catalogue of the Officers and Students of St. John's College for the Academical Year* 1850–51 (New York: Edward Dunigan & Brother, 1851), 24.

95. "Rice Culture & Colleton County," Exhibit at Colleton County Museum, Walterboro, SC.

96. Jones, *The Pinckneys of Ashepoo*, 27.

97. "New York, St. John's College—Rose Hill," *U.S. Catholic Miscellany*, June 1841.

98. "St. John's College, Rosehill, N.Y. First Annual Exhibition—Distributions of Premiums, &c.," *United States Catholic Miscellany*, July 23, 1842. Only the graduation ceremonies of Georgetown were equally covered by the paper; see, e.g., *United States Catholic Miscellany* 21 (July 1841).

99. Archbishop John Hughes, "Sermon on the Occasion of His Return from Cuba, Delivered in St. Patrick's Cathedral, May 1854," in *Complete Works of the Most Rev. John Hughes, D.D., Archbishop of New York, comprising his sermons, letters, lectures, speeches, etc., ed.* Lawrence Kehoe (New York: Lawrence Kehoe, 1866), 2:221. Reprinted on the front page of *United States Catholic Miscellany*, May 13, 1854.

100. Hughes, "Sermon on the Occasion of His Return from Cuba," 222.

101. *The American Ecclesiastical Review*, 1915, 607.

102. Joanne Petro Gury SJ, *Compendium Theologiae Moralis (Juxta Doctrinam S. Alphonsi de Ligorio)*, Tomus Primus (Panormi: Ex Typographiia Bernardi Virzi, 1853), 157.

103. St. John's College Catalogue in the years the boys are attending lists a course in *Butler's Catechism* as required for every year of schooling.

104. *The Most Reverend Doctor James Butler's Catechism, Revised, Enlarged, Improved and Recommended by the Four Roman Catholic Archbishops of Ireland* (D. & J. Sadlier & Co., 1871). Although citations are taken from a later printing, Charles Carmody's research suggests that *Butler's Catechism* underwent stylistic revisions but not substantive ones in its being "frequently reprinted in the United States and incorporated into other American catechisms until 1884." Charles Carmody, "The Roman Catholic Catechesis in the United States, 1784–1930: A Study of Its Theory, Development, and Materials," PhD diss., Loyola University (Chicago), 1975, 39, https://core.ac.uk/download/pdf/48606975.pdf. See also *Butler's Catechism* (New York, n.d.), https://ia902902.us.archive.org/10/items/mostrevoobutl/mostrevoobutl.pdf.

105. *Butler's Catechism*, 58.

106. *Butler's Catechism*, 57.

107. *Butler's Catechism*, 58.

108. *Butler's Catechism*, 57.

109. Anna Lynch, "My Dear Brother."

110. Pinckney, "A happy New Year to my much loved Son."

111. Pinckney, "My dear Son (1852)."

112. Pinckney, "My own dear Son."

113. J. Marshall (Treasurer) to Mrs. E.P. Pinckney," February 26, 1851. Treasurer's Letter Book, Fordham History Collection, Fordham University Archives, Bronx, NY.

114. Pinckney, "My own dear precious Child."

115. J. Larkin SJ, "Prospectus of St. John's College," *U.S. Catholic Miscellany*, October 7, 1854.

116. Charles Connor, "The Northern Catholic Position on Slavery and the Civil War: Archbishop Hughes as a Test Case," *Records of the American Catholic Historical Society of Philadelphia* 96, no. 1/4 (March–December 1985): 35–48.

117. Archbishop John Hughes, "The Abolition Views of Brownson Overthrown," repr. from *The Metropolitan Record* in *The Catholic Mirror*, Baltimore, October 12, 1861. Cited in Rena Mazyck Andrews, "Slavery Views of a Northern Prelate," *Church History* 3, no. 1 (March 1934): 62.

118. Hughes, *Notes on Slavery,* undated manuscript, cited in Andrews, "Slavery Views of a Northern Prelate," 61.

119. Elizabeth Perry Bellinger Pinckney to Eustace Pinckney, "My ever dear Son," October 3, 1851, Pinckney Family Papers, Folder 3, South Caroliniana Library, University of South Carolina, Columbia, SC. Also cited in Powell, *Back over Home,* 92.

120. Pinckney, "A happy New Year to my much loved Son."

121. Gerhard Spieler, "Catholic Hill's Founding Steeped in History," *Beaufort Gazette,* Tuesday, January 12, 1999, 3C, "Newspaper Clippings, 1831–2003," Parish Files, Walterboro, St. James the Greater Mission (2009.02-01-07).

122. Karen Baker-Fletcher, *Dancing with God: The Trinity from a Womanist Perspective* (St. Louis, MO: Chalice, 2006), 128.

123. Baker-Fletcher, *Dancing with God,* 147.

124. Kelly Brown Douglas, *Stand Your Ground: Black Bodies and the Justice of God* (Maryknoll, NY: Orbis, 2015), 149.

125. Jones, *The Pinckneys of Ashepoo,* 20.

126. Jones, *The Pinckneys of Ashepoo,* 20.

127. Marie Jenkins Schwartz, *Birthing a Slave: Motherhood and Medicine in the Antebellum South* (Cambridge, MA: Harvard University Press, 2006).

128. Jones, *The Pinckneys of Ashepoo,* 20.

129. Julia Lynch to Anna Lynch (1860). For a discussion of production and practices in this timeframe, see Edward Baptist, *The Half Has Never Been Told: Slavery and the Making of American Capitalism* (New York: Basic Books, 2014), 111–44.

130. Raymond Schroth, *Fordham: A History and a Memoir,* rev. ed. (New York: Fordham University Press, 2008), 5.

131. Saidiya Hartman, *Lose Your Mother: A Journey along the Atlantic Slave Route* (New York: Farrar, Straus and Giroux, 2007), 170.

## 4. Institutional Networks and Nation Building: Collaborating with the State through Systems of Education

1. Santiago Slabodsky, "It's the Theology, Stupid! Coloniality, Anti-Blackness, and the Bounds of 'Humanity,'" in *Anti-Blackness and Christian Ethics,* ed. Vincent Lloyd and Andrew Prevot (Maryknoll, NY: Orbis, 2017), 31.

2. Slabodsky, "It's the Theology, Stupid!," 31.

3. George Tinker offers a compelling account of the deep cultural differences that framed the Indigenous encounter with European-heritage Christians. George Tinker, "Historic Pain and the Political Present," in *Native American Liberation: A Theology of Sovereignty* (Maryknoll, NY: Orbis, 2008), 1–15.

4. Shannen Dee Williams, *Subversive Habits: Black Catholic Nuns in the Long African American Freedom Struggle* (Durham, NC: Duke University Press, 2022), 27.

5. Oblate Sisters of Providence, Baltimore, Maryland, "Our History," https://www.oblatesisters.com/our-history. The Oblate Sisters of Providence were formally approved by Rome in 1831. Williams, *Subversive Habits*, 53.

6. Black and Indian Mission Office, "Servant of God Mother Mary Lange, O.S.P.," https://blackandindianmission.org/index.php/servant-god-mother-mary-lange-osp.

7. Many White Catholics who fled the Haitian revolution brought with them strong feelings about the necessity of order and resistance to revolution among enslaved people. See, for example, the discussion of William Rodrigue, business partner to Archbishop John Hughes, in John Loughery, *Dagger John: Archbishop John Hughes and the Making of Irish America* (Ithaca, NY: Cornell University Press, 2018), 68.

8. Diane Batts Morrow, *Persons of Color and Religious at the Same Time: The Oblate Sisters of Providence, 1828–1860* (Chapel Hill: University of North Carolina Press, 2002), 155.

9. Williams, *Subversive Habits*, 33.

10. Oblate Sisters of Providence, Baltimore, Maryland, "Our History."

11. Williams, *Subversive Habits*, 33.

12. Marita-Constance Supan, "Dangerous Memory: Mother M. Theresa Maxis Duchemin and the Michigan Congregation of the Sisters, IHM," in *Building Sisterhood: A Feminist History of the Sisters, Servants of the Immaculate Heart of Mary* (Syracuse, NY: Syracuse University Press, 1997), 34.

13. Supan, "Dangerous Memory," 34.

14. The Congregation of the Sisters, Servants of the Immaculate Heart of Mary, "IHM History: Founded November 10, 1845 in Monroe, Michigan by Theresa Maxis Duchemin, IHM and Louis Florent Gillit, CSsR," http://www.sistersofihm.org/who-we-are/ihm-history/.

15. Williams, *Subversive Habits*, 42.

16. Shannen Dee Williams, "What a Forgotten Black Nun Can Teach Us about Racism and Covid-19," *America*, June 8, 2020, https://www.americamagazine.org/faith/2020/04/23/what-forgotten-black-nun-can-teach-us-about-racism-and-covid-19.

17. Morrow, *Persons of Color and Religious at the Same Time*, 145.

18. Morrow, *Persons of Color and Religious at the Same Time*, 145.

19. Morrow, *Persons of Color and Religious at the Same Time*, 191.

20. It may be helpful for our history to name the following locations of the expanding nation: Indiana Territory 1800/statehood 1816; Michigan Territory 1805/statehood 1837; Illinois (part of Indiana Territory until) Territory 1809/statehood 1818; Wisconsin 1836 Territory/statehood 1848; Minnesota Territory 1849/statehood 1858.

21. Genesis 1:28: "God blessed them, and God said to them, 'Be fruitful and multiply, and fill the earth and subdue it; and have dominion over the fish of the sea and over the birds of the air and over every living thing that moves upon the earth'" (NRSV).

22. William Henry Harrison, *Messages and Letters of William Henry Harrison*, Indiana Historical Collection (Indiana Historical Society, 1922), 492–93. For an overview of the impact of papal documents on patterns of domination, including today's ecological crisis, see *The Doctrine of Discovery: Unmasking the Domination Code*, dir. Sheldon Wolfchild (2015), https://vimeo.com/ondemand/dominationcode.

23. Tinker, "Historic Pain and the Political Present," 7–8.

24. Slabodsky, "It's the Theology, Stupid!," 31.

25. Thomas Hart Benton, "Speech of Mr. Benton of Missouri, in the Senate, May 28, 1846, on the Oregon Question," *Congressional Globe* 29, no. 1 (1846): 918.

26. Marco Sioli, "When the Mississippi Was an Indian River: Zebulon Pike's Trip from St. Louis to Its Sources, 1805–1806," *Revue Francaise d'etues Americaines* 98, no. 2 (December 2003): 11. Sioli describes the relationships of East and Midwest as the coordination of a White-serving nation: "Wilkinson noted the reluctance of the Indians to cede the lands, but continued his mission to subdue and pacify the Native American tribes, and to prepare the territory for the coming of the Indians who were to be removed from the East, following Jefferson's plan to move Indian populations around in his agrarian empire."

27. Sioli, "When the Mississippi Was an Indian River," 12.

28. John Carroll to George Washington, March 20, 1792, cited in Catherine O'Donnell, "John Carroll and the Origins of an American Catholic Church," *William and Mary Quarterly* 68, no. 1 (January 2011): 124.

29. Peter Paul Lefevere, "To Bishop John Baptist Purcell," July 19, 1842, University of Notre Dame Archives, Calendar 1842, https://archives.nd.edu/calendar/cal1842.htm.

30. Father Francois Pierz, "To Bishop (Peter Paul) Lefevere," May 26, 1842, University of Notre Dame Archives, Calendar 1842, https://archives.nd.edu/calendar/cal1842.htm.

31. Shannen Dee Williams chronicles the divergent historical records whereby the IHM congregations actively erased the heritage of their OSP foundress, maintaining silence and suppression of their history as each generation navigated its era's racial project, protecting White anti-Blackness. "Mother Theresa Maxis, the exiled and largely forgotten foundress of the IHM in Monroe and in Immaculata and Scranton, Pennsylvania; and Mother Theresa Duchemin, a charter member and former superior general of the OSP, the nation's oldest historically Black Catholic sisterhood, were one in the same person. In other words, the chief foundress of the then exclusively white IHM, one of the nation's largest and most renowned orders of teaching nuns, was a woman of African descent, who had passed for white." Shannen Dee Williams, "Forgotten Habits, Lost Vocations: Black Nuns, Contested Memories, and the 19th Century Struggle to Desegregate U.S. Catholic Religious Life," *Journal of African American History* (Summer 2016): 232.

32. Sisters of IHM, "Bishop Lefevere to Bishop Wood (July 1859)," Paths of Daring, Seeds of Hope, http://www.sistersofihm.org/what-we-do/publications-library/book-excerpts/detail-paths.html?id=287c7221-114a-4b74-906f-63b18bfe7cc0&pageTitle

=IHM%20Book%20Excerpts:%20Theresa%20in%20Monroe:%20Crisis%20of%20Separation.

33. Oblate historian Sarah Willigman, cited in Morrow, *Persons of Color and Religious at the Same Time*, 188–89.

34. Morrow, *Persons of Color and Religious at the Same Time*, 191.

35. Morrow, *Persons of Color and Religious at the Same Time*, 191.

36. Maria Alma, "A Sketch of the Work and History of the Sisters, Servants of the Immaculate Heart of Mary 1845–1920," *Records of the American Catholic Historical Society of Philadelphia* 31, no. 4 (1920): 283.

37. Oblate Sisters of Providence, Baltimore, Maryland, "Our History."

38. Alma, "A Sketch of the Work and History," 286. M. Godfroy Smith (Sister M. Alphonsine) was the sister of the mayor of Monroe.

39. Christopher Lehman, *Slavery's Reach: Southern Slaveholders in the North Star State* (Minnesota Historical Society Press, 2019).

40. William Green, "The Summer Christmas Came to Minnesota: The Case of Eliza Winston, a Slave," *Minnesota Journal of Law and Inequality* 8, no. 1 (March 1990): 151–77.

41. Minnesota Historical Society, "Enslaved African Americans and the Fight for Freedom," Historic Fort Snelling, https://www.mnhs.org/fortsnelling/learn/african-americans.

42. "Enslaved African Americans and the Fight for Freedom."

43. "Enslaved African Americans and the Fight for Freedom."

44. New Advent, "Roger Brooke Taney," in *Catholic Encyclopedia*, https://www.newadvent.org/cathen/14442c.htm.

45. Audra Savage, "The Religion of Race: The Supreme Court as Priests of Racial Politics," *Utah Law Review* 2021, no. 3 (2021): 569–628, https://dc.law.utah.edu/cgi/viewcontent.cgi?article=1295.

46. *The Dred Scott Decision. Opinion of Chief Justice Taney, with an Introduction by Dr. J. H. Van Evrie* (New York: Van Evrie, Horton & Co., 1860), 13.

47. *The Dred Scott Decision*, 19.

48. *The Dred Scott Decision*, 19.

49. Morrow, *Persons of Color and Religious at the Same Time*, 154.

50. Morrow, *Persons of Color and Religious at the Same Time*, 155.

51. Patrick Carey, "Political Atheism: *Dred Scott*, Roger Brooke Taney, and Orestes A. Brownson," *Catholic Historical Review* 88, no. 2 (April 2002): 221.

52. *U.S. Catholic Miscellany*, December 23, 1843.

53. *The Catholic Mirror*, April 20, 1861.

54. Carey, "Political Atheism," 221–22. Carey cites Henry F. Brownson, ed., *The Works of Orestes A. Brownson*, 20 vols. (Detroit, 1882–1887), 13:131.

55. Charles Connor, "The Northern Catholic Position on Slavery and the Civil War: Archbishop Hughes as a Test Case," *Records of the American Catholic Historical Society of Philadelphia* 96, no. 1/4 (March–December 1985): 35–48.

56. *The Dred Scott Decision*, 17.

57. Archives West, "Historical Note," Northern Pacific Railway Company Records 1870–1968, Orbis Cascade Alliance, http://archiveswest.orbiscascade.org/ark:/80444/xv68060: "The first survey for a northern route to the Pacific was conducted by the War Department in 1853."

58. Rev. Cyril Van der Donckt, "The Founders of the Church in Idaho," *American Ecclesiastical Review*, March 1905, 285.

59. Some among the publications that disseminated Catholic opinion/assessment of Indigenous peoples include *The Month and Catholic Review*, *United States Catholic Miscellany*, and *The Indian Sentinel*.

60. Augustus Thebaud SJ, "The Native Tribes of North America and the Catholic Missions," *The Month and Catholic Review* 30 (1877): 145. Emphasis on "settled" in the original. As a reminder of the wider project of White supremacy we might recognize that Thebaud's article comes in a volume that includes an article on comparative theology (1–16), the "races of man" (100–9), and the African slave trade (219).

61. Steven Newcomb, *Pagans in the Promised Land: Decoding the Doctrine of Discovery* (Golden, CO: Fulcrum, 2008); Eric Kades, "History and Interpretation of the Great Case of Johnson v. M'Intosh," *College of William and Mary Law School Faculty Publications* (2001), https://scholarship.law.wm.edu/facpubs/50. The economic benefit of the destruction of Indigenous peoples for White citizens is chronicled also by Richard Henry Pratt: Not only did early-eighteenth-century legislation in South Carolina, North Carolina, and Virginia provide compensation for White settlers who would scalp native peoples, but the educational efforts in the nineteenth century were compensated by the government and infused White communities. Richard Henry Pratt, "The Advantages of Mingling Indians with Whites," *Official Proceedings of the Annual Meeting of the National Conference on Social Welfare* (1892), 49–50, 51–52, https://quod.lib.umich.edu/n/ncosw/ach8650.1892.001/73.

62. National Park Service, "The Dawes Act," in *History and Culture of the Badlands*, https://www.nps.gov/articles/000/dawes-act.htm.

63. Willie James Jennings, *After Whiteness: An Education in Belonging* (Grand Rapids, MI: Eerdmans, 2020), 107.

64. The establishment of twenty-one of the twenty-eight Jesuit institutions of the AJCU within the nineteenth century encourages each institution to ask when and how their land came into their possession (the number varies depending on how we count Loyola Marymount [1911]/St. Vincent's [1865]), but the list is as follows: Georgetown (1789), Saint Louis University (1818), Spring Hill (Mobile, 1830), Xavier (Cincinnati, 1831), Holy Cross (Massachusetts, 1843), St. Joseph's (Philadelphia, 1851), Santa Clara (1851), Loyola Maryland (1852), University of San Francisco (1855), Boston College (1863), Loyola Chicago (1870), Canisius College (Buffalo, 1870), St. Peter's University (Jersey City, 1872), University of Detroit Mercy (1877), Creighton (Omaha, 1878), Regis (Denver, 1877), Marquette (Milwaukee, 1881), John Carroll (Ohio, 1886), Gonzaga (Spokane, 1887), University of Scranton (Pennsylvania, 1888),

Seattle University (1891), Rockhurst (Kansas City, 1910), Loyola Marymount (Los Angeles, 1911), Loyola New Orleans (1912), Fairfield (Connecticut, 1942), LeMoyne College (Syracuse, 1946), Wheeling Jesuit (est. 1954, no longer within the network). The twenty-eighth college now listed is St. John's Belize (1887). AJCU, "Institutions," https://www.ajcunet.edu/institutions.

65. Margaret Archuleta, Brenda Child, and K. Tsianina Lomawaima, eds., *Away from Home: American Indian Boarding School Experiences, 1879–2000* (Phoenix, AZ: Heard Museum, 2000), 16.

66. Archuleta et al., eds., *Away from Home*, 16.

67. Denise Lajimodiere, *Stringing Rosaries: The History, the Unforgivable, and the Healing of Northern Plains American Indian Boarding School Survivors* (Fargo: North Dakota State University Press, 2019), 269. See also Richard Henry Pratt, "The Founding of Carlisle," in *Battlefield and Classroom: Four Decades with the American Indian, 1867–1904* (New Haven, CT: Yale University Press, 1964), 213–29.

68. Pratt, *Battlefield and Classroom*, 222.

69. In the 1892 discussion of Pratt's model, a Father O'Ryan of Denver remarked, "Where the Indians have been civilized, it has been recognized that they have souls." *National Conference on Social Welfare*, 390, https://quod.lib.umich.edu/n/ncosw/ach8650.1892.001/413.

70. The Mosqui Indians were incarcerated at Alcatraz "because of their resistance, including refusing to enroll their children in federal schools" (1895), in Archuleta et al., eds., *Away from Home*, 47. Brenda Child indicates the compulsory attendance of 1898 in Brenda Child, *Boarding School Seasons: American Indian Families, 1900–1940* (Lincoln: University of Nebraska Press, 1998), 56.

71. Pratt, *Battlefield and Classroom*, 215.

72. Richard Henry Pratt, "The Advantages of Mingling Indians with Whites," *Official Proceedings of the Annual Meeting of the National Conference on Social Welfare* (1892). Pratt's famous sentiment is situated in this frame: "A great general has said that the only good Indian is a dead one, and that high sanction of his destruction has been an enormous factor in promoting Indian massacres. In a sense, I agree with the sentiment, but only in this: that all the Indian there is in the race should be dead. Kill the Indian in him, and save the man" (46), https://quod.lib.umich.edu/n/ncosw/ACH8650.1892.001/68. Pratt often points to the parallel missions of elevating the "Negroes of Africa" and Indigenous peoples; in his position paper, he advances one among the causes of Indian "destruction" is "the debasing influences of idleness" (49). Pratt reveals the consistent pattern of White Christian logic that slavery elevated African peoples when he announces, "Inscrutable are the ways of Providence. Horrible as were the experiences of its introduction, and of slavery itself, there was concealed in them the greatest blessing that ever came to the Negro race—seven millions of blacks from cannibalism in darkest Africa to citizenship in free and enlightened America. . . . Left in Africa, surrounded by their fellow-savages, our seven millions of industrious black fellow-citizens would still be savages" (50–51).

73. John Mullan Letter to Lorenzo Palladino SJ and Leopold Van Gorp, April 11, 1885, cited in Gerald McKevitt, *Brokers of Culture: Italian Jesuits in the American West, 1848–1919* (Stanford, CA: Stanford University Press, 2007), 156.

74. McKevitt, *Brokers of Culture*, 211–12.

75. L. B. Palladino SJ, *Indian and White in the Northwest: A History of Catholicity in Montana, 1831–1891*, 2nd ed., rev. and enl. (1894; Lancaster, PA: Wickersham, 1922), 113. The book received the symbolic recognition of "imprimi potest," "nihil obstat," and "imprimatur," affirming its soundness from an institutional Catholic perspective.

76. Gonzaga University, "Gonzaga's History," https://www.gonzaga.edu/about/our-mission-jesuit-values/gonzagas-history.

77. "Then and Now: The Northern Pacific Railway," *Spokesman-Review*, April 14, 2014, https://www.spokesman.com/stories/2014/apr/14/then-and-now-northern-pacific-railway/. "Financing was secured by the 40 million acres of land along the route, which the railroad was granted by the federal government."

78. Gonzaga University, "Gonzaga's History."

79. "War of 1812 Veteran, James Nettle Glover, at Pioneers and Soldiers," Minneapolis Pioneers and Soldiers Memorial Cemetery History Page: Alley Article, http://www.friendsofthecemetery.org/history/alley_articles/glover_james_jan2004.shtml.

80. Palladino, *Indian and White*, 124.

81. Ign. F. Horstmann, Bishop of Cleveland, "A Friend in Need," *Indian Sentinel*, 1902–1903, 11. *The Indian Sentinel* has been digitized and housed in the Special Collections at Marquette University: https://cdm16280.contentdm.oclc.org/digital/collection/p15072coll2/id/435/rec/1.

82. Palladino, *Indian and White*, 114–15.

83. Child, *Boarding School Seasons*, 44.

84. Rev. J. B. Carroll SJ, Missionary to the Piëgans, "The Fourth of July Dishonored," *Indian Sentinel*, 1910, 29.

85. Carroll, "The Fourth of July Dishonored," 33. It is worth pressing further a juxtaposition with the theology articulated by Ignatius of Loyola in the *Spiritual Exercises*: "I will consider how God dwells in creatures; in the elements, giving them existence; in the plants, giving them life; in the animals, giving them sensation; in human beings, giving them intelligence; and finally, how in this way he dwells also in myself, giving me existence, life, sensation, and intelligence; and even further making me his temple, since I am created as a likeness and image of the Divine Majesty." From Saint Ignatius, "Contemplation to Attain Love," in *The Spiritual Exercises of Saint Ignatius: A Translation and Commentary by George E. Ganss, S.J.* (Chicago: Loyola, 1992), 95.

86. *Indian Sentinel* 40, no. 1 (1962), back cover, https://cdm16280.contentdm.oclc.org/digital/collection/p15072coll2/id/10369/rec/1.

87. Amanda Bresie, "Mother Katharine Drexel's Benevolent Empire: The Bureau of Catholic Indian Missions and the Education of Native Americans," *U.S. Catholic Historian* 32, no. 2 (Summer 2014): 6.

88. Bresie, "Mother Katharine Drexel's Benevolent Empire," 5.

89. Bresie, "Mother Katharine Drexel's Benevolent Empire," 10.

90. For one example of the ways in which Catholic institutions of parish and church leadership intersected with government-sponsored programs of Indian education like at Carlisle, see Barbara Landis (presenter), "Carlisle Indian Industrial School (1879–1918), References to St. Patrick's Church, Carlisle, PA," https://home.epix.net/~landis/stpatricks.html.

91. Williams, *Subversive Habits*, 62.

92. Sister Roberta Smith SBS (Archivist), "Summary of Letters in Our Archives (Sisters of the Blessed Sacrament, Cornwells Heights, PA)," Parish Files (Series 142), "Walterboro, St. James the Greater," Diocese of Charleston, Charleston, SC.

93. Williams, *Subversive Habits*, 55.

94. Williams, *Subversive Habits*, 63.

95. Williams, *Subversive Habits*, 68.

96. Willie James Jennings, *After Whiteness: An Education in Belonging* (Grand Rapids, MI: Eerdmans, 2020), 32.

97. Jennings, *After Whiteness*, 32.

98. Tommy Davis, interview in Lajimodiere, *Stringing Rosaries*, 210.

99. "Josephine," aged 5–13, at St. Joseph's Indian Boarding School, Chamberlain, SD, in Lajimodiere, *Stringing Rosaries*, 24.

100. Roger White Owl, St. Joseph's Catholic School in Chamberlain, SD, in Lajimodiere, *Stringing Rosaries*, 42.

101. Interviewees in Lajimodiere, *Stringing Rosaries*, recount various forms of "punishment" across various Indian boarding schools, including broom handles (77, Dennis Decoteau, Wahpeton Indian Boarding School / 217, Tommy Davis, Junipero Serra School); straps or belts (33, "Julia" Chamberlain South Dakota / 77, Dennis Decoteau, Wahpeton Indian Boarding School / 176, Eugene Hale, St. Michael's Day School / 188, Phil St. John, various Catholic schools); rulers (33, "Julia / 210, Tommy Davis); seclusion, 34.

102. Tommy Davis, in Lajimodiere, *Stringing Rosaries*, 219.

103. Phil St. James, in Lajimodiere, *Stringing Rosaries*, 192.

104. Sister Miriam Shindelar was a dorm attendant from 1967 to 1970 at the Marty Indian School, a Roman Catholic institution on the Yankton Sioux reservation in South Dakota. "That first year, I was in charge of 91 high school girls," said Shindelar, who also taught at the school from 1974 to 1984. "You didn't have the kinds of time that a family would have. You ended up being largely a disciplinarian." Matt Kelley, "American Indians Describe School Beatings," Associated Press, April 24, 1999.

105. Child, *Boarding School Seasons*, 82.

106. Archuleta et al., eds., *Away from Home*, 36.

107. Photo of "Shoe-making class, Holy Rosary Mission, SD, 1900." *Bureau of Catholic Indian Missions.* In Lajimodiere, *Stringing Rosaries*, 40. Aaron Pierre SJ has presented the longer history of Jesuits' earliest attempts at boarding schools in

Flourissant, MO, focused on "catechism and skills" (1824) and in Kansas at the Osage Manual Labor School for Boys (1846–1876). Aaron Pierre SJ, research presented at "Unpacking Histories: Reflecting on Relations of Indigenous People and the Jesuits," Jesuit Conference of Canada and the United States, Webinar, December 2, 2021.

108. Anselm Weber, "The Navajo Indians and Saint Michael's Mission [Arizona]," *Indian Sentinel* 1, no. 8 (1918): 13. In 1952, Francis Menager SJ reports the benefits that boys who had learned carpentry and girls "the elements of better housekeeping" had brought to Eskimo communities from St. Mary's mission school. Francis Menager SJ, "A New Chapter," *Indian Sentinel* 32, no. 8 (1952): 122.

109. Mary Ann Cavanaugh (St. Michael's North Dakota), in Lajimodiere, *Stringing Rosaries*, 140.

110. Lajimodiere, *Stringing Rosaries*, shoe-making, 40; making knitting needles for the Red Cross, 70; Child, *Boarding School Seasons*, on selling produce from the school farm but not serving it to the boarders, 35.

111. "Josephine," in Lajimodiere, *Stringing Rosaries*, 24.

112. Lajimodiere, *Stringing Rosaries*, 33, 104, 164.

113. Tommy Davis, in Lajimodiere, *Stringing Rosaries*, 221.

114. Eugene Hale, in Lajimodiere, *Stringing Rosaries*, 175.

115. Students throughout the interviews in *Stringing Rosaries* describe this practice as "being washed with DDT," a phrase similarly used in the documentary *A Good Day to Die: A Film about Dennis Banks and the American Indian Movement*, dir. David Mueller (Kino Lorber Films, 2013).

116. Child, *Boarding School Seasons*, 88.

117. Demus McDonald/Makah Wammi Omni, in Lajimodiere, *Stringing Rosaries*, 162.

118. "Josephine," in Lajimodiere, *Stringing Rosaries*, 26.

119. "Julia," in Lajimodiere, *Stringing Rosaries*, 35.

120. Roger White Owl, in Lajimodiere, *Stringing Rosaries*, 46.

121. Patrick Anderson, "Native American Victims of Sex Abuse at Catholic Boarding Schools Fight for Justice," *Argus Leader*, May 16, 2019, https://www.argusleader.com/story/news/2019/05/16/native-american-sex-abuse-victims-catholic-boarding-schools-south-dakota/1158590001/.

122. Phil St. John, in Lajimodiere, *Stringing Rosaries*, 190.

123. "Genevive," in Lajimodiere, *Stringing Rosaries*, 58.

124. Tommy Davis, in Lajimodiere, *Stringing Rosaries*, 229, 232.

125. Tommy Davis, in Lajimodiere, *Stringing Rosaries*, 212.

126. Eugene Hale, in Lajimodiere, *Stringing Rosaries*, 177–78.

127. For contemporary practices of Indigenous Catholicisms, see the work of the Indigenous Catholic Research Fellowship, https://www.Indigenouscatholic.org/.

128. Pietro Paulo Prando, "St. Xavier Mission," 1887, Prando Papers, Jesuit Oregon Province Archives, Foley Center, Gonzaga University, Spokane, WA, cited

in Gerald McKevitt, *Brokers of Culture: Italian Jesuits in the American West, 1848–1919* (Stanford, CA: Stanford University Press, 2007), 157.

129. Lajimodiere, *Stringing Rosaries*, 204.

## 5. Leveraging Capital: Church Institutions for Change in the Twentieth Century

1. For a fuller discussion of "agonistic" in theopolitical perspective, see Mark Lewis Taylor, *The Theological and the Political: On the Weight of the World* (Minneapolis, MN: Fortress, 2011).

2. Ruth Russo, "A Natural History of 'Agonist,'" *Perspectives in Biology and Medicine* 45, no. 3 (Summer 2002): 351.

3. Russo, "A Natural History of 'Agonist,'" 356.

4. Jeannine Hill Fletcher, *Motherhood as Metaphor: Engendering Interreligious Dialogue* (New York: Fordham University Press, 2013).

5. "The Voice of the Farm Worker," in English, *El Malcriado* 32 (Delano, CA: Farm Worker Press, Inc.) (March 3, 1966).

6. The racial categorization "Latinx" points to the changeability of racial categories throughout America's racial project, as "Latino" or "Latina" became preferred over "Hispanic.". "Latinx" attempts to offer a gender-neutral and gender-queer option for this racial categorization. In scholarly usage, the term "Latine" is also becoming current. I have chosen to employ "Latinx" as a reminder of the fabricated nature of the categories themselves, with the disruptive quality of "x" included.

7. Bryan Massingale, *Racial Justice and the Catholic Church* (Maryknoll, NY: Orbis, 2010), 177.

8. Gustavo Gutierrez, *A Theology of Liberation: History, Politics, and Salvation*, rev. ed. (Maryknoll, NY: Orbis, 1988), 110.

9. Gutierrez, *A Theology of Liberation*, 86.

10. "Immigration to the U.S. in the Late 1800s," *National Geographic*, https://www.nationalgeographic.org/photo/immigration-1870-1900/.

11. Erika Lee, *The Making of Asian America: A History* (New York: Simon and Schuster, 2015), 59.

12. Lee, *The Making of Asian America*, 65.

13. Lee, *The Making of Asian America*, 65.

14. Lee, *The Making of Asian America*, 71.

15. "Report of the Secretary of the Interior," in *Message of the President of the United States and Accompanying Documents at the Commencement of the First Session of the Thirty-Ninth Congress* (Washington, 1865), 990, https://books.google.com/books?id=sEfg31gC6H4C&pg=PA990&lpg=PA990.

16. "Sunday Service aboard a Pacific Mail Steam Ship," *Harper's Weekly*, June 16, 1877, 461. For a vivid photo essay chronicling media as a source of insight into the US racial project in relation to Asian immigrants, see Hsu Chung-mao, "[Photo

story] China-US Relations in the Late 19th Century: Is History Repeating Itself?," *Think China*, March 18, 2020, https://www.thinkchina.sg/photo-story-china-us-relations-late-19th-century-history-repeating-itself.

17. Watomika (James Bouchard), "Biographical Sketch of Wa-tom-i-ka," the autobiographical sketch written by James Bouchard and gifted to Pierre-Jean De Smet; translated and published in Jay Miller, "The Early Years of Watomika (James Bouchard): Delaware and Jesuit," *American Indian Quarterly* 13, no. 2 (Spring 1989): 175.

18. Watomika, "Biographical Sketch of Wa-tom-i-ka," 175.

19. Watomika narrates the role of the seer/conjuror/"chief Pow-wow" consulting "in Solitude, the Great Spirit & ascertain[ing] the cause of his Anger & the means of appeasing the Same." After consultation, the Great Spirit sends a sign through the natural world (in the form of a little bird) that "whispered softly into his ear the startling truths that he was about to reveal." Watomika, "Biographical Sketch of Wa-tom-i-ka," 181–82.

20. Watomika, "Biographical Sketch of Wa-tom-i-ka," 184.

21. Watomika, "Biographical Sketch of Wa-tom-i-ka," 184.

22. John Bernard McGloin, *Eloquent Indian: The Life of James Bouchard California Jesuit* (Stanford, CA: Stanford University Press, 1949).

23. "Fr. James Mary Chrysostom Bouchard: A Sketch of His Life and Labors," *Woodstock Letters* 19, no. 3 (October 1, 1890): 302–11.

24. San Francisco, *Catholic Monitor*, February 22, 1873. Cited in McGloin, *Eloquent Indian*, 177.

25. Miller, "The Early Years of Watomika (James Bouchard)," 165–88.

26. James Bouchard, "Chinaman or White Man, Which?," *San Francisco Catholic Guardian*, March 1, 1873. Cited in McGloin, *Eloquent Indian*, 180.

27. McGloin, *Eloquent Indian*, 178.

28. Denny Chin and Kathy Hirata Chin, "'Kung Flu': A History of Hostility and Violence against Asian Americans," *Fordham Law Review* 90, no. 5 (2022): 1889–944.

29. Terrence McArdle, "The Day 30,000 White Supremacists in KKK Robes Marched in the Nation's Capital," *Washington Post*, August 11, 2018.

30. Alan Ziajka, "The Jesuits and Native Communities," *Pierless Bridges* 3 (2022), https://myusf.usfca.edu/provost/The-Jesuits-and-Native-Communities.

31. Timothy Matovina, "Latino Catholics in the Southwest," in *Roman Catholicism in the United States: A Thematic History*, ed. Margaret M. McGuinness and James T. Fisher (New York: Fordham University Press, 2019), 43.

32. Santiago Slabodsky, "It's the Theology, Stupid! Coloniality, Anti-Blackness, and the Bounds of 'Humanity,'" in *Anti-Blackness and Christian Ethics*, ed. Vincent Lloyd and Andrew Prevot (Maryknoll, NY: Orbis, 2017), 31.

33. Matovina, "Latino Catholics in the Southwest," 49.

34. Matovina, "Latino Catholics in the Southwest," 49.

35. Patrick Verel, "Painting from Fordham Archives Spotlighted at the Met," *Fordham News*, July 19, 2017, https://news.fordham.edu/arts-and-culture/painting-from-fordham-archives-spotlighted-at-the-met/.

36. Matovina, "Latino Catholics in the Southwest," 49.

37. Jeffrey Burns, "Left Coast Catholicism: The Tradition of Dissent in the California Church," in *Roman Catholicism in the United States: A Thematic History*, ed. Margaret M. McGuinness and James T. Fisher (New York: Fordham University Press, 2019), 65–66. Burns is citing Michael Engh, *Frontier Faiths: Church, Temple, and Synagogue in Los Angeles, 1846–1888* (Albuquerque: University of New Mexico Press, 1992), 175.

38. Burns, "Left Coast Catholicism," 65.

39. Maria Root, ed., *Filipino Americans: Transformation and Identity* (Thousand Oaks, CA: Sage, 1991), xii.

40. Juan Gonzalez frames his analysis of the flow of Latinx immigration to the United States through the category of a "harvest of empire" insofar as imperial interests (in military or business acquisitions) on the part of the United States of America in other countries created systems for the flow of migration, often as a "safety valve" to the unrest created by the US presence but always in ways that served US political and economic interests. See "Harvest of Empire," dir. Peter Getzels and Eduardo Lopes (Snag Films, 2012).

41. Peter Bacho, "The Tragic Sense of Filipino History," in *Filipino Americans: Transformation and Identity*, ed. Maria Root (Thousand Oaks, CA: Sage, 1991), 2.

42. Juanita Tamayo Lott, "Demographic Changes Transforming the Filipino American Community," in *Filipino Americans: Transformation and Identity, ed. Maria Root* (Thousand Oaks, CA: Sage, 1991), 12.

43. Lee, *The Making of Asian America*, 175.

44. Lee, *The Making of Asian America*, 176.

45. Lott, "Demographic Changes Transforming the Filipino American Community," 12.

46. Chin and Chin, "'Kung Flu,'" 1905–7.

47. For a history of America's racial project in homeownership, see Richard Rothstein, *The Color of Law: A Forgotten History of How Our Government Segregated America* (New York: Liveright, 2017).

48. Stanley L. McMichael, *McMichael's Appraising Manual: A Real Estate Appraising Handbook for Field Work and Advanced Study Courses* (New York: Prentice-Hall, 1931), 278, https://babel.hathitrust.org/cgi/pt?id=uc1.$b281272&view=1up&seq=306&q1=racial.

49. *McMichael's Appraising Manual*, 4th ed. (ninth printing) (Englewood, NJ: Prentice-Hall, 1962), 160.

50. Mario T. García, ed., *A Dolores Huerta Reader* (Albuquerque: University of New Mexico Press, 2008), xvi.

51. Mario T. García, *A Dolores Huerta Reader*, xvi.

52. Huerta moved to Stockton in 1936. Garcia, A *Dolores Huerta Reader*, 333

53. Stacey K. Sowards, *¡Si, Ella Puede! The Rhetorical Legacy of Dolores Huerta and the United Farm Workers* (Austin: University of Texas Press, 2019), 20.

54. Sowards, *¡Si, Ella Puede!*, 16. Sowards cites Marshall Ganz, *Why David Sometimes Wins: Leadership, Organization, and Strategy in the California Farm Worker Movement* (New York: Oxford University Press, 2009), 24; and Natalia Molina, *How Race Is Made in America: Immigration, Citizenship, and the Historical Power of Racial Scripts* (Berkeley: University of California Press, 2014), 10..

55. Erin F. Doss and Robin Jensen, "Balancing Mystery and Identification: Dolores Huerta's Shifting Transcendent Persona," *Quarterly Journal of Speech* 99, no. 4 (November 2013): 486.

56. Lott, "Demographic Changes Transforming the Filipino American Community," 13.

57. Lee, *The Making of Asian America*, 182.

58. Lee, *The Making of Asian America*, 182.

59. Sowards, *¡Si, Ella Puede!*, 20.

60. Dolores Huerta, "Enacting Change for Social Justice Organizing," presentation delivered at The New Face of California: The Great Central Valley Symposium, UC Berkeley, November 3–5, 2005. *Berkeley La Raza Law Journal* 17, no. 2 (Fall 2006): 278.

61. Alex Fabros, interview in Marissa Aroy, *The Delano Manongs: Forgotten Heroes of the United Farm Workers*, Media Factory, 2014, at 14:16.

62. National Park Service, "Gravesites of Larry Itliogn and Richard Chávez," https://www.nps.gov/places/000/gravesites-of-larry-itliong-and-richard-ch-vez.htm.

63. Craig Sharlin and Lilia Villanueva, *Philip Vera Cruz: A Personal History of Filipino Immigrants and the Farmworker Movement*, 3rd ed. (Seattle: University of Washington Press, 2000), 80.

64. Craig Sharlin and Lilia Villanueva, *Philip Vera Cruz*, 80.

65. Craig Sharlin and Lilia Villanueva, *Philip Vera Cruz*, 81.

66. "Dolores Huerta on Spirituality," interview by Mario Garcia, June 1, 2007, in A *Dolores Huerta* Reader, ed. Mario Garcia (Albuquerque: University of New Mexico Press, 2008), 334.

67. Garcia, "Dolores Huerta on Spirituality," 336.

68. Gutierrez, A *Theology of Liberation*, 110.

69. Burns, "Left Coast Catholicism," 77.

70. Igna Kim, "The 1965–1970 Delano Grape Strike and Boycott," United Farm Workers, https://ufw.org/1965-1970-delano-grape-strike-boycott.

71. "Defense Department Grape Purchases," Madeline Rogero and Roger Pitt Collection, Farmworker Movement Documentation Project, University of California–San Diego Library, https://libraries.ucsd.edu/farmworkermovement/ufwarchives/RogeroPitt/02/DEFENSE%20DEPT%20GRAPE%20PURCHASES.pdf.

72. Craig Sharlin and Lilia Villanueva, *Philip Vera Cruz*, 81–82.

73. Craig Sharlin and Lilia Villanueva, *Philip Vera Cruz*, 81–82.

74. Craig Sharlin and Lilia Villanueva, *Philip Vera Cruz*, 81.

75. Craig Sharlin and Lilia Villanueva, *Philip Vera Cruz*, 81. Bishop Manning was bishop of Fresno in 1967 and archbishop of Los Angeles in 1970; Hugh A. Donohoe was bishop of Stockton from 1962 to 1969 and bishop of Fresno from 1969 to 1980.

76. Garcia, "Dolores Huerta on Spirituality," 339.

77. Schneiders, "Spirituality and the Academy," *Theological Studies* 50 (1989): 684.

78. Burns, "Left Coast Catholicism," 79.

79. Corita Kent, "Chávez," seriagraph (print), 1969, https://collection.corita.org/piece/69-80.

80. Garcia, "Dolores Huerta on Spirituality," 331. See also Claire Wolfteich, "Spirituality, Mothering, and Public Leadership: Women's Life Writing and Generative Directions for Spirituality Studies," *Spiritus* 17, no. 2 (2007): 145–64.

81. Robert Chao Romero, "The Spiritual Practice of César Chávez," *Perspectivas*, Spring 2017, 31.

82. Mario Garcia, *The Gospel of César Chávez: My Faith in Action* (Lanham, MD: Sheed & Ward, 2007), 12, 16; quoted in Romero, "The Spiritual Practice of César Chávez," 31. Romero also cites Huerta, who identified a Mexican cultural and religious practice of "self-inflicted punishment" (33).

83. Dolores Huerta, in "Latinopia Event 1966 UFW Peregrinacion (Pilgrimage)," produced by Jesús Salvador Treviño and David Sandoval (Barrio Dog Productions, Inc., 2013), at 1:03–1:09, http://latinopia.com/latino-history/latinopia-event-1966-ufw-peregrinacion-pilgrimage-march/.

84. Huerta, in "Latinopia" at 1:09–1:31.

85. United States Conference of Catholic Bishops, "Easter Triduum," USCCB.org, https://www.usccb.org/prayer-worship/liturgical-year/triduum. "Though chronologically three days, they are liturgically one day unfolding for us the unity of Christ's Pascal Mystery."

86. Kelly Brown Douglass, *Stand Your Ground: Black Bodies and the Justice of God* (Maryknoll, NY: Orbis, 2015), 171–74.

87. Igna Kim, "Today in History," United Farm Workers, https://ufw.org/today-history-cesar-chavez-began-25-day-water-fast-delano-calif-feb-11-1968/.

88. Igna Kim, "The 1965–1970 Delano Grape Strike and Boycott," United Farm Workers, https://ufw.org/1965-1970-delano-grape-strike-boycott/https://ufw.org/1965-1970-delano-grape-strike-boycott/.

89. Kim, "The 1965–1970 Delano Grape Strike and Boycott."

90. Craig Sharlin and Lilia Villanueva, *Philip Vera Cruz*, 82.

91. Anne Klejment, "Dorothy Day and César Chávez: American Catholic Lives in Nonviolence," *U.S. Catholic Historian* 29 no. 3 (2011): 78. Klejment uses this phrase to capture Day's involvement in the civil rights movement for racial justice, and it is apt for her support of the racial justice efforts of the UFW as well.

92. Dorothy Day, "Chavez, Workers Step Up Boycott," *Catholic Worker*, March–April 1973, 1, 4, DDLW #254, https://catholicworker.org/254-2/.

93. "Day's influence on lay Catholics peaked during the 1960s and early 1970s," coinciding with the UFW struggles and indicating the power the paper might have had. Klejment, "Dorothy Day and César Chávez," 78.

94. Luisa Rollenhagen, "How Labor Activist César Chávez Went on a Hunger Strike and Turned Robert Kennedy into a Fan" *Medium*, March 30, 2018, https://timeline.com/César-Chávez-robert-kennedy-vonviolent-justice-california-789f6354682a.

95. Craig Sharlin and Lilia Villanueva, *Philip Vera Cruz*, 81–82.

96. Dolores Huerta, "We've Got the Power," *Progressive*, July 2009, 36.

97. Dolores Huerta, "Enacting Change for Social Justice in Organizing," *La Raza Law Journal* 17, no. 2 (Fall 2006): 280.

98. Garcia, "Dolores Huerta on Spirituality," 341.

99. Garcia, "Dolores Huerta on Spirituality," 52; Kim, "The 1965–1970 Delano Grape Strike and Boycott."

## 6. Confronting a Culture of White Supremacy: Spiritual Strength for Mobilizing Capital

1. Duke L. Kwon and Gregory Thompson, *Reparations: A Christian Call for Repentance and Repair* (Grand Rapids, MI: Brazos, 2021), 38.

2. Kwon and Thompson, *Reparations*, 42.

3. Kwon and Thompson, *Reparations*, 42.

4. Students in a racially diverse classroom working through Kwon and Thompson's *Reparations* had read the chapter in which the authors present their analysis of American racism as a cultural reality and upon hearing the concluding analysis spoken aloud were asked to select one word to describe what they were feeling. Fordham University, Bronx, NY, January 24, 2023.

5. Although Asian populations historically were the targets of wage theft in industry in the mid-nineteenth century, the refusal of immigration from Asian nations (1882–1965) and subsequent changes in immigration law to prioritize highly skilled workers result in Asian demographics ranking quite high on most calculations of wage disparity across the categories of race.

6. Kwon and Thompson, *Reparations*, 77–78.

7. Kwon and Thompson, *Reparations*, 78.

8. Kwon and Thompson, *Reparations*, 81–82.

9. These are the currency of symbolic capital as described by Mark Lewis Taylor, *The Theological and the Political: On the Weight of the World* (Minneapolis, MN: Fortress, 2011), 88.

10. Kwon and Thompson, *Reparations*, 87.

11. M. Craig Barnes, "Guest Editorial," *Theology Today* 76, no. 4 (2020): 287.

12. State of Iowa General Assembly, "House File 802: An Act Providing for Requirements Related to Racism or Sexism Trainings at, and Diversity and Inclusion Efforts by, Governmental Agencies and Entities, Schools Districts, and

Public PostSecondary Educational Institutions," June 8, 2021, https://www.legis.iowa.gov/legislation/BillBook?ga=89&ba=HF802.

13. Sarah Schwartz, "Map: Where Critical Race Theory Is Under Attack," *Education Week*, June 11, 2021, updated May 5, 2023, https://www.edweek.org/policy-politics/map-where-critical-race-theory-is-under-attack/2021/06.

14. Kevin Jones, "New Iowa 'School Choice' Program a Boon for Catholic Schools, Bishop Says," *Catholic News Agency*, January 27, 2023, https://www.catholicnewsagency.com/news/253483/new-iowa-school-choice-program-a-boon-for-catholic-schools-bishop-says.

15. Edward Graham, "Supreme Court Decision Paves Way for Public Funds to Flow to Religious Schools," *National Education Association NEA Today, July* 21, 2022, https://www.nea.org/advocating-for-change/new-from-nea/supreme-court-decision-paves-way-public-funds-flow-religious-schools.

16. Thomas Reese, "Public Funding of Religious Schools Is Coming. The First Lesson Is Compromise," *National Catholic Reporter*, December 15, 2021, https://www.ncronline.org/news/people/public-funding-religious-schools-coming-first-lesson-compromise.

17. "I have become all things to all people that I might by all means save some" (1 Corinthians 9:22).

18. Gustavo Gutierrez, A *Theology of Liberation: History, Politics, and Salvation*, rev. ed. (Maryknoll, NY: Orbis, 1988), 91.

19. Gutierrez, A *Theology of Liberation*, 91.

20. People's Institute for Survival and Beyond, "Our Principles," https://pisab.org/our-principles/.

21. Deborah Yaffe, "Princeton and Slavery: Our Original Sin," *Princeton Alumni Weekly*, November 8, 2017, https://paw.princeton.edu/article/princeton-and-slavery-our-original-sin.

22. Gregory C. Chisholm SJ, William D. Critchley-Menor SJ, and Timothy P. Kesicki SJ, "Days of Reckoning: Essays on Racism and Slaveholding in the Society of Jesus," *Studies in the Spirituality of the Jesuits* 54, no. 4 (Winter 2022).

23. Nate Tinner-Williams, "Sisters of Charity Foundation Acknowledges Slaveholding in New Statement," *Black Catholic Messenger*, February 19, 2022, https://www.blackcatholicmessenger.com/sisters-of-charity-slaveholding-letter/.

24. Kelly Schmidt, "The Pervasive Institution: Slavery and Its Legacies in U.S. Catholicism," *American Catholic Studies Newsletter* (Spring 2022): 11–22.

25. Jody L. Allen, "How Do Academic Institutions Evaluate Their History: Campus Case Studies I: William and Mary," *Theology Today* 76, no. 4 (2020): 296.

26. Sarah Sunshine Manning, "Jesuits Return 525 Acres to Rosebud Sioux Tribe," *Indian Country Today*, May 19, 2017, updated September 13, 2018, https://ictnews.org/archive/jesuits-return-525-acres-rosebud-sioux-tribe.

27. Martha A. Sandweiss, "How Do Academic Institutions Evaluate Their History? Campus Case Studies III: Princeton University," *Theology Today*, 76 no. 4 (2020): 305.

28. National Native American Boarding School Healing Coalition, https://boardingschoolhealing.org/.

29. Ramona Klein interview, in Denise Lajimodiere, *Stringing Rosaries: The History, the Unforgivable, and the Healing of Northern Plains American Indian Boarding School Survivors* (Fargo: North Dakota State University Press, 2019), 130.

30. Kwon and Thompson, *Reparations*, 75.

31. Kwon and Thompson, *Reparations*, 75.

32. Kwon and Thompson, *Reparations*, 75.

33. emilie townes, *Womanist Ethics and the Cultural Production of Evil* (New York: Palgrave Macmillan, 2006).

34. Harvard University, *Report of the Presidential Committee on Harvard & the Legacy of Slavery*, "Summary of Key Findings," section 1.5, https://legacyofslavery.harvard.edu/report/introduction-and-findings.

35. Adam Rothman, "How Do Academic Institutions Evaluate Their History? Campus Case Studies II: Georgetown University," *Theology Today* 76, no. 4 (2020): 301. See also Rothman and Elsa Barraza Mendoza, eds., *Facing Georgetown's History: A Reader on Slavery, Memory, and Reconciliation* (Washington, DC: Georgetown University Press, 2021).

36. Shannen Dee Williams, *Subversive Habits: Black Catholic Nuns in the Long African American Freedom Struggle* (Durham, NC: Duke University Press, 2022), 85–86.

37. Klein, in Lajimodiere, *Stringing Rosaries*, 127.

38. Linda Fredericks, Dan Jesse, Robert Brave Heart Sr., and Melinda Strickland, "The Lakota Language Project at Red Cloud Indian School: Turning the Tide of Native Language Loss," *Journal of American Indian Education* 57, no. 3 (Fall 2018): 51–71.

39. Joseph Barndt, *Becoming an Anti-Racist Church: Journeying Toward Wholeness* (Minneapolis, MN: Fortress, 2011), 159.

40. Barndt, *Becoming an Anti-Racist Church*, 179–80.

41. Virginia Theological Seminary, "Virginia Theological Seminary Dedicated $1.7 Million as a Reparations Endowment Fund," https://vts.edu/mission/multicultural-ministries/reparations/.

42. 117th Congress (2021–2022), "Commission to Study and Develop Reparation Proposals for African Americans, H.R. 40, 117thth Cong (2021)," https://www.congress.gov/bill/117th-congress/house-bill/40/text.

43. Sandra Schneiders, "Theology and Spirituality: Strangers, Rivals, or Partners?," *Horizons* 13 (1986): 266; cited in Sandra Schneiders, "Spirituality and the Academy," *Theological Studies* 50 (1989): 684.

44. Schneiders, "Spirituality and the Academy," 684.

45. M. Shawn Copeland, *Knowing Christ Crucified: The Witness of African American Religious Experience* (Maryknoll, NY: Orbis, 2018), 40.

46. James Cone, *Black Theology and Black Power* (1969; Maryknoll, NY: Orbis, 1997), 36.

47. Omar Ibn Said, *A Muslim American Slave: The Life of Omar Ibn Said*, ed. and trans. Ala Alryyes (Madison: University of Wisconsin Press, 2011), 51.

48. Tommy Davis, in Lajimodiere, *Stringing Rosaries*, 232.

49. "Genevieve," in Lajimodiere, *Stringing Rosaries*, 58–59.

50. Tommy Davis, in Lajimodiere, *Stringing Rosaries*, 212.

51. Ramona Klein, in Lajimodiere, *Stringing Rosaries*, 129.

52. Roger White Owl, in Lajimodiere, *Stringing Rosaries*, 46–47.

53. Erich Longie, in Lajimodiere, *Stringing Rosaries*, 255.

54. Maryland Province Archives, "'Belonging to us': Fr. Dzierozynski recommends Nelly as housekeeper for Fr. Lancaster, January 1843," Georgetown Slavery Archive, https://slaveryarchive.georgetown.edu/items/show/139. She is "an excellent cook and industrious servant and house keeper and sacristan, belonging to us."

55. Gutierrez, *A Theology of Liberation*, 110.

56. Ignatius of Loyola, "General Confession, with Communion," in *Spiritual Exercises of Saint Ignatius*, trans. Elder Mullan SJ (New York: P. J. Kennedy and Sons, 1914), 17.

57. The sociologists Michael Omi and Howard Winant employ the frame of "racial project" to draw attention to the way in which "the races" are constructed categories designed to order humanity and distribute resources through the categories into which persons are sorted. Michael Omi and Howard Winant, *Racial Formation in the United States*, 3rd ed. (New York: Routledge, 2014).

58. Camara Phyllis Jones, "Levels of Racism: A Theoretic Framework and a Gardener's Tale," *American Journal of Public Health* 90, no. 8 (2000): 1212.

59. For an account of Brave Heart's program as adapted by the Jesuit-affiliated Red Cloud Indian School, see https://www.americamagazine.org/politics-society/2021/10/08/indigenous-peoples-day-orange-shirt-culture-jesuits-boarding-school

60. Perhaps this is the aversion White America is experiencing in book banning and curricular refusal to engage Critical Race Theory.

61. James Baldwin, "A Letter to My Nephew," *Progressive Magazine*, December 1, 1962, https://progressive.org/magazine/letter-nephew/.

62. Bryan Massingale, "The Ignatian Witness to Truth in a Climate of Injustice," *Conversations on Jesuit Higher Education*, August 12, 2017, https://epublications.marquette.edu/conversations/vol52/iss1/3.

63. Ignatius of Loyola, *The Spiritual Exercises of Saint Ignatius: A Translation and Commentary*, ed. and trans. George E. Ganss (Chicago: Loyola, 1992), 39.

64. Loyola, *The Spiritual Exercises of Saint Ignatius*, 143n.

65. Loyola, *The Spiritual Exercises of Saint Ignatius*, 24.

66. Loyola, *The Spiritual Exercises of Saint Ignatius*, 25.

67. The sociologist Deadric Williams succinctly summarizes the insight of scholars who study racial construction and racism with the idea that "racism created the races." Scholarly consensus identifies that modern construction of "the races," as categories into which people would be sorted, was a project that emerged simultaneously with European colonialism precisely as a means by which to sort

non-Europeans into categories of "lesser than." J. Kameron Carter's study of the influential philosopher Immanuel Kant's creation of racial categories helps us see that the formulation of a set of categories into which persons were to be sorted (by "race") was the product of thought projects among philosophers, botanists, and emerging anthropologists at a particular time when European nation-states were pursuing a global project of conquest for the accumulation of natural resources and material production. Thus, the very category of "White" was created in the hierarchically ordered categorization as the category of "best," "most human," "closest to the ideal." The drive of White supremacy and European-driven conquest (racism) created the categories of "the races" (with White on top). J. Kameron Carter, *Race: A Theological Account* (Oxford: Oxford University Press, 2008). See also Omi and Winant, *Racial Formation.*

68. Loyola, *The Spiritual Exercises of Saint Ignatius*, 33.

69. Loyola, *The Spiritual Exercises of Saint Ignatius*, 33.

70. "General Examination of Conscience," Loyola, *The Spiritual Exercises of Saint Ignatius*, 35.

71. Language adopted from *Daily Examen Journal*, prayer steps as described by Mark E. Thibodeaux SJ in *Reimagining the Ignatian Examen: Fresh Ways to Pray from Your Day* (Chicago: Loyola, 2015).

72. Patrick Saint-Jean SJ, *The Spiritual Work of Racial Justice: A Month of Meditations with Ignatius of Loyola* (Vestal, NY: Anamchara, 2021).

73. Saint-Jean, *The Spiritual Work of Racial Justice*, 33.

74. St. Ignatius Parish, San Francisco, *Discernment Series*, https://www.stignatiussf.org/program/discernment-series-racial-justice. For particularly powerful discussions on the use of imagination, see volume 8, and on structural realities of racism, see volume 9. The entire series offers an invaluable resource for this work.

75. Loyola, *The Spiritual Exercises of Saint Ignatius*, 33.

76. Such a consideration of Christ among the crucified people of the world is based on the insights of Ignacio Ellacuria and developed in Jeannine Hill Fletcher, *The Sin of White Supremacy: Christianity, Racism, and Religious Diversity in America* (Maryknoll, NY: Orbis, 2017), 142–43.

77. "The Second Exercise," in *The Second Prelude, in* Loyola, *The Spiritual Exercises of Saint Ignatius*, 43.

78. Loyola, *The Spiritual Exercises of Saint Ignatius*, 43.

79. Loyola, *The Spiritual Exercises of Saint Ignatius*, 43.

80. The Native Governance Project offers resources not only for research but also guidance for establishing relationships of reciprocity and repair. See https://nativegov.org/news/a-guide-to-Indigenous-land-acknowledgment/.

81. For a discussion of how White advantage in accessing mortgage lending in the 1940s experienced an exponential increase in White wealth in the housing markets of the 1970s, see Richard Rothstein, *The Color of Law: A Forgotten History of How Our Government Segregated America* (New York: Liveright, 2017).

82. "Mapping Inequality," https://dsl.richmond.edu/panorama/redlining/.

83. Loyola, *The Spiritual Exercises of Saint Ignatius*, 43.

84. Loyola, *The Spiritual Exercises of Saint Ignatius*, 45.

85. Allan Greer, ed., *The Jesuit Relations: Natives and Missionaries in Seventeenth-Century North America* (Boston: Bedford/St. Martin's, 2000).

86. While the transfer of land to White settlers is part of the national history for every Jesuit institution, those situated in the West and founded after the 1862 Homestead Act might particularly investigate the ways in which our institutions benefited directly from proceeds of sales of land taken from tribes. For specific writings from the Jesuits in the nineteenth century, see Joseph Mobberly (Georgetown, 1820) and Augustus Thebaud (Fordham, 1877).

87. The number could be twenty-one or twenty-two, depending on how we count Loyola Marymount (1911)/St. Vincent's (1865): Georgetown (1789), Saint Louis University (1818), Spring Hill (Mobile, 1830), Xavier (Cincinnati, 1831), Holy Cross (Massachusetts, 1843), St. Joseph's (Philadelphia, 1851), Santa Clara (1851), Loyola Maryland (1852), University of San Francisco (1855), Boston College (1863), Loyola Chicago (1870), Canisius College (Buffalo, 1870), St. Peter's University (Jersey City, 1872), University of Detroit Mercy (1877), Creighton (Omaha, 1878), Regis (Denver, 1877), Marquette (Milwaukee, 1881), John Carroll (Ohio, 1886), Gonzaga (Spokane, 1887), University of Scranton (Pennsylvania, 1888), Seattle University (1891), Rockhurst (Kansas City, 1910), Loyola Marymount (Los Angeles, 1911), Loyola New Orleans (1912), Fairfield (Connecticut, 1942), LeMoyne College (Syracuse, 1946), Wheeling Jesuit (est. 1954, no longer within the network). The twenty-eighth college now listed is St. John's Belize (1887). See https://www.ajcunet.edu/institutions.

88. Association of Catholic Colleges and Universities, "U.S. Catholic Higher Education Data," https://www.accunet.org/data.html.

89. Lorenzo Palladino SJ, *Indian and White in the Northwest: A History of Catholicity in Montana, 1831–1891* (1894; Lancaster, PA: Wickersham, 1922). See also Jesuit contributions to a Catholic understanding of Indigenous peoples in the *Indian Sentinel*, published from 1910 to 1962.

90. Shannen Dee Williams, "Religious Orders Owning Slaves Isn't New—Black Catholics Have Emphasized This History for Years," *America*, August 6, 2019, https://www.americamagazine.org/faith/2019/08/06/religious-orders-owning-slaves-isnt-new-black-catholics-have-emphasized-history.

91. Maryland Province Archives, "James Carroll, 'An account of my negroes,' September 27, 1715," Georgetown Slavery Archive, https://slaveryarchive.georgetown.edu/items/show/135.

92. Jesuit institutions are aided in this work by the Georgetown Slavery Archives and the Midwest Province Slavery, Memory, and Reconciliation project. See, for example, Kelly Schmidt, "A National Legacy of Enslavement: An Overview of the Work of the Slavery, History, Memory, and Reconciliation Project," *Journal of Jesuit Studies* 8 (2021): 81–107; and Adam Rothman, "The Jesuits and Slavery," *Journal of Jesuit Studies* 8 (2021): 1–10. Each institution, however, would need to examine their own histories for a more full picture of institutional complicity.

93. Loyola, *The Spiritual Exercises of Saint Ignatius*, 47.

94. Loyola, *The Spiritual Exercises of Saint Ignatius*, 22.

Bibliography

## Books, Articles, and Documents

Allen, Jody L. "How Do Academic Institutions Evaluate Their History: Campus Case Studies I: William and Mary." *Theology Today* 76, no. 4 (2020): 293–97.

Alma, Maria. "A Sketch of the Work and History of the Sisters, Servants of the Immaculate Heart of Mary: 1845–1920." *Records of the American Catholic Historical Society of Philadelphia* 31, no. 4 (1920): 276–338.

Anderson, Patrick. "Native American Victims of Sex Abuse at Catholic Boarding Schools Fight for Justice." *Argus Leader,* May 16, 2019. https://www.argusleader.com/story/news/2019/05/16/native-american-sex-abuse-victims-catholic-boarding-schools-south-dakota/1158590001/.

Andrews, Rena Mazyck. "Slavery Views of a Northern Prelate." *Church History* 3, no. 1 (March 1934): 60–78.

Araujo, Ana. "Raising the Dead: Walls of Names as Mnemonic Devices to Commemorate Enslaved People." *Current Anthropology* 61, no. 22 (2020): 328–38.

Archives West. "Historical Note." Northern Pacific Railway Company Records, 1870–1968. Orbis Cascade Alliance. http://archiveswest.orbiscascade.org/ark:/80444/xv68060.

Archuleta, Margaret, Brenda Child, and K. Tsianina Lomawaima, eds. *Away from Home: American Indian Boarding School Experiences, 1879–2000.* Phoenix, AZ: Heard Museum, 2000.

Ariel, Yaakov. "A Faith Worth Preserving: An Introduction to Judaism." In *Five Voices, Five Faiths: An Interfaith Primer.* Lanham, MD: Rowman & Littlefield, 2005.

Aroy, Marissa. *The Delano Manongs: Forgotten Heroes of the United Farm Workers.* Featuring Alex Fabros, Dolores Huerta, et al. Media Factory, 2014.

Association of Catholic Colleges and Universities. "U.S. Catholic Higher Education Data." https://www.accunet.org/data.html.

Bacho, Peter. "The Tragic Sense of Filipino History." in *Filipino Americans: Transformation and Identity*, ed. Maria Root. Thousand Oaks, CA: Sage, 1991.

Baker-Fletcher, Karen. *Dancing with God: The Trinity from a Womanist Perspective*. St. Louis, MO: Chalice, 2006.

Baldwin, James. "A Letter to My Nephew." *Progressive Magazine*. December 1, 1962. https://progressive.org/magazine/letter-nephew/.

Baptist, Edward. *The Half Has Never Been Told: Slavery and the Making of American Capitalism*. New York: Basic Books, 2014.

Barndt, Joseph. *Becoming an Anti-Racist Church: Journeying toward Wholeness*. Minneapolis, MN: Fortress, 2011.

Barnes, M. Craig. "Guest Editorial." *Theology Today* 76, no. 4 (2020): 287–92.

Barron, Robert. "John Paul II and 'Taking the Discipline.'" *Our Sunday Visitor*, March 15, 2010. Reprinted at https://www.catholiceducation.org/en/controversy/common-misconceptions/john-paul-ii-and-taking-the-discipline.html.

Barth, Karl. *The Epistle to the Romans*. 1933. Trans. from the 6th ed. by Edwyn C. Hoskyns. London: Oxford University Press, 1968.

Benton, Thomas Hart. "Speech of Mr. Benton of Missouri, in the Senate, May 28, 1846, on the Oregon Question." *Congressional Globe* 29, no. 1 (1846): 917–18.

Black and Indian Mission Office. "Servant of God Mother Mary Lange, O.S.P." https://blackandindianmission.org/index.php/servant-god-mother-mary-lange-osp.

Bourdieu, Pierre. "Symbolic Capital and Social Classes." *Journal of Classical Sociology* 13, no. 2 (2013): 292–302.

Brave Heart, Maria Yellow Horse, et al. "Historical Trauma among Indigenous Peoples of the Americas: Concepts, Research, and Clinical Considerations." *Journal of Psychoactive Drugs* 43, no. 4 (2011): 282–90.

———. "Return to the Sacred Path: Reflections on the Development of Historical Trauma Healing." Indian Health Services. https://www.ihs.gov/sites/telebehavioral/themes/responsive2017/display_objects/documents/slides/historicaltrauma/htreturnsacredpath0513.pdf.

Bresie, Amanda. "Mother Katharine Drexel's Benevolent Empire: The Bureau of Catholic Indian Missions and the Education of Native Americans." *U.S. Catholic Historian* 32, no. 2 (Summer 2014): 1–24.

Burns, Jeffrey. "Left Coast Catholicism: The Tradition of Dissent in the California Church." In *Roman Catholicism in the United States: A Thematic History*, ed. Margaret M. McGuinness and James T. Fisher. New York: Fordham University Press, 2019.

Butler, James. *The Most Reverend Doctor James Butler's Catechism, Revised, Enlarged, Improved and Recommended by the Four Roman Catholic Archbishops of Ireland*. D. & J. Sadlier & Co., 1871.

———. *The Most Reverend Doctor James Butler's Catechism, Revised, Enlarged, Improved and Recommended by the Four Roman Catholic Archbishops of Ireland as a General Catechism*. New York: D. & J. Sadlier & Co., n.d. https://ia902902.us.archive.org/10/items/mostrevoobutl/mostrevoobutl.pdf.

Cannon, Katie Geneva. "Transformative Grace." In *Feminist and Womanist Essays in Reformed Dogmatics*, ed. Amy Plantinga Pauw and Serene Jones. Louisville, KY: Westminster John Knox, 2006.

Carey, Patrick. "Political Atheism: *Dred Scott*, Roger Brooke Taney, and Orestes A. Brownson." *Catholic Historical Review* 88, no. 2 (April 2002): 207–29.

Carmody, Charles. "The Roman Catholic Catechesis in the United States, 1784–1930: A Study of Its Theory, Development, and Materials." PhD diss., Loyola University (Chicago), 1975.

Carroll, Rev. J. B. "The Fourth of July Dishonored." *Indian Sentinel*, 1910, 28–33.

Carruthers, Iva E. "Remembrance—toward Righteousness and Reparations." *Ecumenical Review* 72, no. 1 (2020): 6–18.

Carter, J. Kameron. *Race: A Theological Account*. Oxford: Oxford University Press, 2008.

*A Catalogue of the Officers and Students of St. John's College for the Academical Year 1850–51*. New York: Edward Dunigan & Brother, 1851.

Child, Brenda. *Boarding School Seasons: American Indian Families, 1900–1940*. Lincoln: University of Nebraska Press, 1998.

Chisholm, Gregory C., William D. Critchley-Menor, and Timothy P. Kesicki. "Days of Reckoning: Essays on Racism and Slaveholding in the Society of Jesus." *Studies in the Spirituality of the Jesuits* 54, no. 4 (Winter 2022).

Chung-mao, Hsu. "[Photo story] China-US Relations in the Late 19th Century: Is History Repeating Itself?" *Think China*, March 18, 2020. https://www.thinkchina.sg/photo-story-china-us-relations-late-19th-century-history-repeating-itself.

Chin, Denny, and Kathy Hirata Chin. "'Kung Flu': A History of Hostility and Violence against Asian Americans." *Fordham Law Review* 90, no. 5 (2022): 1889–1944.

"Commission to Study and Develop Reparation Proposals for African Americans, H.R. 40, 117th Cong (2021)." 117th Congress. https://www.congress.gov/bill/117th-congress/house-bill/40/text.

"Compendium Theologia Moralis by J. P. Gury (Review)." *American Ecclesiastical Review* 53 (1915): 607–8.

Cone, James. *Black Theology and Black Power*. 1969. Maryknoll, NY: Orbis, 1997.

———. *The Spirituals and the Blues*. 1979. Maryknoll, NY: Orbis, 1991.

Congregation of the Sisters, Servants of the Immaculate Heart of Mary. "IHM History: Founded November 10, 1845 in Monroe, Michigan by Theresa Maxis Duchemin, IHM and Louis Florent Gillit, CSsR." http://www.sistersofihm.org/who-we-are/ihm-history/.

Connor, Charles. "The Northern Catholic Position on Slavery and the Civil War: Archbishop Hughes as a Test Case." *Records of the American Catholic Historical Society of Philadelphia* 96, no. 1/4 (March–December 1985): 35–48.

Copeland, M. Shawn. *Enfleshing Freedom: Body, Race, and Being*. Minneapolis, MN: Fortress, 2009.

———. *Knowing Christ Crucified: The Witness of African American Religious Experience*. Maryknoll, NY: Orbis, 2018.

Crawley, Ashon. *Blackpentecostal Breath: The Aesthetics of Possibility*. New York: Fordham University Press, 2017.

Curran, Robert Emmett. "'Splendid Poverty': Jesuit Slaveholding in Maryland, 1805–1838." In *Shaping American Catholicism, Maryland and New York, 1805–1915*. Washington, DC: Catholic University of America Press, 2012.

Day, Dorothy. "Chavez, Workers Step Up Boycott." *Catholic Worker*, March–April 1973, 1, 4. https://catholicworker.org/254-2/.

"Defense Department Grape Purchases." Madeline Rogero and Roger Pitt Collection, Farmworker Movement Documentation Project, University of California San Diego Library. https://libraries.ucsd.edu/farmworkermovement/ufwarchives/RogeroPitt/02/DEFENSE%20DEPT%20GRAPE%20PURCHASES.pdf.

Doss, Erin F., and Robin Jensen. "Balancing Mystery and Identification: Dolores Huerta's Shifting Transcendent Persona." *Quarterly Journal of Speech* 99, no. 4 (November 2013): 481–506.

Douglas, Kelly Brown. *Stand Your Ground: Black Bodies and the Justice of God*. Maryknoll, NY: Orbis, 2015.

Ellacuria, Ignacio. "The Crucified People: An Essay in Historical Soteriology." In *Ignacio Ellacuria: Essays on History, Liberation, and Salvation*, ed. Michael E. Lee. Maryknoll, NY: Orbis, 2013.

"Fr. James Mary Chrysostom Bouchard: A Sketch of His Life and Labors." *Woodstock Letters* 19, no. 3 (October 1, 1890): 302–11.

Fredericks, Linda, Dan Jesse, Robert Brave Heart Sr., and Melinda Strickland. "The Lakota Language Project at Red Cloud Indian School: Turning the Tide of Native Language Loss." *Journal of American Indian Education* 57, no. 3 (Fall 2018): 51–71.

García, Mario T., ed. *A Dolores Huerta Reader*. Albuquerque: University of New Mexico Press, 2008.

———. *The Gospel of César Chávez: My Faith in Action*. Lanham, MD: Sheed & Ward, 2007.

Garnett, Diana. "National Register Nomination for St. James the Greater Catholic Mission." Master's thesis, University of South Carolina, 2015. https://scholarcommons.sc.edu/etd/3159.

Geelan, Michael. "Silent Reply: A Selection of Antebellum American Catholic Opinions Dealing with the Issue of Slavery." Master's thesis, University of Dayton, 2007.

Getzels, Peter, and Eduardo Lopes, dirs. *Harvest of Empire*. Snag Films, 2012.

Gordon, Avery. *Ghostly Matters: Haunting and the Sociological Imagination*. Minneapolis: University of Minnesota Press, 2008.

Graham, Edward. "Supreme Court Decision Paves Way for Public Funds to Flow to Religious Schools." *National Education Association NEA Today, July* 21, 2022. https://www.nea.org/advocating-for-change/new-from-nea/supreme-court-decision-paves-way-public-funds-flow-religious-schools.

Green, William. "The Summer Christmas Came to Minnesota: The Case of Eliza Winston, a Slave." *Minnesota Journal of Law and Inequality* 8, no. 1 (March 1990): 151–77.

Greer, Allan, ed. *The Jesuit Relations: Natives and Missionaries in Seventeenth-Century North America*. Boston: Bedford/St. Martin's, 2000.

———. *Mohawk Saint: Catherine Tekawitha and the Jesuits*. Oxford: Oxford University Press, 2005.

Gury SJ, Joanne Petro. *Compendium Theologiae Moralis (Juxta Doctrinam S. Alphonsi de Ligorio)*. Tomus Primus. Panormi: Ex Typographiia Bernardi Virzi, 1853.

Gutierrez, Gustavo. *A Theology of Liberation: History, Politics, and Salvation*. Rev. ed. Maryknoll, NY: Orbis, 1988.

Harrison, William Henry. *Messages and Letters of William Henry Harrison*. Indiana Historical Collection, Indiana Historical Society, 1922.

Hartman, Saidiya. *Lose Your Mother: A Journey along the Atlantic Slave Route*. New York: Farrar, Straus and Giroux, 2007.

———. *Scenes of Subjection: Terror, Slavery, and Self-Making in Nineteenth-Century America*. New York: Oxford University Press, 1997.

Harvard University. *Report of the Presidential Committee on Harvard and the Legacy of Slavery*. https://legacyofslavery.harvard.edu/report/introduction-and-findings.

Hayes, Diana. "Faith of Our Mothers: Catholic Womanist God-Talk." In *Uncommon Faithfulness: The Black Catholic Experience*, ed. M. Shawn Copeland. Maryknoll, NY: Orbis, 2009.

Heisser, David. "Bishop Lynch's Civil War Pamphlet on Slavery." *Catholic Historical Review* 84, no. 4 (October 1998): 681–96.

Heisser, David, and Stephen White. *Patrick N. Lynch, 1817–1882: Third Catholic Bishop of Charleston*. Columbia: University of South Carolina Press, 2015.

Hill Fletcher, Jeannine. *Motherhood as Metaphor: Engendering Interreligious Dialogue*. New York: Fordham University Press, 2013.

———. *The Sin of White Supremacy: Christianity, Racism, and Religious Diversity in America*. Maryknoll, NY: Orbis, 2017.

*The History of the Catholic Church in the United States of America*. New York: The Catholic Editing Company, 1914. https://www.google.com/books/edition/The_Catholic_Church_in_the_United_States/KL4YAAAAYAAJ.

Horsley, Richard. "Jesus and Empire." *Union Seminary Quarterly Review*, January 2005, 44–74.

Horstmann, Ign. F. "A Friend in Need." *Indian Sentinel*, 1902–1903, 10–13.

Huerta, Dolores. "Enacting Change for Social Justice in Organizing." *La Raza Law Journal* 17, no. 2 (Fall 2006): 277–83.

———. "We've Got the Power." *Progressive*, July 2009, 36.

Hughes, John (Archbishop). "Sermon on the Occasion of His Return from Cuba, Delivered in St. Patrick's Cathedral, May 1854." In *Complete Works of the Most Rev. John Hughes, D.D., Archbishop of New York, Comprising His Sermons, Letters, Lectures, Speeches, etc., ed.* Lawrence Kehoe (New York: Lawrence Kehoe, 1866), 2:221. Reprinted on the front page of *United States Catholic Miscellany*, May 13, 1854.

Ignatius of Loyola. "General Confession, with Communion." In *Spiritual Exercises of Saint Ignatius*, trans. Elder Mullan SJ. New York: P. J. Kennedy and Sons, 1914.

———. *The Spiritual Exercises of Saint Ignatius: A Translation and Commentary by George E. Ganss, S.J.* Chicago: Loyola, 1992.

Jennings, Willie James. *After Whiteness: An Education in Belonging*. Grand Rapids, MI: Eerdmans, 2020.

Johnson, Sylvester A. *African American Religions, 1500–2000: Colonialism, Democracy, and Freedom*. Cambridge: Cambridge University Press, 2015.

Jones, Camara Phyllis. "Levels of Racism: A Theoretic Framework and a Gardener's Tale." *American Journal of Public Health* 90, no. 8 (2000): 1212–15.

Jones, Kevin. "New Iowa 'School Choice' Program a Boon for Catholic Schools, Bishop Says." *Catholic News Agency*, January 27, 2023. https://www.catholicnewsagency.com/news/253483/new-iowa-school-choice-program-a-boon-for-catholic-schools-bishop-says.

Jones, Mary Claire Pinckney. *The Pinckneys of Ashepoo*. Lithographed by Furlong Publishing, 1988. South Carolinian Library, Special Collections, University of South Carolina, Columbia.

Jones-Rogers, Stephanie. *They Were Her Property: White Women as Slave Owners in the American South*. New Haven, CT: Yale University Press, 2019.

Kades, Eric. "History and Interpretation of the Great Case of Johnson v. M'Intosh." *College of William and Mary Law School Faculty Publications*, 2001. https://scholarship.law.wm.edu/facpubs/50.

Kang, Joy. "Write Their Names," Georgetown Slavery Archive, 2021. https://slaveryarchive.georgetown.edu/items/show/516.

Kaczorowski, Robert. "The Supreme Court and Congress's Power to Enforce Constitutional Rights: An Overlooked Moral Anomaly." *Fordham Law Review* 73, no. 1, art. 10 (2004).

Kelley, Matt. "American Indians Describe School Beatings." Associated Press, April 24, 1999.

Kent, Corita. "Chavez." Seriagraph (print). 1969. https://collection.corita.org/piece/69-80.

Kim, Igna. "The 1965–1970 Delano Grape Strike and Boycott." United Farm Workers. https://ufw.org/1965-1970-delano-grape-strike-boycott.

———. "Today in History." United Farm Workers. https://ufw.org/today-history-cesar-chavez-began-25-day-water-fast-delano-calif-feb-11-1968/.

Klejment, Anne. "Dorothy Day and César Chávez: American Catholic Lives in Nonviolence." *U.S. Catholic Historian* 29, no. 3 (2011): 67–90.

Krebsbach, Suzanne. "Black Catholics in Antebellum Charleston." *South Carolina Historical Magazine* 108, no. 2 (April 2007): 143–59.

Kwon, Duke, and Gregory Thompson. *Reparations: A Christian Call for Repentance and Repair.* Grand Rapids, MI: Brazos, 2021.

Lajimodiere, Denise. *Stringing Rosaries: The History, the Unforgivable, and the Healing of Northern Plains American Indian Boarding School Survivors.* Fargo: North Dakota State University Press, 2019.

Landis, Barbara. "Carlisle Indian Industrial School (1879–1918), References to St. Patrick's Church, Carlisle, PA." https://home.epix.net/~landis/stpatricks.html.

Larkin SJ, J. "Prospectus of St. John's College." *United States Catholic Miscellany.* October 7, 1854.

Lee, Erika. *The Making of Asian America: A History.* New York: Simon and Schuster, 2015.

Lefevre, Peter Paul. "To Bishop John Baptist Purcell." July 19, 1842. University of Notre Dame Archives. https://archives.nd.edu/calendar/cal1842.htm.

Lehman, Christopher. *Slavery's Reach: Southern Slaveholders in the North Star State.* Minnesota Historical Society Press, 2019.

Lockley, Tim. "The Forming and Fracturing of Families on a South Carolina Rice Plantation, 1812–1865." *History of the Family* 23, no. 1 (2017): 75–89.

Lott, Juanita Tamayo. "Demographic Changes Transforming the Filipino American Community." In *Filipino Americans: Transformation and Identity*, ed. Maria Root. Thousand Oaks, CA: Sage, 1991.

Loughery, John. *Dagger John: Archbishop John Hughes and the Making of Irish America.* Ithaca, NY: Cornell University Press, 2018.

Manning, Sarah Sunshine. "Jesuits Return 525 Acres to Rosebud Sioux Tribe." *Indian Country Today*, May 19, 2017, updated September 13, 2018. https://ictnews.org/archive/jesuits-return-525-acres-rosebud-sioux-tribe.

Massingale, Bryan. "The Ignatian Witness to Truth in a Climate of Injustice." *Conversations in Jesuit Higher Education*, August 12, 2017. http://www.conversationsmagazine.org/web-features/2017/8/12/the-ignatian-witness-to-truth-in-a-climate-of-injustice.

———. *Racial Justice and the Catholic Church.* Maryknoll, NY: Orbis, 2010.

Matovina, Timothy. "Latino Catholics in the Southwest." In *Roman Catholicism in the United States: A Thematic History*, ed. Margaret M. McGuinness and James T. Fisher. New York: Fordham University Press, 2019.

Maxwell, John Francis. *Slavery and the Catholic Church: The History of Catholic Teaching Concerning the Moral Legitimacy of the Institution of Slavery.* London: Barry Rose, 1975.

McArdle, Terrence. "The Day 30,000 White Supremacists in KKK Robes Marched in the Nation's Capital." *Washington Post*, August 11, 2018.

McGloin, John Bernard. *Eloquent Indian: The Life of James Bouchard California Jesuit.* Stanford, CA: Stanford University Press, 1949.

McGreevy, John. "Catholicism and Abolition: A Historical (and Theological) Problem." In *Figures in the Carpet: Finding the Human Person in the American Past,* ed. Wilfred McClay. Grand Rapids, MI: Eerdmans, 2007.

McKevitt, Gerald. *Brokers of Culture: Italian Jesuits in the American West, 1848–1919.* Stanford, CA: Stanford University Press, 2007.

McMichael, Stanley L. *McMichael's Appraising Manual: A Real Estate Appraising Handbook for Field Work and Advanced Study Courses.* New York: Prentice-Hall, 1931. https://babel.hathitrust.org/cgi/pt?id=uc1.$b281272.

———. *McMichael's Appraising Manual.* 4th ed., 9th printing. Englewood, NJ: Prentice-Hall, 1962.

*Mechtild of Hakeborn. The Booke of Gostlye Grace of Mechtild of Hakeborn.* Ed. Theresa A. Halligan. Toronto: Pontifical Institute of Medieval Studies, 1979.

———, *ill. The Love of the Sacred Heart.* Foreword by the Lord Bishop of Salford. London: Burns, Oates & Washbourne, Ltd., 1922.

Menager, Francis. "A New Chapter." *Indian Sentinel* 32, no. 8 (1952): 122–24.

Miller, Jay. "The Early Years of Watomika (James Bouchard): Delaware and Jesuit." *American Indian Quarterly* 13, no. 2 (Spring 1989): 165–88.

Miller, Seumas. "Social Institutions." In *The Stanford Encyclopedia of Philosophy, ed.* Edward N. Zalta. Summer 2019 ed. https://plato.stanford.edu/archives/sum2019/entries/social-institutions/.

Minnesota Historical Society. "Enslaved African Americans and the Fight for Freedom." Historic Fort Snelling. https://www.mnhs.org/fortsnelling/learn/african-americans.

Minneapolis Pioneers and Soldiers Memorial Cemetery. "War of 1812 Veteran, James Nettle Glover, at Pioneers and Soldiers." http://www.friendsofthecemetery.org/history/alley_articles/glover_james_jan2004.shtml.

Morrow, Diane Batts. *Persons of Color and Religious at the Same Time: The Oblate Sisters of Providence, 1828–1860.* Chapel Hill: University of North Carolina Press, 2002.

Mueller, David, dir. *A Good Day to Die: A Film about Dennis Banks and the American Indian Movement.* Kino Lorber Films, 2013.

Murphy, Thomas. *Jesuit Slaveholding in Maryland, 1717–1838.* New York: Routledge, 2001.

Naranjo-Huebl, Linda. "'Take, Eat': Food Imagery, the Nurturing Ethic, and Christian Identity in *The Wide, Wide World, Uncle Tom's Cabin,* and *Incidents in the Life of a Slave Girl.*" *Christianity and Literature* 56, no. 4 (Summer 2007): 597–631.

National Geographic. "Immigration to the U.S. in the Late 1800s." https://www.nationalgeographic.org/photo/immigration-1870-1900/.

National Park Service. "The Dawes Act." History and Culture of the Badlands. https://www.nps.gov/articles/000/dawes-act.htm.

———. "Gravesites of Larry Itliogn and Richard Chávez." https://www.nps.gov/places/000/gravesites-of-larry-itliong-and-richard-ch-vez.htm.

Native Governance Project. "A Guide to Indigenous Land Acknowledgment." https://nativegov.org/news/a-guide-to-Indigenous-land-acknowledgment/.

New Advent. "Roger Brooke Taney." *Catholic Encyclopedia*. https://www.newadvent.org/cathen/14442c.htm.

Newcomb, Steven. *Pagans in the Promised Land: Decoding the Doctrine of Discovery*. Golden, CO: Fulcrum, 2008.

O'Connell, Jeremiah Joseph. *Catholicity in the Carolinas and Georgia: Leaves of Its History, 1820–1878*. New York: D. & J. Sadlier & Co, 1879. https://babel.hathitrust.org/cgi/pt?id=mdp.39015068629461.

O'Donnell, Catherine. "John Carroll and the Origins of an American Catholic Church." *William and Mary Quarterly* 68, no. 1 (January 2011): 101–26.

Öğütle, Vefa Saygin. "Institution as Mediation between Social Structure and Agency: Toward a Realist Social Ontology of Institutions." *Journal for the Theory of Social Behavior* 51 (2021): 489–507.

O'Hara, Matthew. "The Supple Whip: Innovation and Tradition in Mexican Catholicism." *American Historical Review*, December 2012, 1373–1401.

Omi, Michael, and Howard Winant. *Racial Formation in the United States*. 3rd ed. New York: Routledge, 2014.

Palladino, L. B. *Indian and White in the Northwest: A History of Catholicity in Montana, 1831–1891*. 2nd ed. Lancaster, PA: Wickersham, 1922.

People's Institute for Survival and Beyond. "Our Principles." https://pisab.org/our-principles/.

Pierz, Father Francois. "To Bishop (Peter Paul) Lefevere." May 26, 1842. University of Notre Dame Archives. https://archives.nd.edu/calendar/cal1842.htm.

Powell, Mary Pinckney. *Back over Home—the Heritage of Pinckneys of Pinckney Colony Bluffton, South Carolina*. Columbia, SC: R. L. Bryan Company, 1996.

Pratt, Richard Henry. "The Advantages of Mingling Indians with Whites." In *Official Proceedings of the Annual Meeting of the National Conference on Social Welfare*, 1892. https://quod.lib.umich.edu/n/ncosw/ACH8650.1892.001/68.

———. "The Founding of Carlisle." In *Battlefield and Classroom: Four Decades with the American Indian, 1867–1904*. New Haven, CT: Yale University Press, 1964.

Quallen, Matthew. "Beyond the 272 Sold in 1838, Plotting the National Diaspora of Jesuit-Owned Slaves." *The Hoya* (Georgetown University), April 30, 2016. http://features.thehoya.com/beyond-the-272-sold-in-1838-plotting-the-national-diaspora-of-jesuit-owned-slaves.

Raphael, Melissa. *The Female Face of God in Auschwitz: A Jewish Feminist Theology of the Holocaust*. London: Routledge, 2003.

Red Cloud Indian School (now Mahpiya Luta), "Truth and Healing," https://mahpiyaluta.org/the-missions/initiatives/truth-and-healing/

Reese, Thomas. "Public Funding of Religious Schools Is Coming. The First Lesson Is Compromise." *National Catholic Reporter*, December 15, 2021. https://www

.ncronline.org/news/people/public-funding-religious-schools-coming-first-lesson-compromise.

"Report of the Secretary of the Interior." In *Message of the President of the United States and Accompanying Documents at the Commencement of the First Session of the Thirty-Ninth Congress*. Washington, DC, 1865, 990. https://books.google.com/books?id=sEfg31gC6H4C.

Reynolds, Jon. "Tuition." *Georgetown Magazine*, November–December 1982. https://library.georgetown.edu/special-collections/archives/essays/tuition.

Rieger, Jeorg. "Christian Theology and Empires." In *Empire and the Christian Tradition*, ed. Kwok Pui-lan, Don Compier, and Jeorg Rieger. Minneapolis, MN: Fortress, 2007.

Rollenhagen, Luisa. "How Labor Activist Cesar Chavez Went on a Hunger Strike and Turned Robert Kennedy into a Fan." *Medium*, March 30, 2018. https://timeline.com/cesar-chavez-robert-kennedy-vonviolent-justice-california-789f6354682a.

Romero, Robert Chao. "The Spiritual Practice of César Chávez." *Perspectivas*, Spring 2017, 24–40.

Root, Maria, ed. *Filipino Americans: Transformation and Identity*, Thousand Oaks, CA: Sage, 1991.

Rothman, Adam. *Beyond Freedom's Reach: A Kidnapping in the Twilight of Slavery*. Cambridge, MA: Harvard University Press, 2015.

———. "How Do Academic Institutions Evaluate Their History? Campus Case Studies II: Georgetown University." *Theology Today* 76, no. 4 (2020): 301.

———. "The Jesuits and Slavery." *Journal of Jesuit Studies* 8 (2021): 1–10.

Rothman, Adam, and Elsa Barraza Mendoza, eds. *Facing Georgetown's History: A Reader on Slavery, Memory, and Reconciliation*. Washington, DC: Georgetown University Press, 2021.

Rothstein, Richard. *The Color of Law: A Forgotten History of How Our Government Segregated America*. New York: Liveright, 2017.

Russo, Ruth. "A Natural History of 'Agonist.'" *Perspectives in Biology and Medicine* 45, no. 3 (Summer 2002): 350–58.

Said, Omar Ibn. *A Muslim American Slave: The Life of Omar Ibn Said*. Ed. and trans. Ala Alryyes. Madison: University of Wisconsin Press, 2011.

Saint-Jean, Patrick. *The Spiritual Work of Racial Justice: A Month of Meditations with Ignatius of Loyola*. Vestal, NY: Anamchara, 2021.

St. Ignatius Parish, San Francisco. Discernment Series. https://www.stignatiussf.org/program/discernment-series-racial-justice.

St. James the Greater Catholic Church. "In this Sacred Place, St. James the Greater Catholic Church." YouTube video. https://www.youtube.com/watch?v=YvsZoWckksI.

———. *St. James the Greater: Catholic Hill, South Carolina, Est. 1826*. N.d. Pamphlet available at St. James the Greater, Ritter, SC.

Sandweiss, Martha A. "How Do Academic Institutions Evaluate Their History? Campus Case Studies III: Princeton University." *Theology Today* 76, no. 4 (2020): 305.

Savage, Audra. "The Religion of Race: The Supreme Court as Priests of Racial Politics." *Utah Law Review* 2021, no. 3 (2021): 569–628. https://dc.law.utah.edu/cgi/viewcontent.cgi?article=1295&context=ulr.

Schmidt, Kelly L. "Enslaved Faith Communities in the Jesuits' Missouri Missions." *U.S. Catholic Historian* 37, no. 2 (Spring 2019): 49–81.

———. "A National Legacy of Enslavement: An Overview of the Work of the Slavery, History, Memory, and Reconciliation Project." *Journal of Jesuit Studies* 8, no. 1 (2021): 81–107.

———. "The Pervasive Institution: Slavery and Its Legacies in U.S. Catholicism." *American Catholic Studies Newsletter*, Spring 2022, 11–22.

———. "Sexual Abuse of Enslaved People in the U.S. Catholic Church." Paper presented at Taking Responsibility, Gonzaga University, Spokane, WA, April 1, 2022.

Schneiders, Sandra. "Spirituality and the Academy." *Theological Studies* 50 (1989): 676–97.

Schroeder, Paul. "Is the U.S. an Empire?" Op-ed following his address to the American Historical Association, n.d. *History News Network* (of the Columbian College of Arts and Sciences at the George Washington University). https://historynewsnetwork.org/article/1237.

Schroth, Raymond. *Fordham: A History and a Memoir.* Rev. ed. New York: Fordham University Press, 2008.

Schwartz, Marie Jenkins. *Birthing a Slave: Motherhood and Medicine in the Antebellum South.* Cambridge, MA: Harvard University Press, 2006.

Schwartz, Sarah. "Map: Where Critical Race Theory Is Under Attack." *Education Week*, June 11, 2021, updated May 5, 2023. https://www.edweek.org/policy-politics/map-where-critical-race-theory-is-under-attack/2021/06.

Sharlin, Craig, and Lilia Villanueva. *Philip Vera Cruz: A Personal History of Filipino Immigrants and the Farmworker Movement.* 3rd ed. Seattle: University of Washington Press, 2000.

Sioli, Marco. "When the Mississippi Was an Indian River: Zebulon Pike's Trip from St. Louis to Its Sources, 1805–1806." *Revue Francaise d'etues Americaines* 98, no. 2 (December 2003): 9–19.

Sisters of IHM. "Bishop Lefevere to Bishop Wood (July 1859)." Paths of Daring, Seeds of Hope. http://www.sistersofihm.org/what-we-do/publications-library/book-excerpts/detail-paths.html?id=287c7221-114a-4b74-906f-63b18bfe7cc0.

Slabodsky, Santiago. "It's the Theology, Stupid! Coloniality, Anti-Blackness, and the Bounds of 'Humanity.'" In *Anti-Blackness and Christian Ethics*, ed. Vincent Lloyd and Andrew Prevot. Maryknoll, NY: Orbis, 2017.

Smith, Henry. "The Baronies of South Carolina." *South Carolina Historical and Genealogical Magazine* 15, no. 4 (October 1914): 149–65.

Sowards, Stacey K. *¡Si, Ella Puede! The Rhetorical Legacy of Dolores Huerta and the United Farm Workers*. Austin: University of Texas Press, 2019.

Spieler, Gerhard. "Catholic Hill's Founding Steeped in History." *Beaufort Gazette*, Tuesday, January 12, 1999, 3C. "Newspaper Clippings, 1831–2003," Parish Files, Walterboro, St. James the Greater Mission, 2009.02-01-07.

State of Iowa General Assembly. "House File 802: An Act Providing for Requirements Related to Racism or Sexism Trainings at, and Diversity and Inclusion Efforts by, Governmental Agencies and Entities, Schools Districts, and Public PostSecondary Educational Institutions." June 8, 2021. https://www.legis.iowa.gov/legislation/BillBook?ga=89&ba=HF802.

Stockton, Nancy. "'I Wonder Who Will Think to Pray for Me When I'm Dead?' Elite Catholic Women in Nineteenth-Century South Carolina." Master's thesis, The Citadel, 2004.

"Sunday Service aboard a Pacific Mail Steam Ship." *Harper's Weekly*, June 16, 1877.

Supan, Marita-Constance. "Dangerous Memory: Mother M. Theresa Maxis Duchemin and the Michigan Congregation of the Sisters, IHM." In *Building Sisterhood: A Feminist History of the Sisters, Servants of the Immaculate Heart of Mary*, 31–68. Syracuse, NY: Syracuse University Press, 1997.

Swarns, Rachel. *The 272: The Families Who Were Enslaved and Sold to Build the American Catholic Church*. New York: Random House, 2023.

Taney, Roger. *The Dred Scott Decision. Opinion of Chief Justice Taney, with an Introduction by Dr. J. H. Van Evrie*. New York: Van Evrie, Horton & Co., 1860.

Taylor, Mark Lewis. *The Executed God: The Way of the Cross in Lockdown America*. 2nd ed., rev. and exp. Minneapolis, MN: Fortress, 2015.

———. *The Theological and the Political: On the Weight of the World*. Minneapolis. MN: Fortress, 2011.

Thebaud, Augustus. "The Native Tribes of North America and the Catholic Missions." *Month and Catholic Review* 30 (1877): 145–62.

"Then and Now: The Northern Pacific Railway." *Spokesman-Review*, April 14, 2014. https://www.spokesman.com/stories/2014/apr/14/then-and-now-northern-pacific-railway/.

Thibodeaux, Mark E. *Reimagining the Ignatian Examen: Fresh Ways to Pray from Your Day*. Chicago: Loyola, 2015.

Thurman, Howard. *Jesus and the Disinherited*. 1949. Boston: Beacon, 1996.

Tinker, George. *Native American Liberation: A Theology of Sovereignty*. Maryknoll, NY: Orbis, 2008.

Tinner-Williams, Nate. "Sisters of Charity Foundation Acknowledges Slaveholding in New Statement." *Black Catholic Messenger*, February 19, 2022. https://www.blackcatholicmessenger.com/sisters-of-charity-slaveholding-letter/.

Tisby, Jamar. *The Color of Compromise: The Truth about the American Church's Complicity in Racism*. Grand Rapids, MI: Zondervan, 2019.

Tonstad, Linn. *Queer Theology: Beyond Apologetics*. Eugene, OR: Cascade, 2018.

townes, emilie. *Womanist Ethics and the Cultural Production of Evil.* New York: Palgrave Macmillan, 2006.

Treviño, Jesús Salvador, and David Sandoval. "Latinopia Event 1966 UFW Peregrinacion (Pilgrimage)." Barrio Dog Productions, Inc., 2013. http://latinopia.com/latino-history/latinopia-event-1966-ufw-peregrinacion-pilgrimage-march/.

*United States Catholic Miscellany.* "The Catholic Church—Domestic Slavery, and the Slave Trade." December 23, 1843.

———. *The Catholic Mirror,* April 20, 1861, issue.

———. "Church of St. James—Colleton." May 16, 1840.

———. "Colleton." January 29, 1848.

———. "Colleton and Beaufort." January 9, 1841.

———. December 23, 1843, issue.

———. "Episcopal Visitation." April 19, 1845.

———. "New York, St. John's College—Rose Hill."

———. "St. John's College, Rosehill, N.Y. First Annual Exhibition—Distributions of Premiums, &c." July 23, 1842.

———. "South Carolina. Charleston." January 23, 1831.

United States Conference of Catholic Bishops. "Easter Triduum." USCCB.org. https://www.usccb.org/prayer-worship/liturgical-year/triduum.

United States Federal Census. 1850. St. Bartholomews Parish, Colleton County, South Carolina. Real estate 10000, Line Number 23, Dwelling Number 633, Family Number 633, Elizabeth Pinckney household.

———. 1850. Slave Schedules, St. Barth's [Bartholomew's] Parish, Colleton County, South Carolina, #761, column 1, lines 20–42 (plus one added), "Elizabeth Pinckney," and column 2, lines 1–14, "Elizabeth Pinckney."

———. 1850. Slave Schedules, St. Barth's [Bartholomew's] Parish, Colleton County, South Carolina, #759, column 2, lines 16–42 (plus one added), "Sarah Bellinger," and #761, column 1, lines 1–19, "Sarah Bellinger."

University of Richmond. "Mapping Inequality." https://dsl.richmond.edu/panorama/redlining/.

Van der Donckt, Cyril. "The Founders of the Church in Idaho." *American Ecclesiastical Review* 32 (March 1905): 280–91.

Verel, Patrick. "Painting from Fordham Archives Spotlighted at the Met." *Fordham News,* July 19, 2017. https://news.fordham.edu/arts-and-culture/painting-from-fordham-archives-spotlighted-at-the-met/.

Virginia Theological Seminary. "Virginia Theological Seminary Dedicated $1.7 Million as a Reparations Endowment Fund." https://vts.edu/mission/multicultural-ministries/reparations/.

"The Voice of the Farm Worker." *El Malcriado* 32, March 3, 1996. Delano, CA: Farm Worker Press, Inc.

Weber, Anselm. "The Navajo Indians and Saint Michael's Mission [Arizona]." *Indian Sentinel* 1, no. 8 (April 1918): 8–13.

Wells-Oghoghomeh, Alexis. *The Souls of Womenfolk: The Religious Cultures of Enslaved Women in the Lower South*. Chapel Hill: University of North Carolina Press, 2021.

Wilder, Craig Steven. *Ebony and Ivy: Race, Slavery, and the Troubled History of America's Universities*. New York: Bloomsbury, 2013.

Williams, Shannen Dee. "Forgotten Habits, Lost Vocations: Black Nuns, Contested Memories, and the 19th Century Struggle to Desegregate U.S. Catholic Religious Life." *Journal of African American History*, Summer 2016, 231–60.

———. "Religious Orders Owning Slaves Isn't New—Black Catholics Have Emphasized This History for Years." *America*, August 6, 2019. https://www.americamagazine.org/faith/2019/08/06/religious-orders-owning-slaves-isnt-new-black-catholics-have-emphasized-history.

———. *Subversive Habits: Black Catholic Nuns in the Long African American Freedom Struggle*. Durham, NC: Duke University Press, 2022.

———. "What a Forgotten Black Nun Can Teach Us about Racism and Covid-19." *America*, June 8, 2020. https://www.americamagazine.org/faith/2020/04/23/what-forgotten-black-nun-can-teach-us-about-racism-and-covid-19.

Wingard, George, dir. *We Came a Long Way by Faith: Catholic Hill and St. James the Greater Catholic Church*. 2020. https://vimeo.com/415619367.

Wolfchild, Sheldon, dir. *The Doctrine of Discovery: Unmasking the Domination Code*. Co-prod. Steven Newcomb. 2015. https://vimeo.com/ondemand/dominationcode.

Wolfteich, Claire. "Spirituality, Mothering, and Public Leadership: Women's Life Writing and Generative Directions for Spirituality Studies." *Spiritus* 17, no. 2 (2007): 145–64.

"Women as Sacristans." *American Ecclesiastical Review* 14, no. 2 (1889): 177. https://babel.hathitrust.org/cgi/pt?id=hvd.ah68l3&view=1up&seq=215.

Woods, James M. *A History of the Catholic Church in the American South, 1513–1900*. Gainesville: University Press of Florida, 2011.

Wright, Jeremiah. "Confusing God and Government." Sermon delivered April 13, 2003. https://forums.sluggy.com/viewtopic.php?p=315691&sid=4b3e97ace4ee8ceeo2bd6850e52f50b7.

Yaffe, Deborah. "Princeton and Slavery: Our Original Sin." *Princeton Alumni Weekly*, November 8, 2017. https://paw.princeton.edu/article/princeton-and-slavery-our-original-sin.

Ziajka, Alan. "The Jesuits and Native Communities." *Pierless Bridges* 3 (2022). https://myusf.usfca.edu/provost/The-Jesuits-and-Native-Communities.

## Archives of the Diocese of Charleston

Louis (no surname) to Tom (no surname). "Here Is a Rough Copy of the History of St. James," June 24, 1976 (II:2, page 11), Walterboro, St. James, the Greater Mission (Series 142), Files Re: history of St. James, The Greater Mission, from the Archives at St. Elizabeth's Convent, Cornwell Heights, PA (2009.02-01-09), Parish Files, Catholic Diocese of Charleston Archives, Charleston, SC.

Fr. D. Barberich PSM to Rev. A. Walter PSM, February 4, 1895 [Translation of letter found in Archives of the Generalate of the Pallottine Fathers—Piazza V. Pallotti, 204, Rome, Italy; composed by G. J. Carcich SAC, Provincial, on Letterhead *Pallottine Fathers* dated September 21, 1959], Walterboro, St. James, the Greater Mission (Series 142), Newspaper Clippings, 1831–2003 (2009.02-01-07), Parish Files (Series 142), Catholic Diocese of Charleston Archives, Charleston, SC.

"St. James Church Approaching 150th Anniversary." *Press and Standard*, Thursday July 3, 1975, 9-A. Newspaper Clippings, 1831–2003 (2009.02-01-07), Parish Files (Series 142), Catholic Diocese of Charleston Archives, Charleston, SC.

"St. James Church—Walterboro, S.C., Church Records 1839–1854." Digitized Microfiche, Catholic Diocese of Charleston Archives, Charleston, SC.

Sister Roberta Smith SBS (Archivist), "Summary of Letters in Our Archives (Sisters of the Blessed Sacrament, Cornwells Heights, PA)," Parish Files (Series 142), "Walterboro, St. James the Greater," Diocese of Charleston, Charleston, SC.

## Fordham Archives

"J. Marshall (Treasurer) to Mrs. E.P. Pinckney." February 26, 1851. Treasurer's Letter Book, Fordham History Collection, Fordham University Archives, Bronx, NY.

## Georgetown University Archives

Archivum Romanum Societatis Iesu. "'As bad as a Priest's Slave': Letter from Fr. Beschter, March 27, 1829." Georgetown Slavery Archive. https://slaveryarchive.georgetown.edu/items/show/469.

———. "Slavery at St. Thomas Manor: Fr. Grivel to Fr. Roothaan, 1831." Georgetown Slavery Archive. https://slaveryarchive.georgetown.edu/items/show/292.

———. "'The unhappy idea of Fr. Thomas F. Mulledy': Letter from Fr. Vespre to Fr. Roothaan, 12 Jan. 1843." Georgetown Slavery Archive. https://slaveryarchive.georgetown.edu/items/show/463

Diggs, Louis. "'I know that my Bennett ancestors were slaves to the Jesuits . . .': Interviews with descendants in Maryland from Louis Diggs' Surviving in America." Georgetown Slavery Archive. https://slaveryarchive.georgetown.edu/items/show/60.

Georgetown Memory Project. "The Lost Jesuit Slaves of Maryland: Searching for 91 people left behind in 1838." April 30, 2018. https://www.georgetownmemoryproject.org/wp-content/uploads/Research-Memo-Lost-Jesuit-Slaves.pdf.

Georgetown Slavery Archive. "Proslavery oration by Rev. James Ryder, SJ, August 30, 1835." Georgetown Slavery Archive. https://slaveryarchive.georgetown.edu/items/show/88.

Georgetown University Archives. "'Present State of the College,' 1820." Georgetown Slavery Archive. https://slaveryarchive.georgetown.edu/items/show/190.
Jesuit Plantation Project. "List of people sold by Fr. Thomas Mulledy in 1838." Georgetown Slavery Archive. http://slaveryarchive.georgetown.edu/items/show/9.
Joseph P. Mobberly SJ Papers. "Br. Mobberly recounts the whipping of Sucky, an enslaved woman at St. Inigoes, The Mobberly Diaries, Part I, 1820." Georgetown Slavery Archive. https://slaveryarchive.georgetown.edu/items/show/148.
———. "'Masters must answer,' *The Mobberly Diaries*, part I, 1820." Georgetown Slavery Archive. https://slaveryarchive.georgetown.edu/items/show/152.
Kenney, Peter. 1820 Consultation Report. Archives of the Maryland Province of the Society of Jesus (GTM.000119). Box 38, Folder 15. http://hdl.handle.net/10822/1062955.
Maryland Province Archives. "Articles of agreement between Thomas F. Mulledy, of Georgetown, District of Columbia, of one part, and Jesse Beatty and Henry Johnson, of the State of Louisiana, of the other part. 19th June 1838." Georgetown Slavery Archive. https://slaveryarchive.georgetown.edu/items/show/1.
———. "'Belonging to us': Fr. Dzierozynski recommends Nelly as housekeeper for Fr. Lancaster, January 1843." Georgetown Slavery Archive. https://slaveryarchive.georgetown.edu/items/show/139.
———. "Bill of sale for 56 persons from Thomas Mulledy to Henry Johnson, November 10, 1838." Georgetown Slavery Archive. https://slaveryarchive.georgetown.edu/items/show/12.
———. "Distribution of shoes at St. Inigoes, March 1818." Georgetown Slavery Archive. https://slaveryarchive.georgetown.edu/items/show/228.
———. "'A Dreadful Whipping': Fr. Beschter to Fr. Leavy on the whipping of a female slave at St. Inigoes, January 7th, 1836." Georgetown Slavery Archive. https://slaveryarchive.georgetown.edu/items/show/103.
———. "Fr. Francis Neale describes difficulties arranging slave marriages and British pillaging during the War of 1812." Georgetown Slavery Archive. https://slaveryarchive.georgetown.edu/items/show/368.
———. "Fr. Roothaan, S.J. lays out the conditions for the sale of enslaved persons, 27 December 1836." Georgetown Slavery Archive. https://slaveryarchive.georgetown.edu/items/show/94.
———. "'I have parted from Nelly': Fr. Woodley to Fr. Brocard, September 25, 1850." Georgetown Slavery Archive. https://slaveryarchive.georgetown.edu/items/show/165.
———. "'I would be willing to take $450': Fr. Mulledy to Fr. McElroy on pricing slaves, June 12, 1838." Georgetown Slavery Archive. https://slaveryarchive.georgetown.edu/items/show/100.
———. "James Carroll, 'An account of my negroes, September 27, 1715.'" Georgetown Slavery Archive. https://slaveryarchive.georgetown.edu/items/show/135.
———. "List of enslaved persons remaining on Estate and exchanged, no date—perhaps 1839." Georgetown Slavery Archive. https://slaveryarchive.georgetown.edu/items/show/64.

———. "A 'Multiplicity of Deaths': Fr. Mobberly to Fr. Grassi, on a series of deaths that occurred at St. Inigoes, 1812." Georgetown Slavery Archive. https://slaveryarchive.georgetown.edu/items/show/113.
———. "Nancy buys her daughter Sophia to set her free, September 19, 1803." Georgetown Slavery Archive. https://slaveryarchive.georgetown.edu/items/show/235.
———. "St. Inigoes tax assessment, 1804." Georgetown Slavery Archive. https://slaveryarchive.georgetown.edu/items/show/344.
———. "'She will not Rule Me': Fr. Steinbacher airs his grievances against the female slaves of Newtown, April, 1848." Georgetown Slavery Archive. https://slaveryarchive.georgetown.edu/items/show/144.
———. "'To Humane and Christian Masters. The Disposal of Sarah's Children, June 1809." Georgetown Slavery Archive. https://slaveryarchive.georgetown.edu/items/show/194.
———. "'We are in the dark as long as we keep slaves': Br. Joseph Mobberly, S.J. calculates the cost savings from emancipation, February 5, 1815." Georgetown Slavery Archive. https://slaveryarchive.georgetown.edu/items/show/66.
Maryland State Archives. "List of slaves taxed at White Marsh in 1833." *Georgetown Slavery Archive*. https://slaveryarchive.georgetown.edu/items/show/314.
———. "St. Inigoes Tax Assessment, 1831." Georgetown Slavery Archive. https://slaveryarchive.georgetown.edu/items/show/78.
Mobberly, Joseph. *Treatise on Slavery—Cham*. 1 of 2. Georgetown University Manuscripts, Booth Family Center for Special Collections, Washington, DC http://hdl.handle.net/10822/1060288.
———. *Treatise on Slavery—Cham*. 2 of 2. 1823. http://hdl.handle.net/10822/1060291.
National Archives, Fort Worth, TX. "Manifest of the Katherine Jackson, 1838." Georgetown Slavery Archive. https://slaveryarchive.georgetown.edu/items/show/2.

## South Caroliniana Library, University of South Carolina, Columbia, SC, Archives

Anna Lynch to Bishop Patrick Lynch. "My dear brother [from Walterboro]." December 27, 1860. Charleston Diocesan Archives, Item #13T8. https://lcdl.library.cofc.edu/lcdl/catalog/lcdl:41719.
Elizabeth Perry Bellinger Pinckney to Charles Pinckney. "To My Beloved Son [from Edgefield]." October 9, 1854. Folder 5. Pinckney Family Papers.
Elizabeth Perry Bellinger Pinckney to Eustace Pinckney [St. John's College Fordham]. "A happy New Year to my much loved Son." January 8, 1852. Folder 3. Pinckney Family Papers.
Elizabeth Perry Bellinger Pinckney to Eustace Pinckney [St. John's College Fordham]. "My Beloved Son." November 1, 1850.
Elizabeth Perry Bellinger Pinckney to Eustace Pinckney [St. John's College Fordham]. "My dear Son, [signed May God bless you my ever dear Boy prays your affectionate Mother]." June 20, 1852.

Elizabeth Perry Bellinger Pinckney to Eustace Pinckney. "My Dear Son." August 15, 1860.
Elizabeth Perry Bellinger Pinckney to Eustace Pinckney [St. John's College Fordham]. "My ever dear Son." October 3, 1851. Pinckney Family Papers, Folder 3.
Elizabeth Perry Bellinger Pinckney to Eustace Pinckney [St. John's College Fordham]. "My own dear precious Child." October 3, 1852. Folder 4. Pinckney Family Papers.
Elizabeth Perry Bellinger Pinckney to Eustace Pinckney [St. John's College Fordham]. "My own dear Son." December 18, 1852. Folder 5. Pinckney Family Papers.
Julia Lynch Pinckney to Anna Lynch. "My dear Sister." January 8, 1860.

# Index


Agricultural Workers Organizing Committee, 198
agonistic, 1, 3–5, 12, 142, 170–172, 174–176, 181, 188, 190, 195, 199–200, 202–205, 285n1
anachronism, 169
ancestor(s), 3, 11, 28, 39, 44, 50, 64, 69, 74, 76, 122, 162; on elders becoming ancestors, 9, 210, 256, 273n71; enslaved, 7–9, 44, 69, 237; of future generations, 212; Jesuit, 72, 74; as models, 205, 236–237; in relation to ghosts, 37, 221; restoring of, 223; in South Carolina, 237; West African, 104. *See also* ghosts
anti-Asian violence, 1, 184–185
anti-Blackness, 1, 12, 111, 129, 145, 185, 278n31
antiracism, 165, 205, 217, 230–231, 252
archives, 40–44, 50, 64, 67–69, 89, 94, 155; access to, 162, 225–226; limits of, 8
Ashepoo River (and plantation), 80, 106, 120, 123,
Asian, 178–185, 191, 208, 214–215, 227–228; racialization of, 213; in the United Farm Workers, 196
Association of Catholic Colleges and Universities, 224
Association of Jesuit Colleges and Universities, 224

Baker-Fletcher, Karen, 122
Baltimore, 108–109, 130–134, 137–139, 142–144, 164, 170, 191
Baptist, Edward, 261n12
Barberich, Fr. Daniel (also spelled Berberich), 81, 86, 89–90, 92, 104, 154
Barndt, Joseph, 25–26, 230–231
Barth, Karl, 36
Bellinger, 82, 85, 93–94,100, 106, 113, 120, 124, 189, 268n7
Bellinger, John, 94, 174n93, 270n32
Bellinger, Sarah, 83–84, 94, 97, 107
Bellinger, Susan, 84, 94, 174n86
Benton, Thomas Hart, 136
Beschter SJ, John, 46–47, 49, 53–58
Black Catholics, 59, 67, 106, 111, 113, 119, 121, 154, 168–169, 228, 289n17; in Baltimore, 130–134, 164; as educators, 156; enslaved to the Jesuits, 47, 62–64 73; in South Carolina, 85–96, 234
Bolton SJ, Fr., 46–47, 60–61
Bouchard, James, 181–187
Bourdieu, Pierre, 16, 19–22
Brave Heart, Maria Yellow Horse, 9–13, 50, 79, 130, 162–165 186, 220–223, 227, 239
Brown University, 223
Brownson, Orestes, 145–146
Butler's Catechism, 117–119

Cannon, Katie, 68–69
capital: African Americans and, 234; agriculture workers and, 173, 176, 203, 209; archives and, 41, 44; Bourdieu on, 19; the Catholic Church in America and, 27, 50, 64, 78, 84, 86, 90–92, 108, 119, 126, 129–130, 140, 144, 154, 164, 169, 173–175, 183, 187, 199–202, 209, 221, 248; Catholic media and, 206; the cross and, 30, cultural, 20–21, 131; economic, 53, 44, 131, 182–185; enslaved and, 50, 60–63, 73, 91;

capital *(continued)*
enslavers and, 50, 62–63, 96, 112, 116, 119, 127; fetish and, 103; Filipinos and, 196; flow of, 120; Indigenous people and, 162, 235; institutions and, 14–15, 20–24, 27, 37, 42–43, 80, 145, 165, 169, 221, 231; Jesus and, 35, 174; labor and, 180; land as, 191; leveraging, 40, 93, 111, 129, 131, 134, 175, 178, 207–208, 225; media and, 108, 117; racialization and, 237; relics and, 104; restitution of, 215; social, 131, 145, 182, 238; sociopolitical, 114; spiritual, 73, 88–89, 95, 102, 131, 145, 183–185, 202, 205, 233, 237–238; the state and, 135; symbolic, 10, 21–22, 46, 57, 74, 81–85, 112, 144–145, 182–185, 214; Whiteness and, 127, 133, 138–139, 165, 197, 200
Carey, Patrick, 144–145
Carlisle Indian School, 149–150, 158
Carroll, James, 249
Carroll, J.B., 153
Carroll, John, 130, 137
Carruthers, Iva E., 10–11
Cataldo SJ, Fr. Joseph, 151–152
*Catholic Guardian*, 183
Catholic media networks, 24, 81, 115, 127, 140, 144–145, 187, 200, 206, 224. See also *Catholic Guardian*; *Catholic Worker*; *Indian Sentinel*; *Month and Catholic Review*; *United States Catholic Miscellany*
*Catholic Worker*, 206
Central Pacific Railroad, 179
Charleston, 80–86, 90–91, 93, 95–96, 98–102, 113–115, 120–121, 130, 155, 310; slave trade in, 96
Chávez, César, 174, 198, 200, 202–206, 209, 218
Chief Spotted Tail, 149
Child, Brenda, 281n70
Chinese, 151, 181; anti-Chinese legislation, 185, 187; in Stockton, CA, 195; as workers, 179–180, 184
Christology, 29–37
Civil War, 87–89
complicity, 5, 28, 76, 79, 80, 227; of northern institutions, 145; refusal to face, 240
Cone, James, 234
Copeland, M. Shawn, 48, 53, 65, 68, 86, 234
Crawley, Ashon, 28, 48–49, 58–60
Critical Race Theory, 3, 9, 25, 225, 293n60
Crucified People, 30, 36–39, 197, 204; Ignacio Ellacuria on, 30, 36, 294n76

Davis, Cyprian, 86, 91
Davis, Tommy, 157, 159, 235
Davis, Vincent of Paul, 86
Dawes Act, 148
Day, Dorothy, 206, 218
defense of slavery: John England (bishop),108; John Hughes (archbishop), 116; Joseph Mobberly, SJ, 51, 75; Ignatius Reynolds (bishop), 112; James Ryder, SJ, 75
Delano, CA, 199, 201, 203, 205, 208
De Paul University, 223
Donckt, Cyril Van der, 147
Douglas, Kelly Brown, 122
Dred Scott v. Sandford, 142–144
Drexel, Katharine, 90, 154–156, 170
Duchemin, Almaide Maxis, 132–133, 138. *See also* Maxis, Theresa
Dzierozynski SJ, Fr. Francis, 55–58, 69, 71–74

Easter, 173–174, 203–204, 218
ecclesiology, 72, 98, 126–127, 169
Ellacuria, Ignacio, 30, 35–36, 294n76
empire: Christians and, 36, 39–42; Katharine Drexel and, 282n87; Thomas Jefferson and, 278n26; Jesus and, 34–35, 174; Roman, 31–32, 38; United States of America as, 187, 191–192, 287n40
England, John (bishop), 80, 83, 94, 108–109, 144, 268n3, 269n13
Enlightenment, 59, 143, 194
enslaved Catholics: Catholic constructions of, 54 116; in Church-building, 39, 61,63, 67, 73, 78, 107, 249; as Church founders, 45, 62, 101; erasure of, 3–5, 168, 172, 191, 214, 221–222, 226, 258; as ghosts, 8, 52; hermeneutics and, 66; by Jesuits, 52, 58, 75, 184; Jesus and, 48; law and, 143; legal battles of, 41, 142; practices of, 71, 99; re-membering, 43–44, 77, 98; revolution and, 130–132; self-emancipation and, 100, 118, 140–141; spirituality and, 65, 68, 71, 169, 234–237; as workers, 127
enslavers: and Bellinger, 97, 100, 107, 113, 124, 274n93; Catholic bishops and, 144; Catholic catechism and, 118; Catholics in Charleston, 114; economic calculating and, 63; John England and (bishop) 108; Jesuits and, 51–53; Pinckney, 97, 102, 118, 122–123; St. John's Fordham and, 115, 120, 274n93; violence of, 56, 261n12, 263n43
Examination of Conscience, 242

Fabros, Alex, 197
Federal Housing Administration, 194
fetish, 103–104

Filipino(s), 192–193, 196–199, 202, 207, 213; in Stockton, 195; in the United Farm Workers, 200
flagellation, self-, 39, 46–49, 56–57; term, 47
Fordham University, 14, 117, 120, 256. *See also* St. John's Fordham
fragments, 44
free women of color, 131–135. *See also* Duchemin, Almaide Maxis; Oblate Sisters of Providence
Forsyth, John (secretary of state), 108–109, 115, 144
Fugitive Slave Clause, 107, 140, 272n85

Gandhi (Mohandas), 203, 205
Garnett, Diana, 101, 104
Georgetown University, 2, 7–8, 40, 61, 69, 75, 78–79, 114–115, 223, 226–227, 232, 255; archives, 42–43, 56, 169; slavery and, 62
ghosts, 27; Gordon on, 27–28 ; Swarns on, 8; theology of, 27–29. *See also* ancestors
Glover, James, 151
Gonzaga University, 151–152
Gordon, Avery, 27–28
grace: in face of White supremacy, 67–69
grandmothers, Indigenous, 163–164
Grape Strike, 201–203
Great Depression, 193
Great Northern Railroad, 151
Gury SJ, Joanne Petro, 117, 119
Gutierrez, Gustavo, 177, 210, 219, 226

Haitian Revolution, 131–132; and White Catholics, 277n7
Hartman, Saidiya, 99, 125
Harvard University, 223, 227
Hayes, Diana, 68
Henrietta of St. James the Greater (Hetty), 29, 90–100, 107, 112–113, 118–120, 124, 126, 172, 176, 218
hermeneutic(s), 66–67, 117, 143, 165, 234–235; of suspicion, 51, 74
hierarchy: Catholic Church and, 98, 172, 191; God and, 51, 116; of humanity, 129, 133,146, 227; as justification for slavery, 51, 98; mortgage lending and, 194, 197, 215, 245; power and, 116; racial, 164, 197, 215; racialization and, 262n41
historical trauma, 4, 9–13, 40–41, 79–80, 90, 220–221, 239, 251
Homestead Act, 147–148, 214, 295n86
Horsley, Richard, 30–33
Horstmann, Ignatius (bishop), 152
House Resolution 40, 242, 249
Hoyt, Homer, 194
Huerta, Dolores, 195–203, 207–209
Hughes, John (archbishop), 100, 115–116, 120, 145

Ignatius of Loyola, 239, 282n85
IHM. *See* Sisters, Servants of the Immaculate Heart of Mary
*imago Dei*, 68
*Imitatio Christi*, 50
Indian Appropriations Act, 147
Indian Boarding Schools, 149–150, 152, 157–162
*Indian Sentinel*, 153, 207
institutional abandonment (by the Catholic Church): in Baltimore, 135, 190; in South Carolina, 86, 102, 190; in Texas, 189–190
institutional ontology, 14
institutionalized racism, 239
institutions, 15–17; capital in, 19–22, 23–25; as connections in history, 18–19; as places of practice, 26; and White supremacy, 25–27
Itliong, Larry, 198, 200, 208, 218

Jacobs, Harriet, 72, 234
Jennings, Willie James, 44, 148, 157
Jesus Movement, 30, 33–34, 82, 200
Jesus of Nazareth, 30–36
Jim Crow, 90; laws, 231
*Johnson v. M'Intosh*, 136, 146, 148
Jones, Camara Phyllis, 239
Joubert, James Fr., 131–132

Kang, Joy, 7–8, 69
Kennedy, Robert, 205, 207, 218
kenosis (kenotic), 220
Kenrick, Francis, 108, 110, 112, 117. See also *Theologia Moralis*
Kent, Corita, 202
Kim, Igna, 200
King, Rev. Dr. Martin Luther, 205
Klein, Ramona, 236
Krebsbach, Suzanne, 81
Kwon, Duke, 76, 211–215, 220–222, 225, 227, 230, 233

Lajimodiere, Denise, 281n67, 283nn98–103, 292n29, 293nn48–53
Leavy, Fr., 46, 54–55
Lee, Erika, 179, 192
Lefevere, Peter Paul (bishop), 137–138
Lehman, Christopher, 141
Lord Baltimore, 42–43
Loretto Sisters, 223
Lott, Juanita Tamayo, 192–193, 196

Louisiana, 70–71, 190
Louisiana Purchase, 179
L'Ouverture, Toussaint, 130
Lynch, Patrick (bishop), 82, 85, 93–96, 99–100, 113, 120–121

Mahoney, Harry, 64, 71
Mahoney, Nelly, 69–75, 237
Maphiya Luta, 239
Maryland, 39, 43, 63, 113, 134; Baltimore, 138; Port Tobacco, 151; province of Jesuits, 232
Massingale, Bryan, 175, 240
mastery, 22, 54, 61, 67, 129, 138, 148–149, 151, 153, 159, 162, 169, 178, 191–192, 213–216, 229
Matovina, Timothy, 188–189
Maxis, Theresa, 132–134, 138, 170–172. *See also* Duchemin, Almaide Maxis
McGreevy, John, 111
*McMichael's Appraising Manual*, 194
Mechtild of Hakeborn, 30, 36
media. *See* Catholic media networks
Mexican-American War, 179, 188, 245
Michigan, 138–140
Minnesota, 141, 151
missiology, 5
Mobberly SJ, Joseph, 46, 49–53, 55–58, 62, 75
*Month and Catholic Review*, 147, 206
Morrow, Diana Batts, 131, 134, 138, 143
Mulledy SJ, Thomas, 63, 70–71, 74–75
multiracial, 3, 94, 100, 154, 157, 162, 164–165, 167, 173, 175, 178, 185, 197, 207, 209–210, 212, 217, 226, 228, 230, 243
Murphy SJ, Thomas, 46, 55–57, 66–67

Nancy (at Georgetown), 64–65, 77–79
National Labor Relations Board, 196
National Native American Boarding School Hearing Coalition, 226
New Deal, 193, 196

Oblate Sisters of Providence, 131–136, 138–139, 144
O'Connell, Jeremiah Joseph, 82–84, 86, 93, 268n6, 270n32
Ögütle, Vefa Saygin, 18
Omi, Michael, 258n3, 293n57
Onondaga nation, 225
Oregon Territory, 136, 147
otherwise possibilities, 26, 28–30, 34, 37, 48, 58–61, 64, 67–69, 74, 76, 98, 118, 141, 144–145, 167, 169, 174, 195, 198–199, 202, 204, 206, 208–210, 218, 221, 225, 232
Owl, Roger White, 158, 161, 235

Palladino, Lorenzo, 150–152
Pascal Mystery, 289n85
Philippines, 191–193, 196
Pike, Zebulon, 136
pilgrimage, 175–176, 203–207
Pinckney, Elizabeth Perry Bellinger, 83–85, 94, 96–99, 102, 106–107, 118–124
Pinckney, Eustace, 95–96, 98–100, 113, 119, 121–122, 124
Pinckney Jones, Mary Claire, 114, 122–124
pneumatology, 48
Pope Gregory, 108
Pratt, Richard Henry, 149–150

rabbis, 208
race, 8, 51, 136, 140, 143–147, 156, 175, 180, 183, 184, 187, 194–195, 213, 216, 226–227, 239–240, 262n41, 293n67
race-evasive, 186
racial discrimination, 20
racial hierarchy, 129, 146, 194, 215, 227, 245, 252
racial project, 129, 137–138, 140, 143–146, 148, 155, 180–181, 184, 189, 192, 195, 197, 216, 230, 232–233, 239, 278n32, 285n16, 293n67; homeownership and, 287n47. *See also* multiracial
racialization, 156, 219, 181
racism, 10, 13, 25, 76, 156, 200, 214, 230, 240–241, 243, 245; as historic trauma, 10, 212, 239, 251; as institutional, 25, 231, 239, 248; as internalized, 242; as sin, 247; US culture of, 211–216, 233
racist, 142, 154–156, 184, 216, 222, 231, 242, 250–251
Raphael, Melissa, 71
*ratio studiorum*, 150
reckoning, 28, 59, 78, 124, 140, 186, 223, 227, 238, 251
Reconstruction, 87, 89–92, 231, 237
Red Cloud Indian School (now Maphiya Luta), 229
Red Summer, 185
Redemptorists, 117, 135–138
Reiger, Jeorg, 31
relics, 102–104, 107
religio-racial project, 140, 180–181
re-membering, 11, 44–46, 50, 61, 65, 70, 76, 228, 261n12
reparations, 215, 231–232, 245, 249, 309
Reynolds, Ignatius (bishop), 82–83, 108, 111–112, 144
romanticization, 76, 186, 213, 222, 258n8
Rosebud Sioux Tribe, 224

Rosewood, FL, 187
Rothman, Adam, 255, 260
Russo, Ruth, 170–171

Said, Omar Ibn, 235
Saint-Jean, Patrick, 242
San Francisco, CA, 179, 183–186, 201, 243
Sandford, John, 142, 144
Schmidt, Kelly, 223, 263, 266n11
Schneiders, Sandra, 88, 127, 233
Scott, Etheldred, 141–142, 144
segregation, 211, 230–231
settler-colonialism, 128, 135–138, 147–151, 162, 168, 170, 188–191, 244, 248
Sisters of Charity, 223
Sisters of the Blessed Sacrament for Indians and Colored People, 154–155
Sisters, Servants of the Immaculate Heart of Mary (IHM), 138, 140, 144, 170, 278n31
Slabodsky, Santiago, 128
Sowards, Stacey, 195–196
*Spiritual Exercises*, 241–251
spirituality, 65, 88–89, 104–105, 120–122, 127, 163, 169, 202–203, 206, 233–234, 236, 239, 248, 251
Spokane, WA, 151
Stations of the Cross, 173–175, 203–204, 207
Steinbacher, SJ, Fr., 61
Stockton, CA, 195–196
Stockton, Nancy, 98
Stony Point Presbyterian Church, 225
St. Ignatius (Indian Mission), 150
St. Ignatius Church (San Francisco), 186, 243
St. Ignatius College (San Francisco), 186
St. Inigoes, 52, 57, 45–46, 62, 64, , 69–73
St. James the Greater, 80–82, 86–90, 97, 100–102, 107, 127, 154–155, 237; on National Registry of Historic Places, 101, 104
St. John's Fordham, 113–119 121–124, 128, 147, 189
St. Philip Church (Walterboro, SC), 82–83, 85, 96
Sucky (Susannah) at Georgetown, 39–41, 45–46, 51, 60, 64, 70, 237; Beschter and, 58; Mobberly and, 50; Murphy on, 55–56; her scream, 47–54; interpreting her scream, 57–59
surrogacy, 99
Swarns, Rachel, 62, 64, 71, 74–75
systemic, 16–19, 132, 156

Taney, Roger, 142–146
Temple-State, 32–34
Texas, 181, 185, 188–190
Thebaud, Augustus, 147
theft, 54, 76, 212–215, 222, 227–230, 233; of history, 76, 213, 222, 227; of identity, 213, 230; of power, 214–215, 230; of wealth, 212–215
*Theologia Moralis*, 108, 110–112, 117, 144
Thompson, Gregory, 76, 211–215, 220–222, 225, 227, 230, 233
Tisby, Jamar, 259n24
townes, emilie, 227
truth-telling, 9–10, 12, 40–41, 75, 79, 209, 214; 222, 239; as anachronism, 169; analysis and, 163; bearing fruit of, 212; in Catholic education, 216; ghosts and, 221; healing and, 90, 248, institutional inheritance and, 166; institutional resources and, 42; institutional transformation and, 78; as liberatory, 217, 225; as a nation, 232; Nelly (at Georgetown) and, 74; for otherwise possibilities, 141, 171–172; re-membering and, 11, 228; reparation and, 220; as spiritual exercise, 249
Tulsa, OK, 185
Turner, Nat, 134

United Farm Workers, 175, 198–207
*United States Catholic Miscellany*, 81–83, 108–109, 113, 117, 115, 119, 169, 207, 280
United States of Mexico, 147, 179, 187, 191
Universities Studying Slavery, 223
University of San Francisco, 186
University of Virginia, 223

Vincent of Paul, 84–86, 91–94, 102
violence, 185
Virgin of Guadalupe, 202
Virginia Theological Seminary, 231

Walterboro, SC, 80–86, 96, 99–100, 107, 113, 118, 120–122, 268n7
War of 1812, 64–67, 137
Watomika, 181–182. *See also* Bouchard, James
Watsonville, CA, 193, 196
*We Came a Long Way by Faith*, 83
Wells-Oghoghomeh, Alexis, 272n52
White following, 205–208
White supremacy, 52, 146, 238, 251; benefits accrued from, 220, 236, 250; Chinese exclusion and, 184–186; as culture, 234; as disordered affection, 241; in education, 26, 129, 131, 230; grace in the face of, 67–69, 226; as historical trauma, 4, 9–10, 13, 80, 90, 188, 221; institutions and, 25–27,

White supremacy *(continued)*
231, 239, 244; knowledge systems and, 228; legislation and, 143; militarism and, 140; mortgage lending and, 194; in "race science," 51; romanticization and, 222; as sin, 10; stations of the cross and, 175; in structures, 12, 131–132, 174, 189, 215; as theft, 213–214, 227; violence and, 190; White-centering and, 26, 134; willful ignorance and, 240; withstanding assaults of, 235
Wilder, Craig Steven, 1–2, 28, 42, 223
William and Mary, The College of, 223
Williams, Shannen Dee, 42, 130, 133, 155–156, 248, 278n31
Winant, Howard, 258n3, 293n57

Ziajka, Alan, 186

**Jeannine Hill Fletcher** is professor of theology at Fordham University. She is the author of *The Sin of White Supremacy: Christianity, Racism, and Religious Diversity in America* (Orbis, 2017).